It's 2006. I believe the serialization began in 1999, so that means we've entered our seventh year of publication! Long enough for kids that were just entering elementary school to now be in junior high... I recently started noticing how it seems like the years pass quicker and quicker. Where in the world did the time go?! When in the world did I become middle-aged?! Yikes...

—*Masashi Kishimoto, 2006*

Author/artist Masashi Kishimoto was born in 1974 in rural Okayama Prefecture, Japan. After spending time in art college, he won the Hop Step Award for new manga artists with his manga **Karakuri** (Mechanism). Kishimoto decided to base his next story on traditional Japanese culture. His first version of **Naruto**, drawn in 1997, was a one-shot story about fox spirits; his final version, which debuted in **Weekly Shonen Jump** in 1999, quickly became the most popular ninja manga in Japan.

NARUTO VOL. 32
The SHONEN JUMP Manga Edition

This graphic novel contains material that was originally published in English in **SHONEN JUMP** #69-70. Artwork in the magazine may have been slightly altered from that presented here.

STORY AND ART BY MASASHI KISHIMOTO

Translation/Mari Morimoto
English Adaptation/Deric A. Hughes & Benjamin Raab
Touch-up Art & Lettering/Sabrina Heep
Design/Sean Lee
Editor/Joel Enos

Editor in Chief, Books/Alvin Lu
Editor in Chief, Magazines/Marc Weidenbaum
VP of Publishing Licensing/Rika Inouye
VP of Sales/Gonzalo Ferreyra
Sr. VP of Marketing/Liza Coppola
Publisher/Hyoe Narita

Printed in the U.S.A.

Published by VIZ Media, LLC
P.O. Box 77010
San Francisco, CA 94107

SHONEN JUMP Manga Edition
10 9 8 7 6 5 4 3 2 1
First printing, November 2008

THE WORLD'S MOST POPULAR MANGA

www.viz.com

www.shonenjump.com

SHONEN JUMP MANGA EDITION

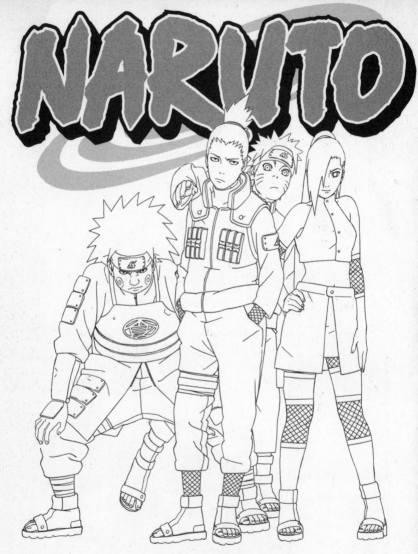

NARUTO

VOL. 32
THE SEARCH FOR SASUKE

STORY AND ART BY
MASASHI KISHIMOTO

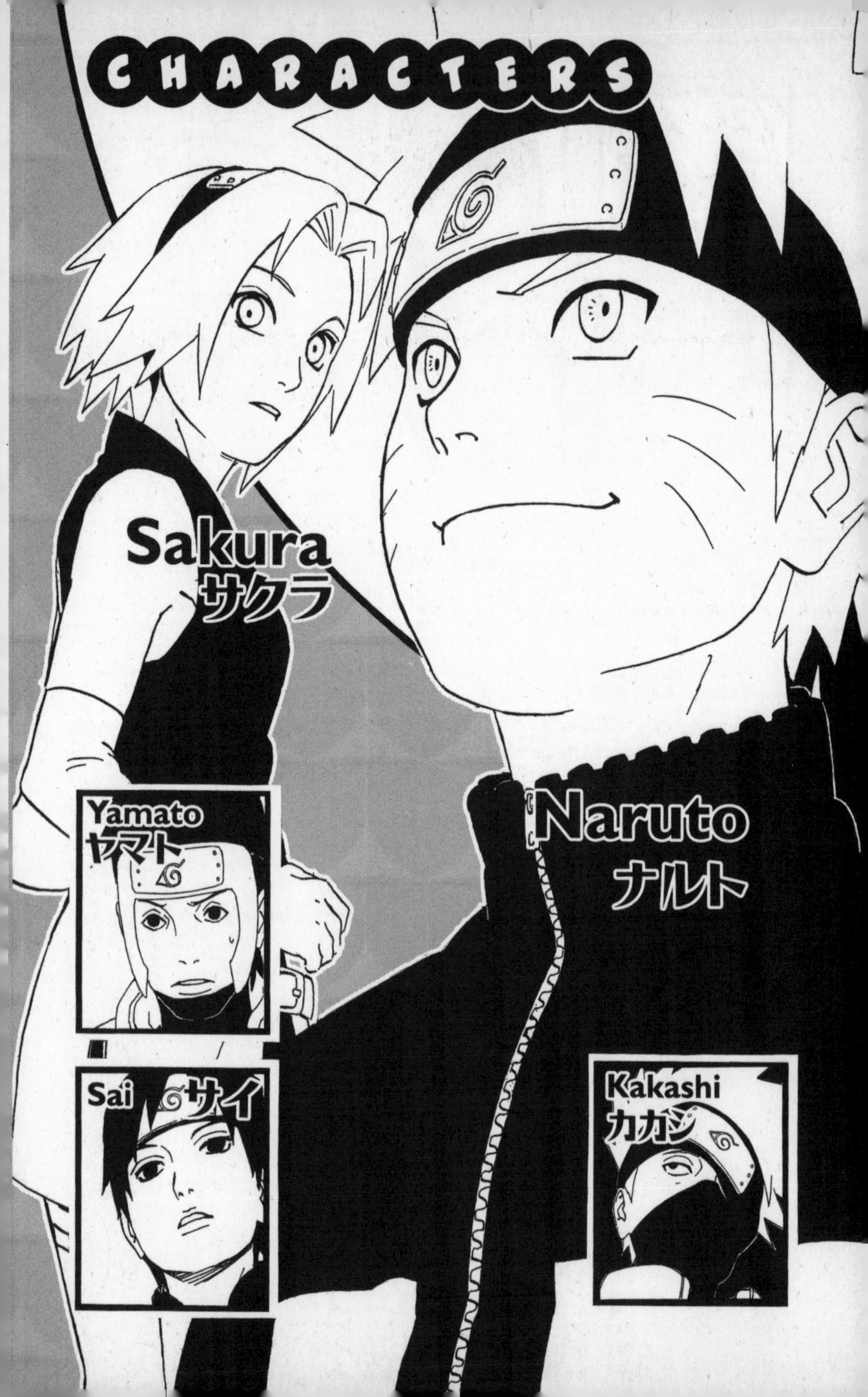
CHARACTERS
Naruto
ナルト
Sakura
サクラ
Kakashi
カカシ
Yamato
ヤマト
Sai
サイ

Danzo ダンゾウ
Shizune シズネ
Tsunade 綱手
Ino いの
Choji チョウジ
Shikamaru シカマル

The Story So Far...

Naruto, the biggest troublemaker at the Ninja Academy in Konohagakure, finally becomes a ninja along with his classmates Sasuke and Sakura. During the Chûnin Selection Exams, Orochimaru and his henchmen launch *Operation Destroy Konoha*. To stop the attack and prevent the deaths of any more of Konoha's shinobi, Sarutobi, the Third Hokage, sacrifices his own life. In the wake of this tragedy, Lady Tsunade is sought out and declared Fifth Hokage.

Sasuke—lured by the Sound Ninja Four of Orochimaru—leaves Konohagakure. Naruto fights valiantly against Sasuke, but cannot stop his friend from following the possible path of darkness...

After two years, Naruto and his comrades reunite, each having grown and matured in attitude and aptitude. Gaara of the Sand has become Kazekage, and falls into the hands of the mysterious organization known as the Akatsuki.

After several fierce battles, Naruto and the others defeat rogue ninja Sasori and Deidara and recover Gaara. But their victory looks to be a bitter one as Gaara is dead. Or so it seems until Granny Chiyo, using a reincarnation jutsu, sacrifices her own life to resurrect the fallen Kazekage!

NARUTO

VOL. 32
THE SEARCH FOR SASUKE

CONTENTS

Number 281: The Search for Sasuke!!

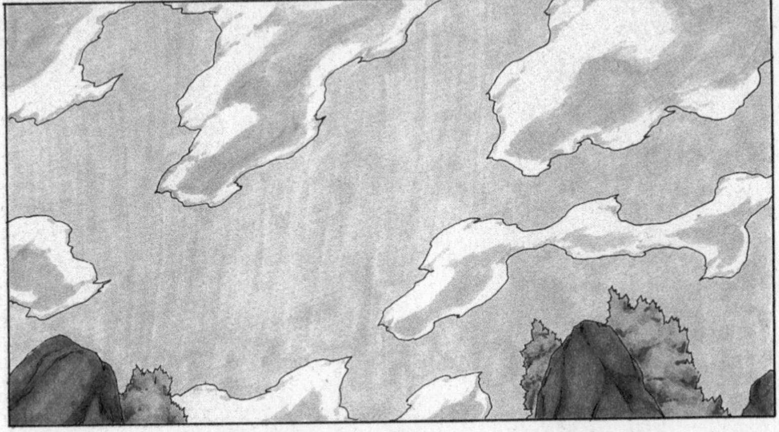

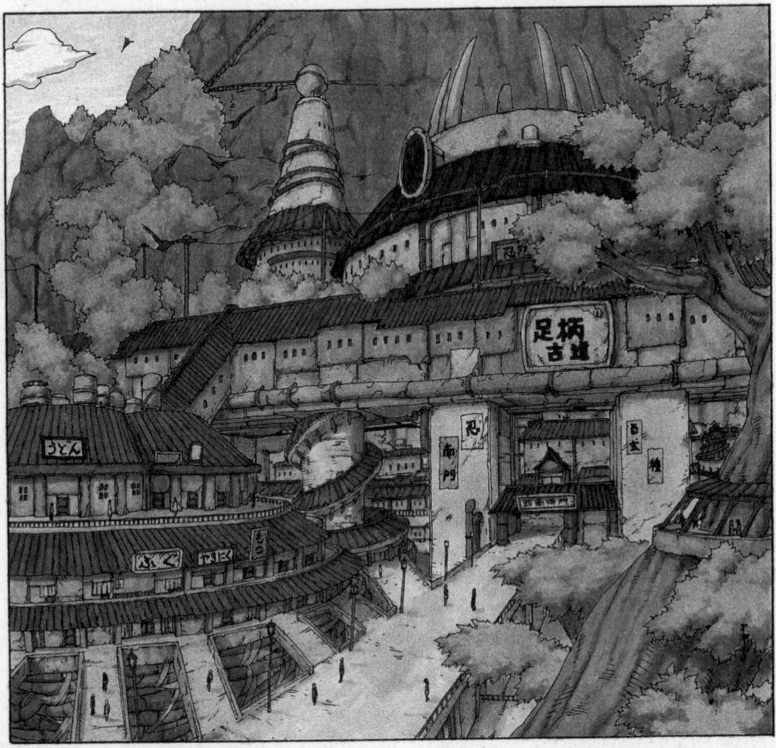
うどん

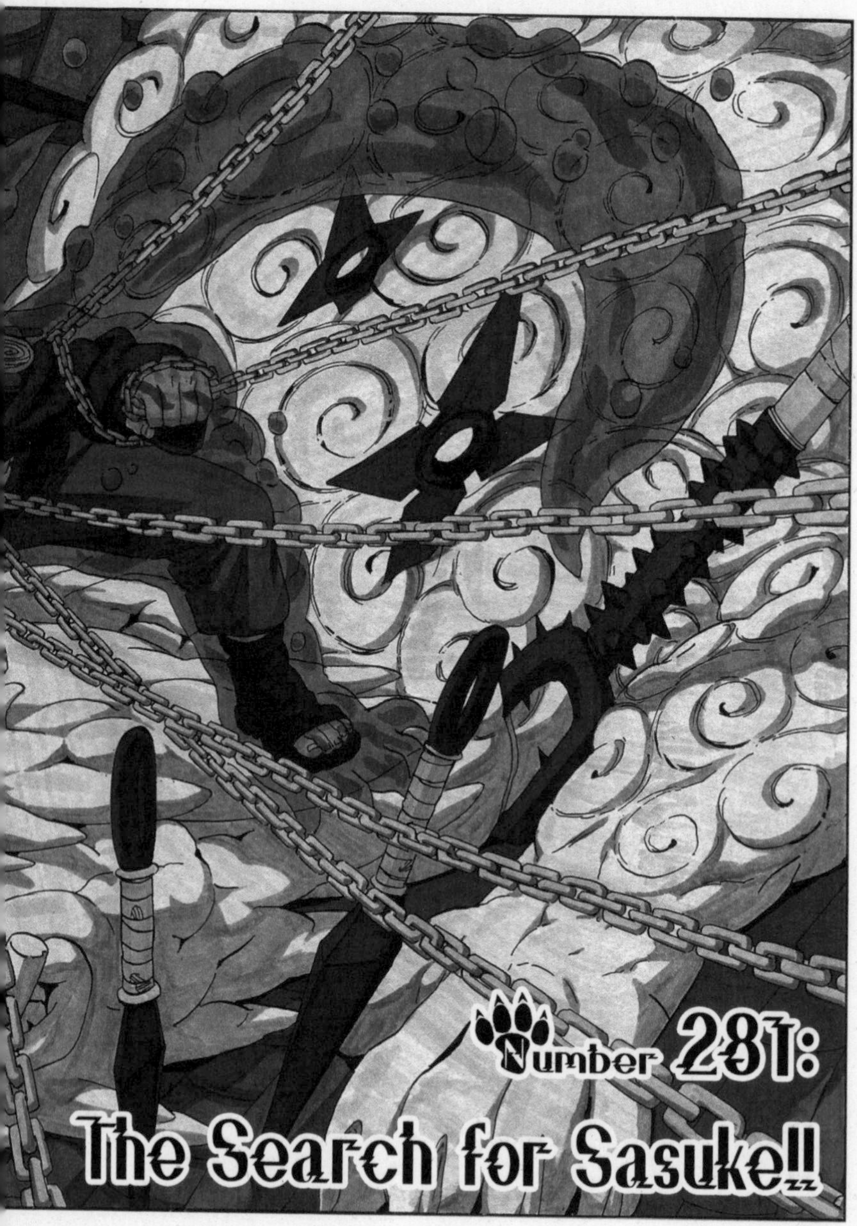
Number 281:
The Search for Sasuke!!

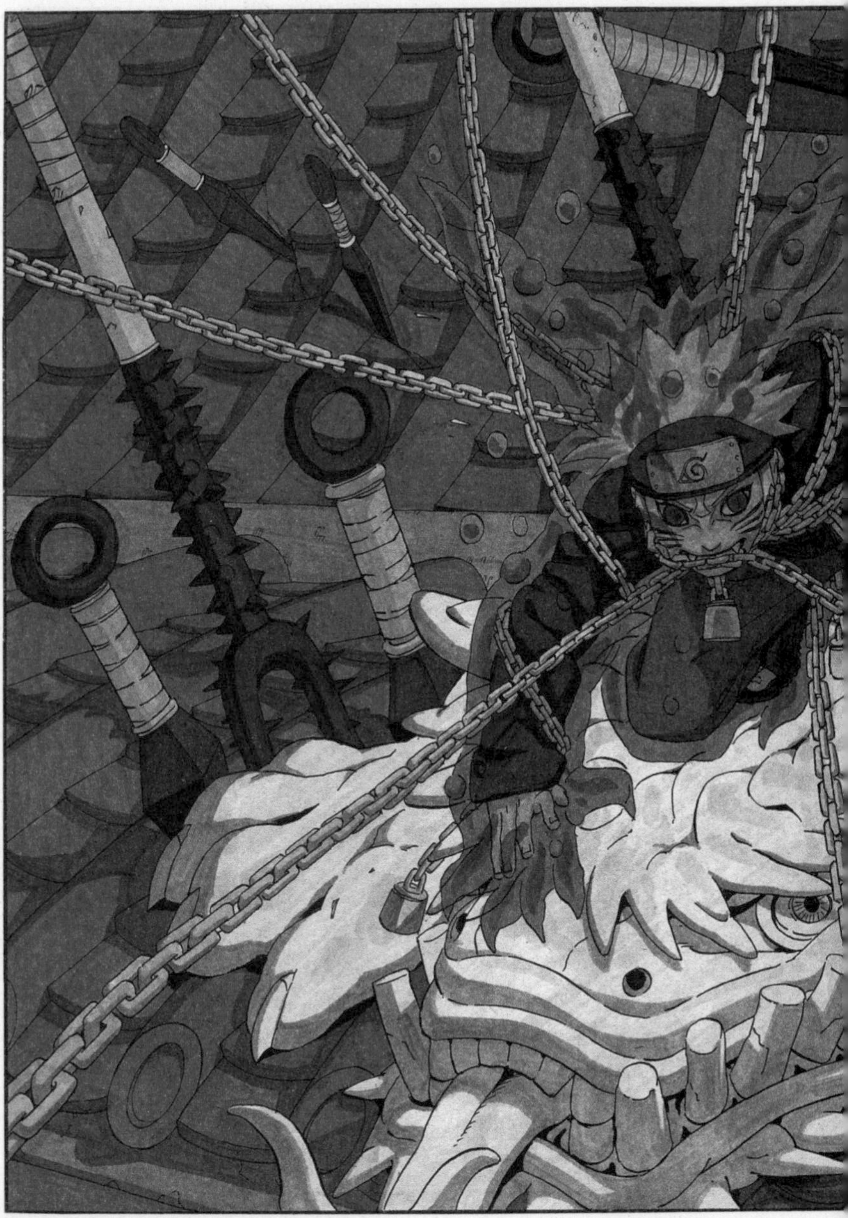

NARUTO

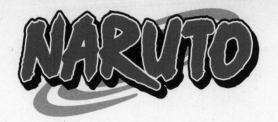

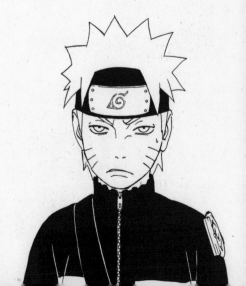

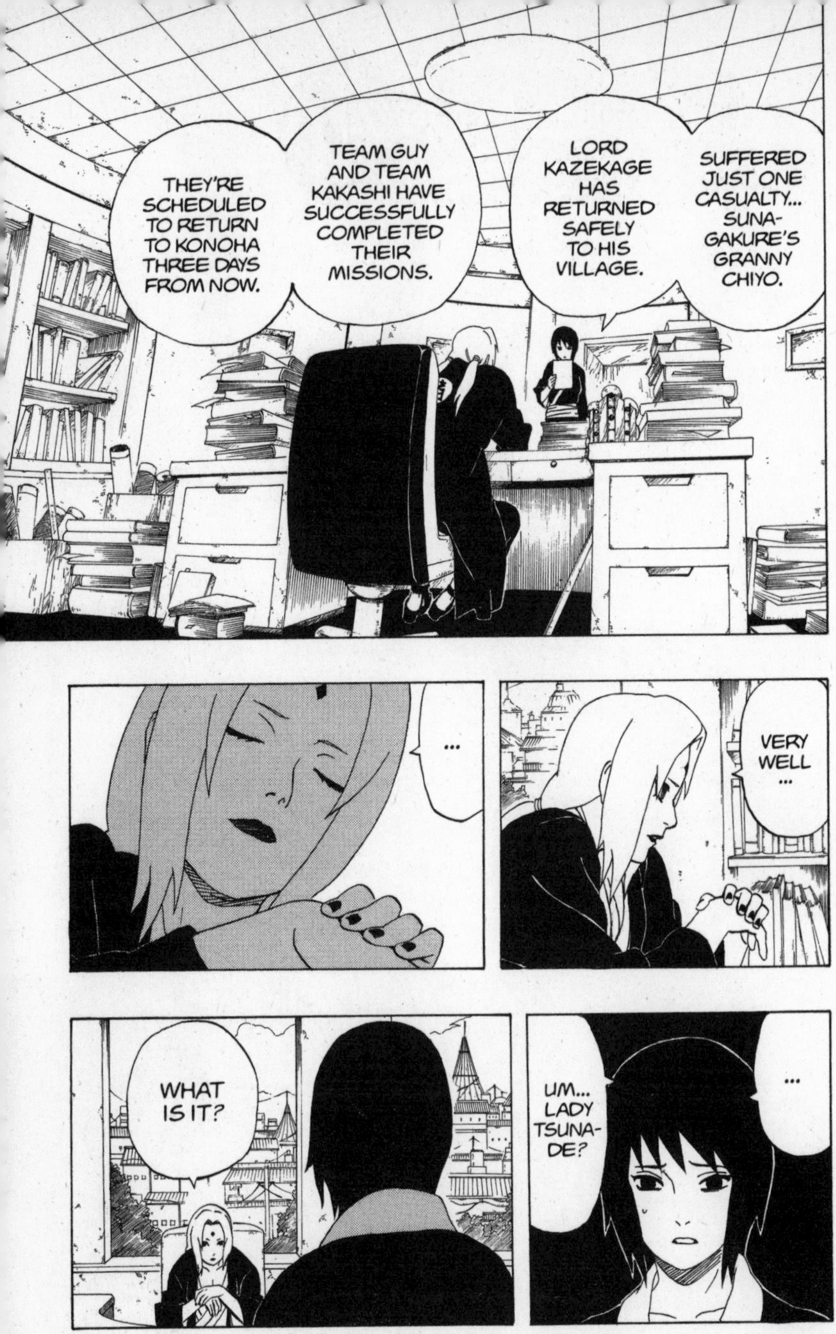

LORD KAZEKAGE HAS RETURNED SAFELY TO HIS VILLAGE.
SUFFERED JUST ONE CASUALTY... SUNA-GAKURE'S GRANNY CHIYO.
TEAM GUY AND TEAM KAKASHI HAVE SUCCESSFULLY COMPLETED THEIR MISSIONS.
THEY'RE SCHEDULED TO RETURN TO KONOHA THREE DAYS FROM NOW.
VERY WELL ...
...
...
UM... LADY TSUNA-DE?
WHAT IS IT?

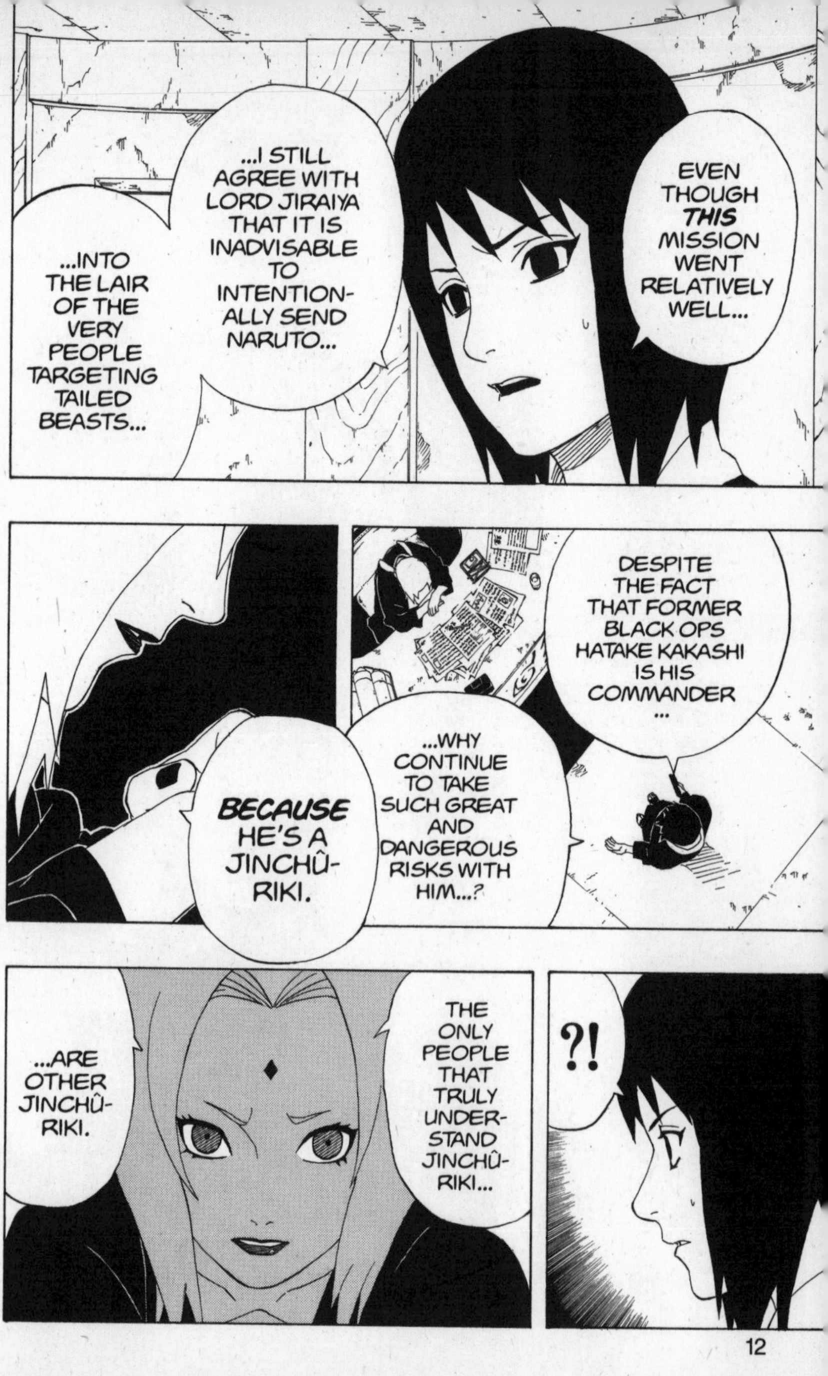
EVEN THOUGH *THIS* MISSION WENT RELATIVELY WELL...
...I STILL AGREE WITH LORD JIRAIYA THAT IT IS INADVISABLE TO INTENTIONALLY SEND NARUTO...
...INTO THE LAIR OF THE VERY PEOPLE TARGETING TAILED BEASTS...
DESPITE THE FACT THAT FORMER BLACK OPS HATAKE KAKASHI IS HIS COMMANDER...
...WHY CONTINUE TO TAKE SUCH GREAT AND DANGEROUS RISKS WITH HIM...?
BECAUSE HE'S A JINCHÛRIKI.
?!
THE ONLY PEOPLE THAT TRULY UNDERSTAND JINCHÛRIKI...
...ARE OTHER JINCHÛRIKI.

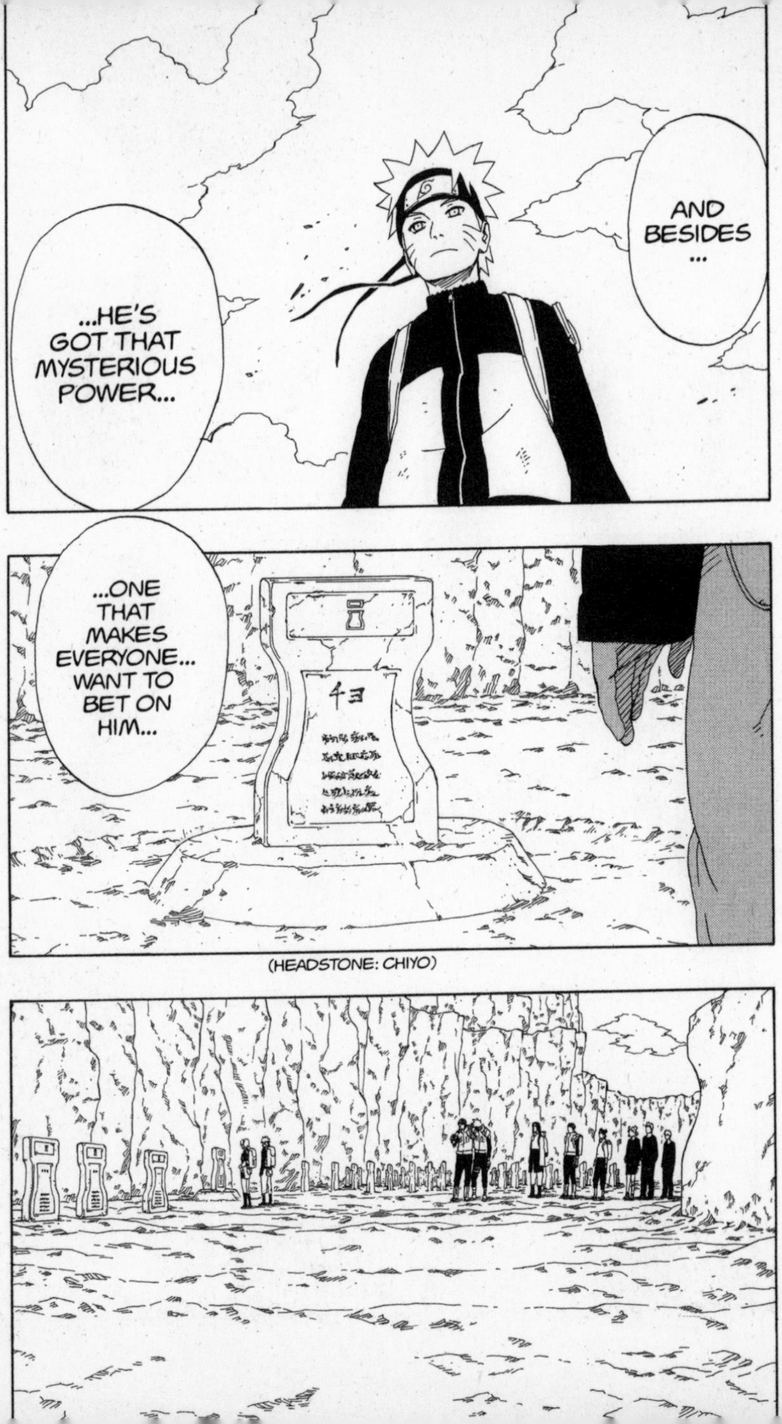
AND BESIDES...
...HE'S GOT THAT MYSTERIOUS POWER...
...ONE THAT MAKES EVERYONE... WANT TO BET ON HIM...
(HEADSTONE: CHIYO)

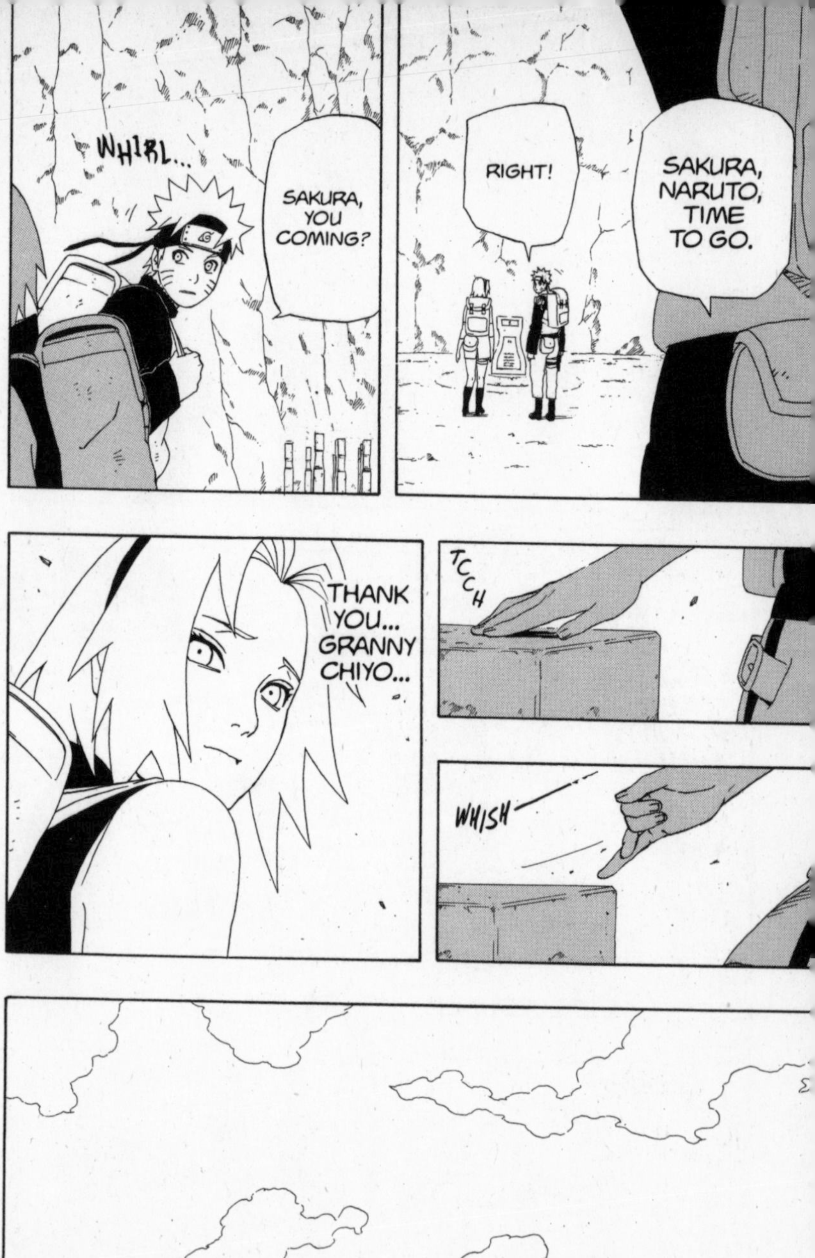
SAKURA, NARUTO, TIME TO GO.
RIGHT!
WHIRL...
SAKURA, YOU COMING?
TCCH
WHISH
THANK YOU... GRANNY CHIYO...

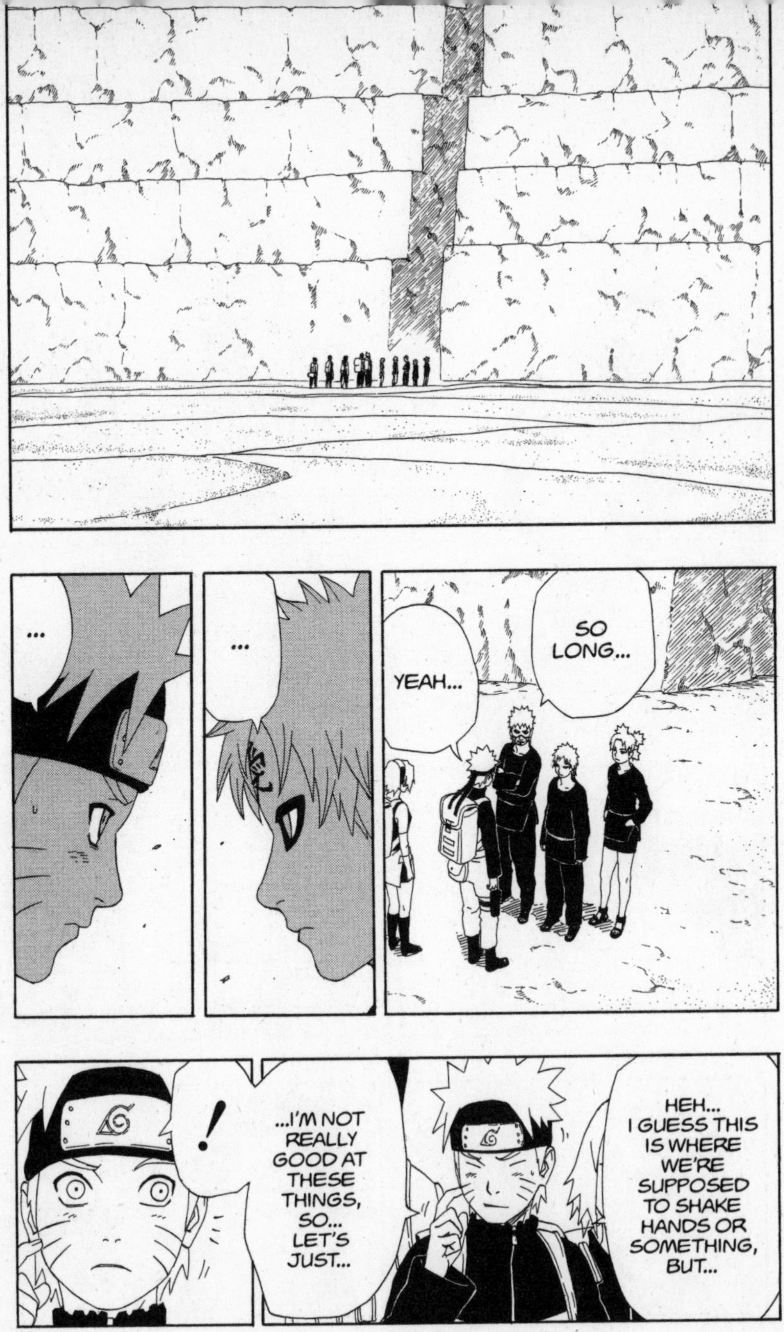
SO LONG...
YEAH...
...
...
HEH... I GUESS THIS IS WHERE WE'RE SUPPOSED TO SHAKE HANDS OR SOMETHING, BUT...
...I'M NOT REALLY GOOD AT THESE THINGS, SO... LET'S JUST...
!

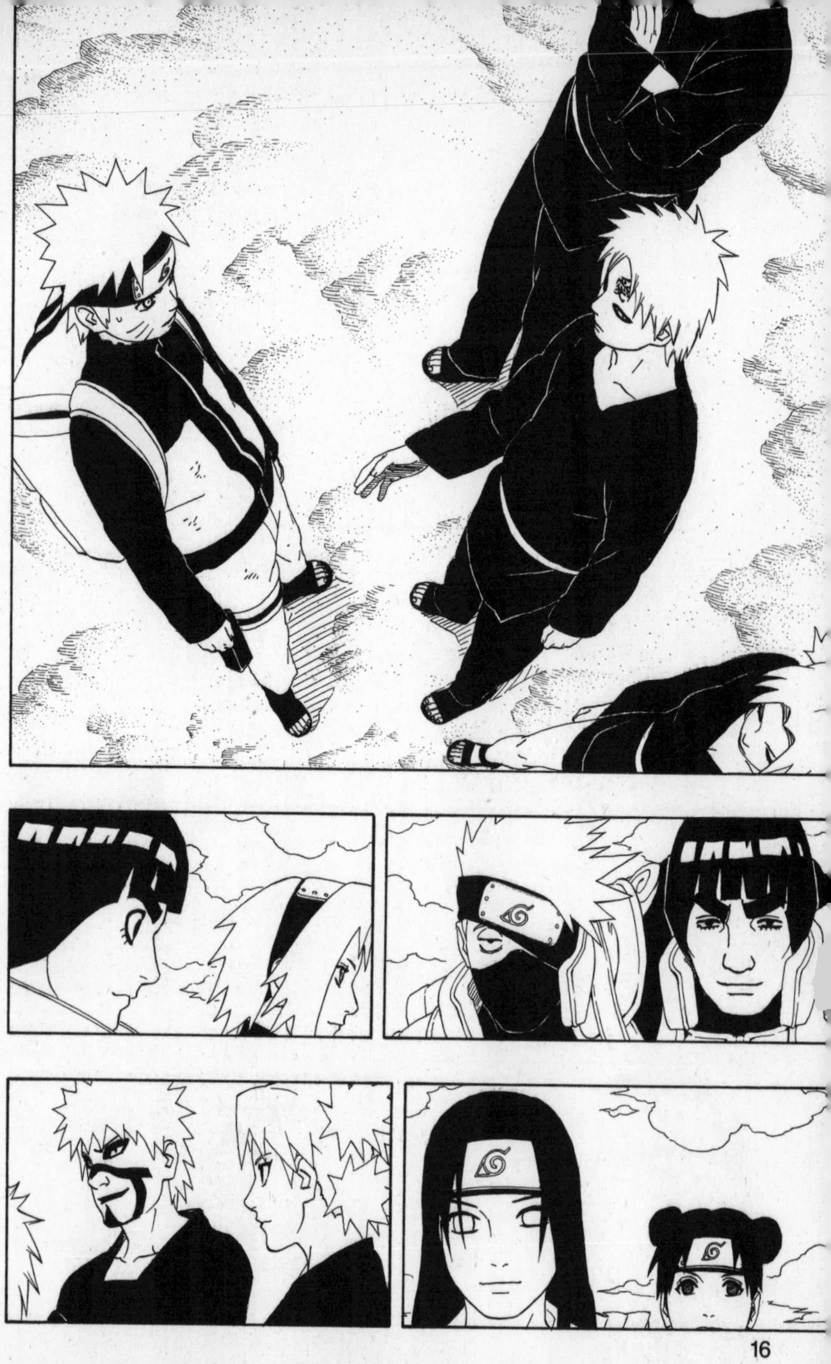

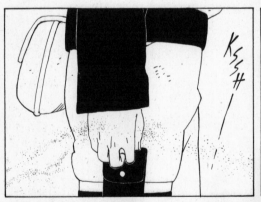

KSSH

!

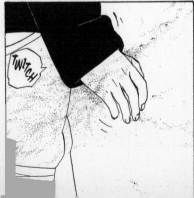

TWITCH

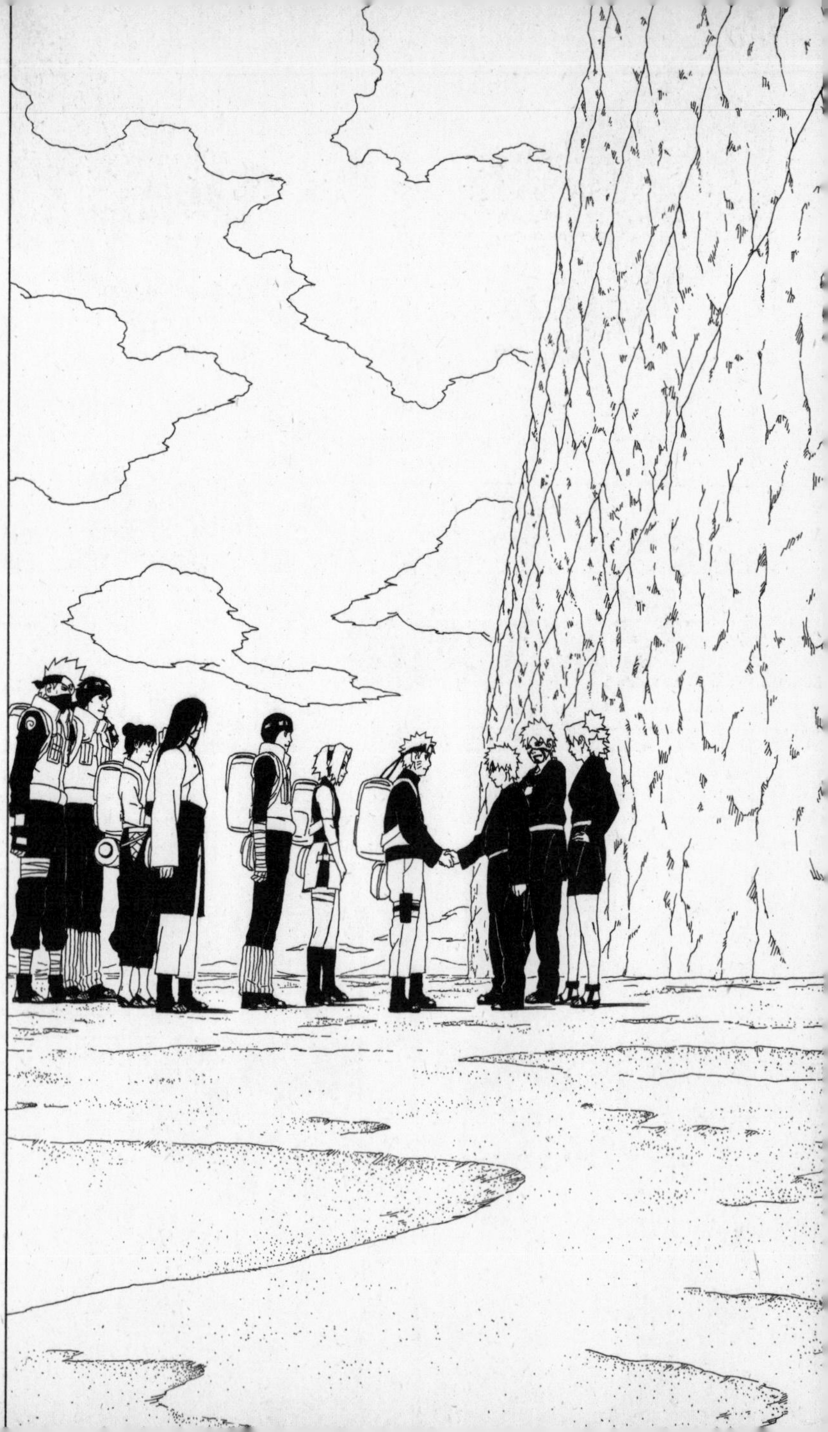

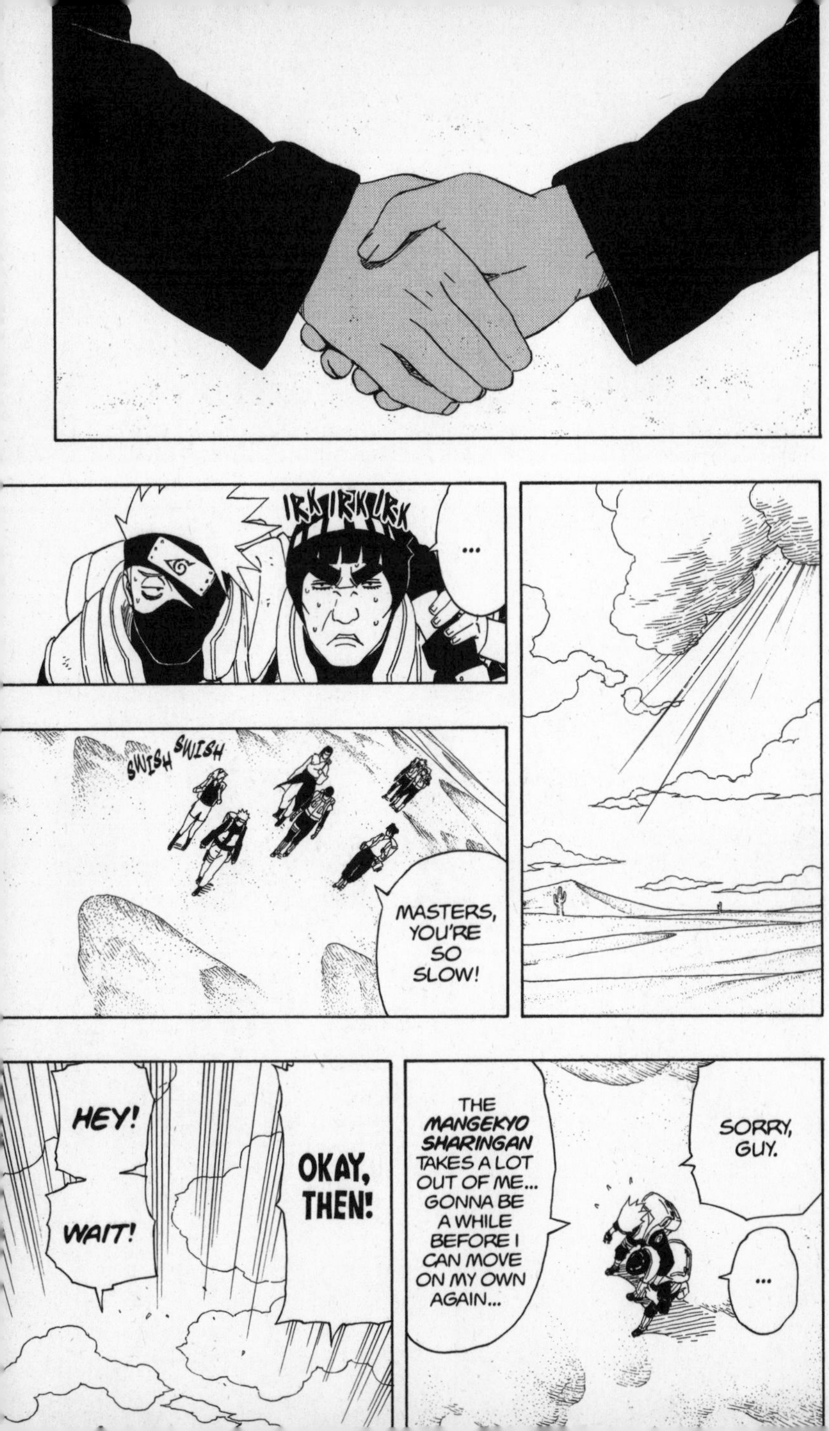
...
IRK IRK IRK IRK
MASTERS, YOU'RE SO SLOW!
SWISH SWISH
SORRY, GUY.
THE *MANGEKYO SHARINGAN* TAKES A LOT OUT OF ME... GONNA BE A WHILE BEFORE I CAN MOVE ON MY OWN AGAIN...
...
OKAY, THEN!
HEY!
WAIT!

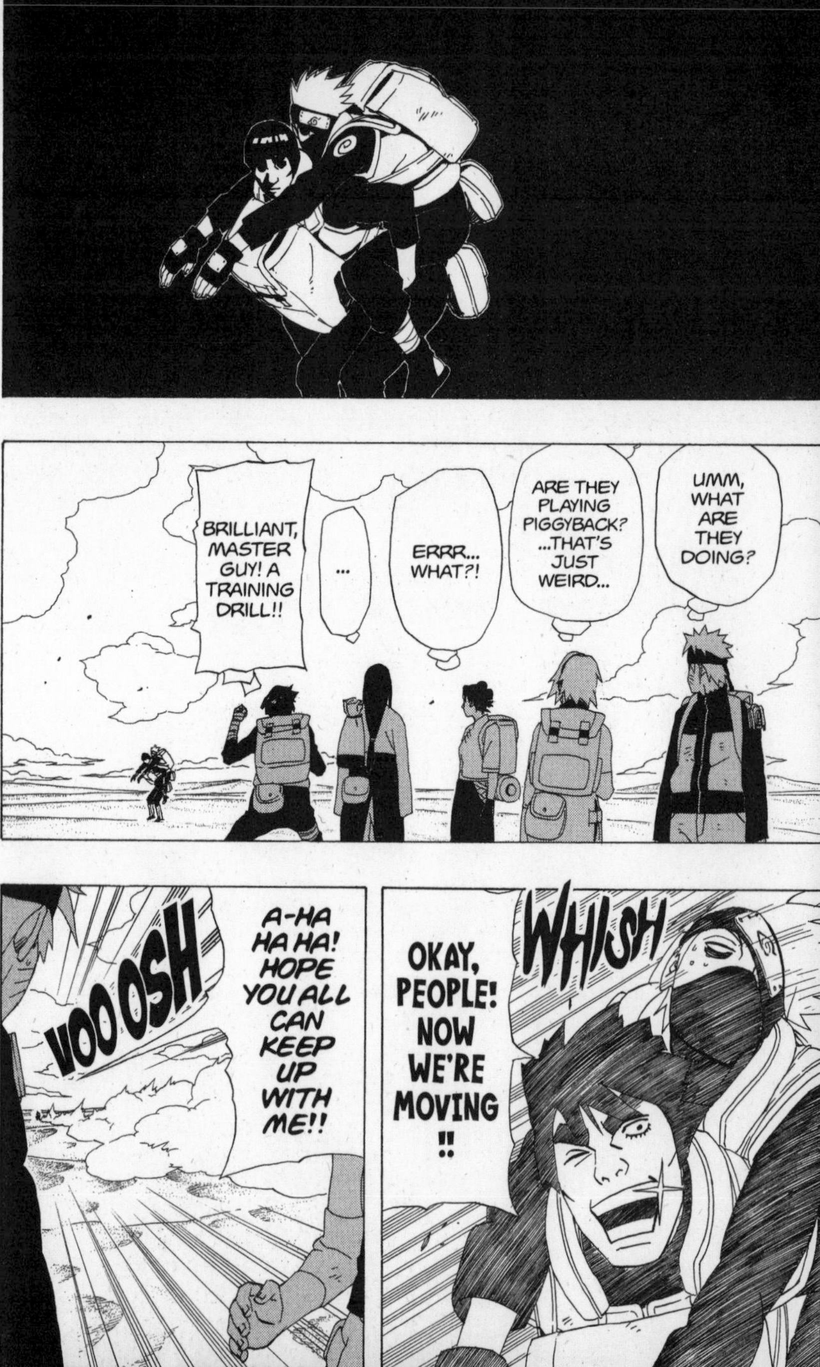
UMM, WHAT ARE THEY DOING?
ARE THEY PLAYING PIGGYBACK? ...THAT'S JUST WEIRD...
ERRR... WHAT?!
...
BRILLIANT, MASTER GUY! A TRAINING DRILL!!
WHISH
OKAY, PEOPLE! NOW WE'RE MOVING!!
A-HA HA HA! HOPE YOU ALL CAN KEEP UP WITH ME!!
VOOOSH

READ THIS WAY

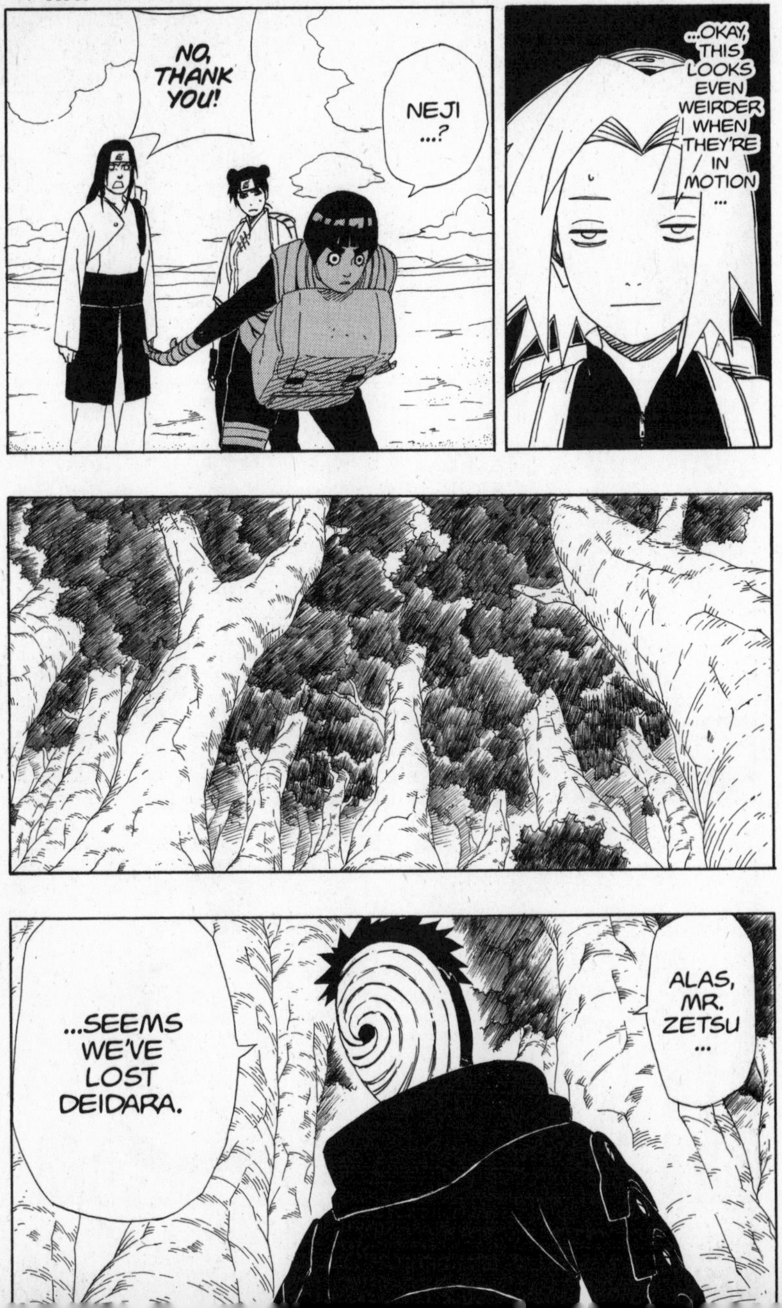
...OKAY, THIS LOOKS EVEN WEIRDER WHEN THEY'RE IN MOTION ...
NEJI ...?
NO, THANK YOU!
ALAS, MR. ZETSU ...
...SEEMS WE'VE LOST DEIDARA.

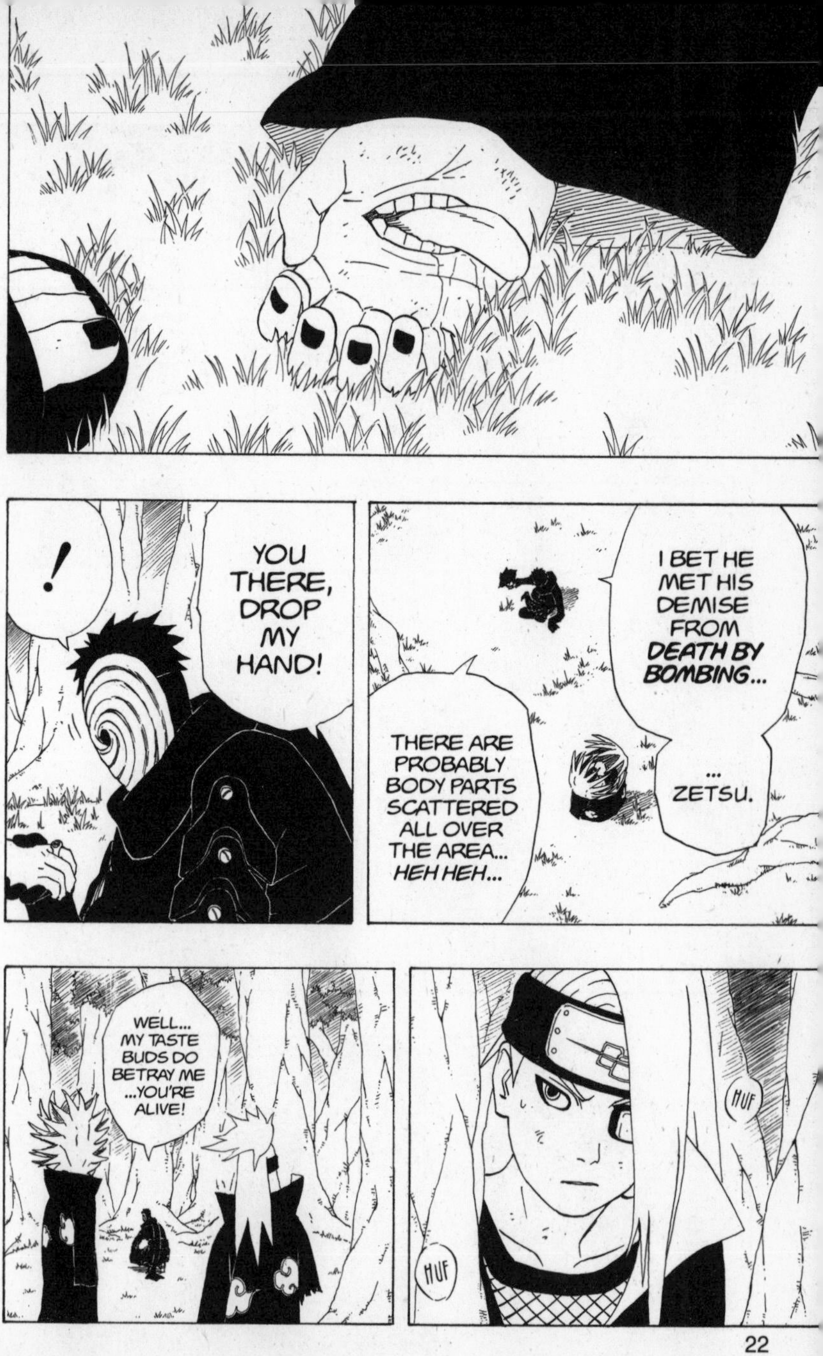
I BET HE MET HIS DEMISE FROM *DEATH BY BOMBING...*
... ZETSU.
THERE ARE PROBABLY BODY PARTS SCATTERED ALL OVER THE AREA... *HEH HEH...*
YOU THERE, DROP MY HAND!
!
HUF
HUF
WELL... MY TASTE BUDS DO BETRAY ME ...YOU'RE ALIVE!

READ THIS WAY

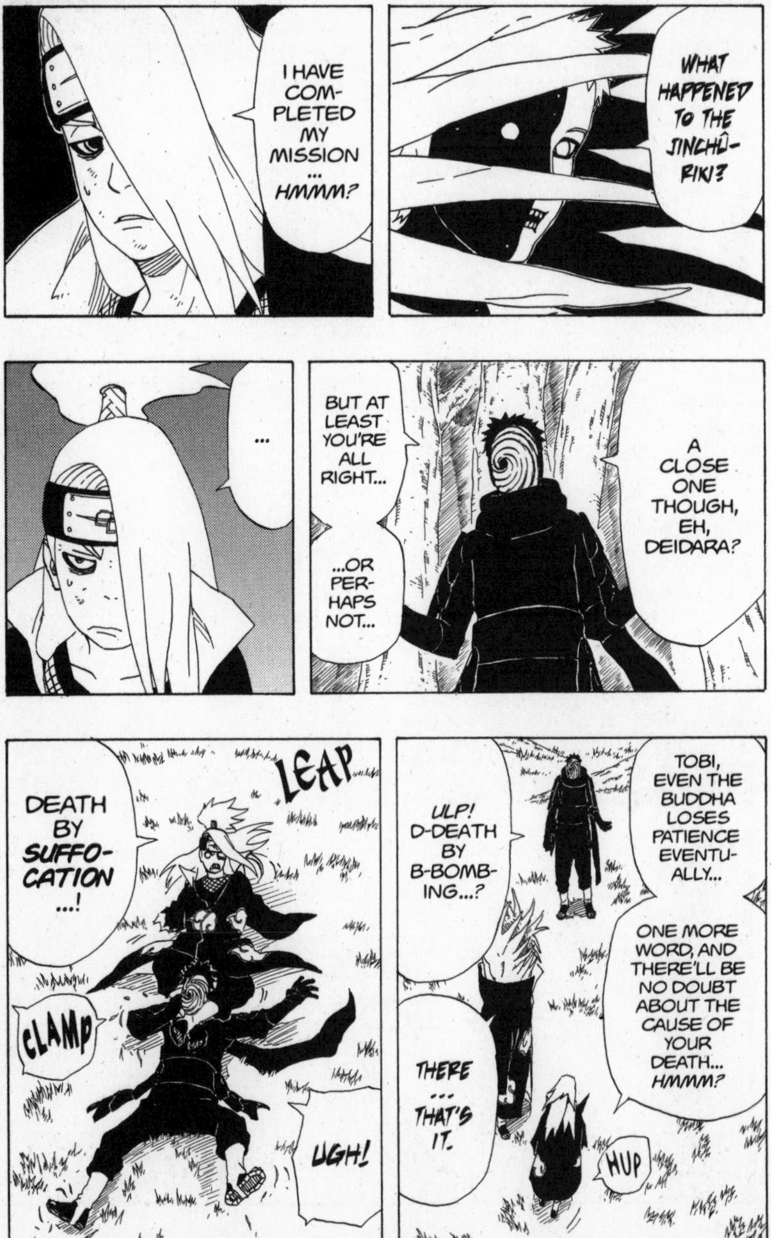
WHAT HAPPENED TO THE JINCHÛ-RIKI?
I HAVE COMPLETED MY MISSION ... HMMM?
A CLOSE ONE THOUGH, EH, DEIDARA?
BUT AT LEAST YOU'RE ALL RIGHT...
...OR PERHAPS NOT...
...
TOBI, EVEN THE BUDDHA LOSES PATIENCE EVENTUALLY...
ONE MORE WORD, AND THERE'LL BE NO DOUBT ABOUT THE CAUSE OF YOUR DEATH... HMMM?
ULP! D-DEATH BY B-BOMBING...?
HUP
THERE ... THAT'S IT.
LEAP
DEATH BY SUFFOCATION ...!
CLAMP
UGH!

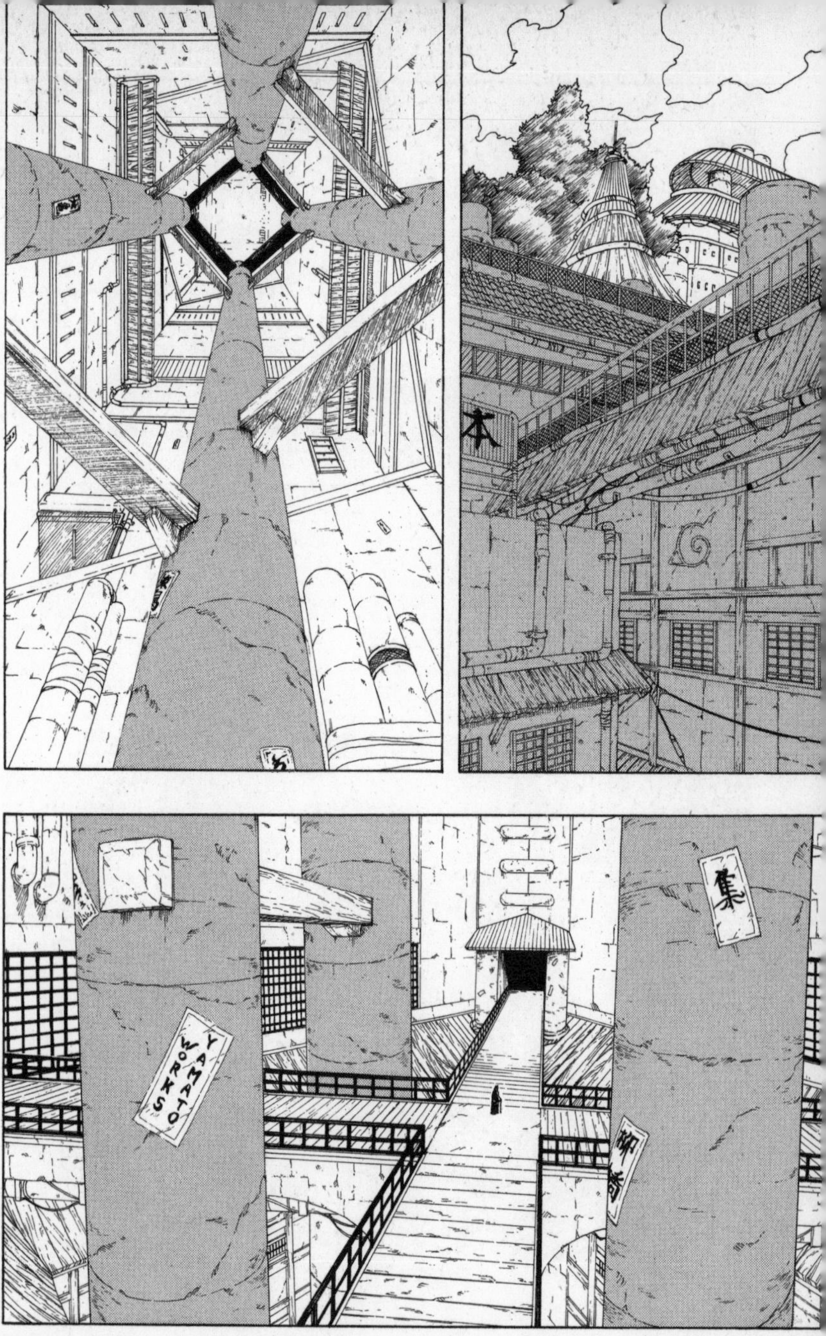
本
YAMATO WORKS
集

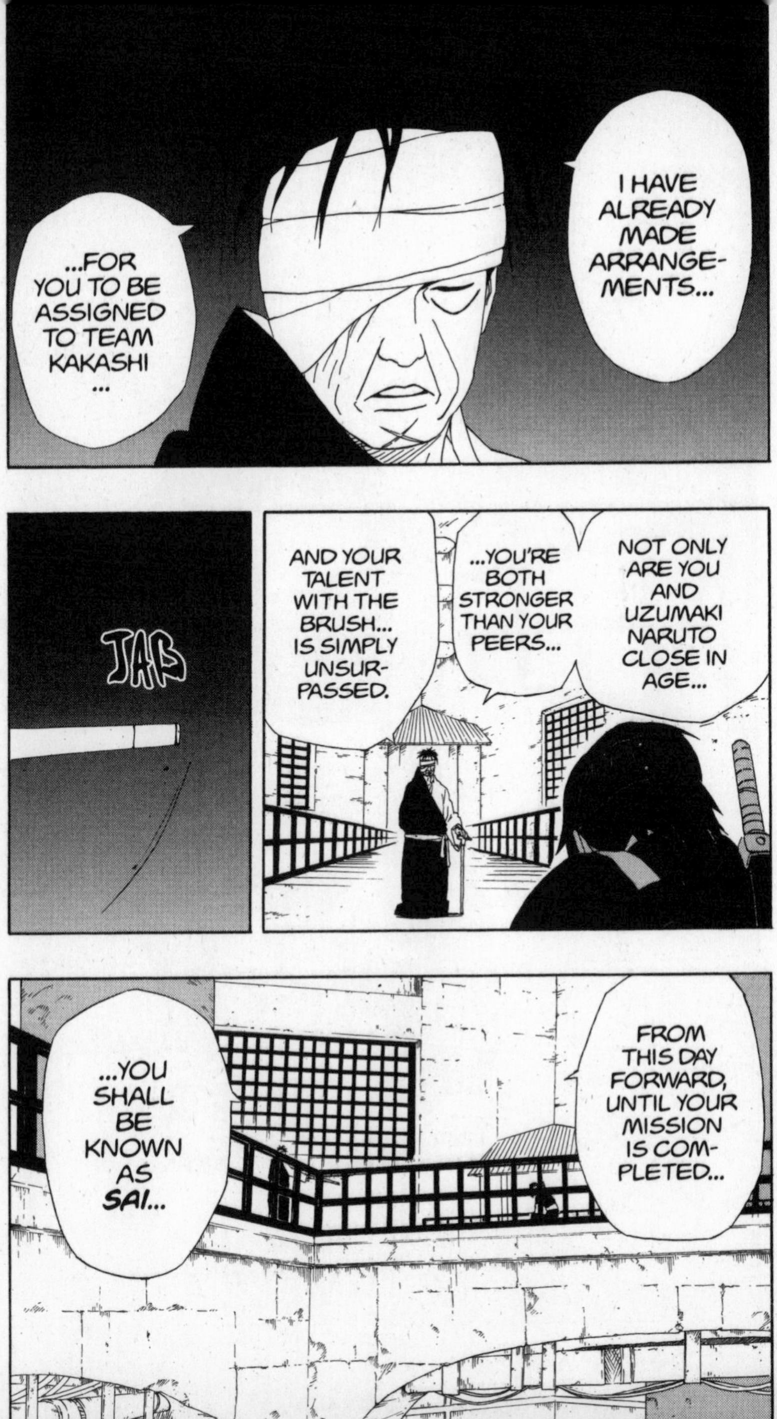
I HAVE ALREADY MADE ARRANGE-MENTS...
...FOR YOU TO BE ASSIGNED TO TEAM KAKASHI ...
NOT ONLY ARE YOU AND UZUMAKI NARUTO CLOSE IN AGE...
...YOU'RE BOTH STRONGER THAN YOUR PEERS...
AND YOUR TALENT WITH THE BRUSH... IS SIMPLY UNSUR-PASSED.
JAB
FROM THIS DAY FORWARD, UNTIL YOUR MISSION IS COM-PLETED...
...YOU SHALL BE KNOWN AS *SAI*...

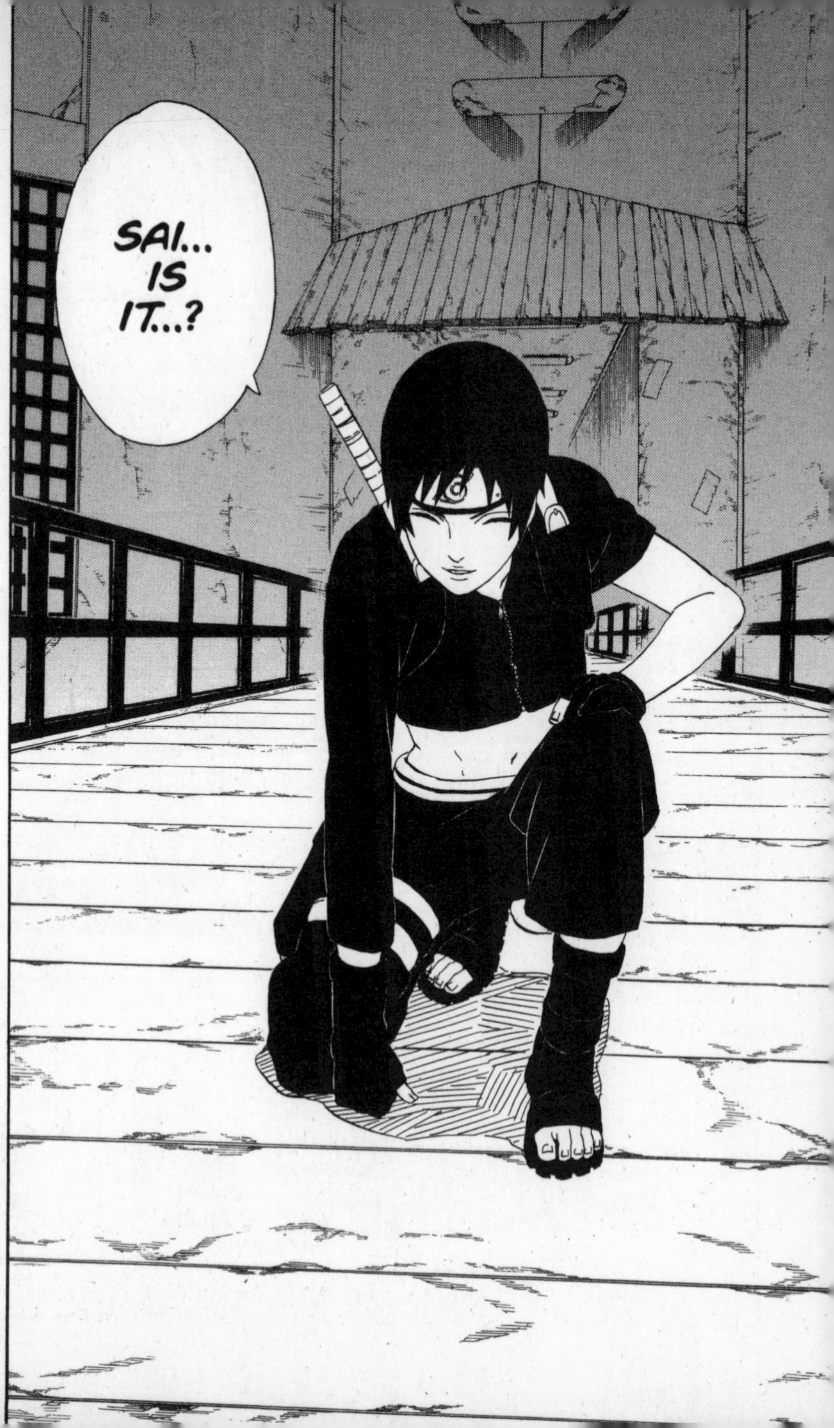
SAI... IS IT...?

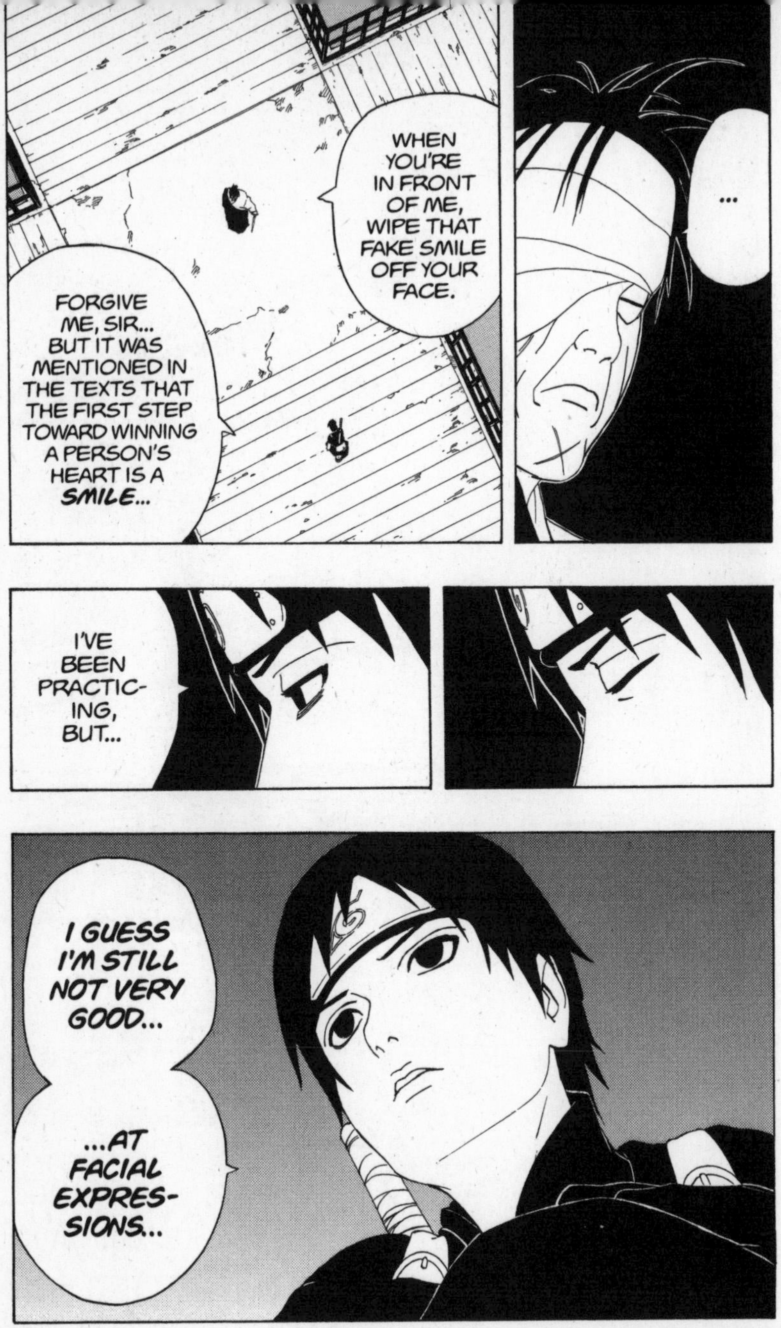
...
WHEN YOU'RE IN FRONT OF ME, WIPE THAT FAKE SMILE OFF YOUR FACE.
FORGIVE ME, SIR... BUT IT WAS MENTIONED IN THE TEXTS THAT THE FIRST STEP TOWARD WINNING A PERSON'S HEART IS A SMILE...
I'VE BEEN PRACTIC-ING, BUT...
I GUESS I'M STILL NOT VERY GOOD...
...AT FACIAL EXPRES-SIONS...

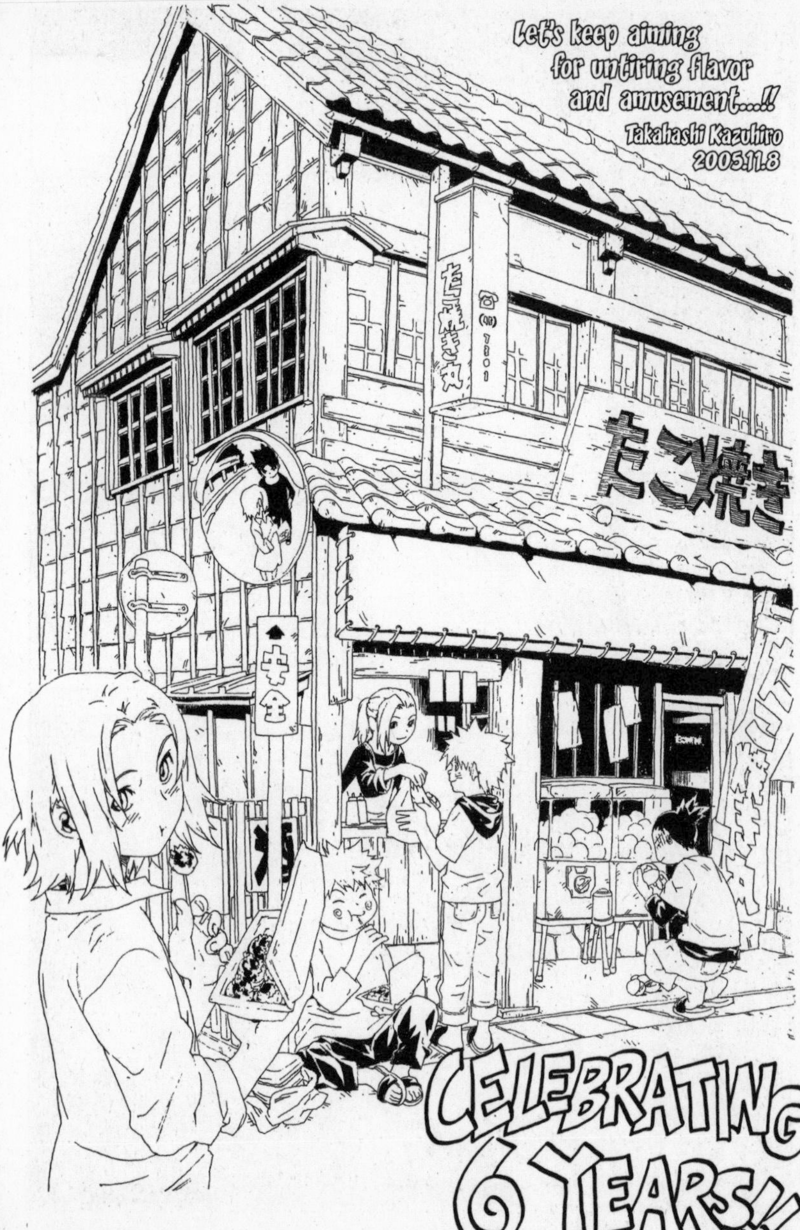
Let's keep aiming for untiring flavor and amusement...!!
Takahashi Kazuhiro
2005.11.8
たこ焼き
CELEBRATING 6 YEARS!!

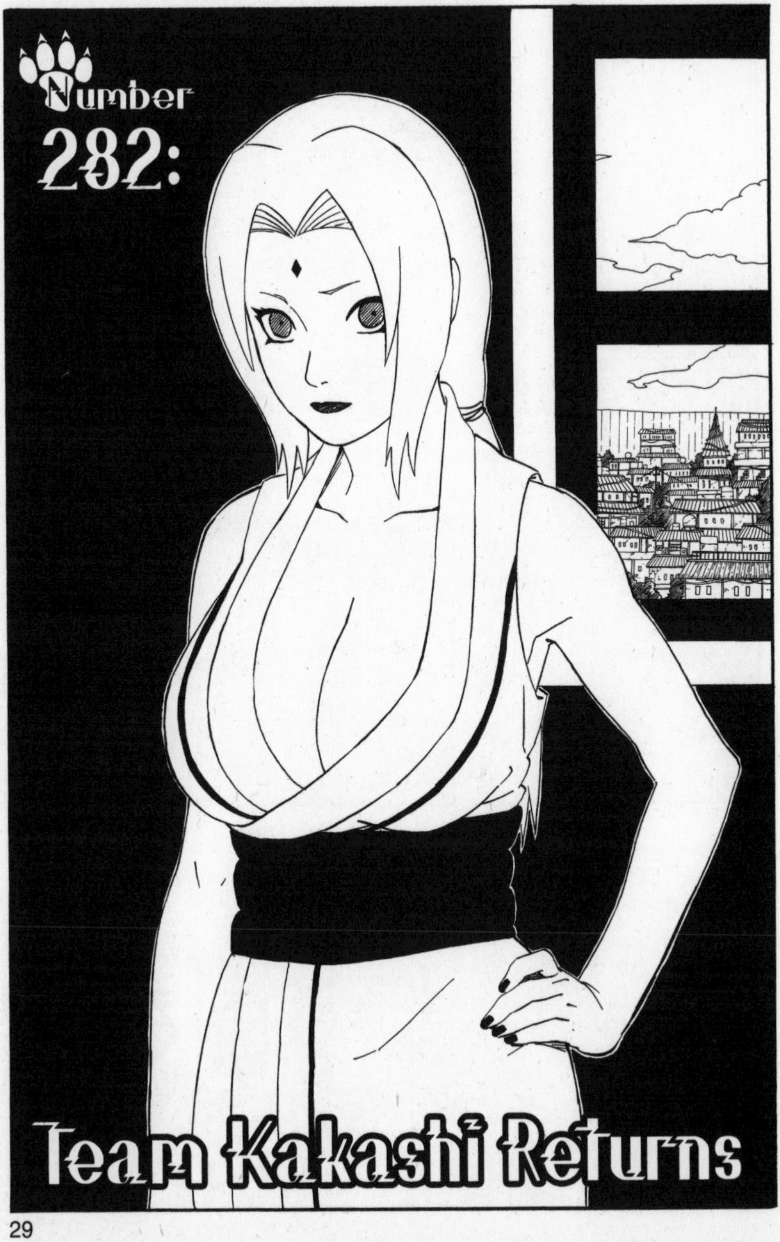
Number
282:
Team Kakashi Returns

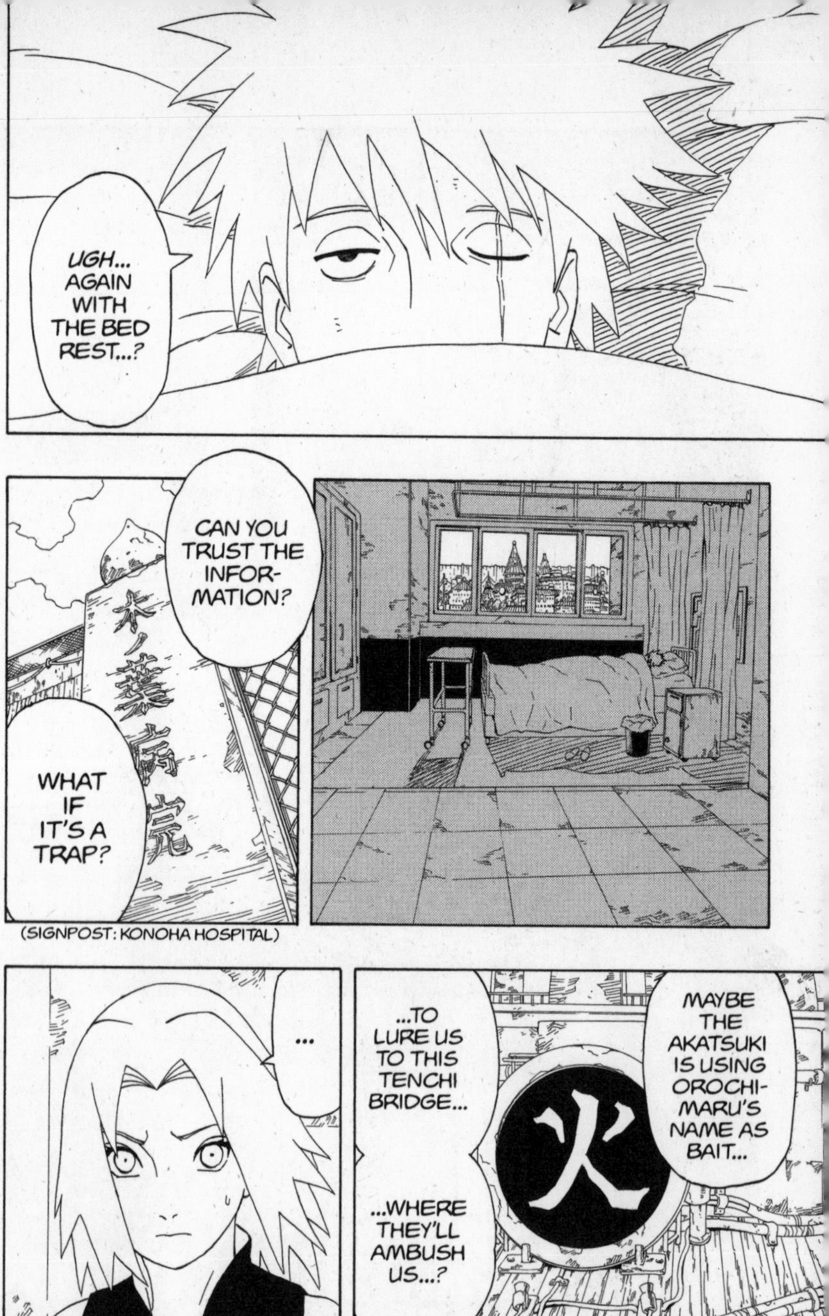
UGH... AGAIN WITH THE BED REST...?
CAN YOU TRUST THE INFORMATION?
WHAT IF IT'S A TRAP?
(SIGNPOST: KONOHA HOSPITAL)
MAYBE THE AKATSUKI IS USING OROCHIMARU'S NAME AS BAIT...
...TO LURE US TO THIS TENCHI BRIDGE...
...WHERE THEY'LL AMBUSH US...?
...

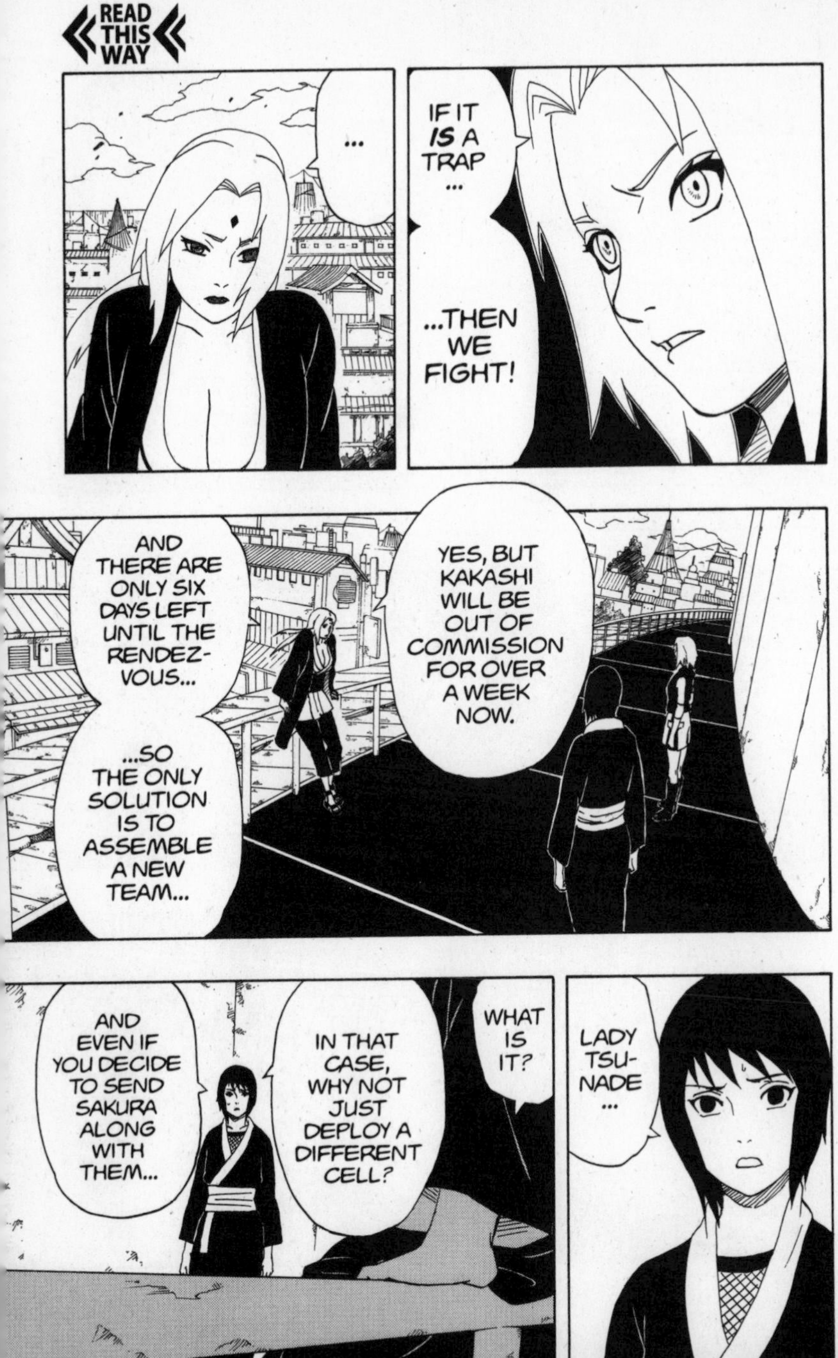
READ THIS WAY
IF IT IS A TRAP ...
...THEN WE FIGHT!
...
YES, BUT KAKASHI WILL BE OUT OF COMMISSION FOR OVER A WEEK NOW.
AND THERE ARE ONLY SIX DAYS LEFT UNTIL THE RENDEZ-VOUS...
...SO THE ONLY SOLUTION IS TO ASSEMBLE A NEW TEAM...
LADY TSU-NADE ...
WHAT IS IT?
IN THAT CASE, WHY NOT JUST DEPLOY A DIFFERENT CELL?
AND EVEN IF YOU DECIDE TO SEND SAKURA ALONG WITH THEM...

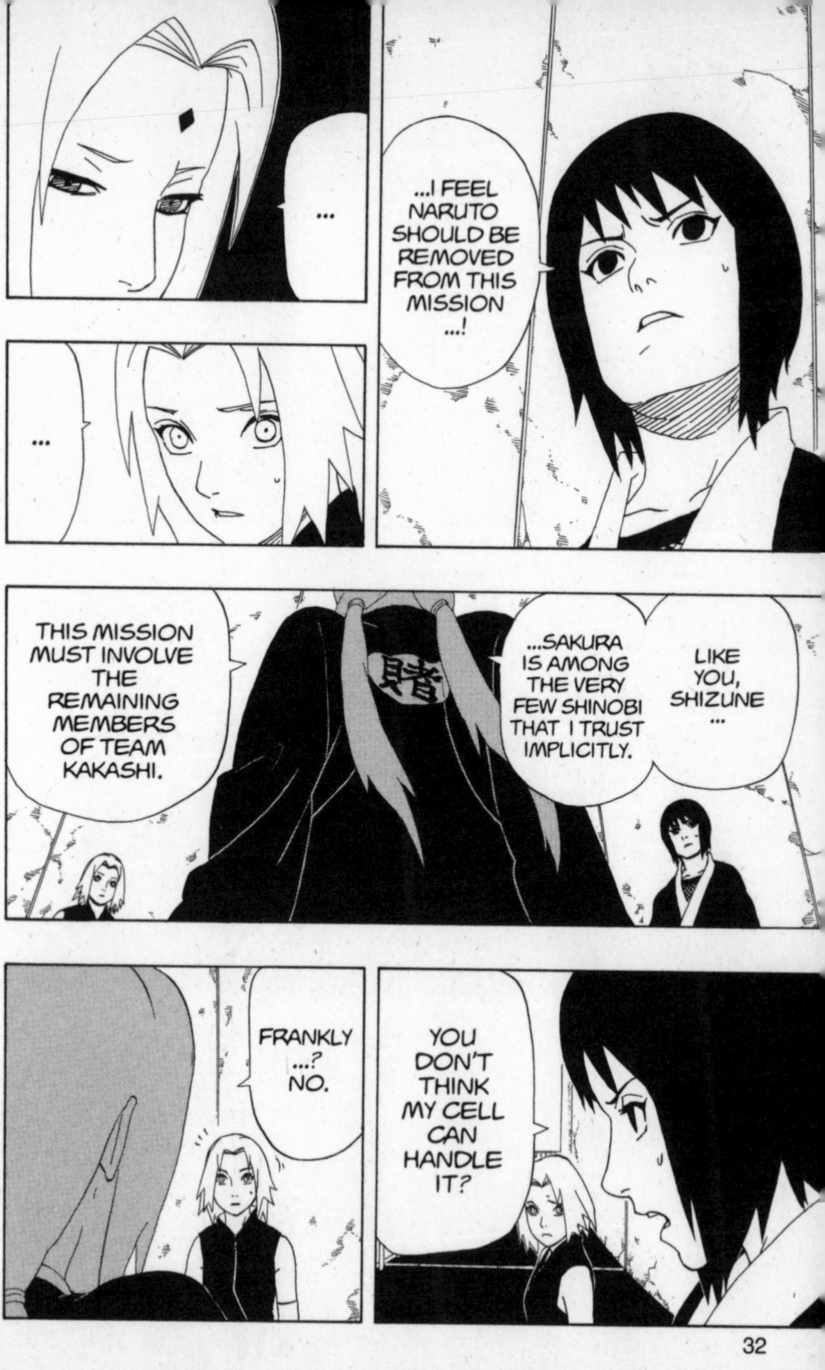
...I FEEL NARUTO SHOULD BE REMOVED FROM THIS MISSION ...!
...
...
LIKE YOU, SHIZUNE ...
...SAKURA IS AMONG THE VERY FEW SHINOBI THAT I TRUST IMPLICITLY.
THIS MISSION MUST INVOLVE THE REMAINING MEMBERS OF TEAM KAKASHI.
YOU DON'T THINK MY CELL CAN HANDLE IT?
FRANKLY ...? NO.

READ THIS WAY

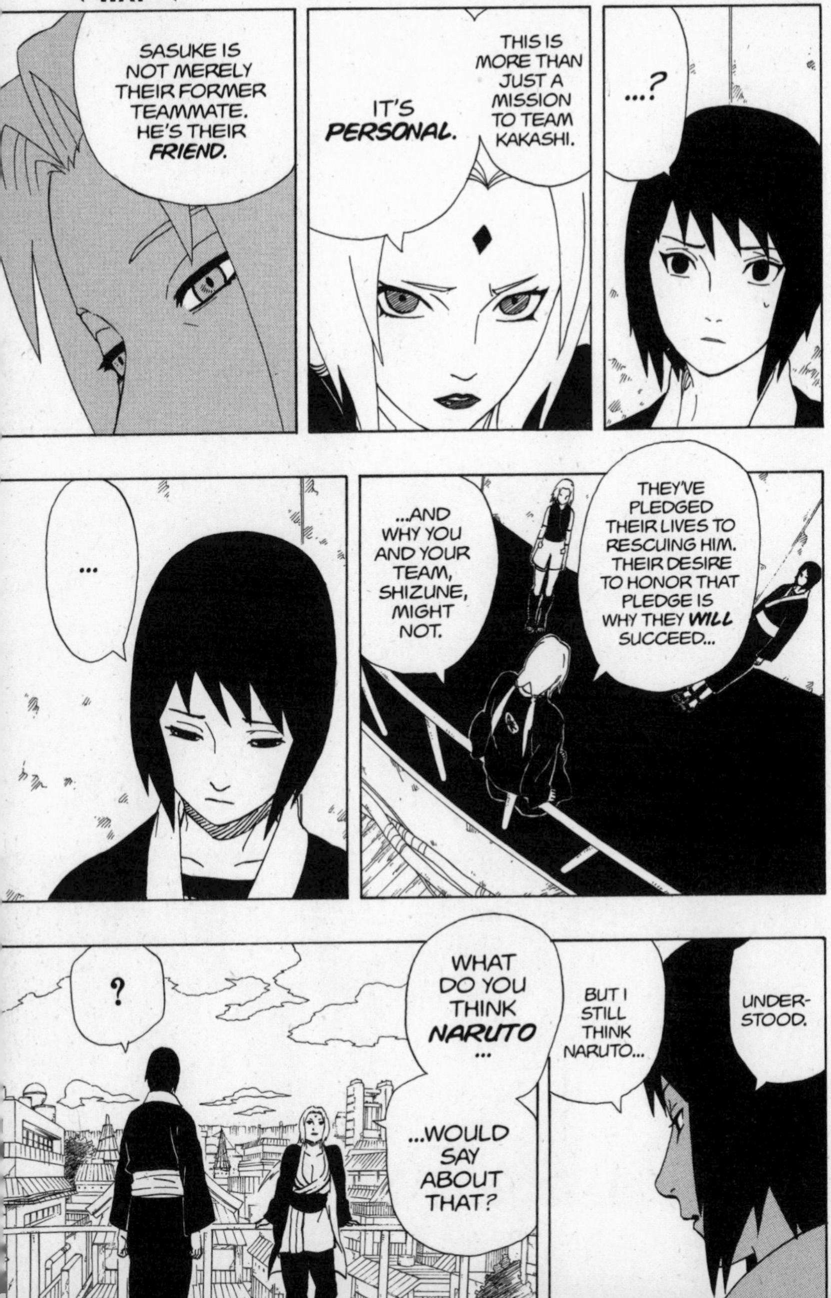

...?
THIS IS MORE THAN JUST A MISSION TO TEAM KAKASHI.
IT'S **PERSONAL.**
SASUKE IS NOT MERELY THEIR FORMER TEAMMATE. HE'S THEIR **FRIEND.**
THEY'VE PLEDGED THEIR LIVES TO RESCUING HIM. THEIR DESIRE TO HONOR THAT PLEDGE IS WHY THEY **WILL** SUCCEED...
...AND WHY YOU AND YOUR TEAM, SHIZUNE, MIGHT NOT.
...
UNDER-STOOD.
BUT I STILL THINK NARUTO...
WHAT DO YOU THINK **NARUTO** ...
...WOULD SAY ABOUT THAT?
?

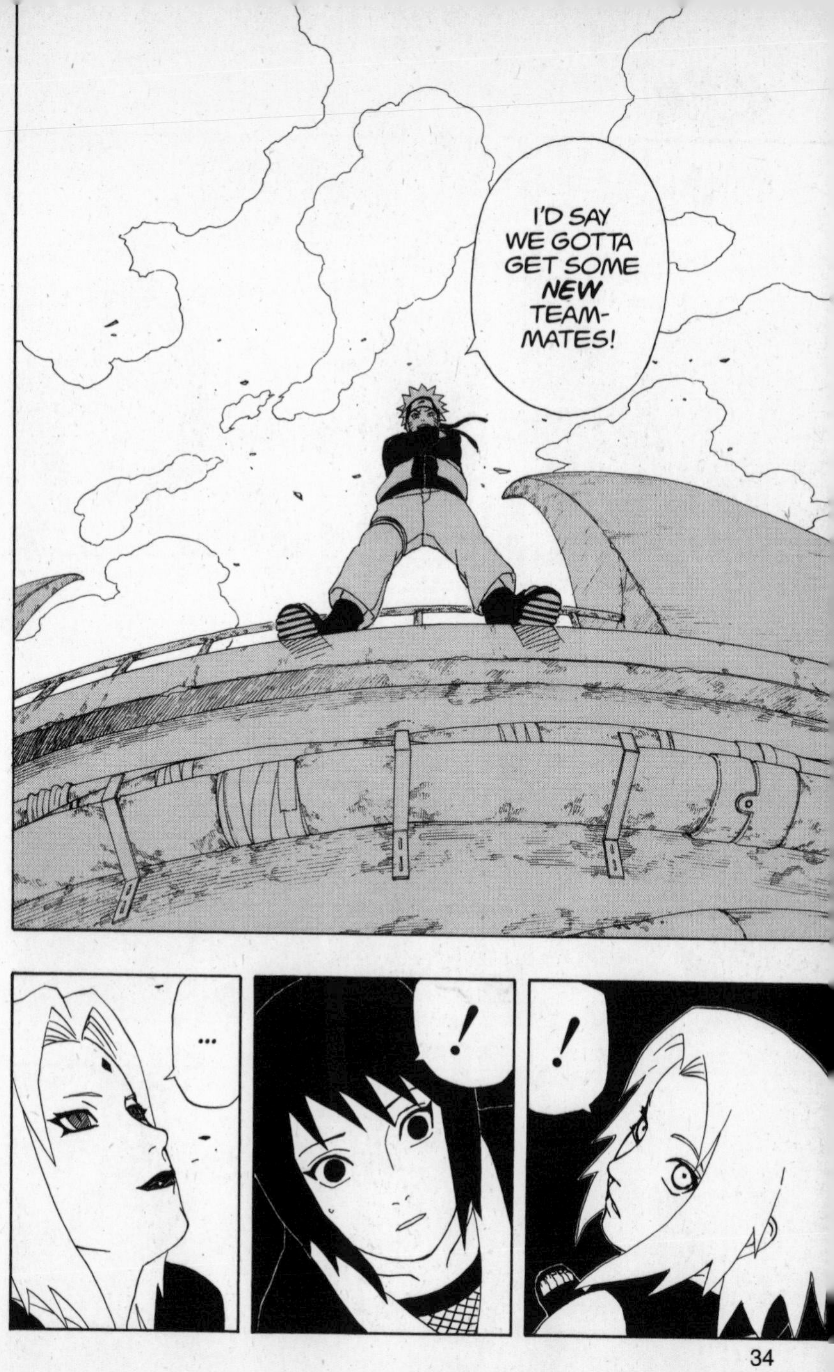
I'D SAY WE GOTTA GET SOME *NEW* TEAM-MATES!
!
!
...

READ THIS WAY

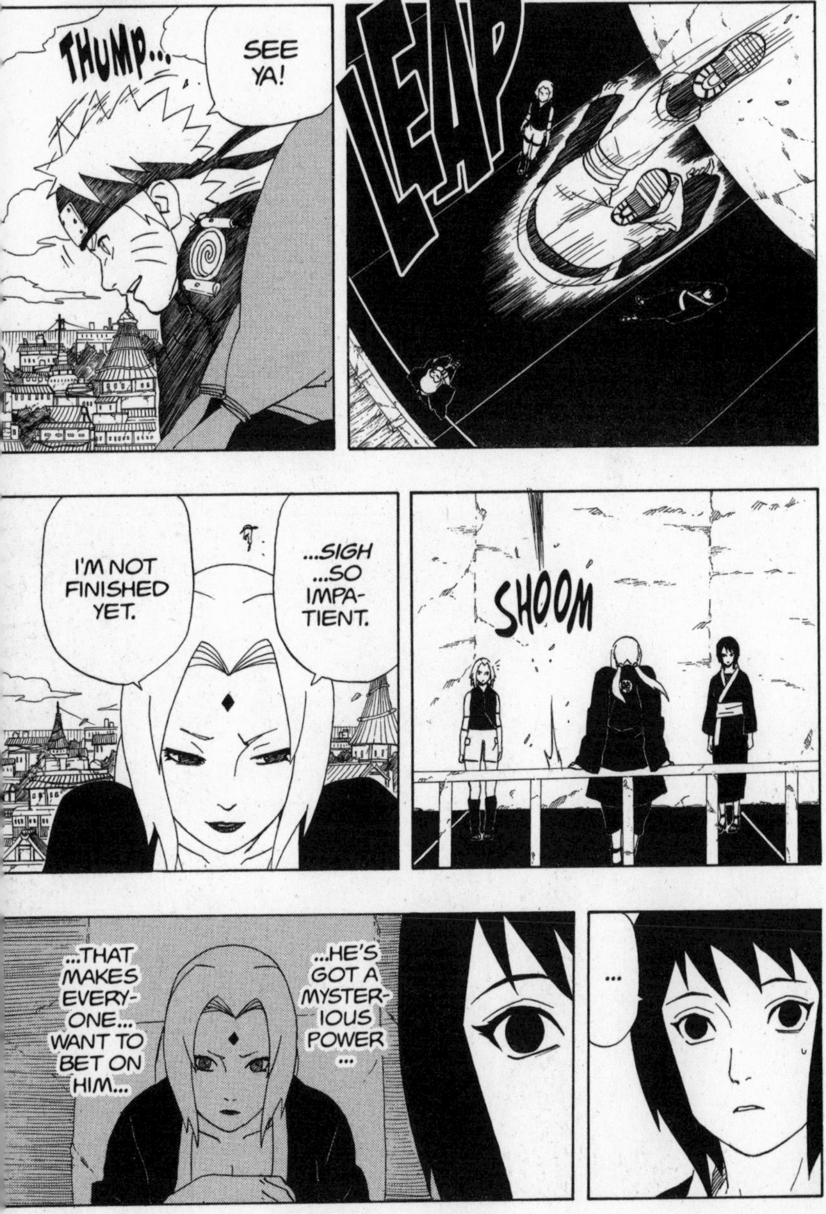
LEAP
SEE YA!
THUMP...
SHOOM
...SIGH ...SO IMPA-TIENT.
I'M NOT FINISHED YET.
...
...HE'S GOT A MYSTER-IOUS POWER ...
...THAT MAKES EVERY-ONE... WANT TO BET ON HIM...

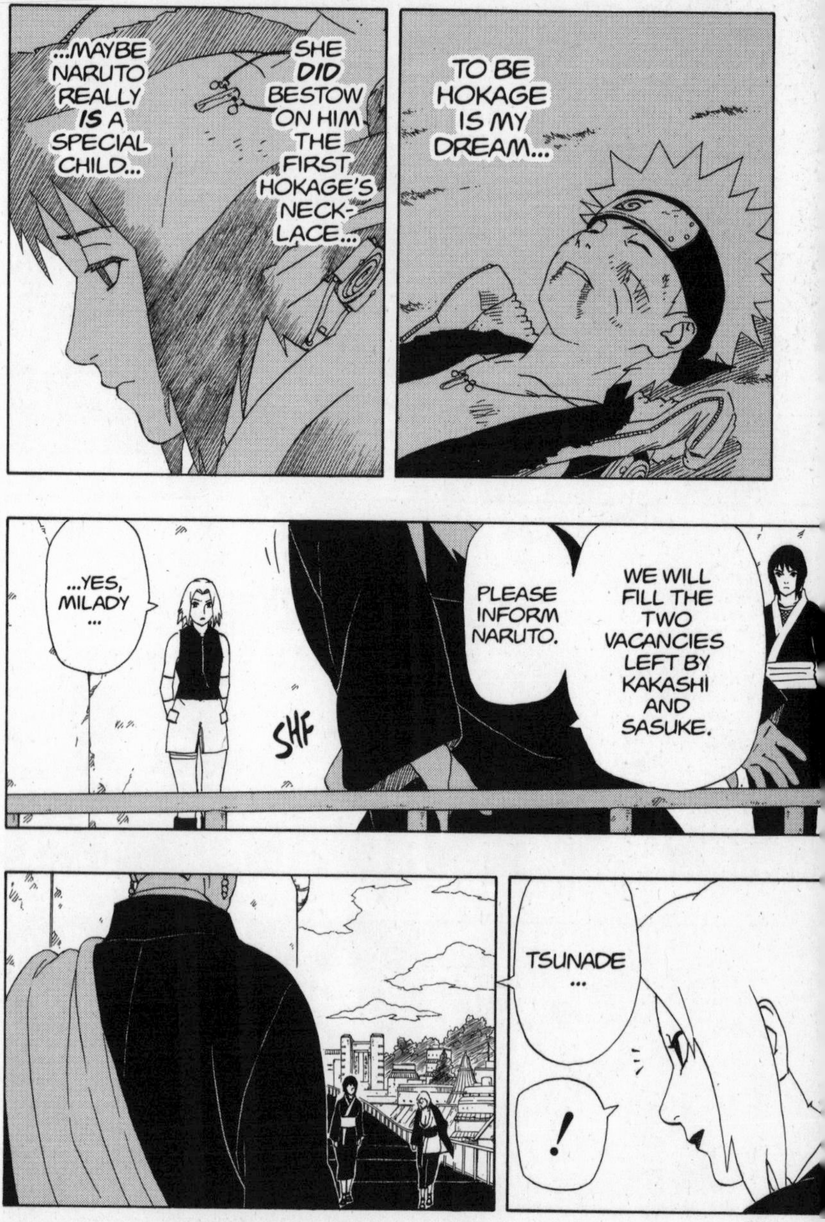
TO BE HOKAGE IS MY DREAM...
SHE DID BESTOW ON HIM THE FIRST HOKAGE'S NECK-LACE...
...MAYBE NARUTO REALLY IS A SPECIAL CHILD...
WE WILL FILL THE TWO VACANCIES LEFT BY KAKASHI AND SASUKE.
PLEASE INFORM NARUTO.
SHF
...YES, MILADY ...
TSUNADE ...
!

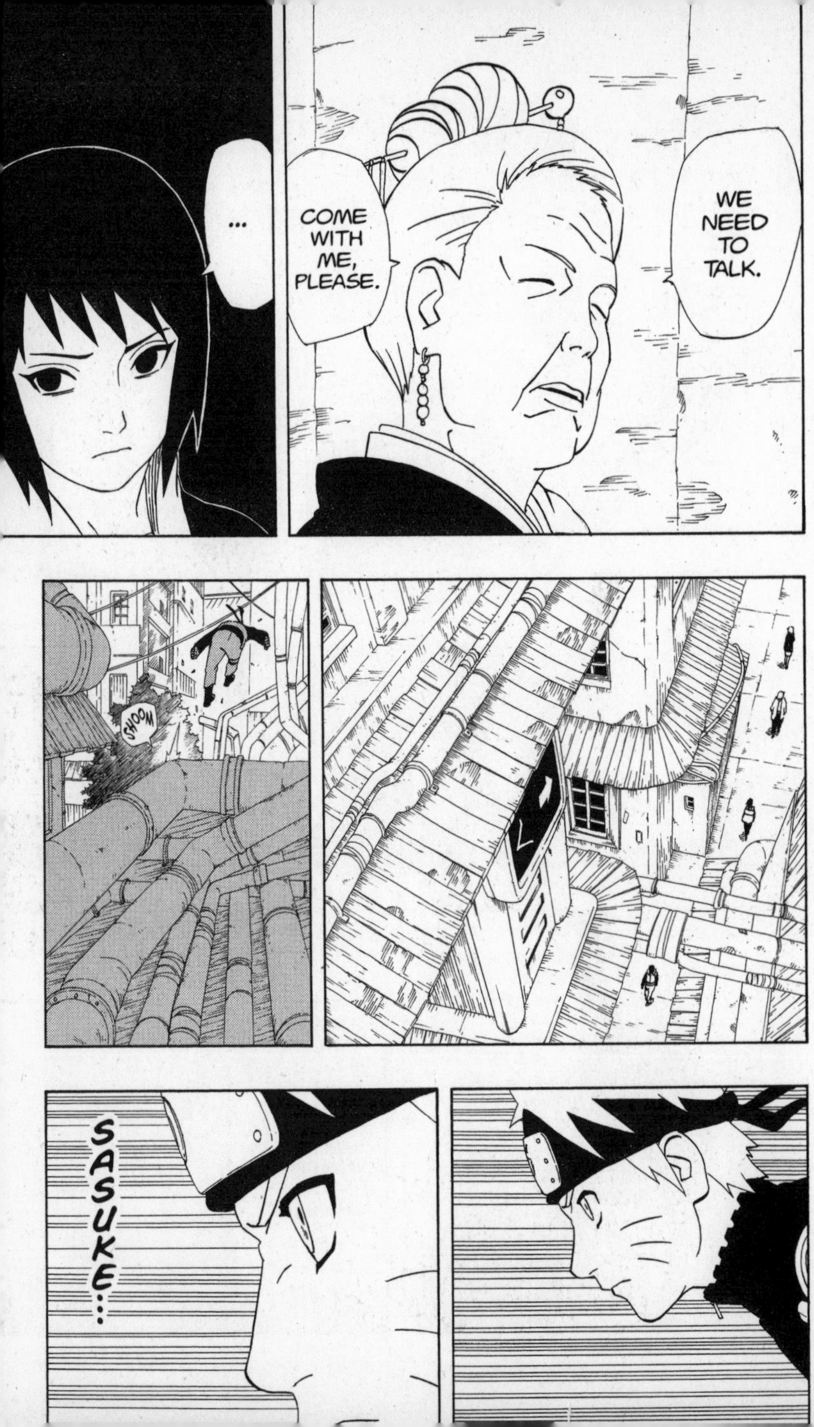
WE NEED TO TALK.
COME WITH ME, PLEASE.
...
SHOOM
SASUKE...

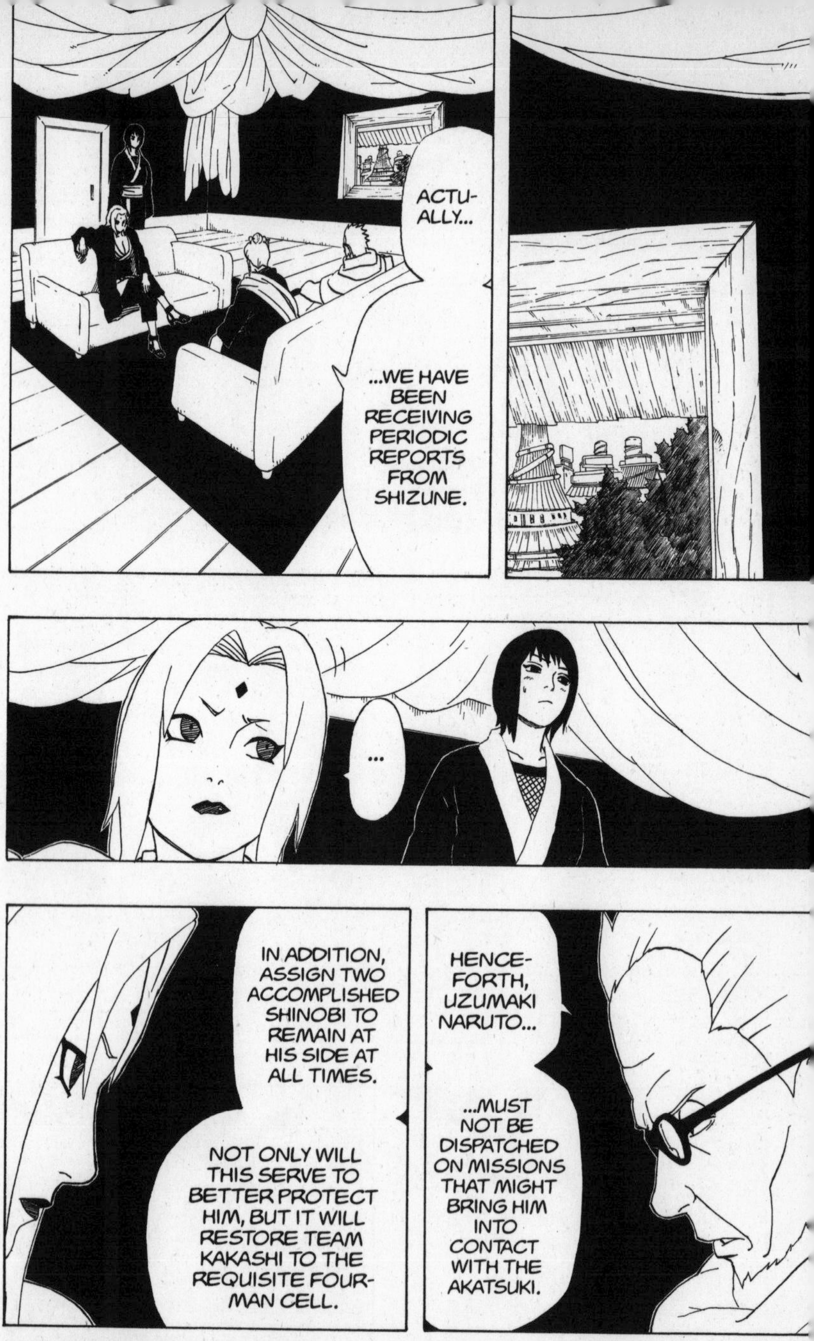
ACTU-ALLY...
...WE HAVE BEEN RECEIVING PERIODIC REPORTS FROM SHIZUNE.
...
HENCE-FORTH, UZUMAKI NARUTO...
...MUST NOT BE DISPATCHED ON MISSIONS THAT MIGHT BRING HIM INTO CONTACT WITH THE AKATSUKI.
IN ADDITION, ASSIGN TWO ACCOMPLISHED SHINOBI TO REMAIN AT HIS SIDE AT ALL TIMES.
NOT ONLY WILL THIS SERVE TO BETTER PROTECT HIM, BUT IT WILL RESTORE TEAM KAKASHI TO THE REQUISITE FOUR-MAN CELL.

READ THIS WAY

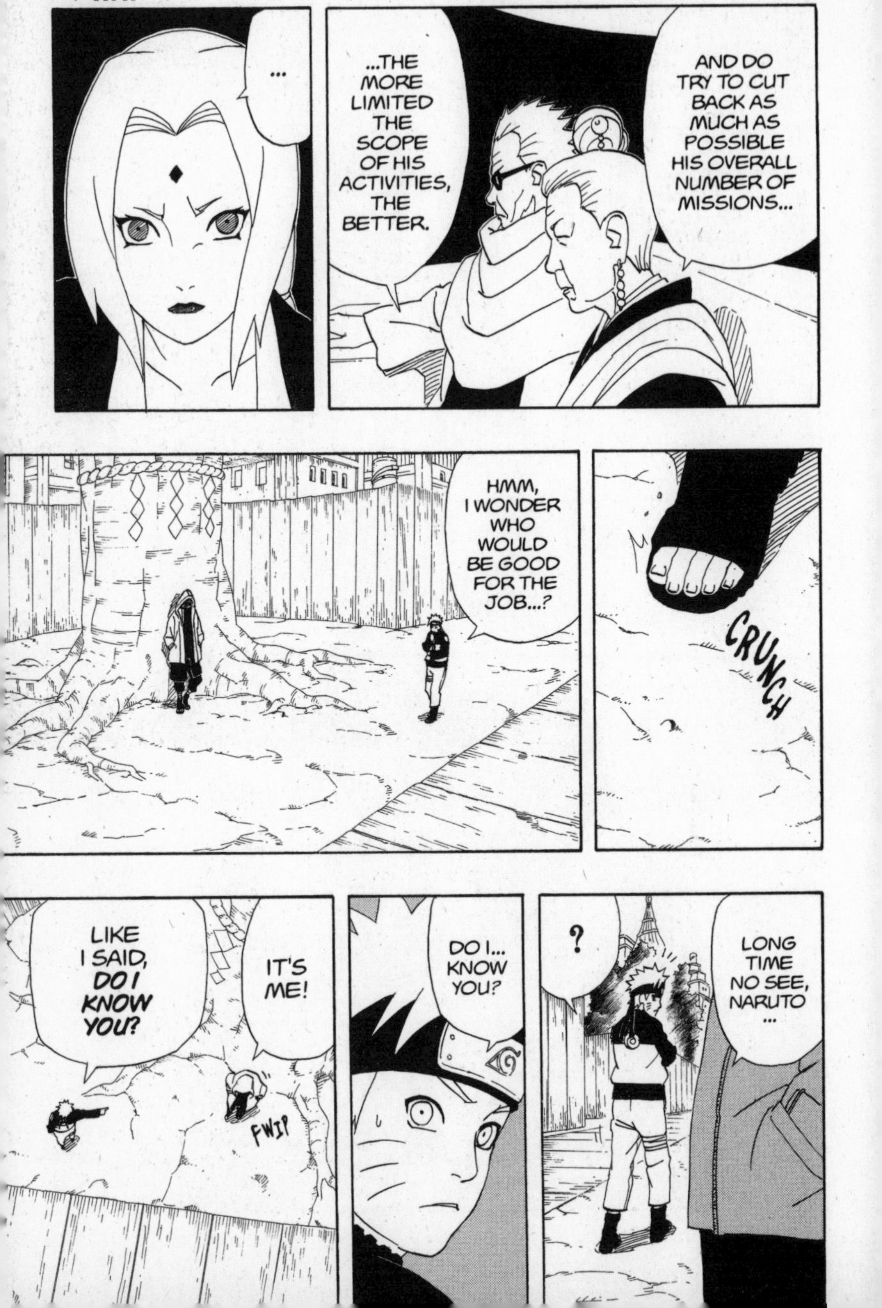
AND DO TRY TO CUT BACK AS MUCH AS POSSIBLE HIS OVERALL NUMBER OF MISSIONS...
...THE MORE LIMITED THE SCOPE OF HIS ACTIVITIES, THE BETTER.
...
CRUNCH
HMM, I WONDER WHO WOULD BE GOOD FOR THE JOB...?
LONG TIME NO SEE, NARUTO ...
?
DO I... KNOW YOU?
IT'S ME!
LIKE I SAID, **DO I KNOW YOU?**
FWIP

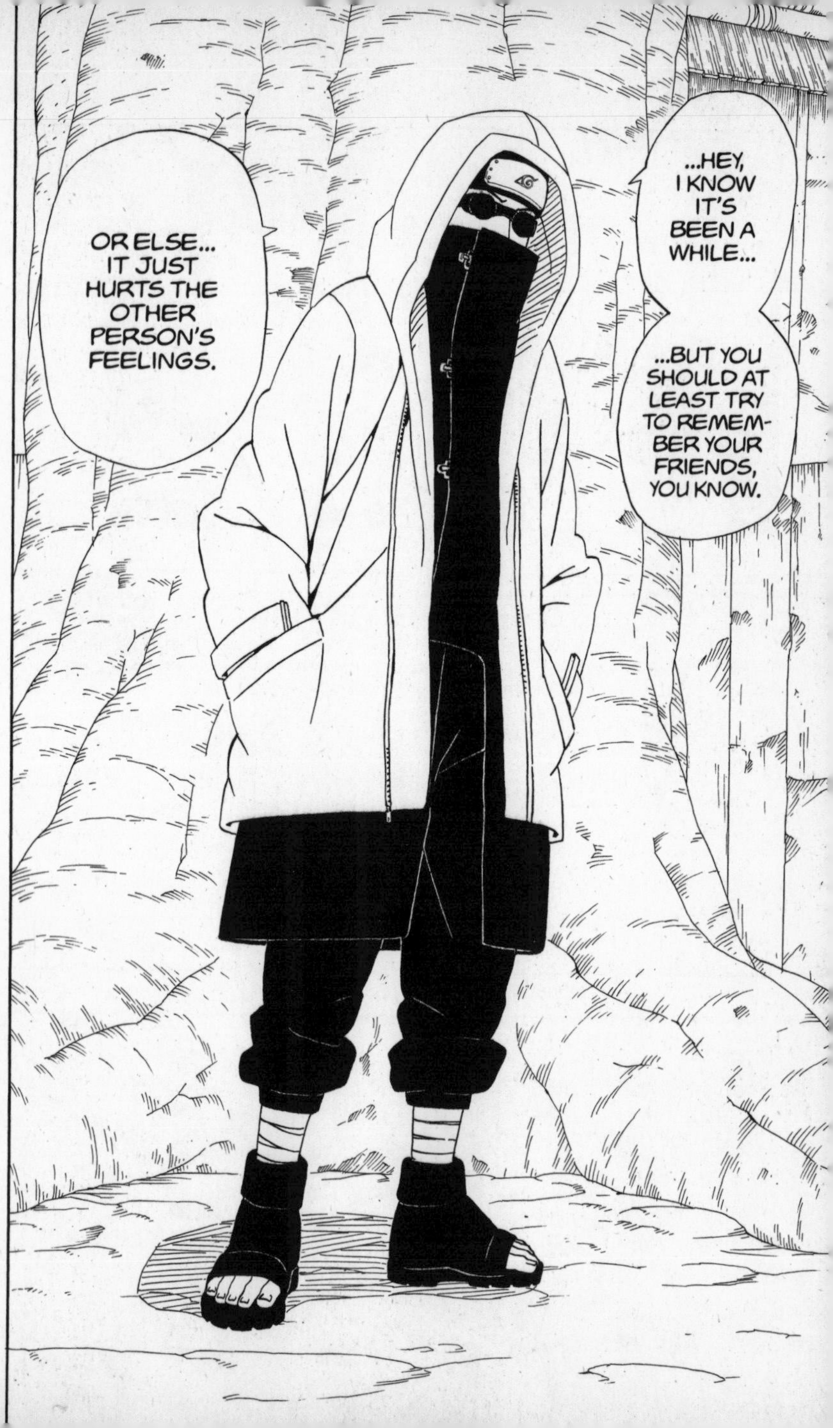
...HEY, I KNOW IT'S BEEN A WHILE...
...BUT YOU SHOULD AT LEAST TRY TO REMEM-BER YOUR FRIENDS, YOU KNOW.
OR ELSE... IT JUST HURTS THE OTHER PERSON'S FEELINGS.

READ THIS WAY

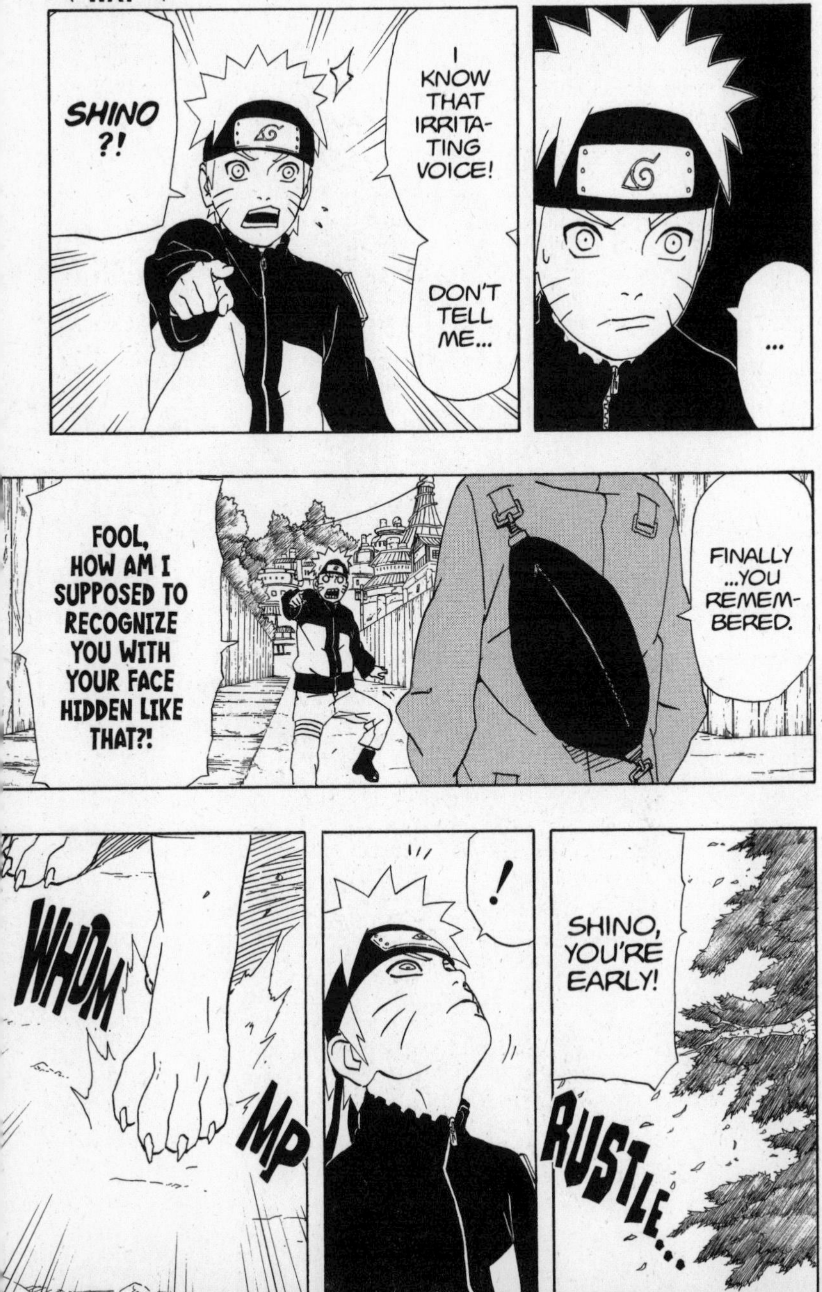
...
I KNOW THAT IRRITATING VOICE!
DON'T TELL ME...
SHINO?!
FINALLY ...YOU REMEMBERED.
FOOL, HOW AM I SUPPOSED TO RECOGNIZE YOU WITH YOUR FACE HIDDEN LIKE THAT?!
SHINO, YOU'RE EARLY!
RUSTLE...
!
WHOMP

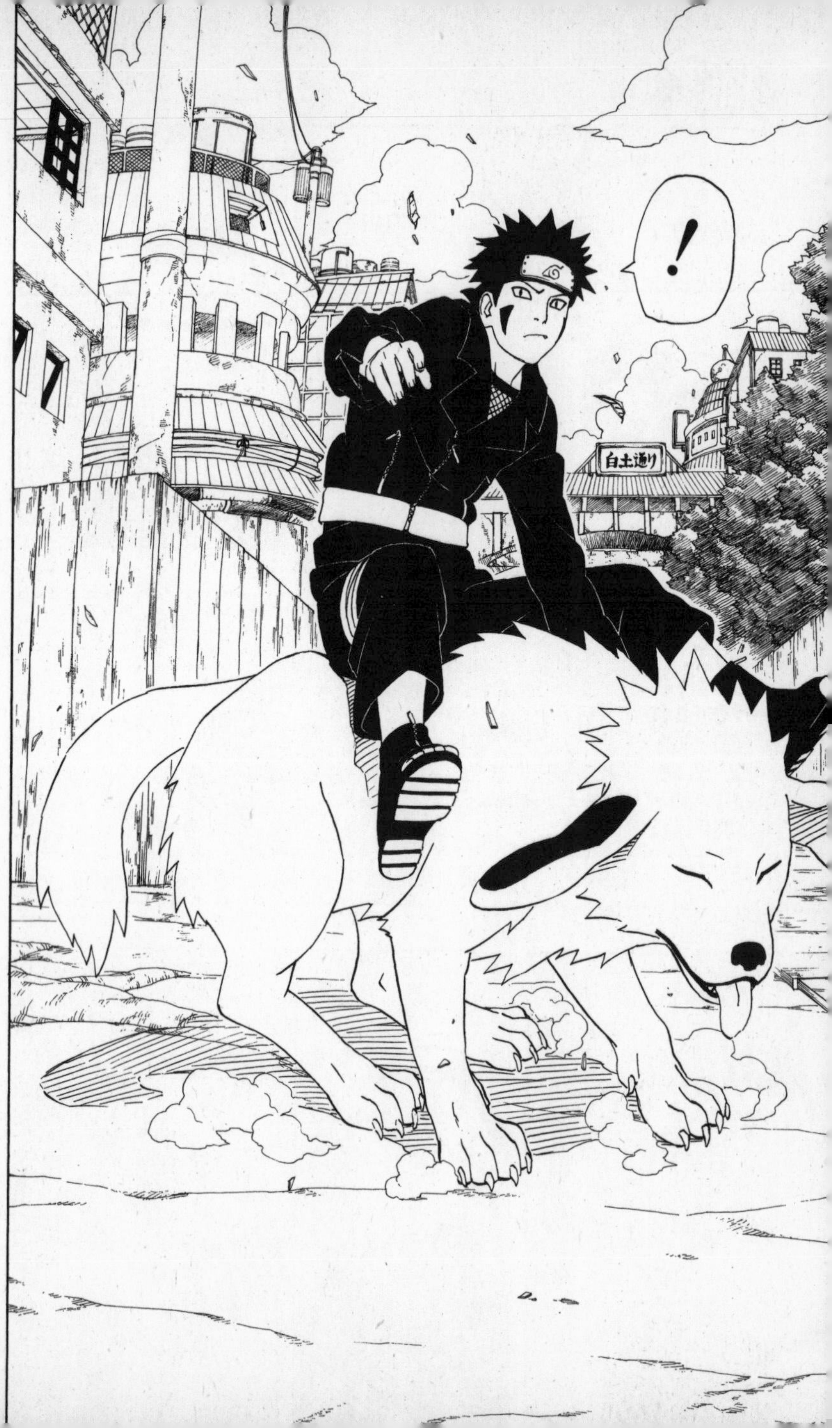
!
白土通り

READ THIS WAY

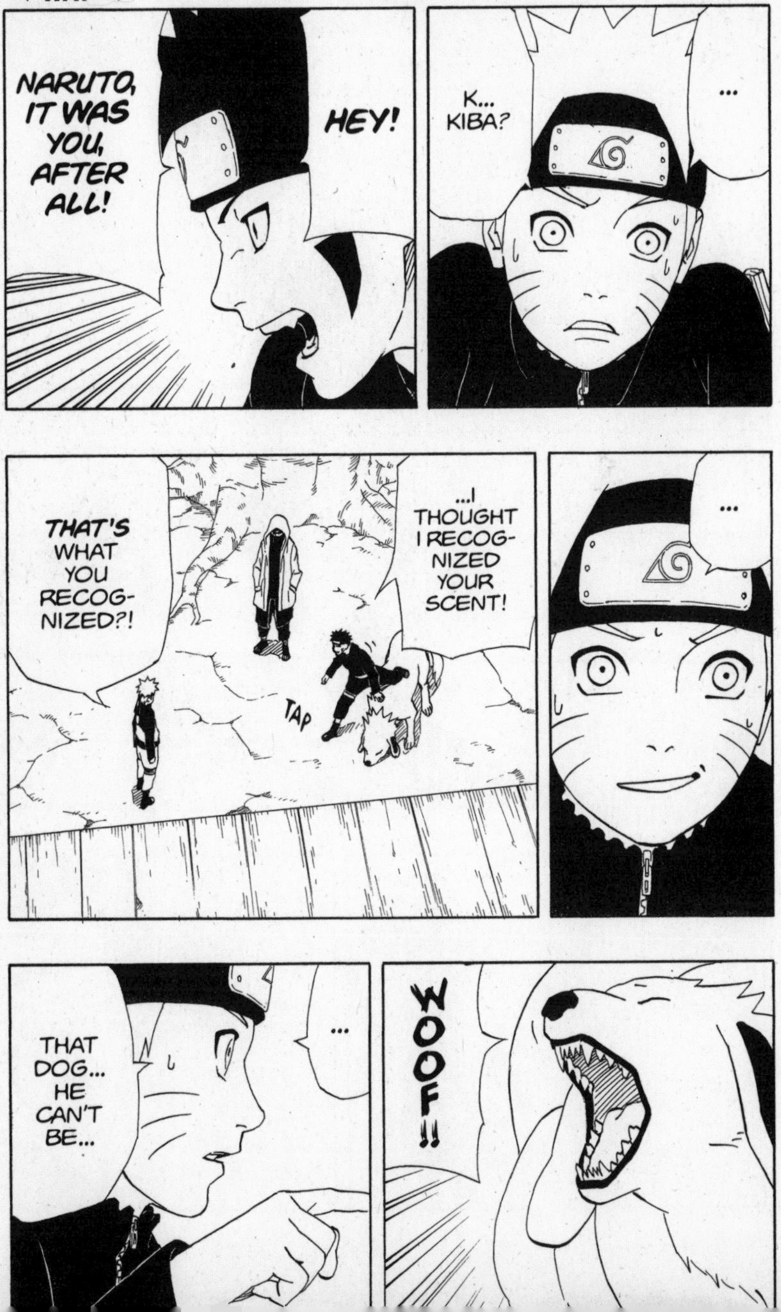
...
K... KIBA?
HEY!
NARUTO, IT WAS YOU, AFTER ALL!
...
...I THOUGHT I RECOG-NIZED YOUR SCENT!
TAP
THAT'S WHAT YOU RECOG-NIZED?!
WOOF!!
...
THAT DOG... HE CAN'T BE...

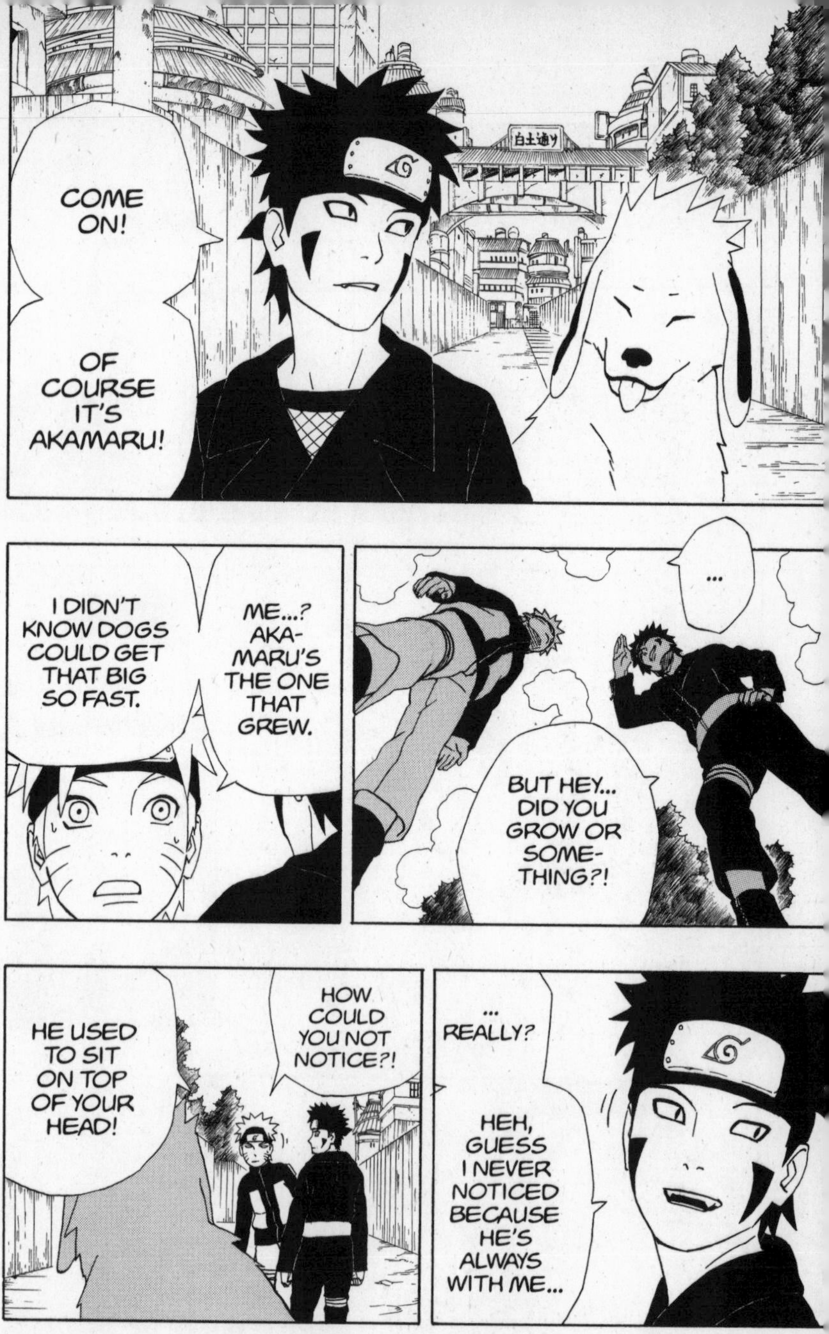
COME ON!
OF COURSE IT'S AKAMARU!
...
BUT HEY... DID YOU GROW OR SOME-THING?!
ME...? AKA-MARU'S THE ONE THAT GREW.
I DIDN'T KNOW DOGS COULD GET THAT BIG SO FAST.
... REALLY?
HEH, GUESS I NEVER NOTICED BECAUSE HE'S ALWAYS WITH ME...
HOW COULD YOU NOT NOTICE?!
HE USED TO SIT ON TOP OF YOUR HEAD!

READ THIS WAY

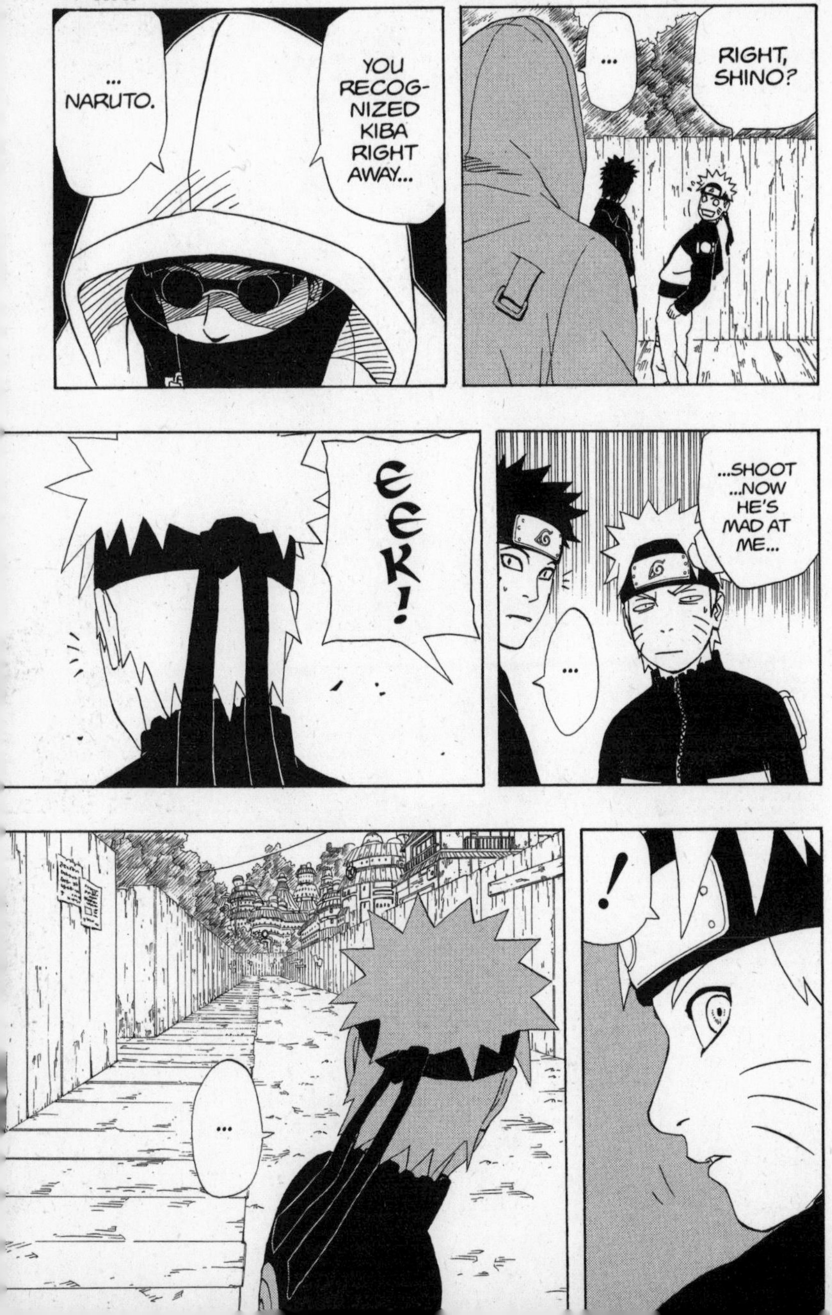
RIGHT, SHINO?
...
YOU RECOG-NIZED KIBA RIGHT AWAY...
... NARUTO.
...SHOOT ...NOW HE'S MAD AT ME...
...
EEK!
!
...

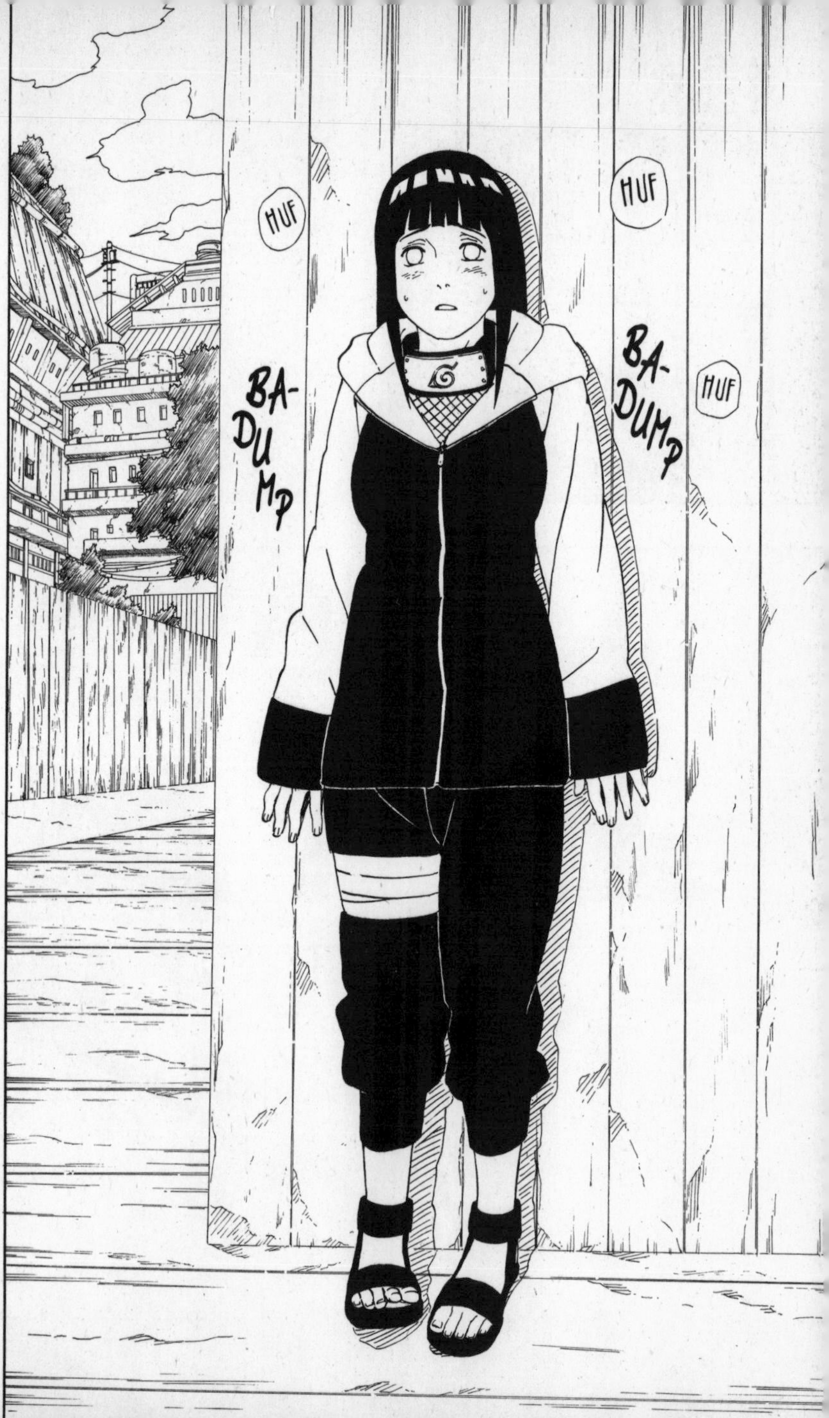
HUF
BA-DUMP
HUF
HUF
BA-DUMP

READ THIS WAY

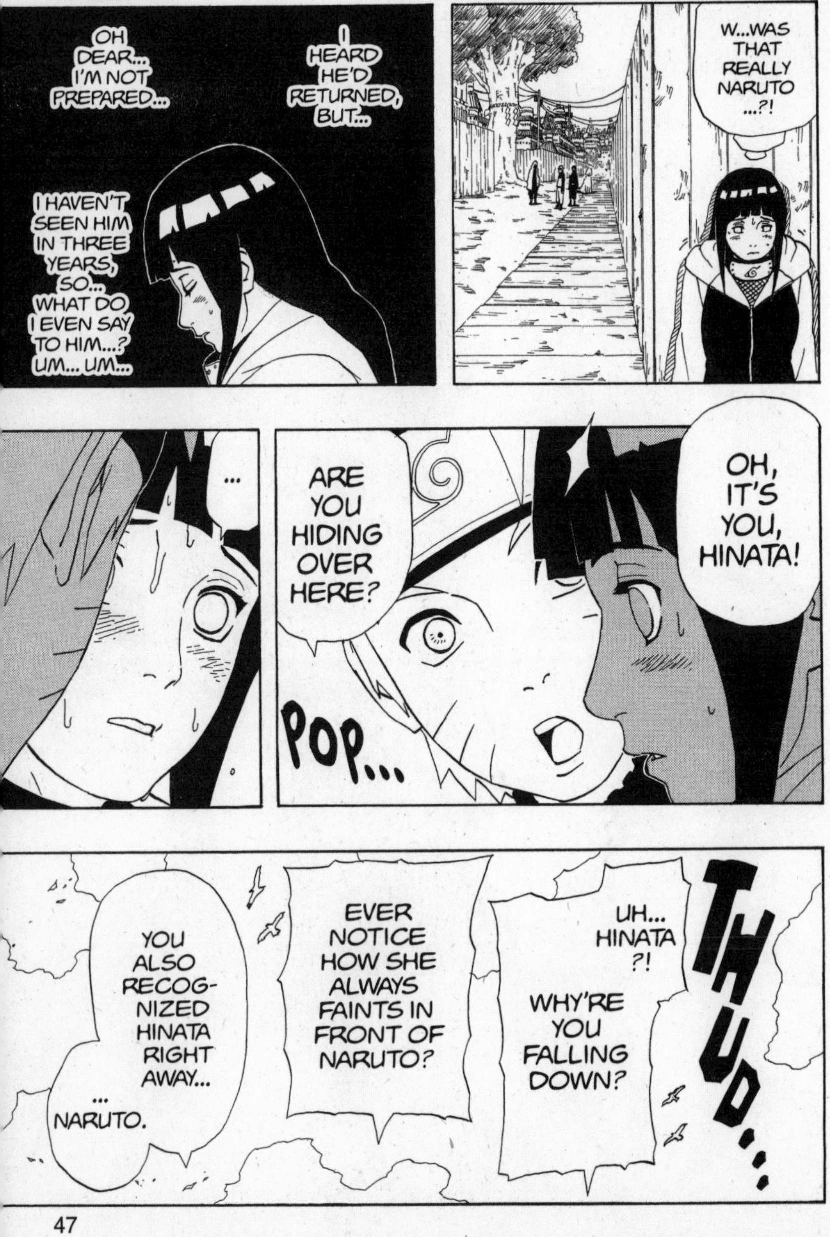

W...WAS THAT REALLY NARUTO ...?!
I HEARD HE'D RETURNED, BUT...
OH DEAR... I'M NOT PREPARED...
I HAVEN'T SEEN HIM IN THREE YEARS, SO... WHAT DO I EVEN SAY TO HIM...? UM... UM...
OH, IT'S YOU, HINATA!
ARE YOU HIDING OVER HERE?
POP...
...
THUD...
UH... HINATA ?!
WHY'RE YOU FALLING DOWN?
EVER NOTICE HOW SHE ALWAYS FAINTS IN FRONT OF NARUTO?
YOU ALSO RECOG-NIZED HINATA RIGHT AWAY...
... NARUTO.

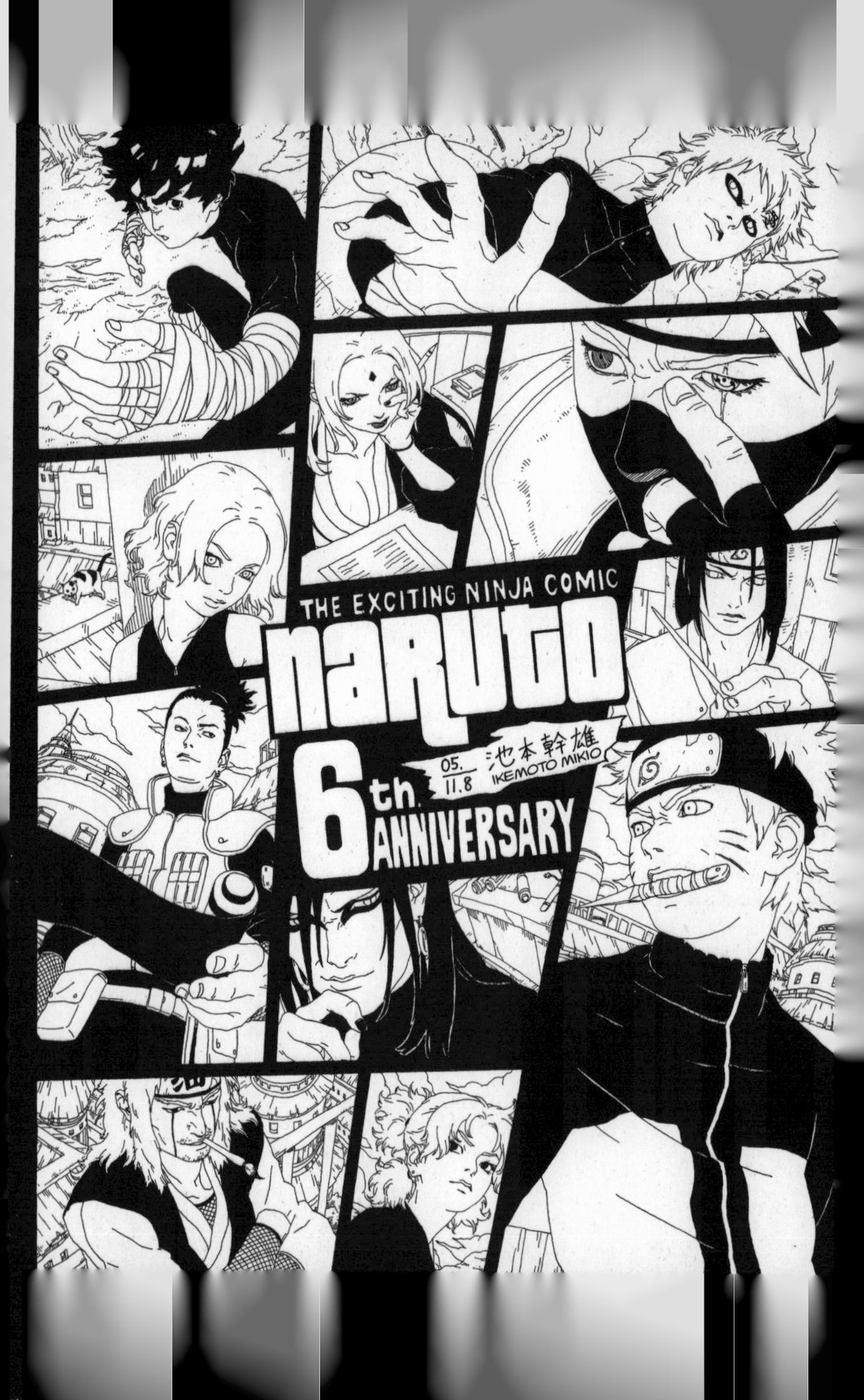
THE EXCITING NINJA COMIC
NARUTO
6th ANNIVERSARY
05. 11.8
池本幹雄
IKEMOTO MIKIO

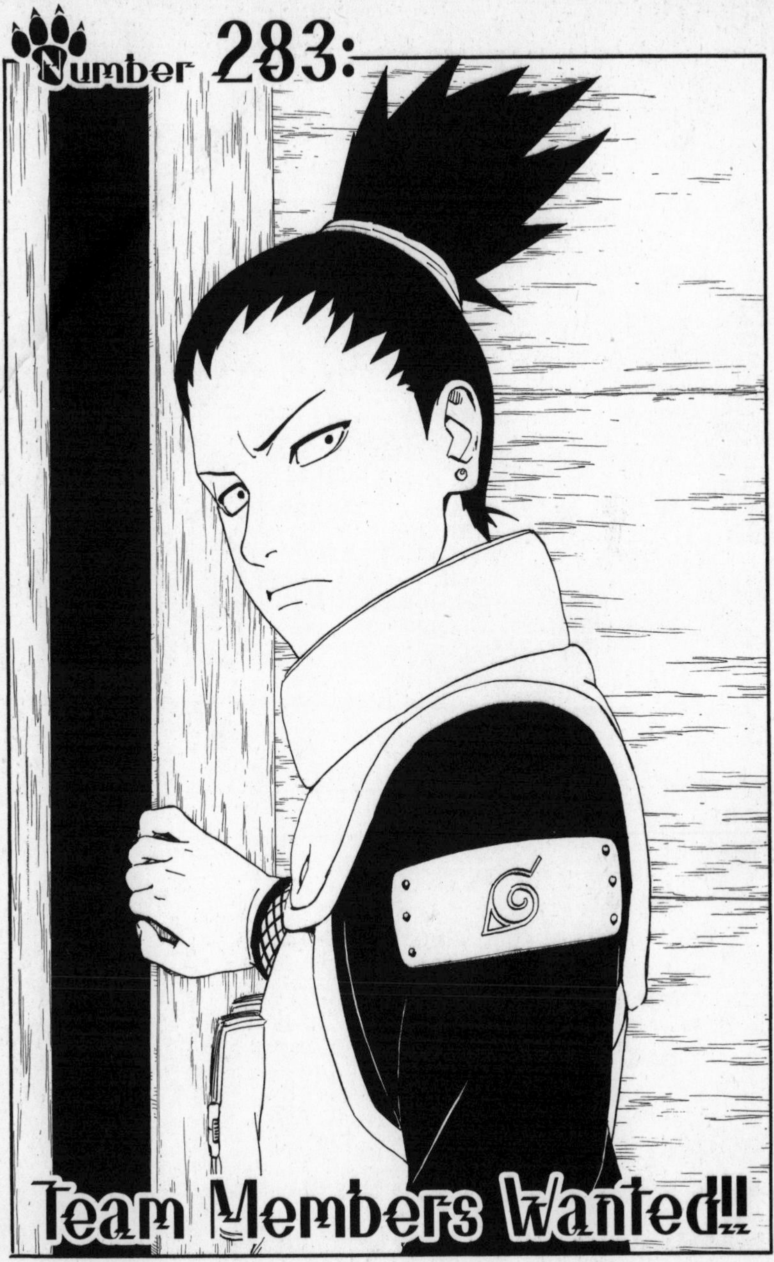
Number 283:
Team Members Wanted!!

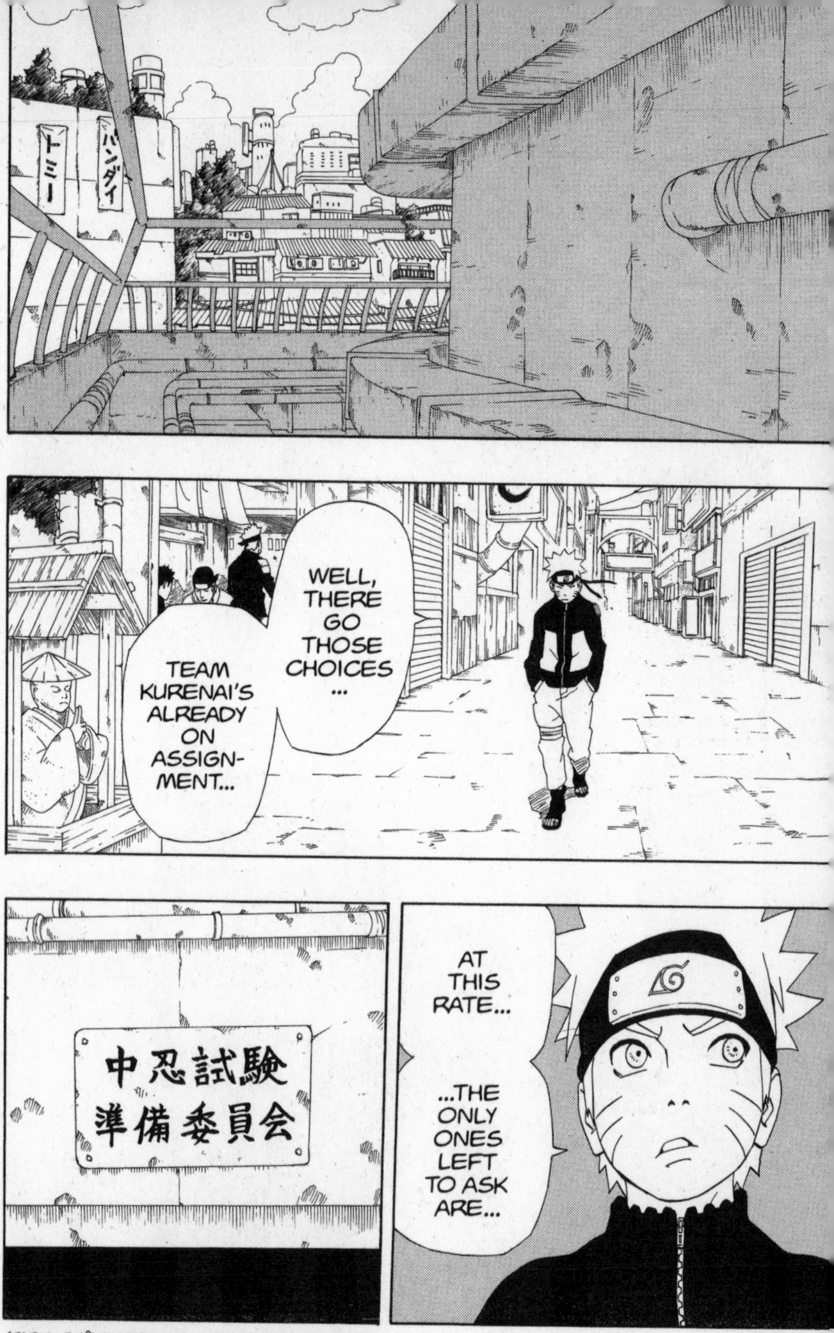
バンダイ
トミー
WELL, THERE GO THOSE CHOICES...
TEAM KURENAI'S ALREADY ON ASSIGNMENT...
AT THIS RATE...
...THE ONLY ONES LEFT TO ASK ARE...
中忍試験
準備委員会
(SIGN: CHŪNIN EXAM PLANNING COMMITTEE)

READ THIS WAY

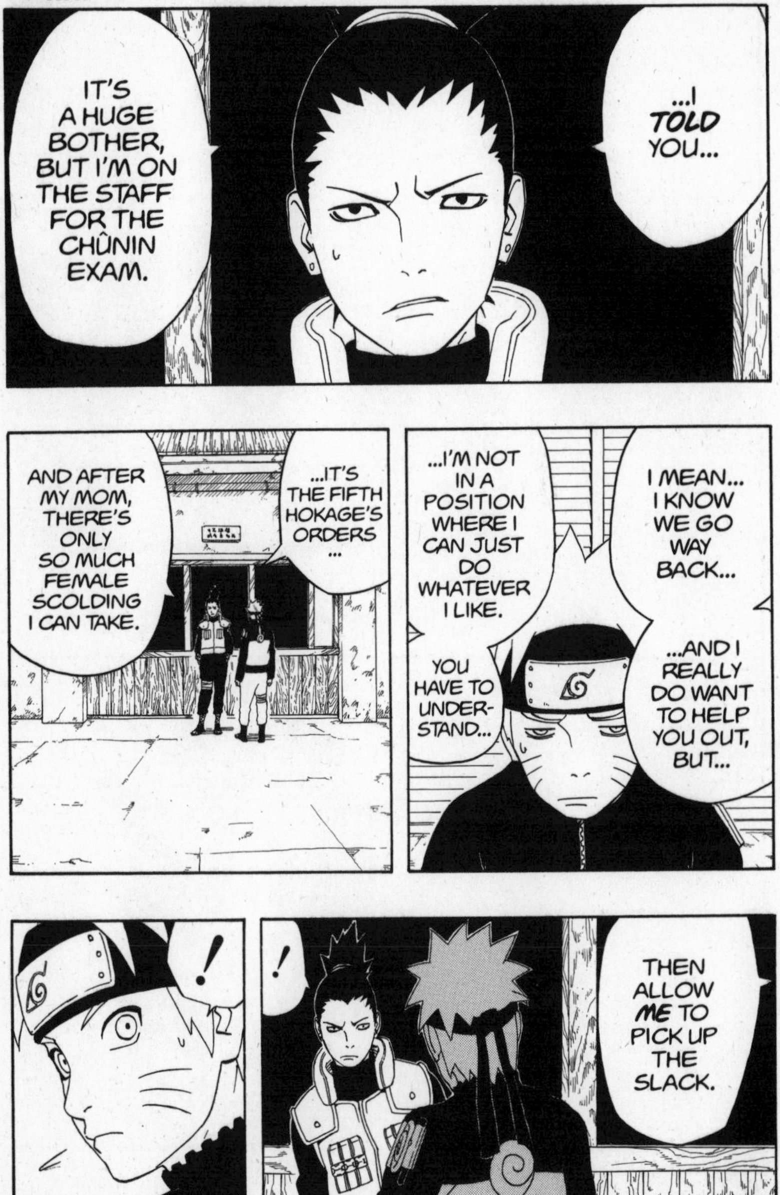

...I *TOLD* YOU...
IT'S A HUGE BOTHER, BUT I'M ON THE STAFF FOR THE CHÛNIN EXAM.
I MEAN... I KNOW WE GO WAY BACK...
...AND I REALLY DO WANT TO HELP YOU OUT, BUT...
...I'M NOT IN A POSITION WHERE I CAN JUST DO WHATEVER I LIKE.
YOU HAVE TO UNDER-STAND...
...IT'S THE FIFTH HOKAGE'S ORDERS...
AND AFTER MY MOM, THERE'S ONLY SO MUCH FEMALE SCOLDING I CAN TAKE.
THEN ALLOW *ME* TO PICK UP THE SLACK.
!
!

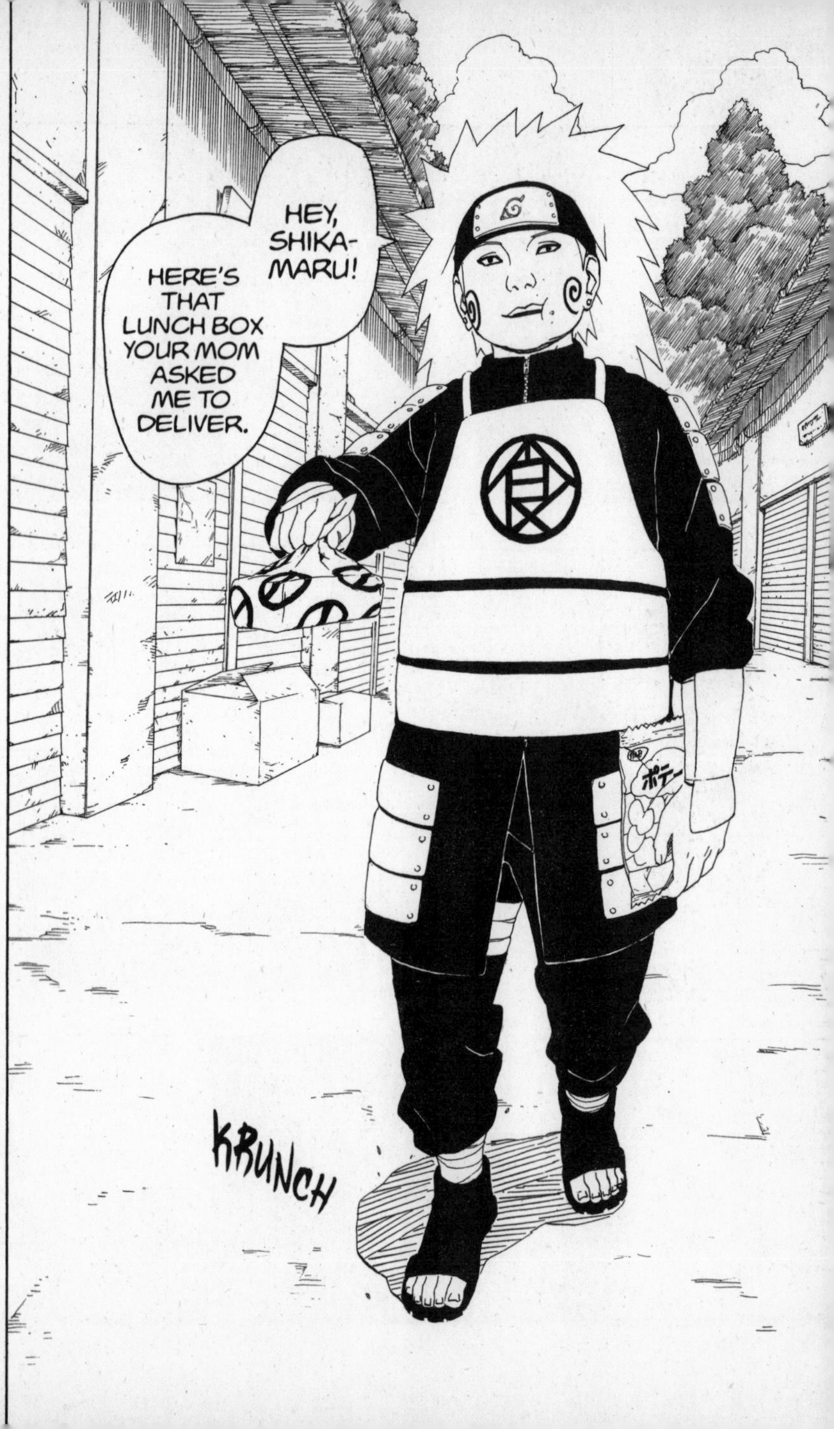
HEY, SHIKA-MARU!
HERE'S THAT LUNCH BOX YOUR MOM ASKED ME TO DELIVER.
KRUNCH

READ THIS WAY

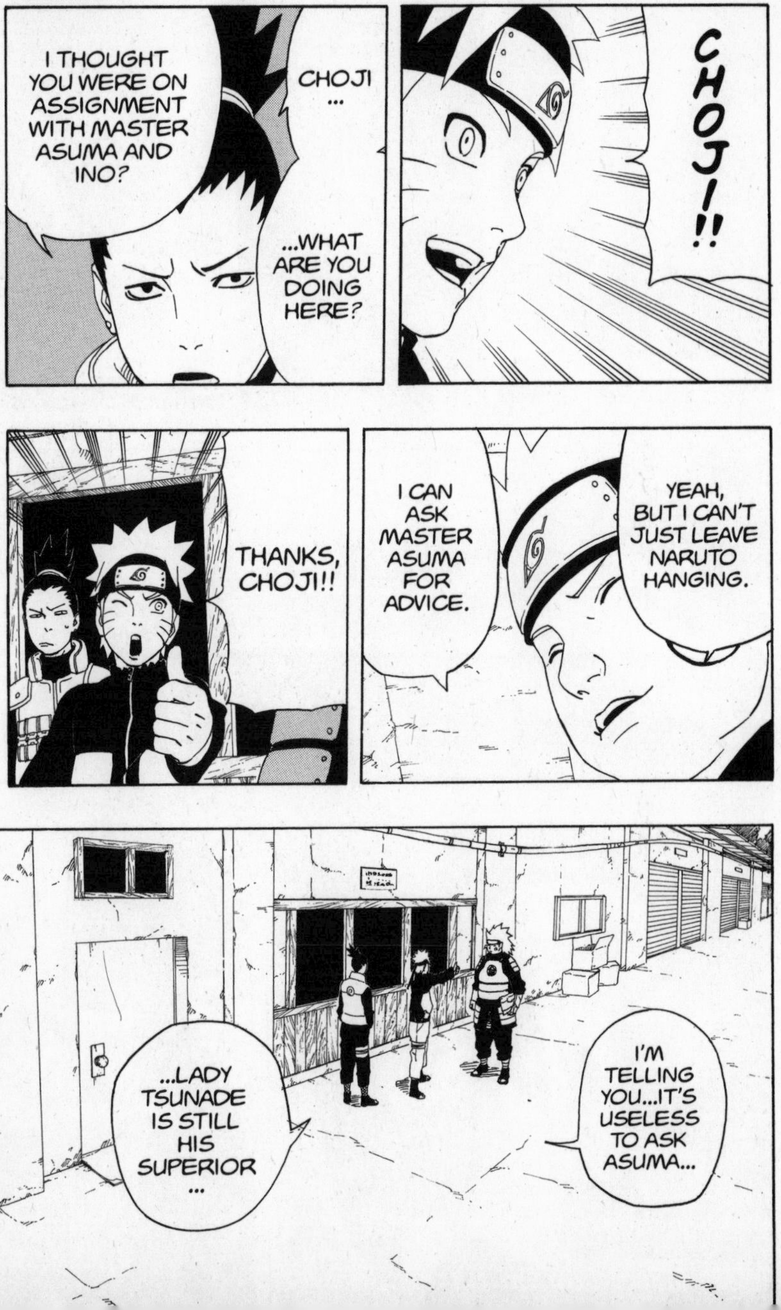
CHOJI!!
CHOJI ...
I THOUGHT YOU WERE ON ASSIGNMENT WITH MASTER ASUMA AND INO?
...WHAT ARE YOU DOING HERE?
YEAH, BUT I CAN'T JUST LEAVE NARUTO HANGING.
I CAN ASK MASTER ASUMA FOR ADVICE.
THANKS, CHOJI!!
I'M TELLING YOU...IT'S USELESS TO ASK ASUMA...
...LADY TSUNADE IS STILL HIS SUPERIOR ...

SQUIK SQUIK
PLIP
WHIRL
KLIK
TUG
SPLISH

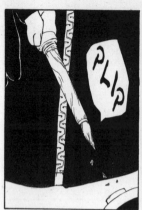

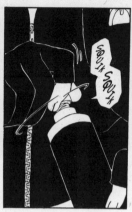

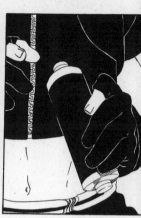

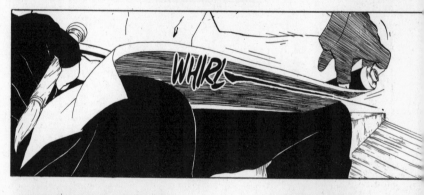

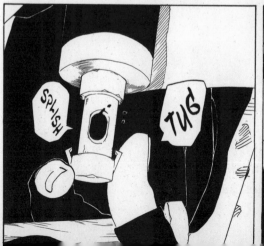

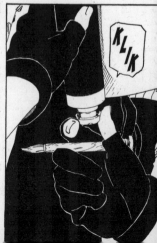

READ THIS WAY

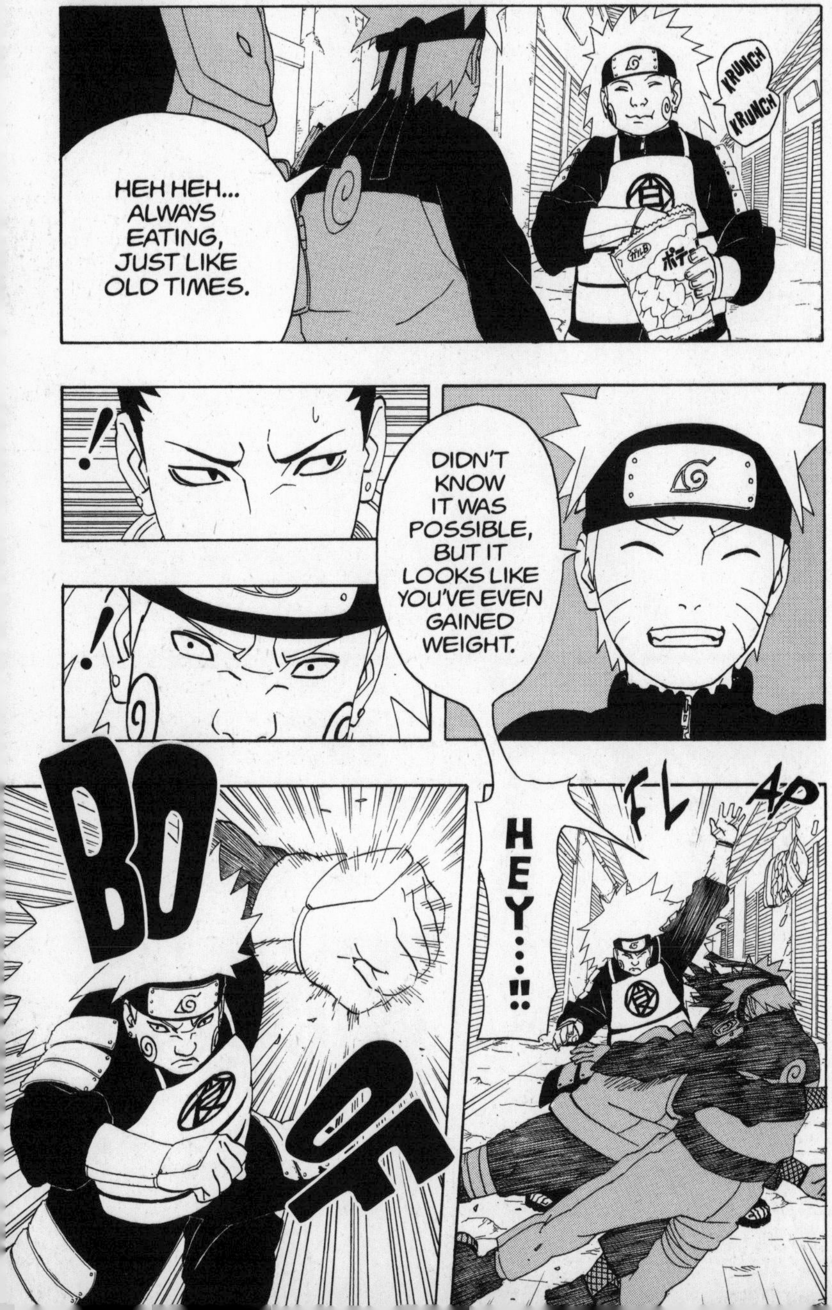
KRUNCH
KRUNCH
HEH HEH... ALWAYS EATING, JUST LIKE OLD TIMES.
DIDN'T KNOW IT WAS POSSIBLE, BUT IT LOOKS LIKE YOU'VE EVEN GAINED WEIGHT.
!
!
FLAP
HEY...!!
BOOF

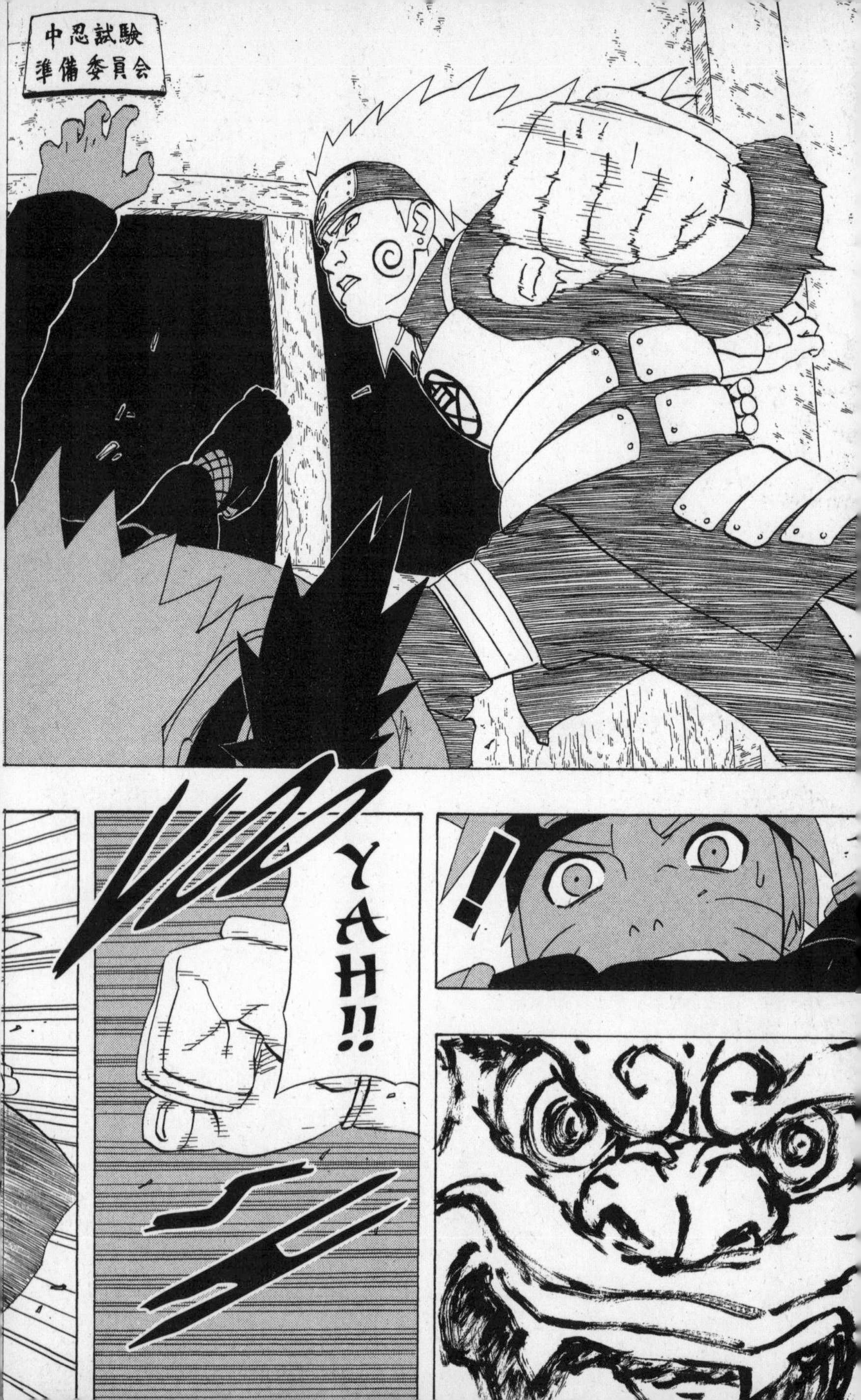
中忍試験
準備委員会
!
VOO
YAH!!

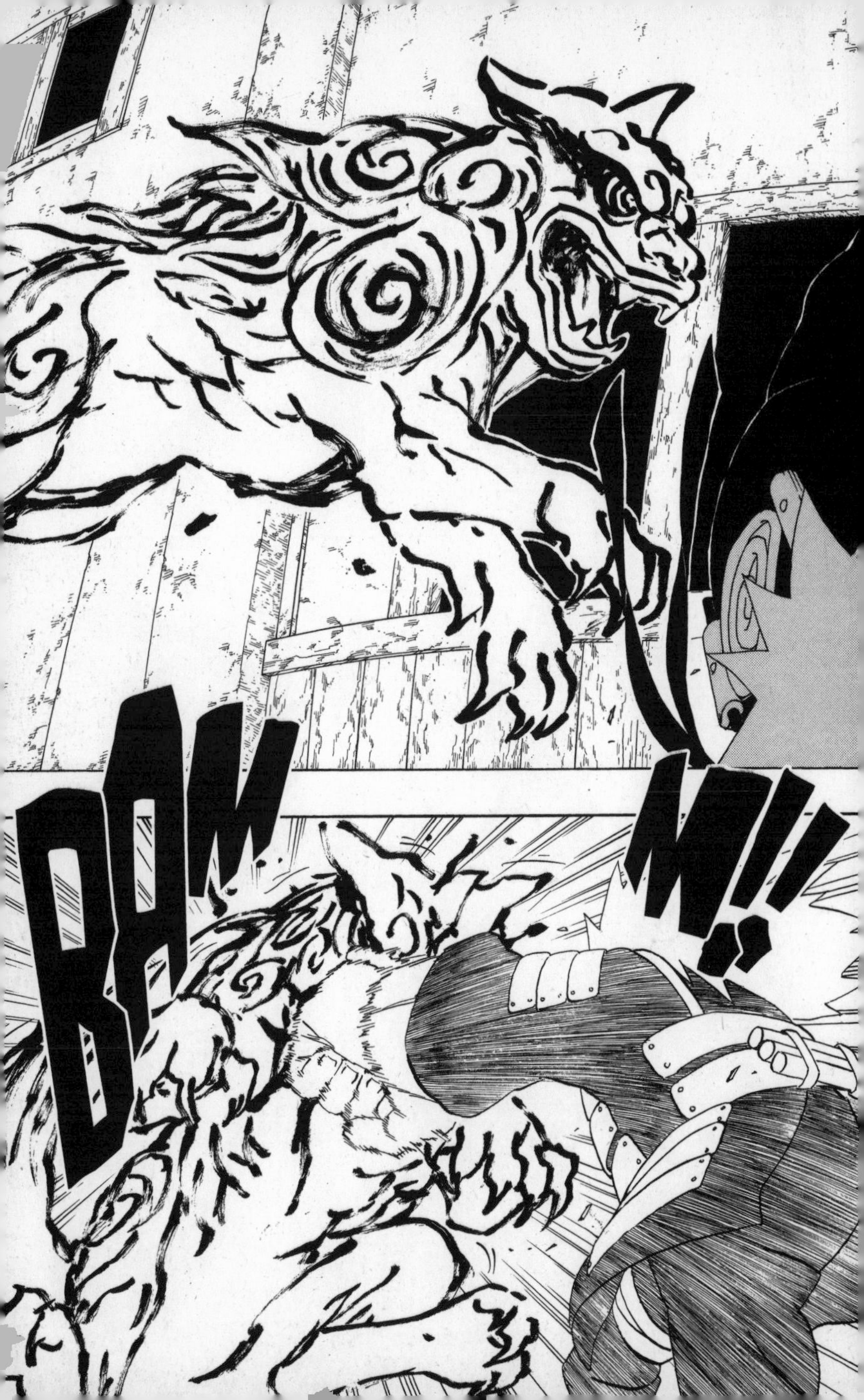
BAM!!

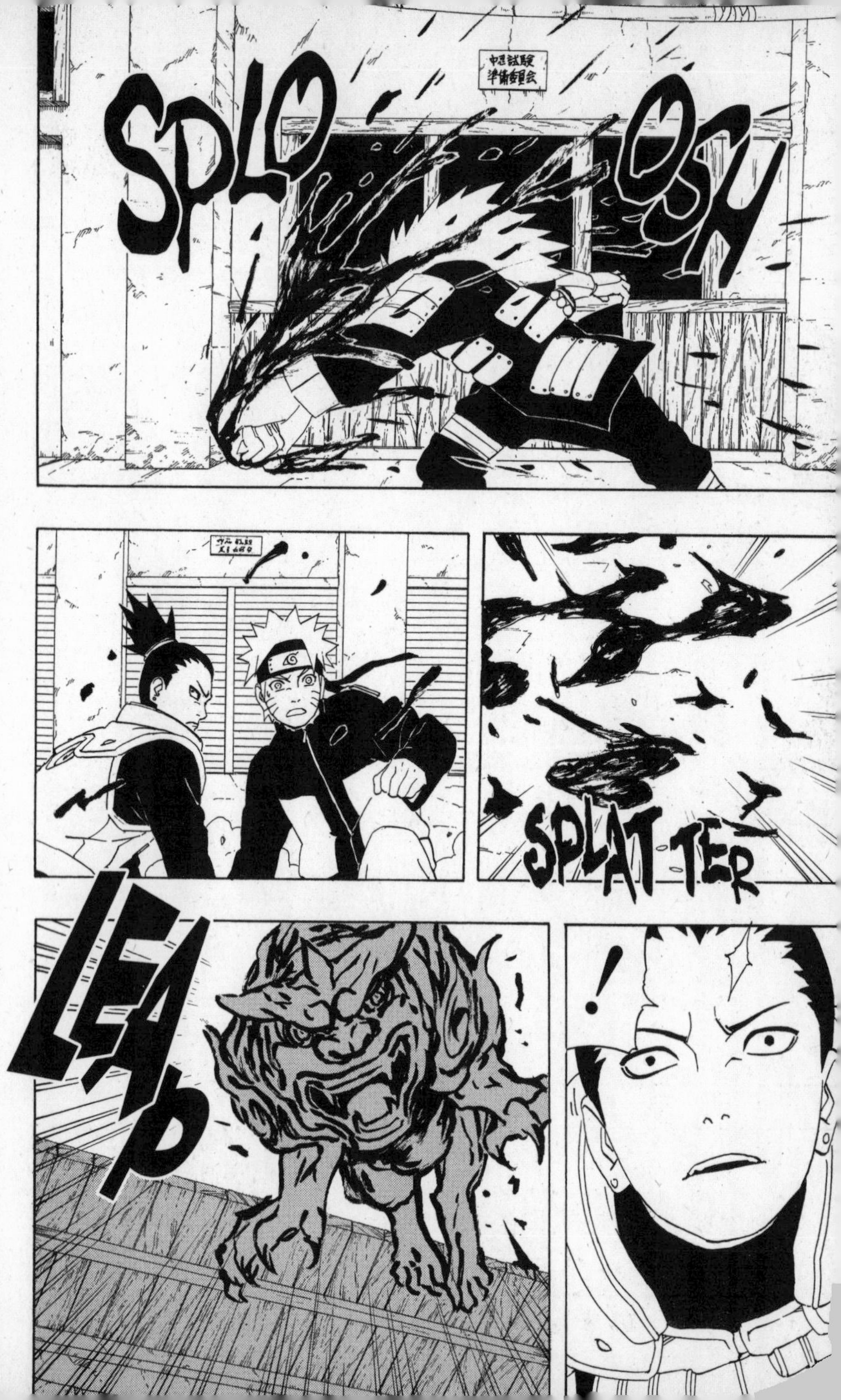
SPLOOSH
SPLATTER
!
LEAP

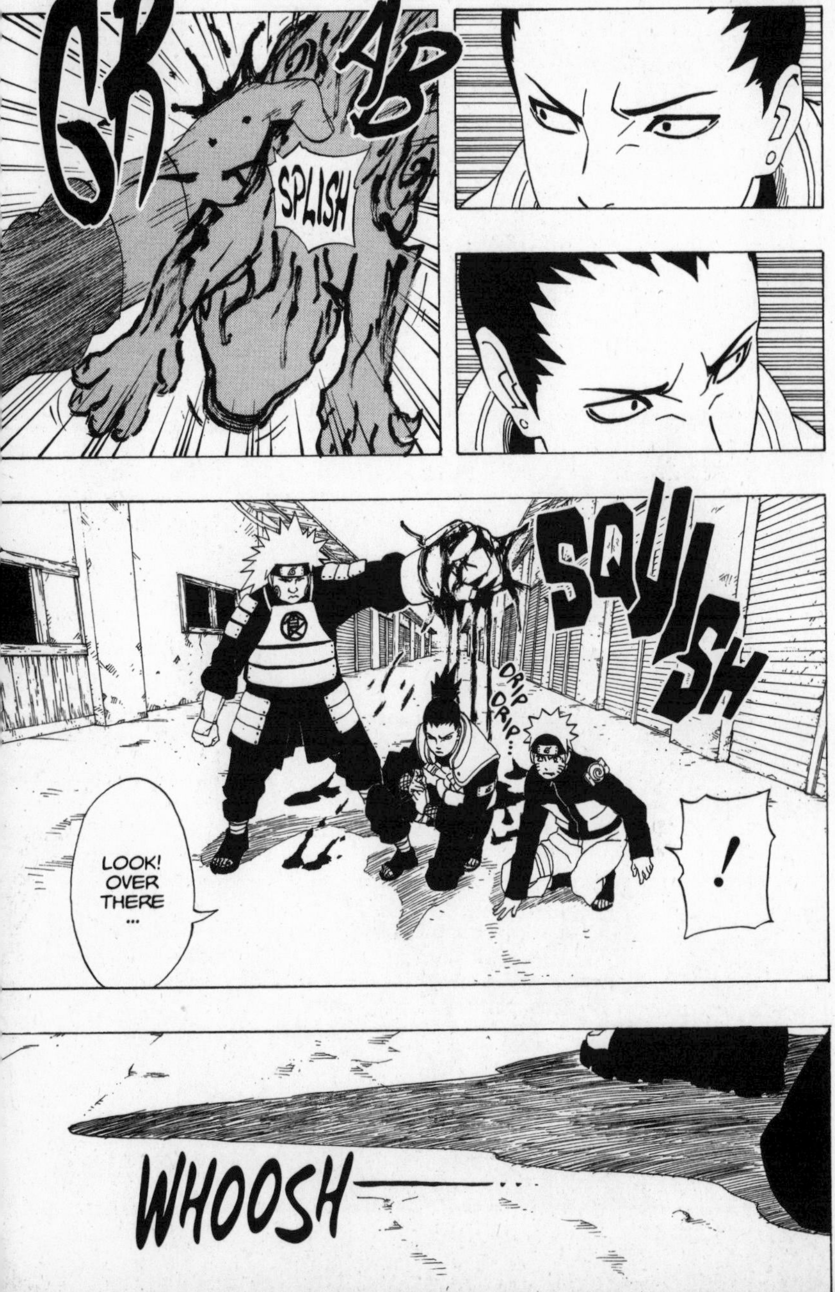
GRAB
SPLISH
SQUISH
DRIP DRIP...
!
LOOK! OVER THERE ...
WHOOSH

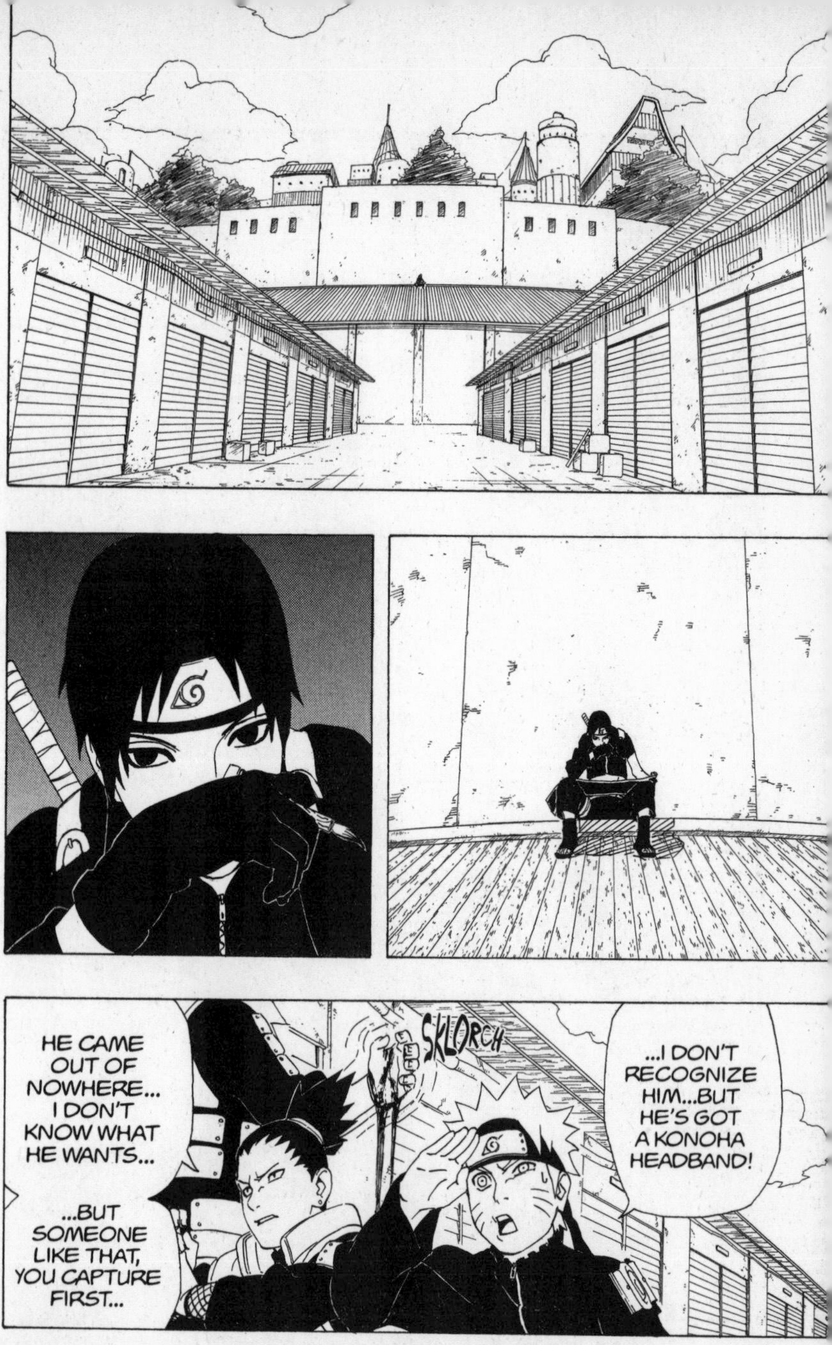
...I DON'T RECOGNIZE HIM...BUT HE'S GOT A KONOHA HEADBAND!
SKLORCH
HE CAME OUT OF NOWHERE... I DON'T KNOW WHAT HE WANTS...
...BUT SOMEONE LIKE THAT, YOU CAPTURE FIRST...

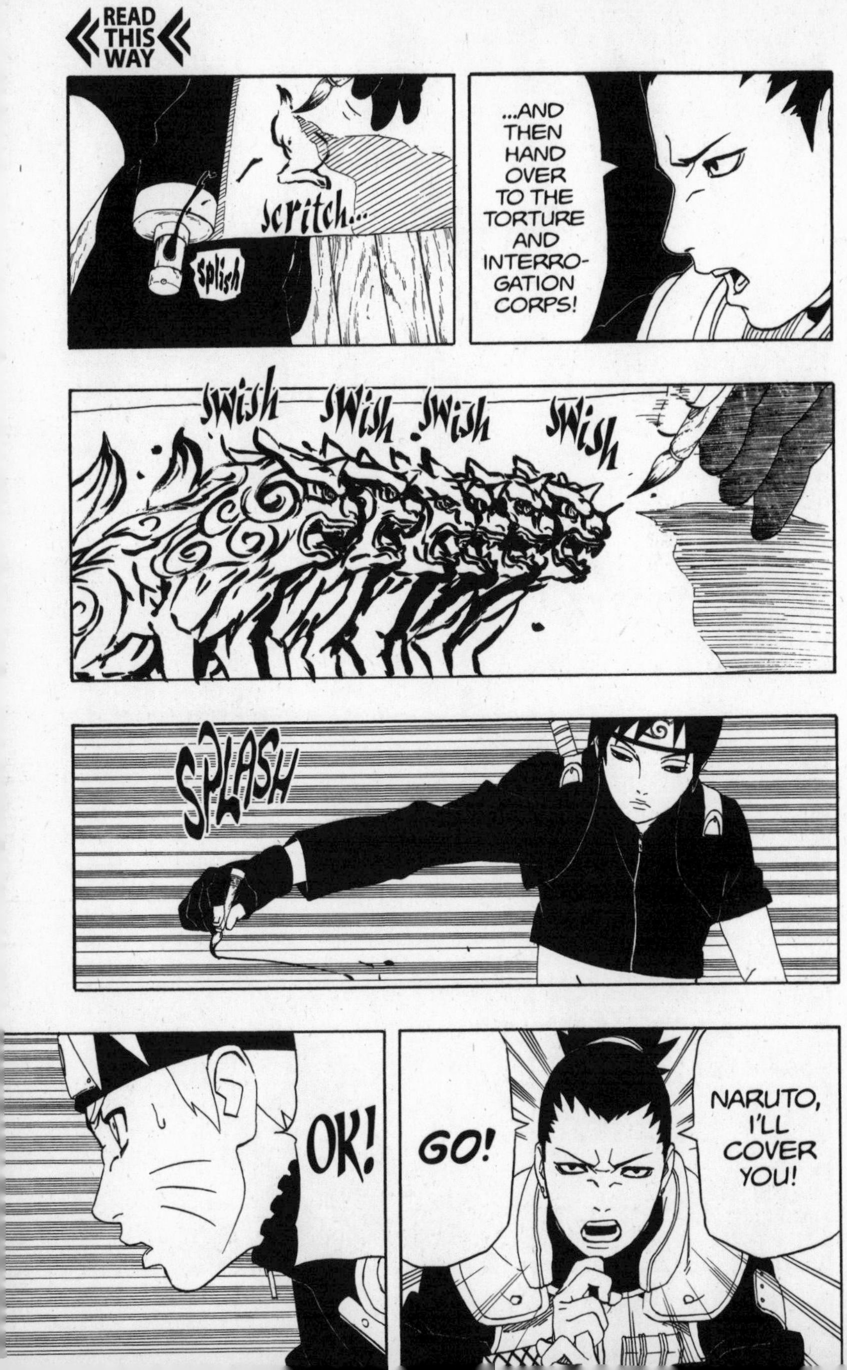
READ THIS WAY
...AND THEN HAND OVER TO THE TORTURE AND INTERROGATION CORPS!
scritch...
splish
SWISH
SWISH
SWISH
SWISH
SPLASH
NARUTO, I'LL COVER YOU!
GO!
OK!

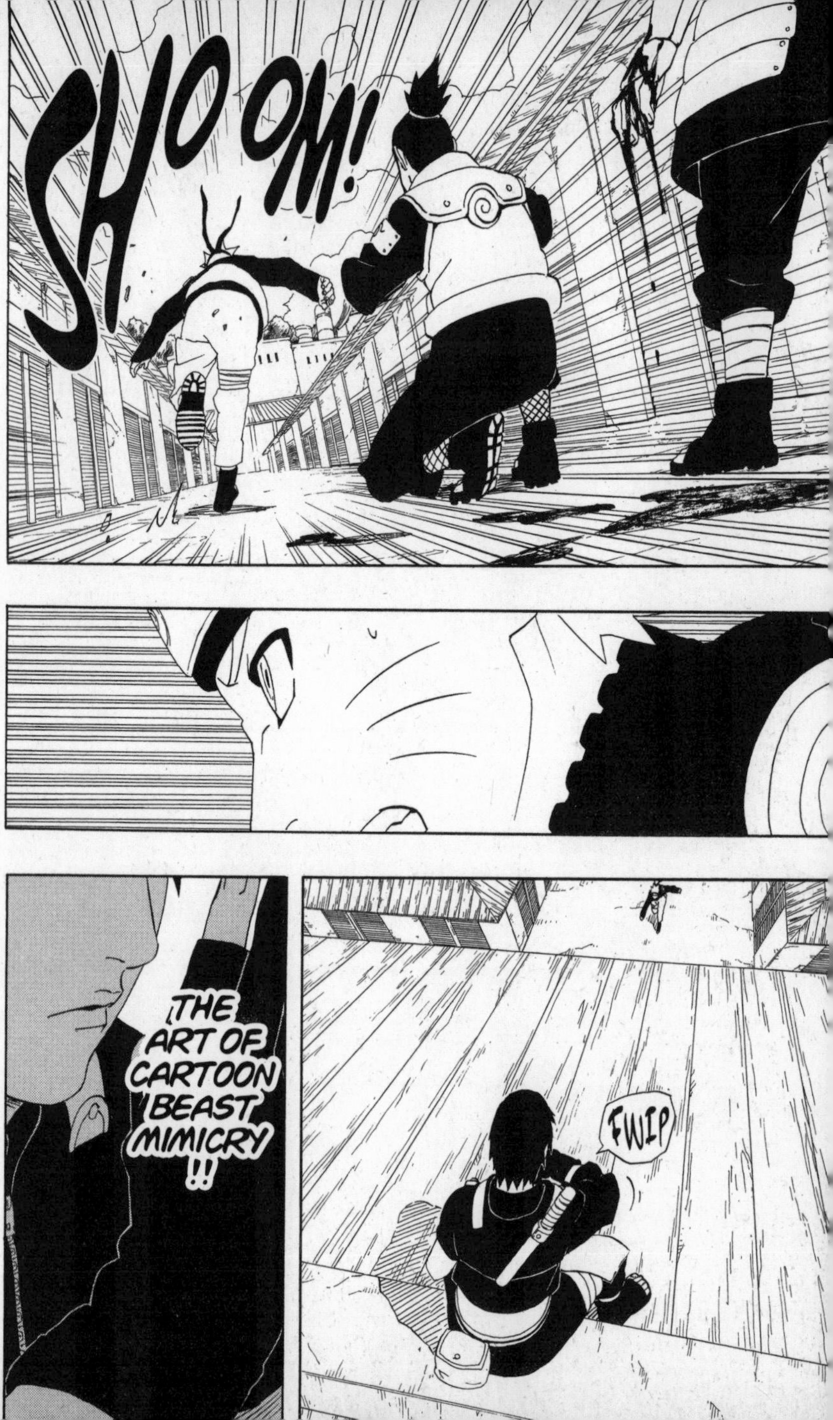
SHOOM!
FWIP
THE ART OF CARTOON BEAST MIMICRY!!

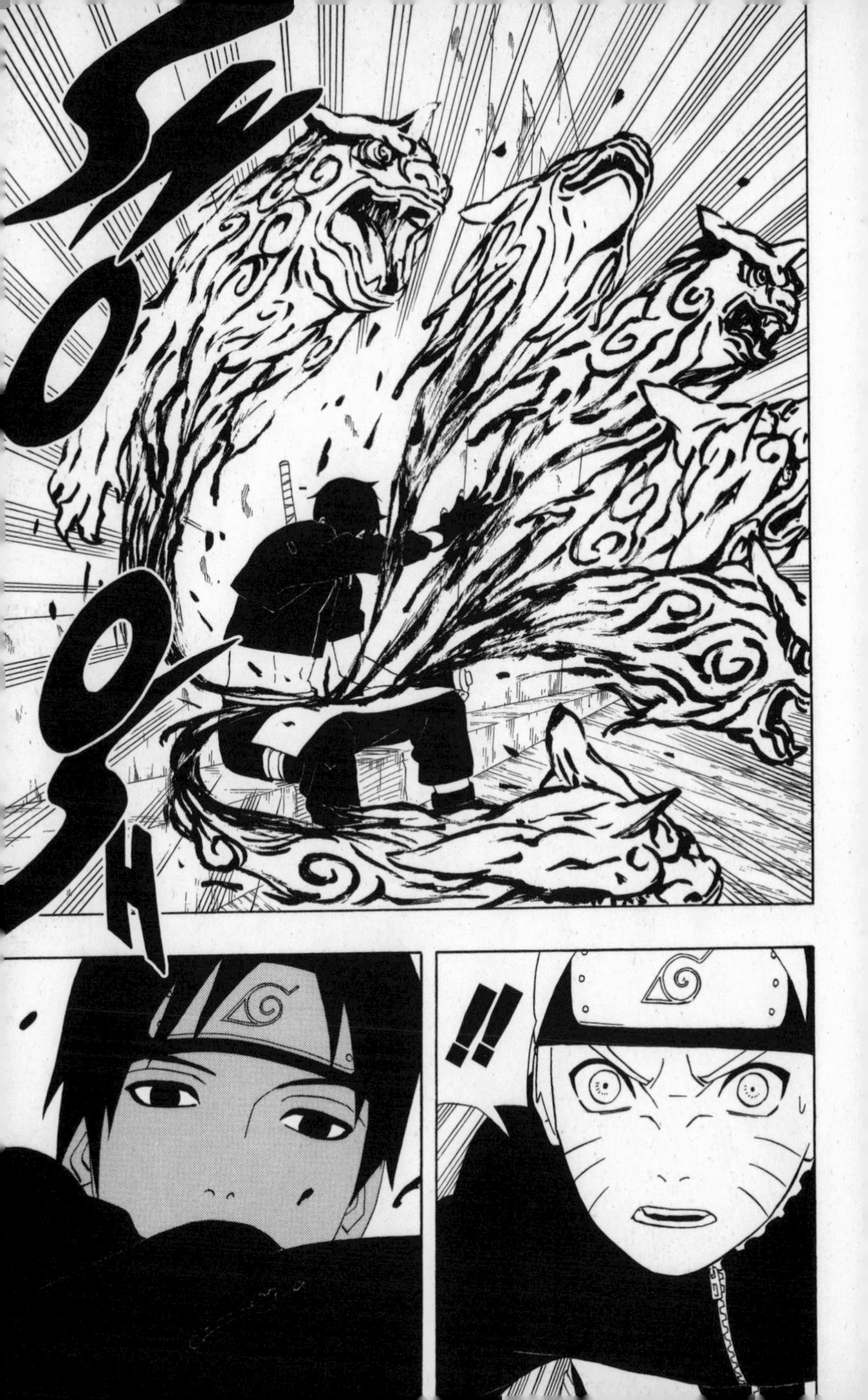
SWOOSH
!!

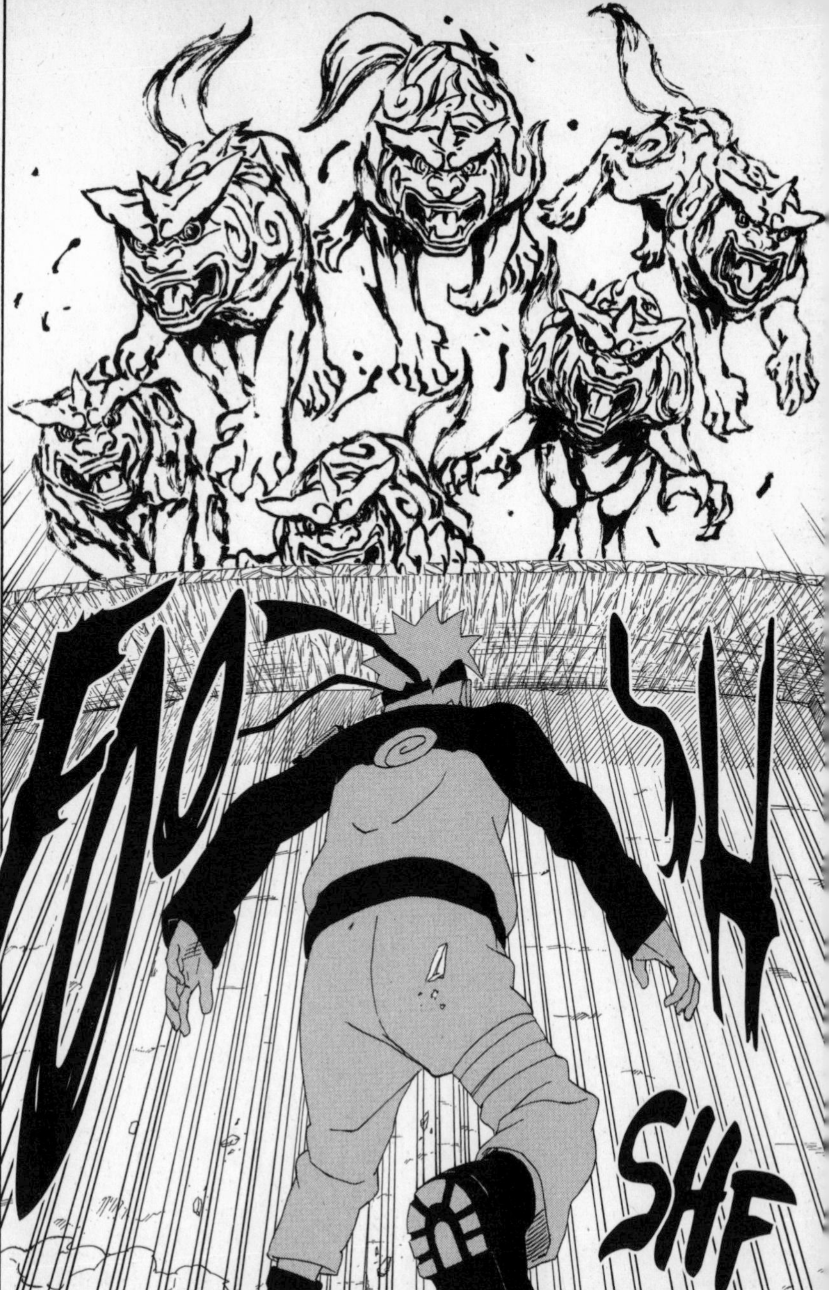
FWOOSH
SHF

READ THIS WAY

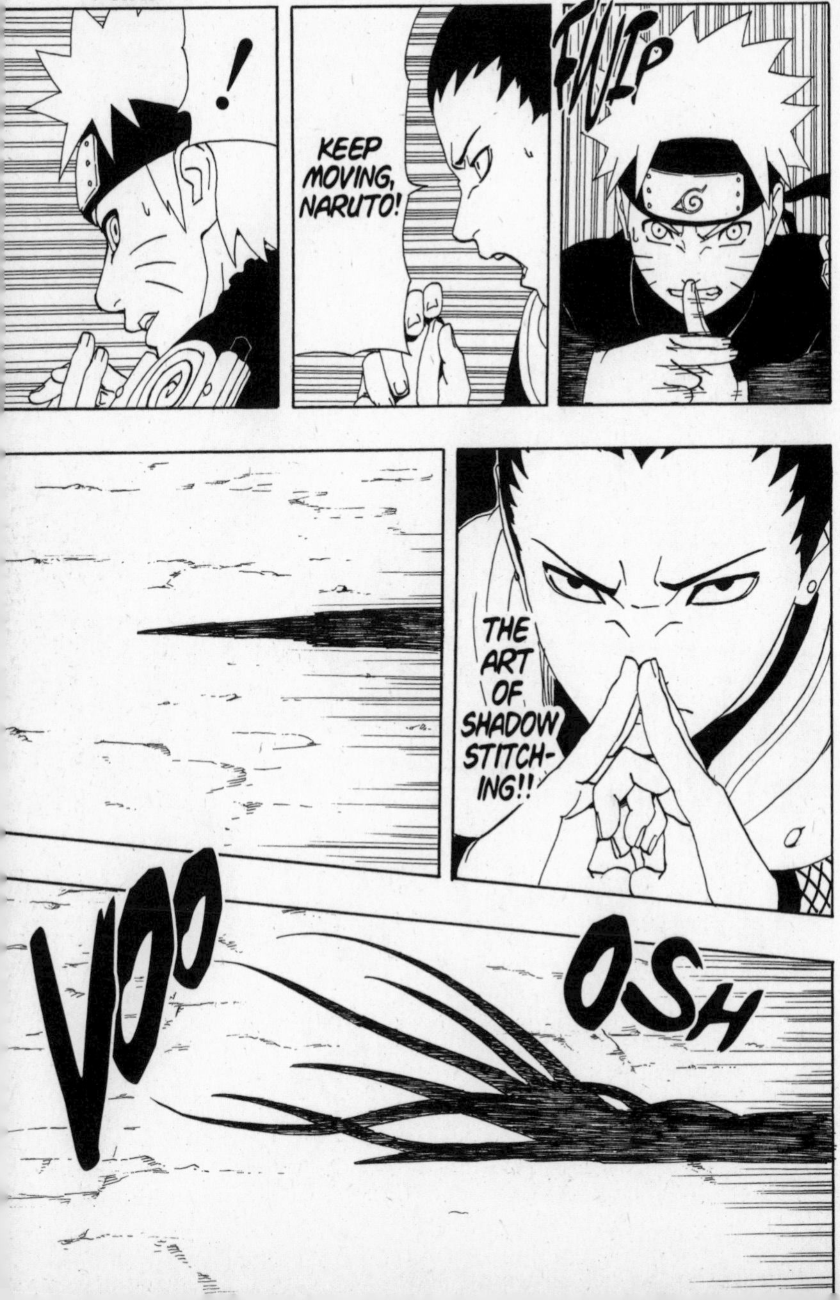
FWIP
KEEP MOVING, NARUTO!
!
THE ART OF SHADOW STITCHING!!
VOO
OSH

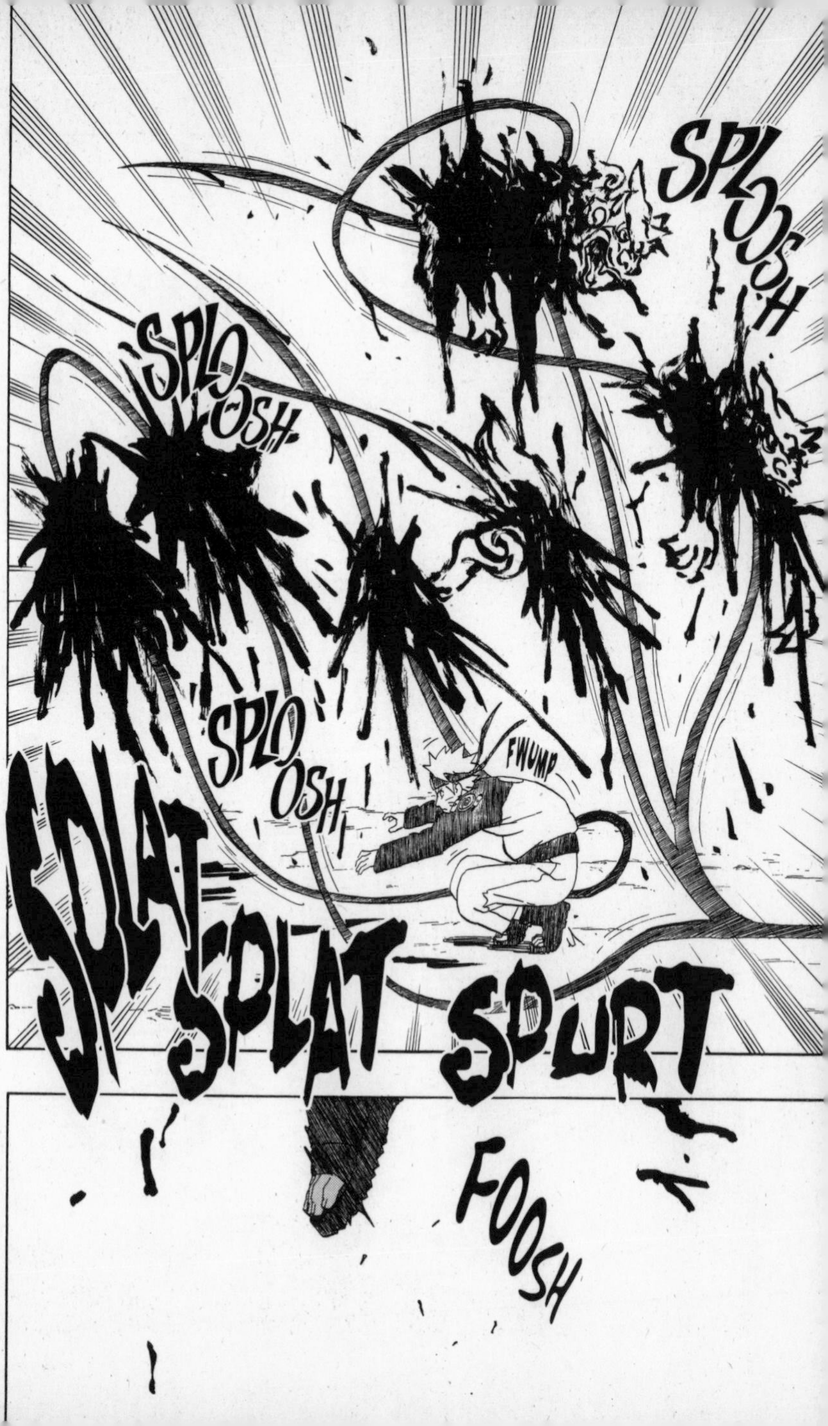
SPLOOSH
SPLOOSH
FWUMP
SPLOOSH
SPURT
SPLAT
SPLAT
FOOSH

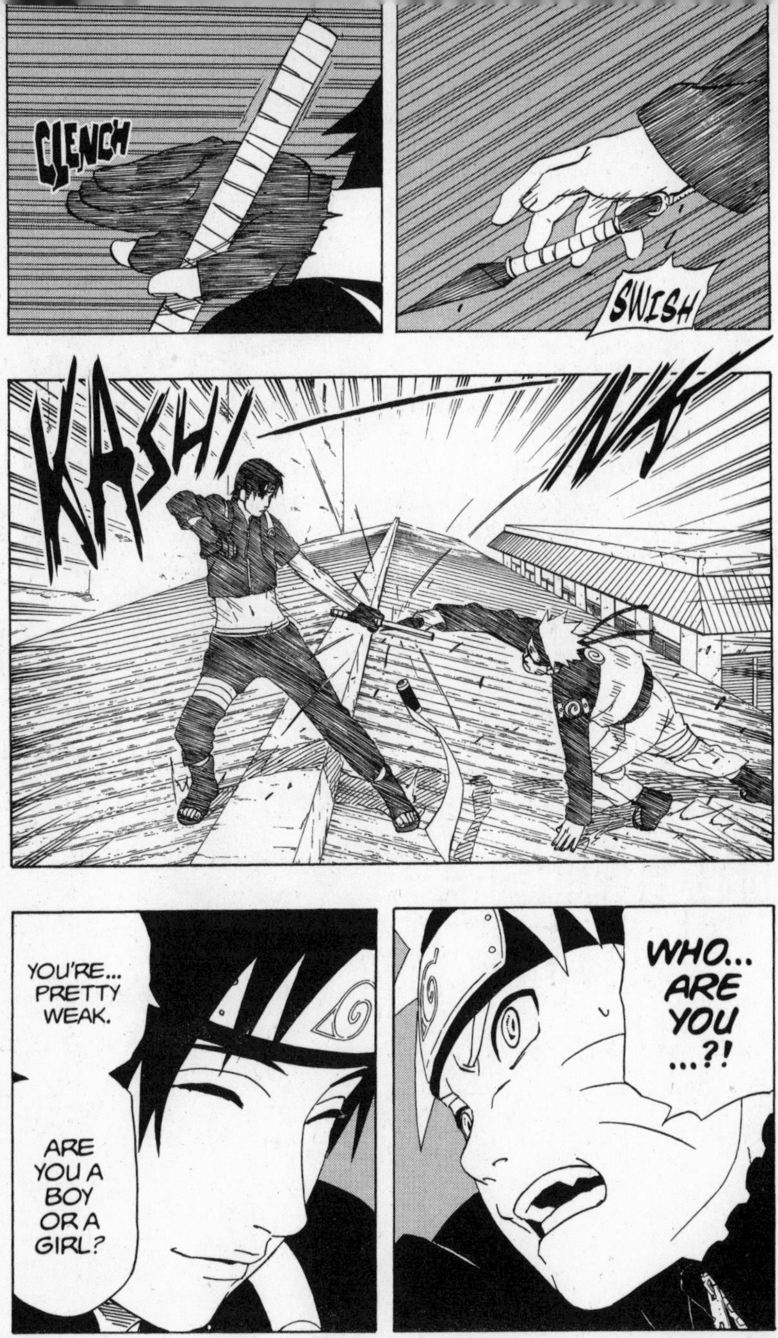
SWISH
CLENCH
KASHINK
WHO... ARE YOU ...?!
YOU'RE... PRETTY WEAK.
ARE YOU A BOY OR A GIRL?

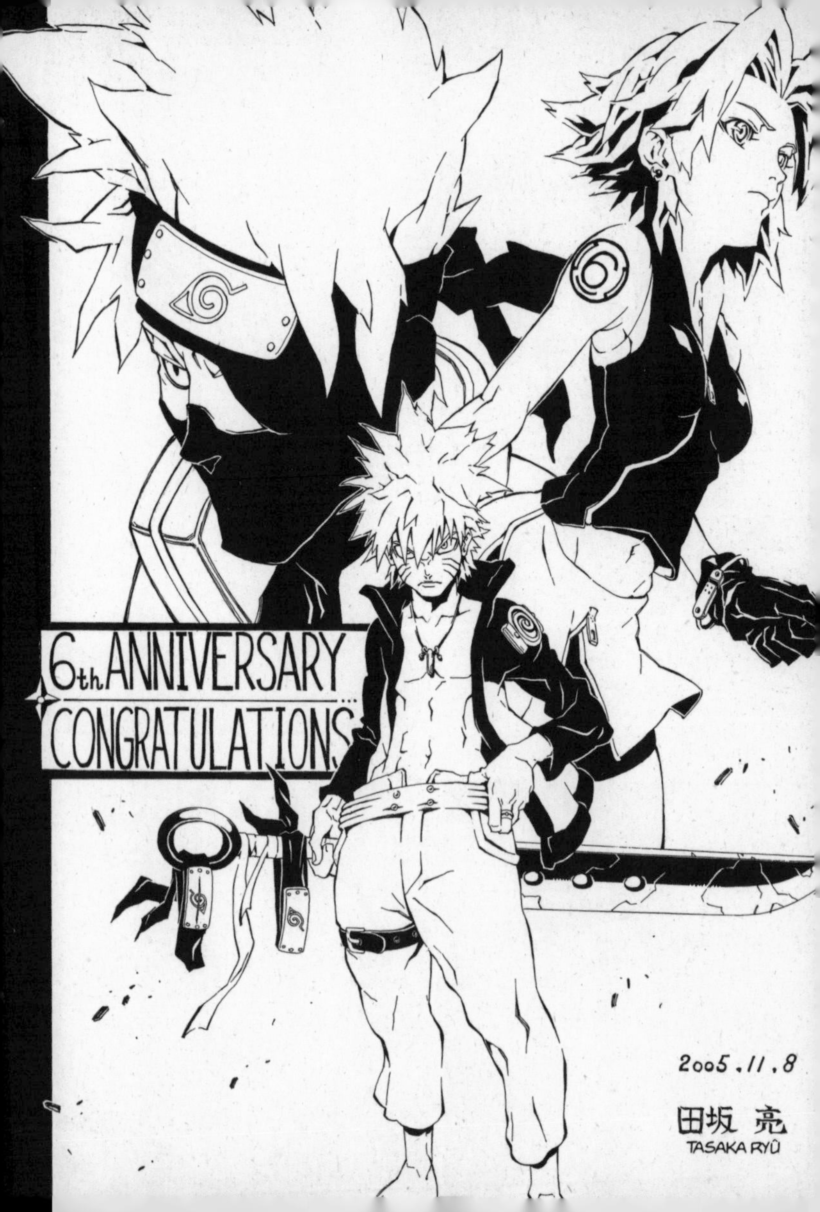
6th ANNIVERSARY
CONGRATULATIONS
2005.11.8
田坂 亮
TASAKA RYÛ

Number 284: The New Cell...!!

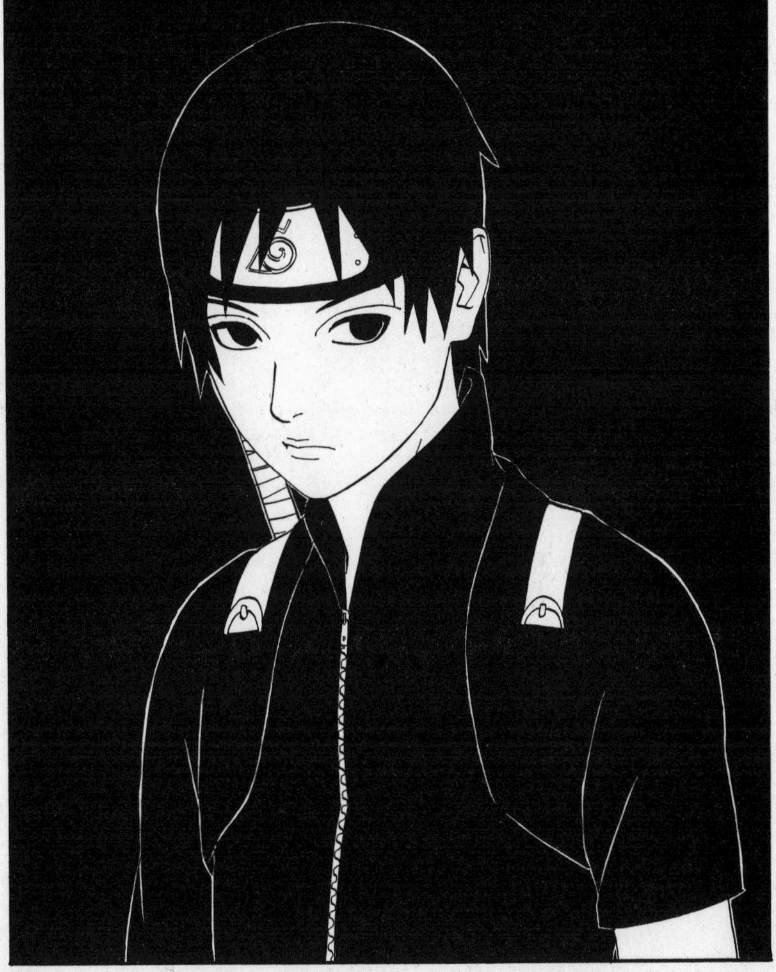

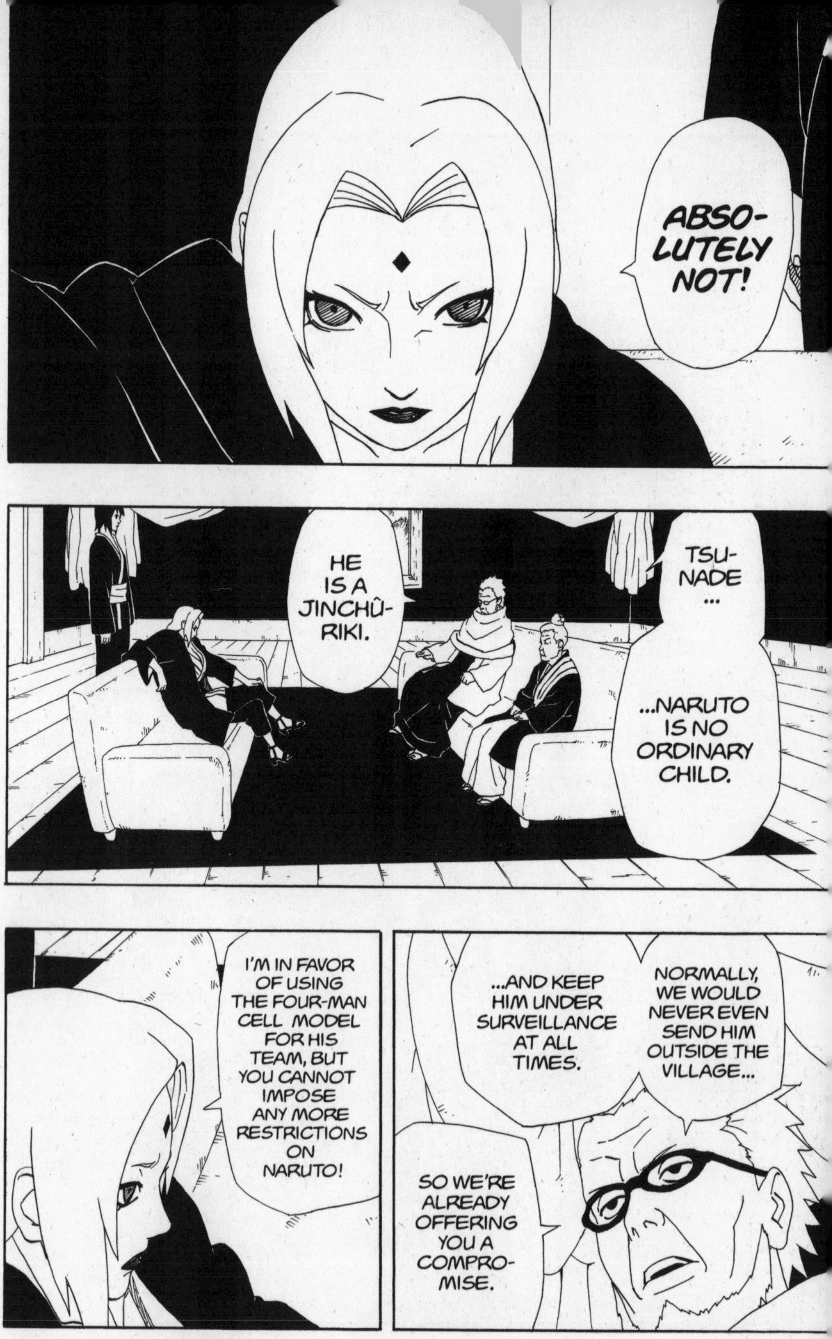
ABSO-LUTELY NOT!
TSU-NADE...
...NARUTO IS NO ORDINARY CHILD.
HE IS A JINCHÛ-RIKI.
NORMALLY, WE WOULD NEVER EVEN SEND HIM OUTSIDE THE VILLAGE...
...AND KEEP HIM UNDER SURVEILLANCE AT ALL TIMES.
SO WE'RE ALREADY OFFERING YOU A COMPRO-MISE.
I'M IN FAVOR OF USING THE FOUR-MAN CELL MODEL FOR HIS TEAM, BUT YOU CANNOT IMPOSE ANY MORE RESTRICTIONS ON NARUTO!

READ THIS WAY

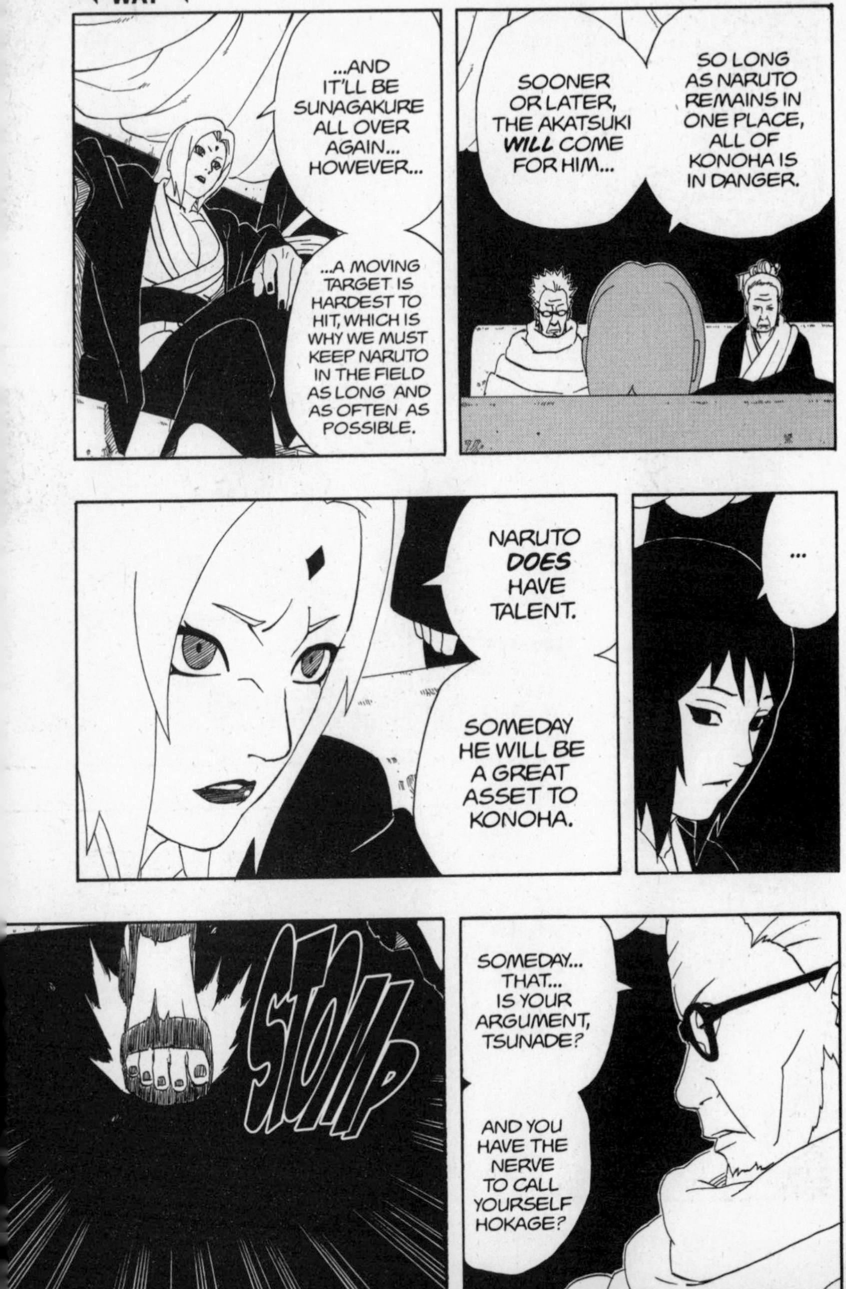
SO LONG AS NARUTO REMAINS IN ONE PLACE, ALL OF KONOHA IS IN DANGER.
SOONER OR LATER, THE AKATSUKI **WILL** COME FOR HIM...
...AND IT'LL BE SUNAGAKURE ALL OVER AGAIN... HOWEVER...
...A MOVING TARGET IS HARDEST TO HIT, WHICH IS WHY WE MUST KEEP NARUTO IN THE FIELD AS LONG AND AS OFTEN AS POSSIBLE.
...
NARUTO **DOES** HAVE TALENT.
SOMEDAY HE WILL BE A GREAT ASSET TO KONOHA.
SOMEDAY... THAT... IS YOUR ARGUMENT, TSUNADE?
AND YOU HAVE THE NERVE TO CALL YOURSELF HOKAGE?
STOMP

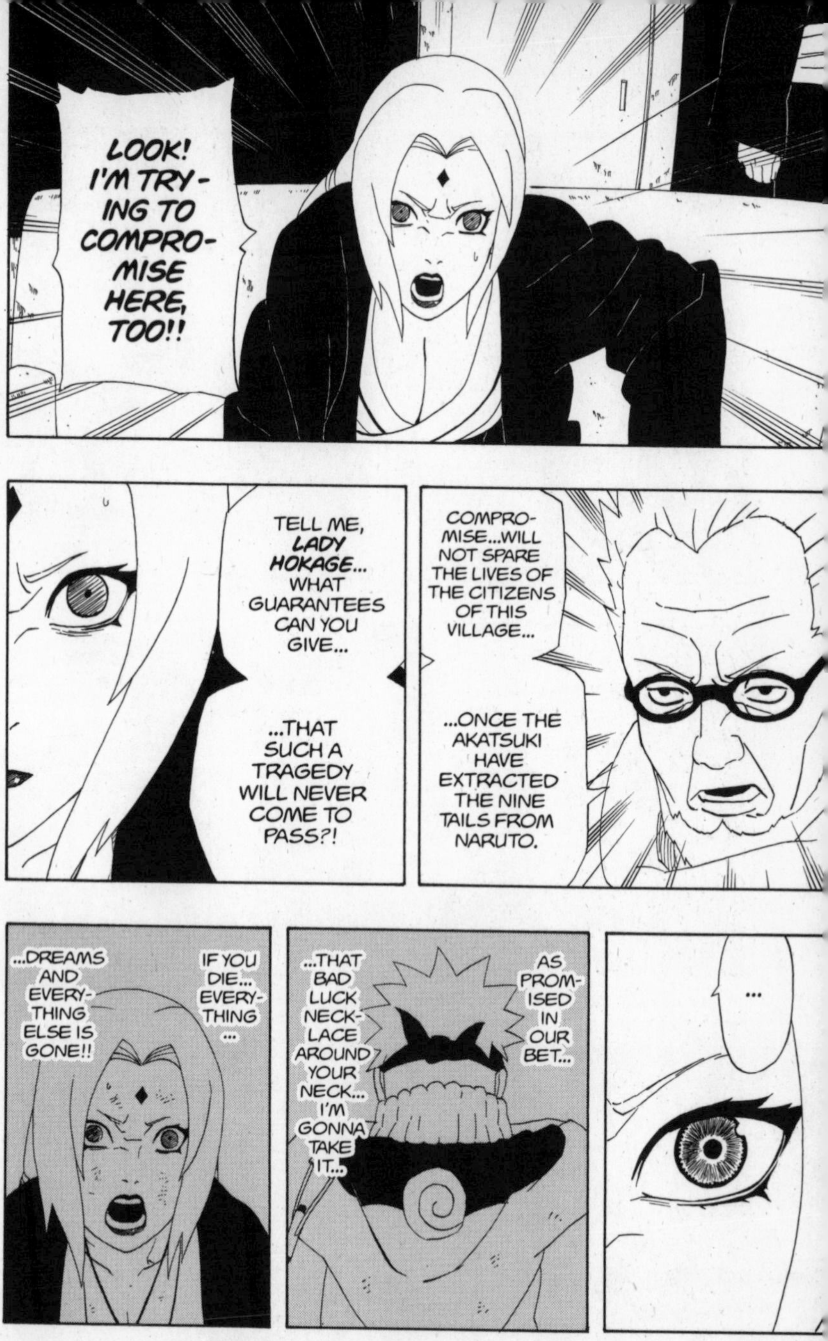
LOOK! I'M TRYING TO COMPROMISE HERE, TOO!!
COMPROMISE...WILL NOT SPARE THE LIVES OF THE CITIZENS OF THIS VILLAGE...
...ONCE THE AKATSUKI HAVE EXTRACTED THE NINE TAILS FROM NARUTO.
TELL ME, LADY HOKAGE... WHAT GUARANTEES CAN YOU GIVE...
...THAT SUCH A TRAGEDY WILL NEVER COME TO PASS?!
...
AS PROMISED IN OUR BET...
...THAT BAD LUCK NECKLACE AROUND YOUR NECK... I'M GONNA TAKE IT...
IF YOU DIE... EVERYTHING...
...DREAMS AND EVERYTHING ELSE IS GONE!!

READ THIS WAY

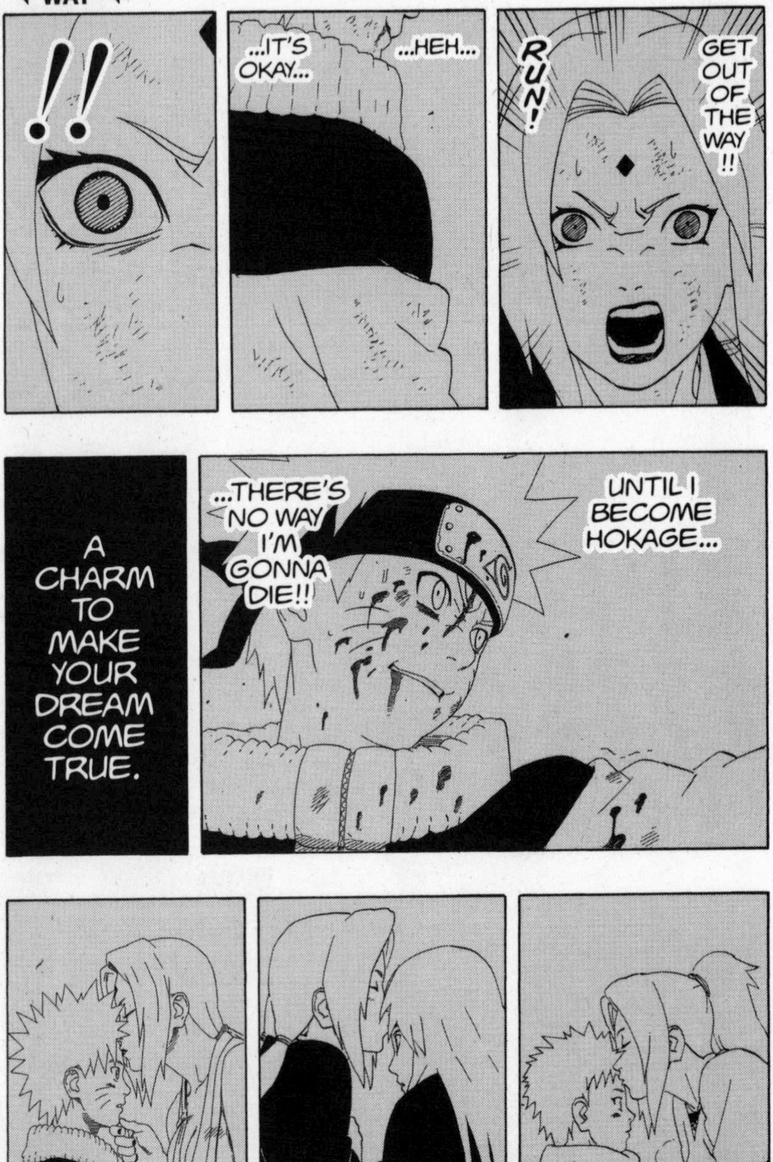
GET OUT OF THE WAY!!
RUN!
...HEH...
...IT'S OKAY...
!!
UNTIL I BECOME HOKAGE...
...THERE'S NO WAY I'M GONNA DIE!!
A CHARM TO MAKE YOUR DREAM COME TRUE.

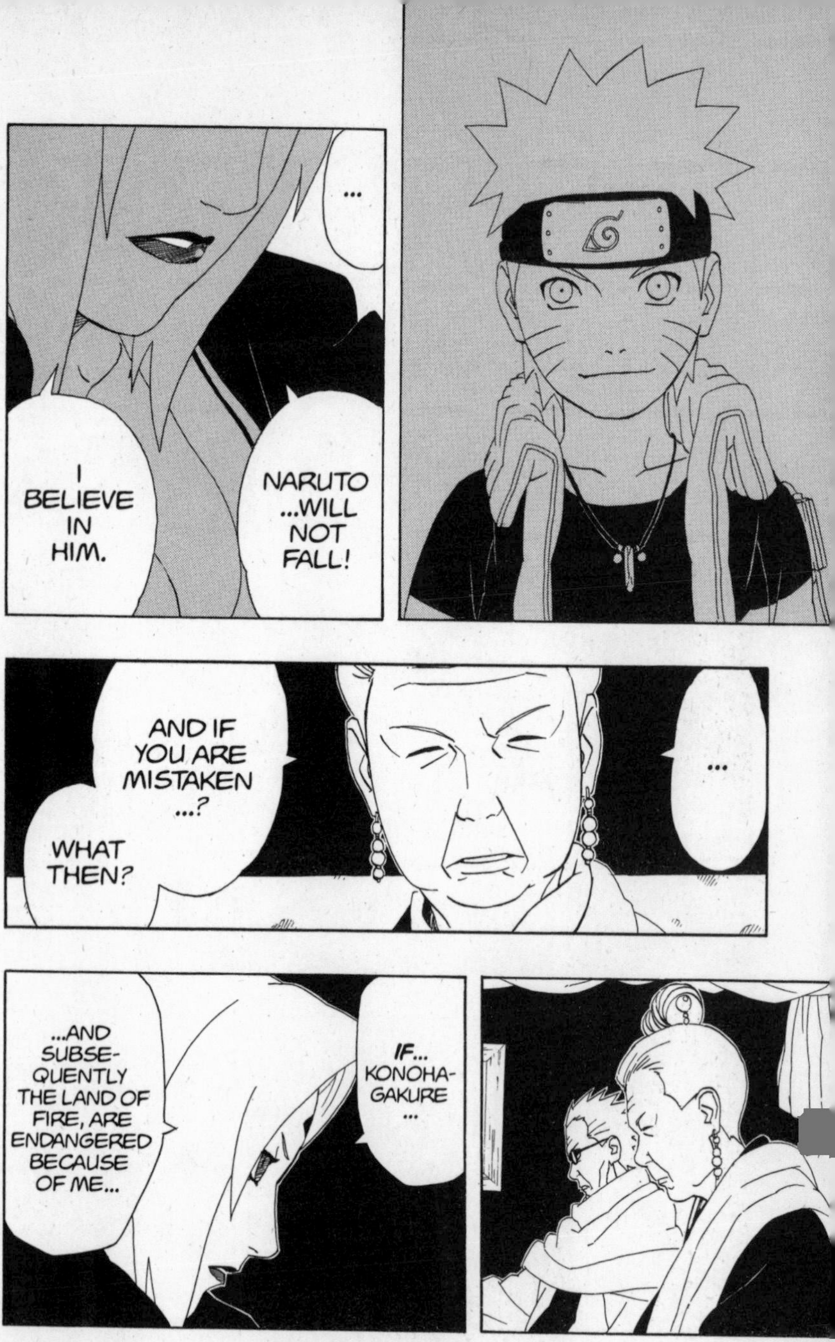
...
NARUTO ...WILL NOT FALL!
I BELIEVE IN HIM.
...
AND IF YOU ARE MISTAKEN ...?
WHAT THEN?
IF... KONOHA-GAKURE ...
...AND SUBSE-QUENTLY THE LAND OF FIRE, ARE ENDANGERED BECAUSE OF ME...

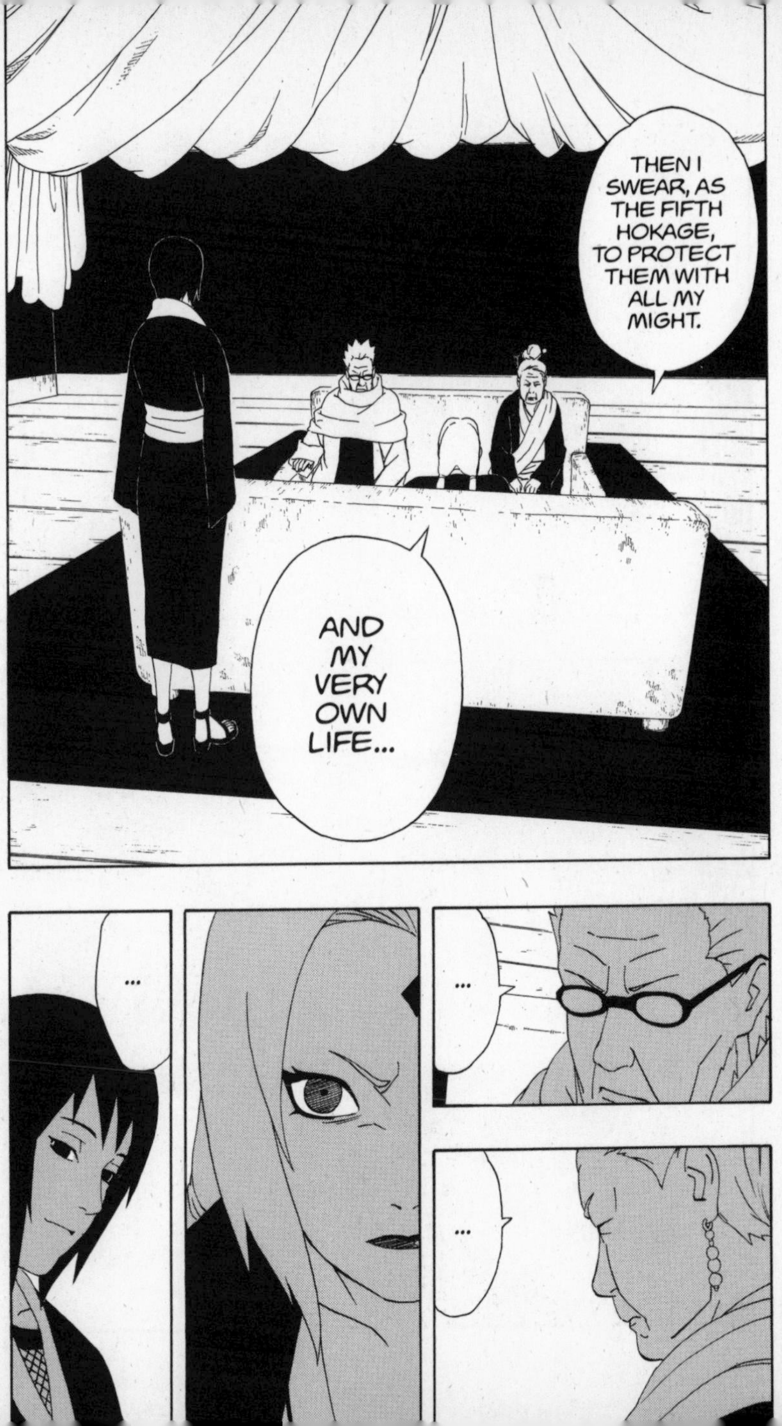
THEN I SWEAR, AS THE FIFTH HOKAGE, TO PROTECT THEM WITH ALL MY MIGHT.
AND MY VERY OWN LIFE...
...
...
...

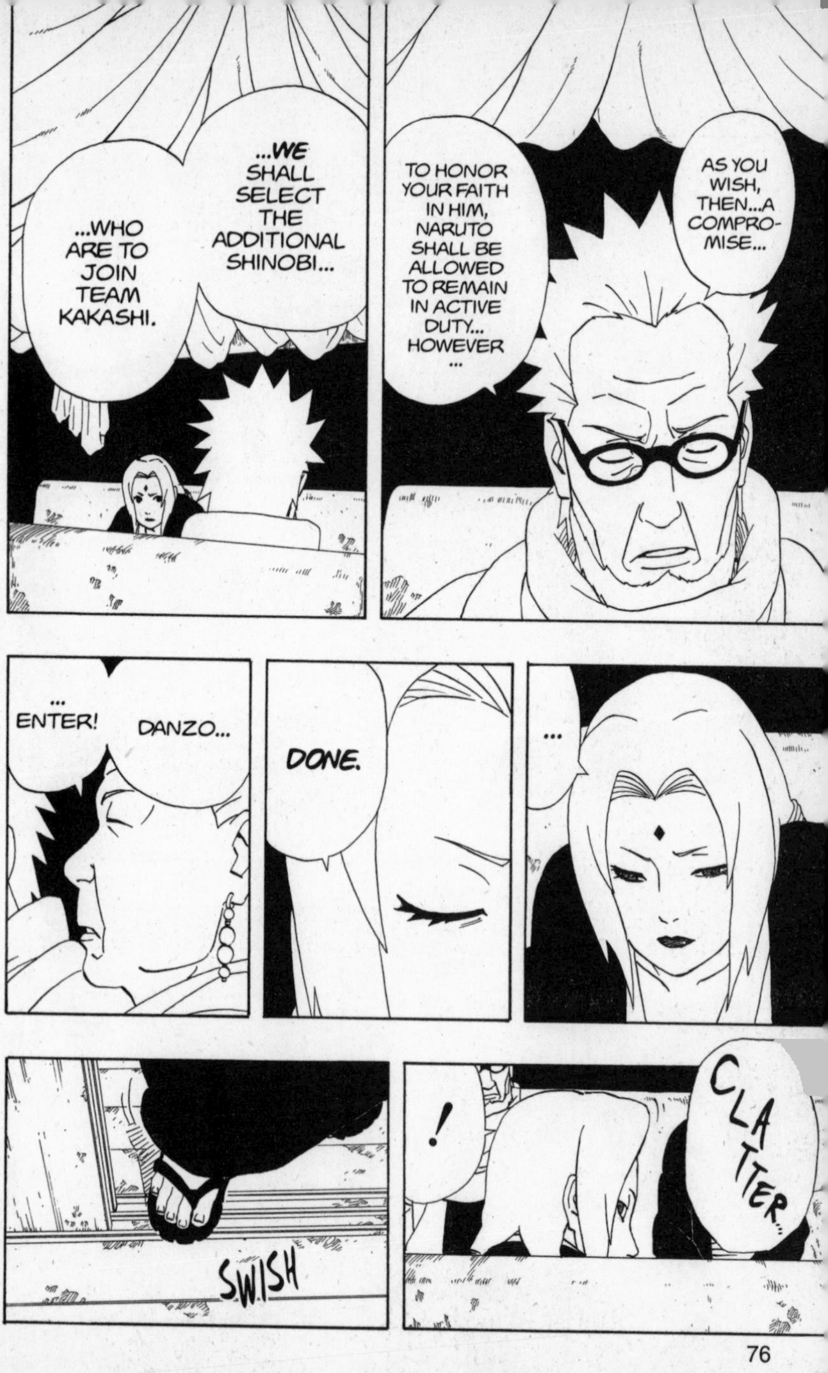
AS YOU WISH, THEN...A COMPROMISE...
TO HONOR YOUR FAITH IN HIM, NARUTO SHALL BE ALLOWED TO REMAIN IN ACTIVE DUTY... HOWEVER ...
...WE SHALL SELECT THE ADDITIONAL SHINOBI...
...WHO ARE TO JOIN TEAM KAKASHI.
...
DONE.
DANZO...
... ENTER!
!
CLATTER...
SWISH

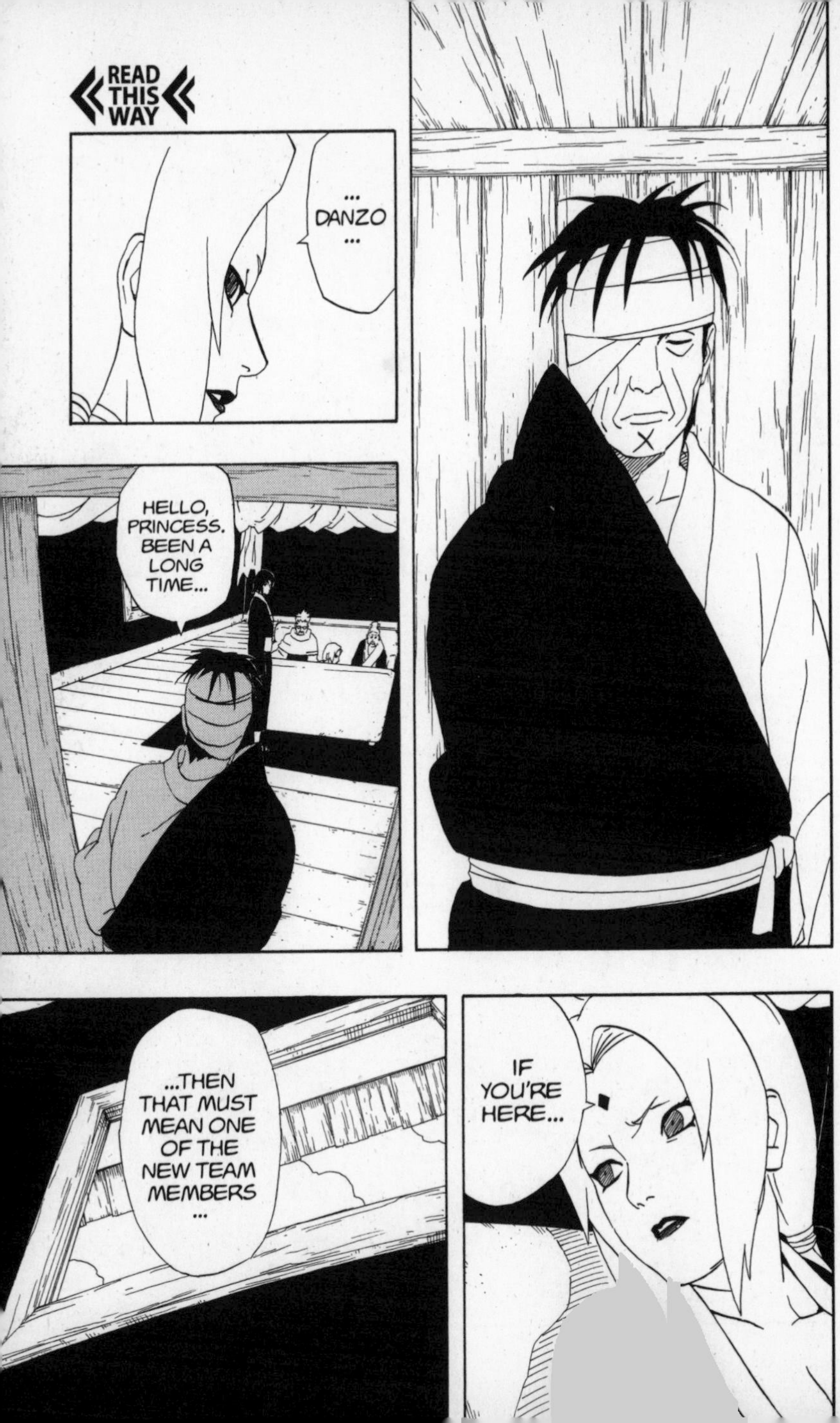
READ THIS WAY
... DANZO ...
HELLO, PRINCESS. BEEN A LONG TIME...
IF YOU'RE HERE...
...THEN THAT MUST MEAN ONE OF THE NEW TEAM MEMBERS ...

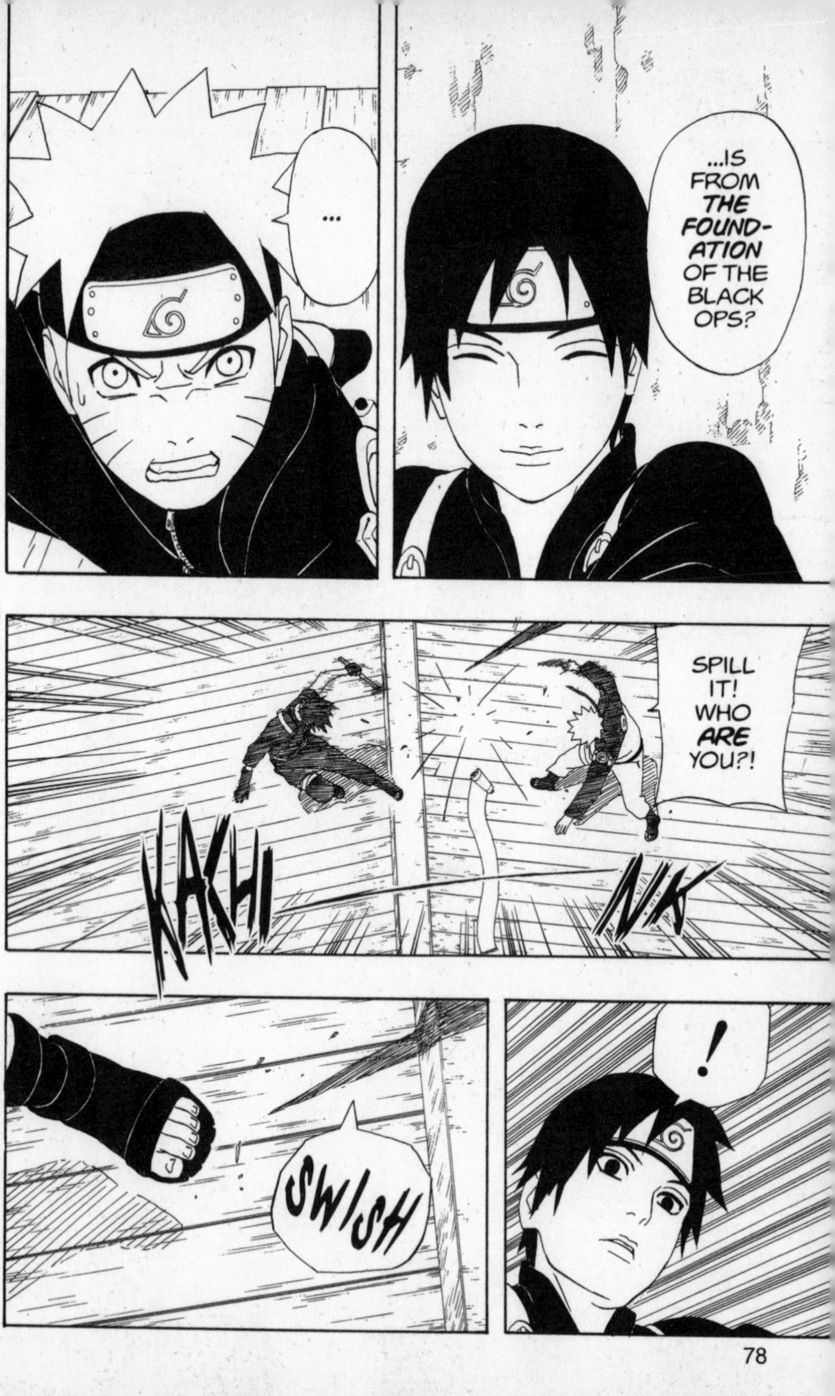
...IS FROM THE FOUNDATION OF THE BLACK OPS?
...
SPILL IT! WHO ARE YOU?!
KACHI
NK
!
SWISH

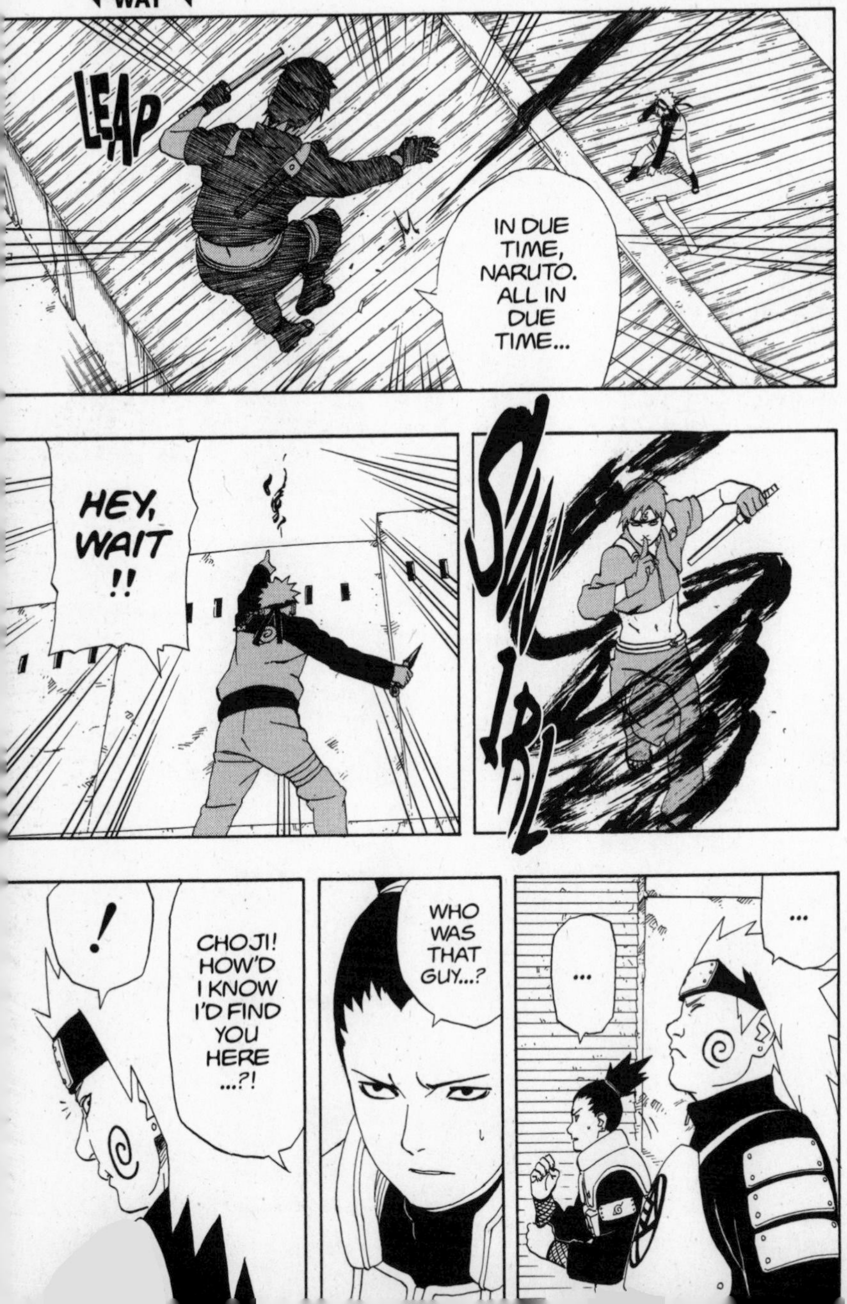

READ THIS WAY
LEAP
IN DUE TIME, NARUTO. ALL IN DUE TIME...
SWIRL
HEY, WAIT !!
...
...
WHO WAS THAT GUY...?
!
CHOJI! HOW'D I KNOW I'D FIND YOU HERE ...?!

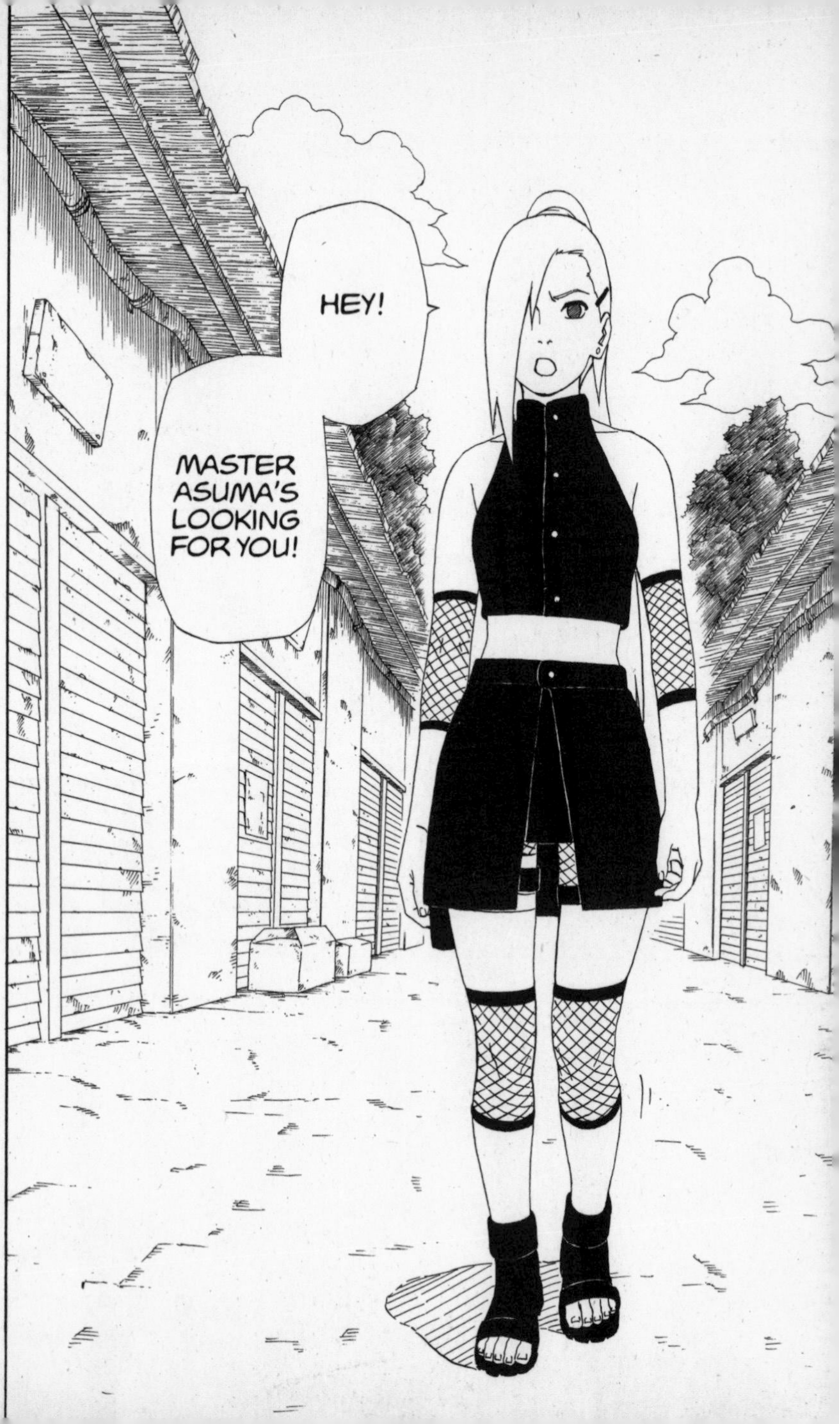
HEY!
MASTER ASUMA'S LOOKING FOR YOU!

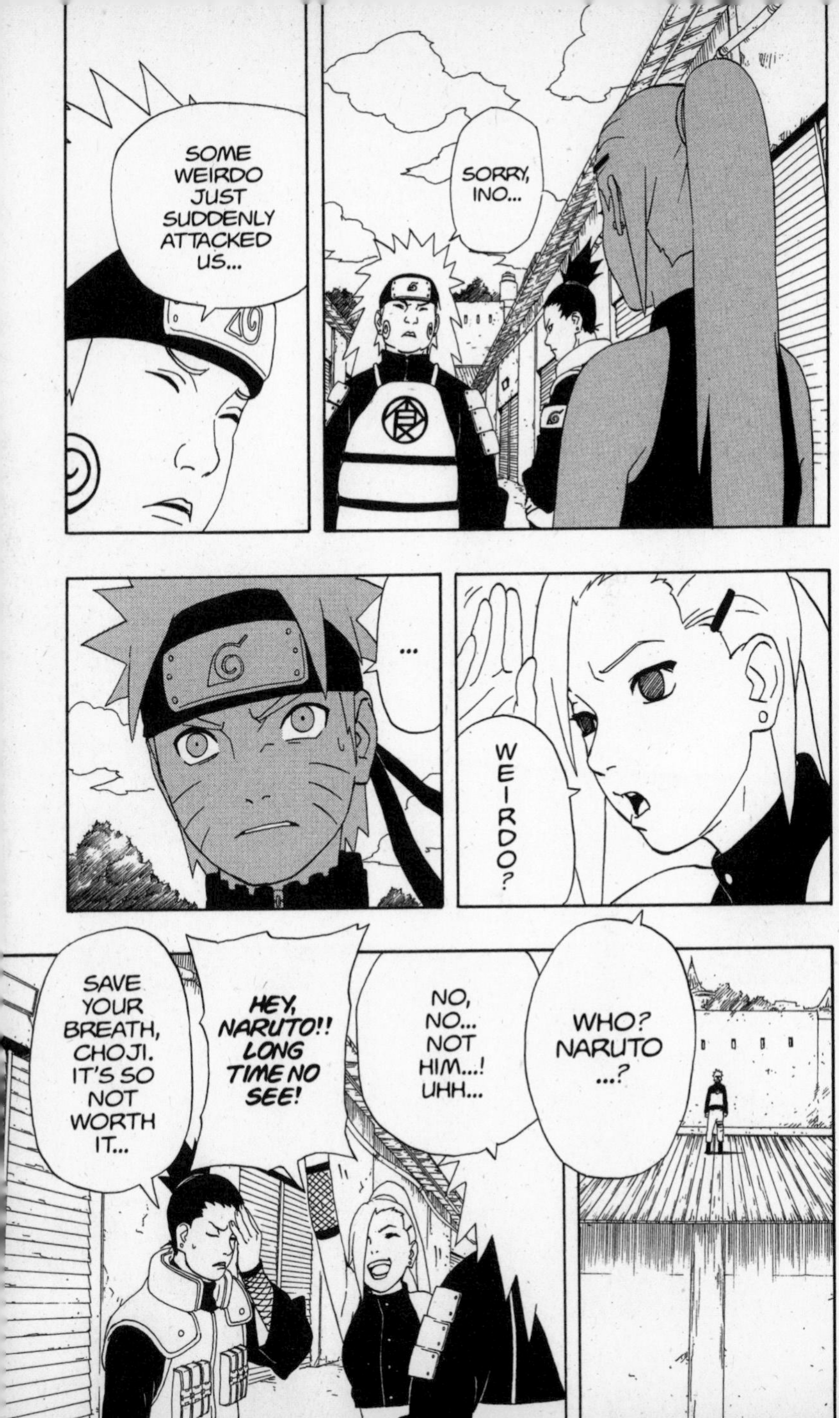
SORRY, INO...
SOME WEIRDO JUST SUDDENLY ATTACKED US...
WEIRDO?
...
WHO? NARUTO ...?
NO, NO... NOT HIM...! UHH...
HEY, NARUTO!! LONG TIME NO SEE!
SAVE YOUR BREATH, CHOJI. IT'S SO NOT WORTH IT...

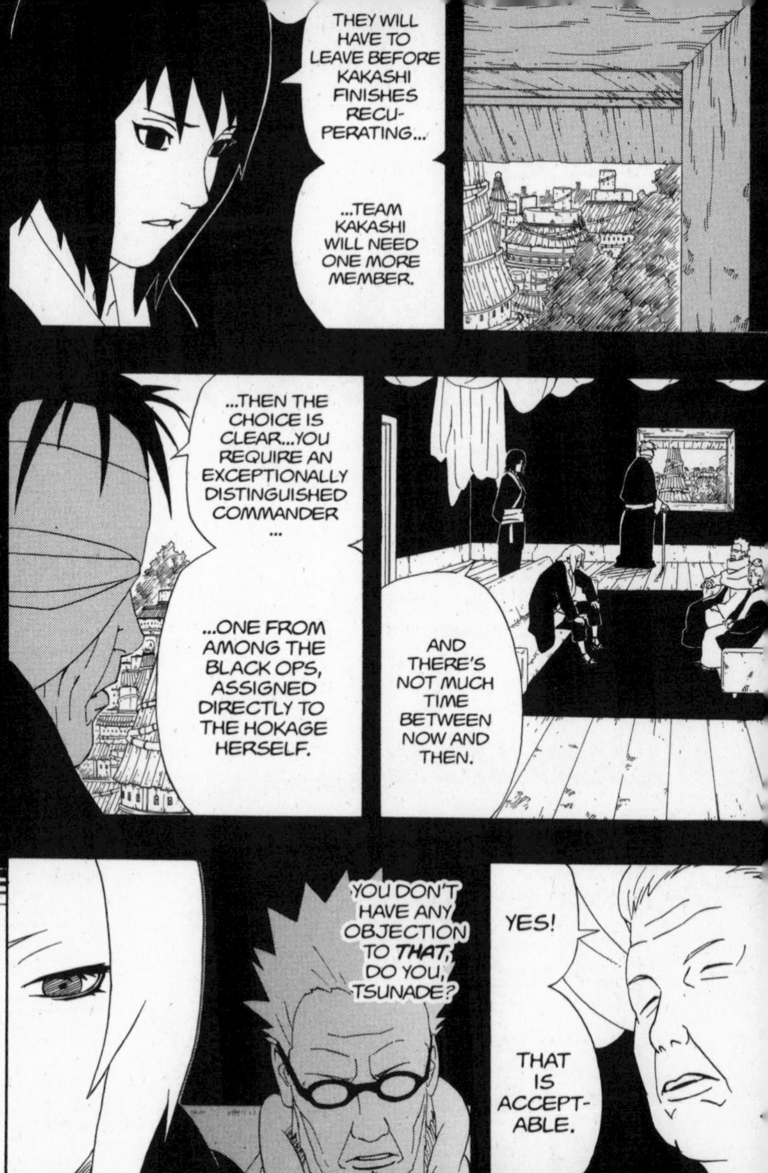
THEY WILL HAVE TO LEAVE BEFORE KAKASHI FINISHES RECU-PERATING...
...TEAM KAKASHI WILL NEED ONE MORE MEMBER.
AND THERE'S NOT MUCH TIME BETWEEN NOW AND THEN.
...THEN THE CHOICE IS CLEAR...YOU REQUIRE AN EXCEPTIONALLY DISTINGUISHED COMMANDER...
...ONE FROM AMONG THE BLACK OPS, ASSIGNED DIRECTLY TO THE HOKAGE HERSELF.
YES!
THAT IS ACCEPT-ABLE.
YOU DON'T HAVE ANY OBJECTION TO *THAT*, DO YOU, TSUNADE?

READ THIS WAY

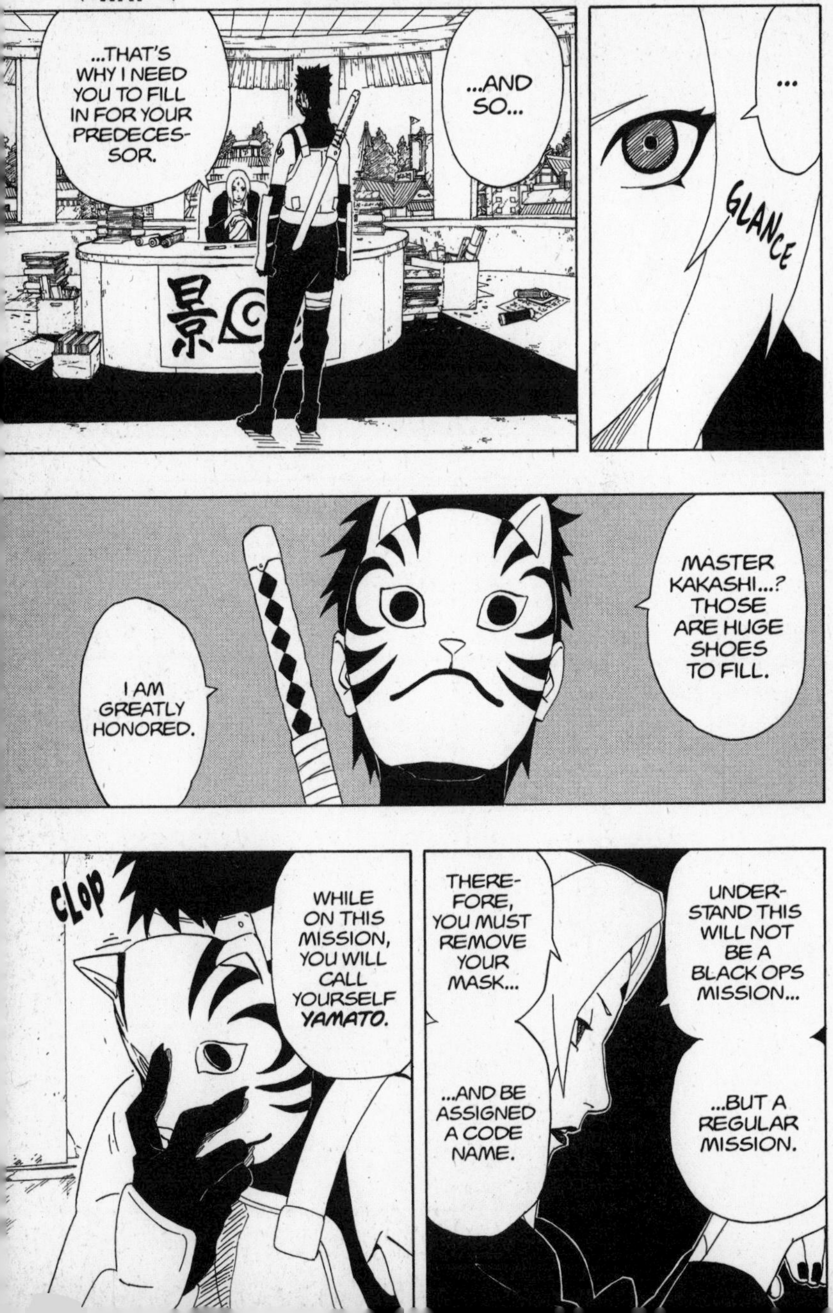
...
GLANCE
...AND SO...
...THAT'S WHY I NEED YOU TO FILL IN FOR YOUR PREDECES-SOR.
MASTER KAKASHI...? THOSE ARE HUGE SHOES TO FILL.
I AM GREATLY HONORED.
UNDER-STAND THIS WILL NOT BE A BLACK OPS MISSION...
...BUT A REGULAR MISSION.
THERE-FORE, YOU MUST REMOVE YOUR MASK...
...AND BE ASSIGNED A CODE NAME.
WHILE ON THIS MISSION, YOU WILL CALL YOURSELF *YAMATO*.
CLOP

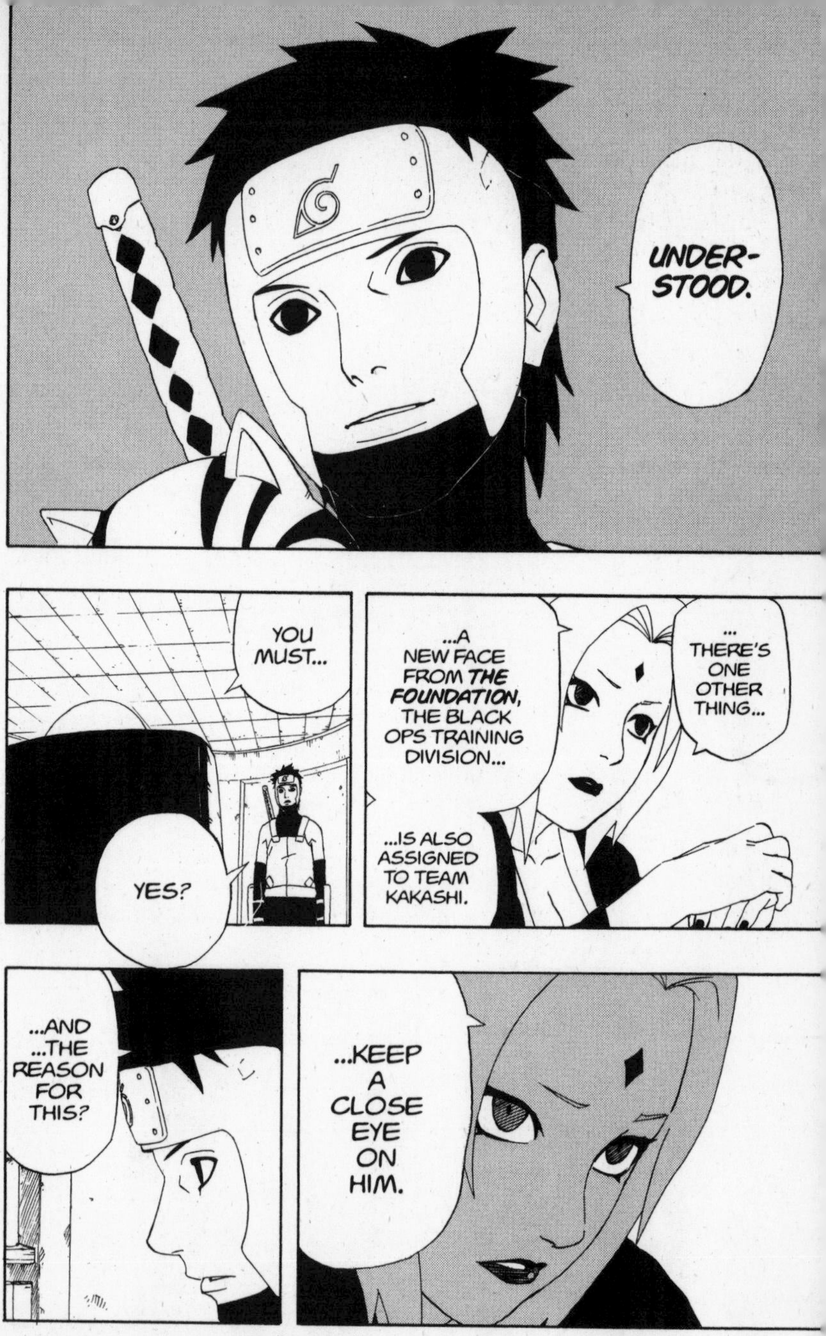
UNDER-STOOD.
... THERE'S ONE OTHER THING...
...A NEW FACE FROM THE FOUNDATION, THE BLACK OPS TRAINING DIVISION...
...IS ALSO ASSIGNED TO TEAM KAKASHI.
YOU MUST...
YES?
...KEEP A CLOSE EYE ON HIM.
...AND ...THE REASON FOR THIS?

READ THIS WAY

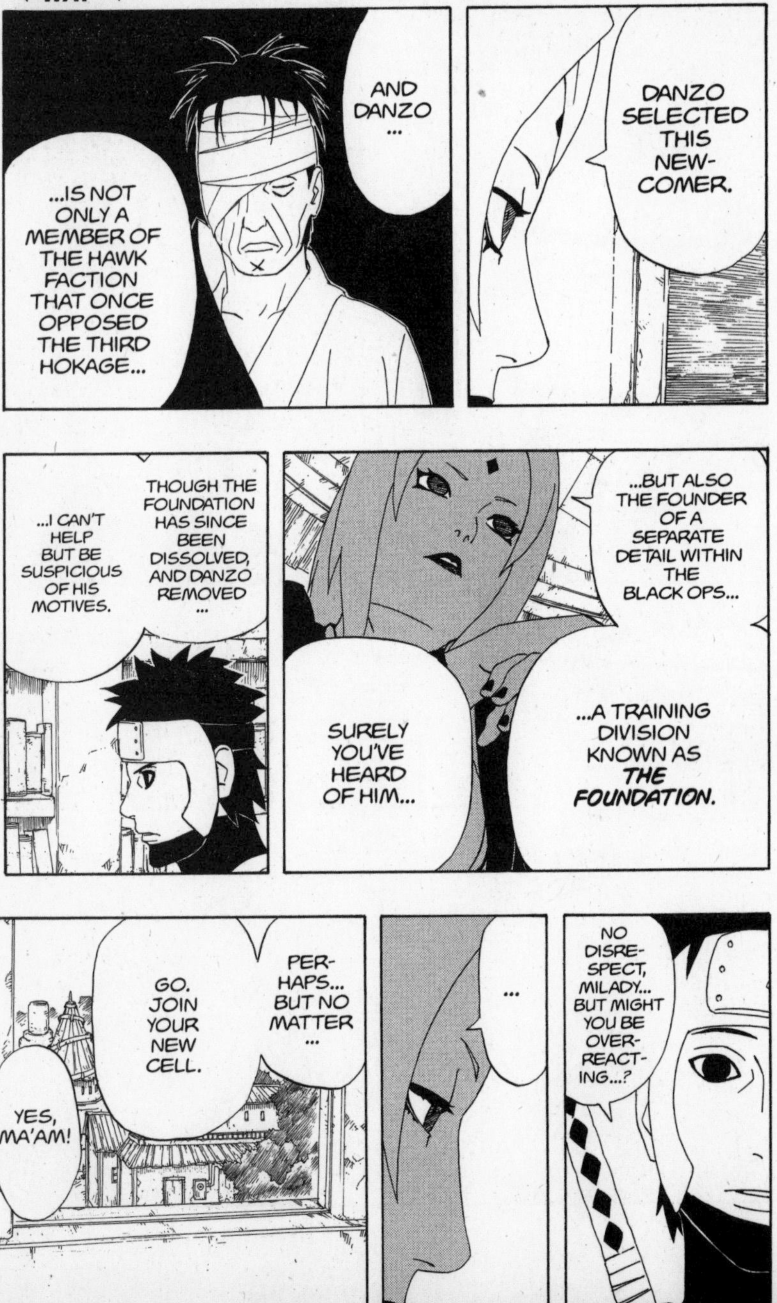
DANZO SELECTED THIS NEWCOMER.
AND DANZO ...
...IS NOT ONLY A MEMBER OF THE HAWK FACTION THAT ONCE OPPOSED THE THIRD HOKAGE...
...BUT ALSO THE FOUNDER OF A SEPARATE DETAIL WITHIN THE BLACK OPS...
...A TRAINING DIVISION KNOWN AS ***THE FOUNDATION***.
SURELY YOU'VE HEARD OF HIM...
THOUGH THE FOUNDATION HAS SINCE BEEN DISSOLVED, AND DANZO REMOVED ...
...I CAN'T HELP BUT BE SUSPICIOUS OF HIS MOTIVES.
NO DISRESPECT, MILADY... BUT MIGHT YOU BE OVERREACTING...?
...
PERHAPS... BUT NO MATTER ...
GO. JOIN YOUR NEW CELL.
YES, MA'AM!

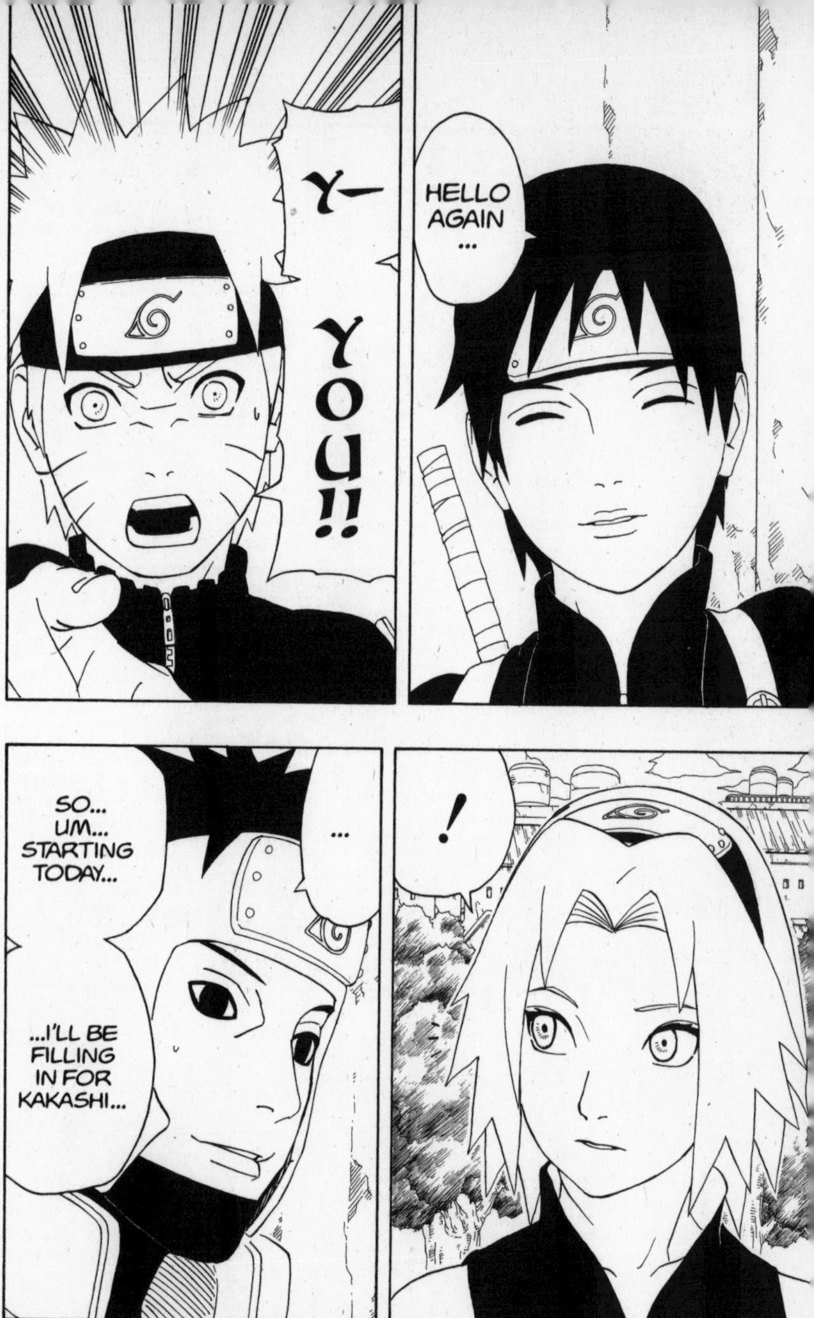
HELLO AGAIN ...
Y— YOU!!
!
...
SO... UM... STARTING TODAY...
...I'LL BE FILLING IN FOR KAKASHI...

READ THIS WAY

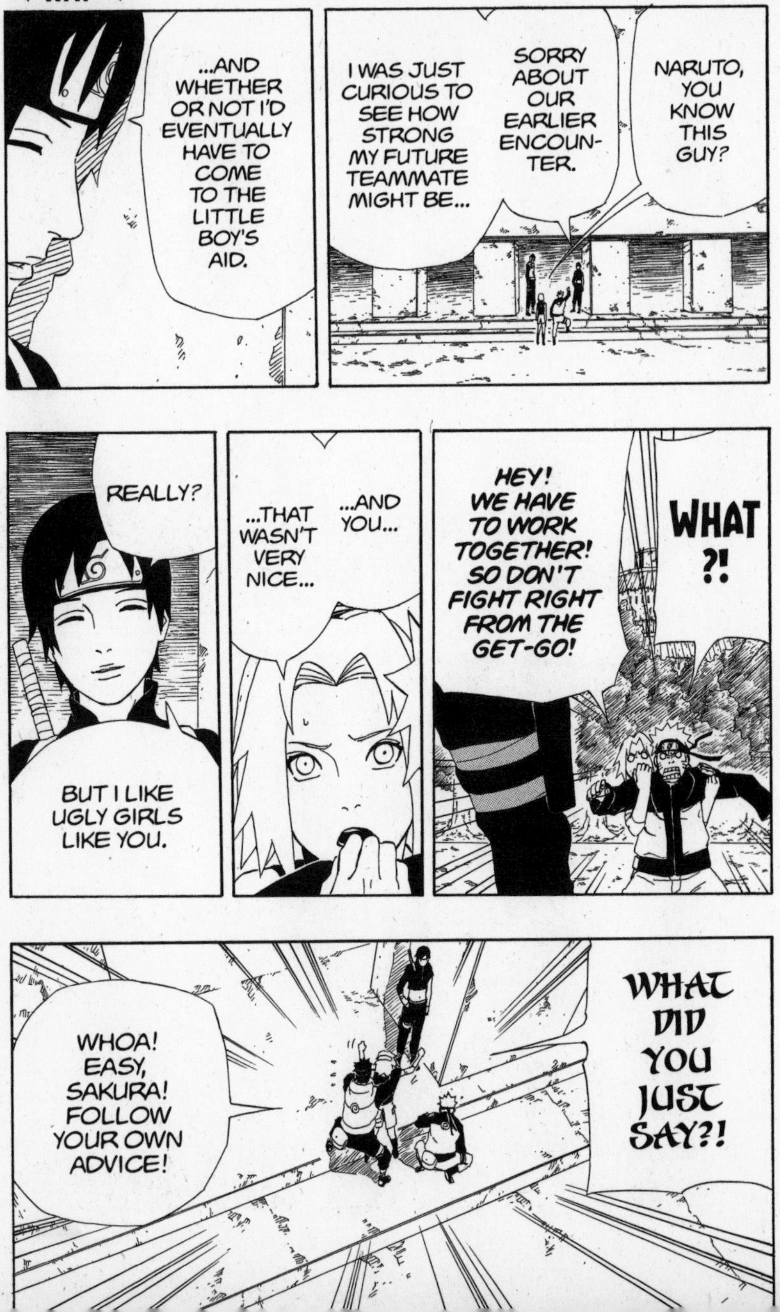
NARUTO, YOU KNOW THIS GUY?
SORRY ABOUT OUR EARLIER ENCOUNTER.
I WAS JUST CURIOUS TO SEE HOW STRONG MY FUTURE TEAMMATE MIGHT BE...
...AND WHETHER OR NOT I'D EVENTUALLY HAVE TO COME TO THE LITTLE BOY'S AID.
WHAT ?!
HEY! WE HAVE TO WORK TOGETHER! SO DON'T FIGHT RIGHT FROM THE GET-GO!
...AND YOU...
...THAT WASN'T VERY NICE...
REALLY?
BUT I LIKE UGLY GIRLS LIKE YOU.
WHAT DID YOU JUST SAY?!
WHOA! EASY, SAKURA! FOLLOW YOUR OWN ADVICE!

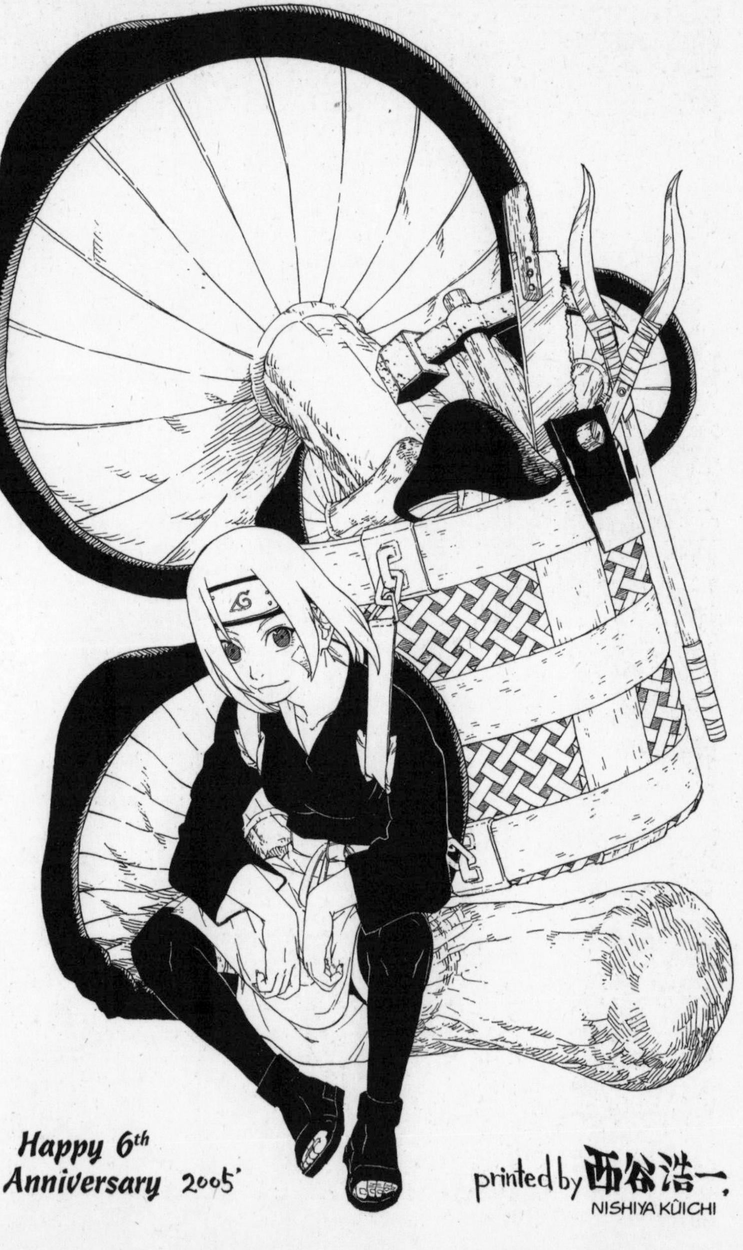
Happy 6th
Anniversary 2005'
printed by 西谷浩一
NISHIYA KÛICHI

Number 285: The Foundation

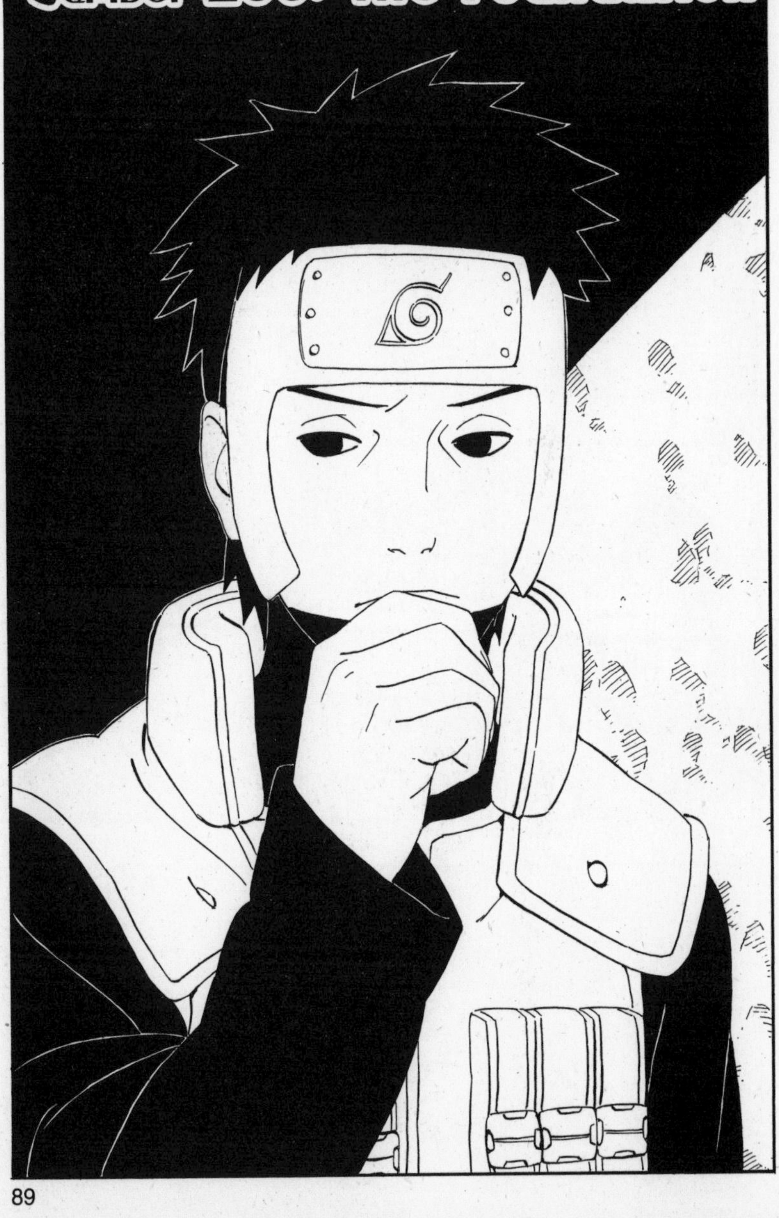

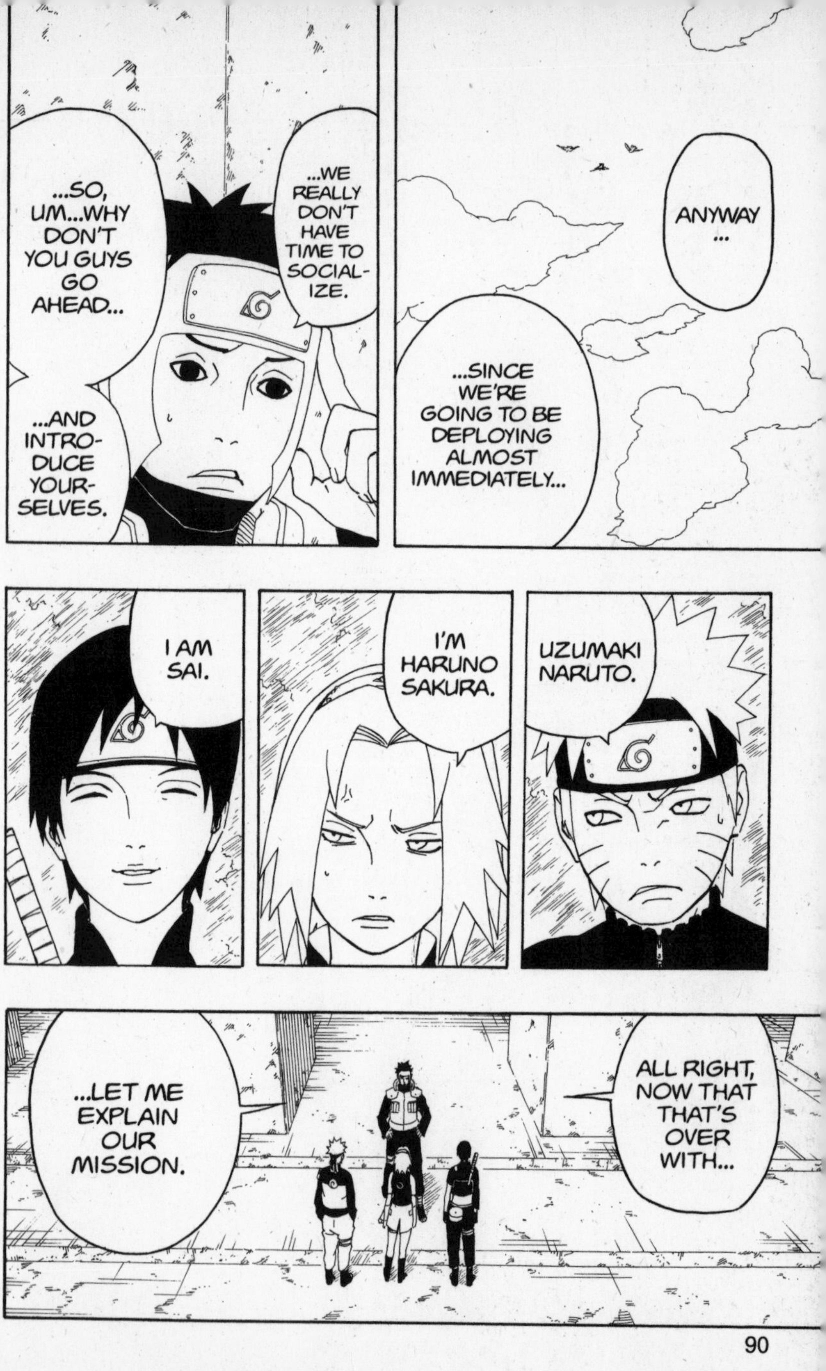
ANYWAY...
...SINCE WE'RE GOING TO BE DEPLOYING ALMOST IMMEDIATELY...
...WE REALLY DON'T HAVE TIME TO SOCIAL-IZE.
...SO, UM...WHY DON'T YOU GUYS GO AHEAD...
...AND INTRO-DUCE YOUR-SELVES.
UZUMAKI NARUTO.
I'M HARUNO SAKURA.
I AM SAI.
ALL RIGHT, NOW THAT THAT'S OVER WITH...
...LET ME EXPLAIN OUR MISSION.

READ THIS WAY

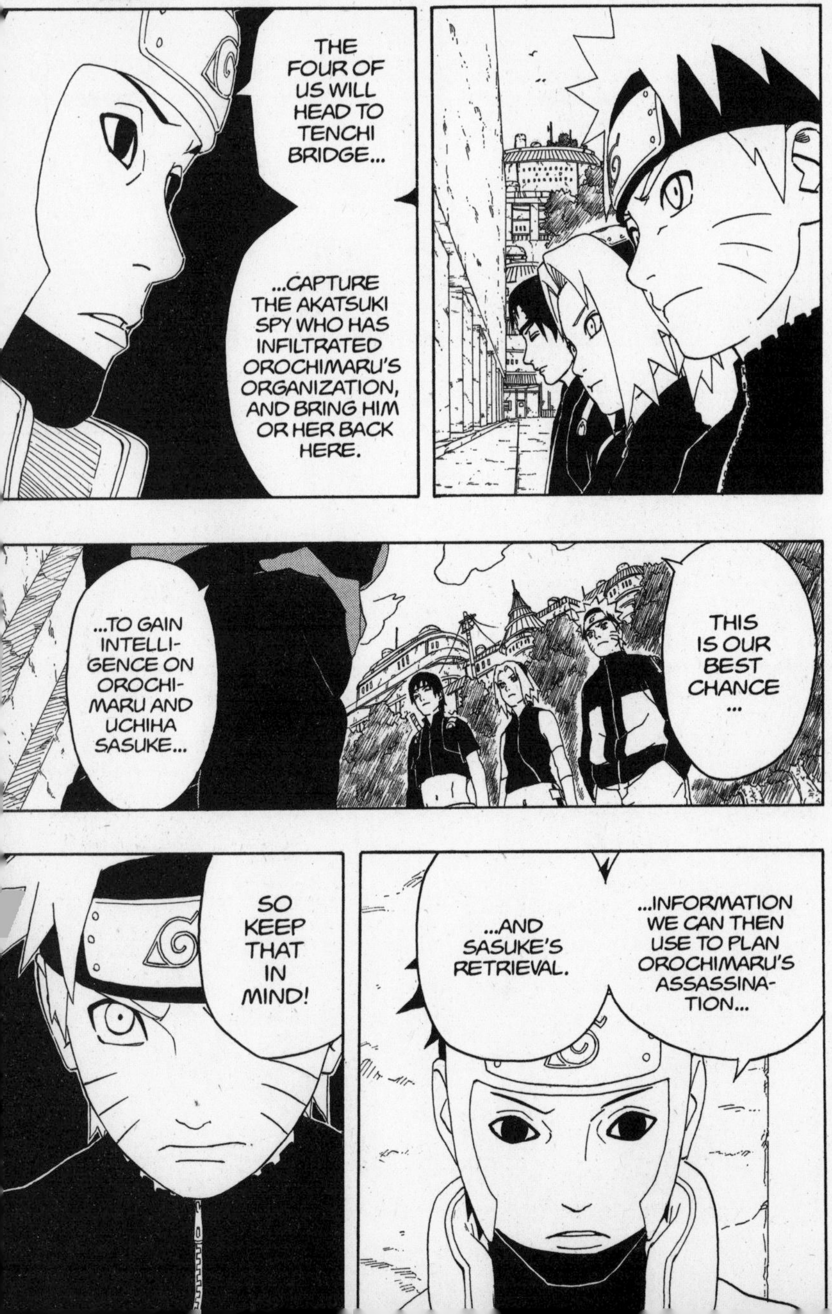
THE FOUR OF US WILL HEAD TO TENCHI BRIDGE...
...CAPTURE THE AKATSUKI SPY WHO HAS INFILTRATED OROCHIMARU'S ORGANIZATION, AND BRING HIM OR HER BACK HERE.
THIS IS OUR BEST CHANCE ...
...TO GAIN INTELLI-GENCE ON OROCHI-MARU AND UCHIHA SASUKE...
...INFORMATION WE CAN THEN USE TO PLAN OROCHIMARU'S ASSASSINA-TION...
...AND SASUKE'S RETRIEVAL.
SO KEEP THAT IN MIND!

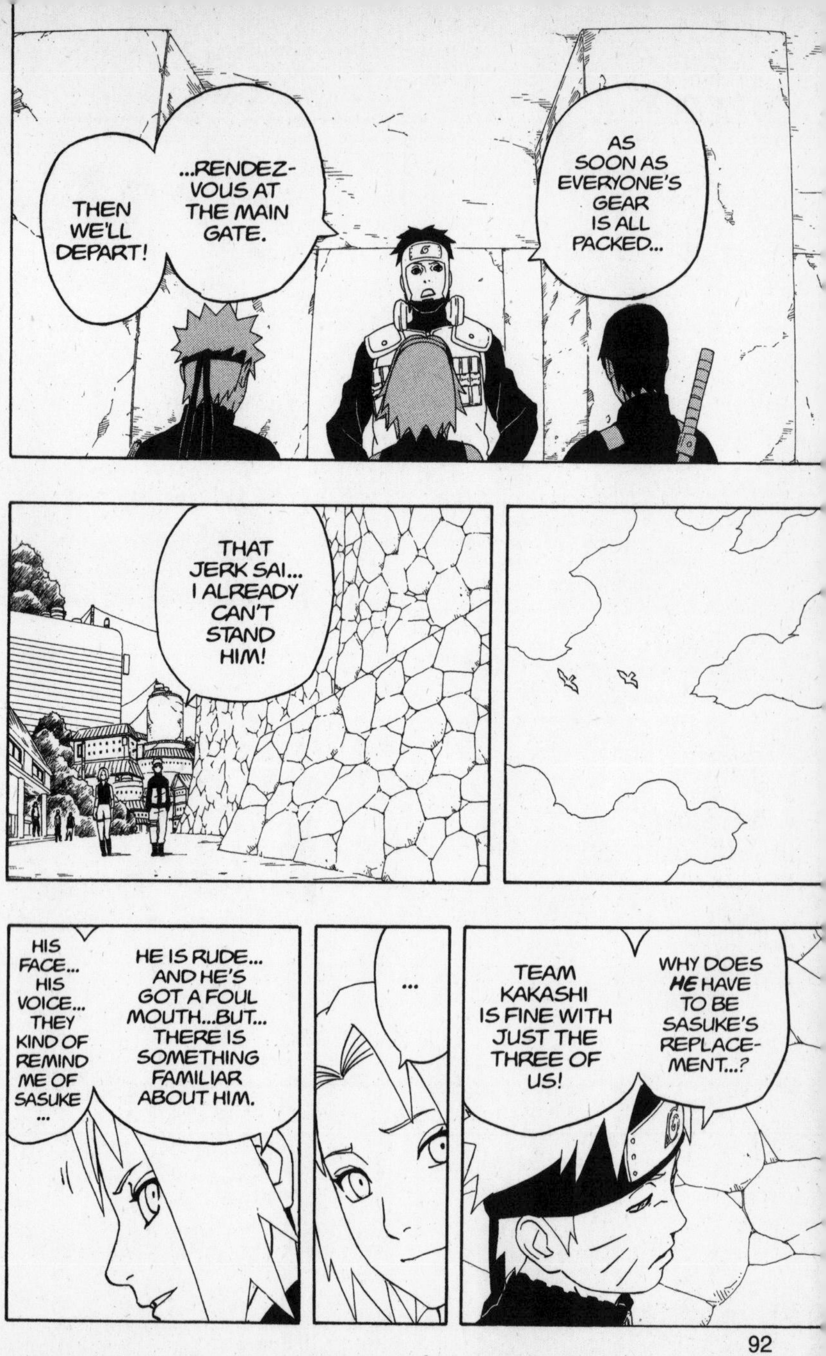
AS SOON AS EVERYONE'S GEAR IS ALL PACKED...
...RENDEZ-VOUS AT THE MAIN GATE.
THEN WE'LL DEPART!
THAT JERK SAI... I ALREADY CAN'T STAND HIM!
WHY DOES *HE* HAVE TO BE SASUKE'S REPLACE-MENT...?
TEAM KAKASHI IS FINE WITH JUST THE THREE OF US!
...
HE IS RUDE... AND HE'S GOT A FOUL MOUTH...BUT... THERE IS SOMETHING FAMILIAR ABOUT HIM.
HIS FACE... HIS VOICE... THEY KIND OF REMIND ME OF SASUKE...

READ THIS WAY

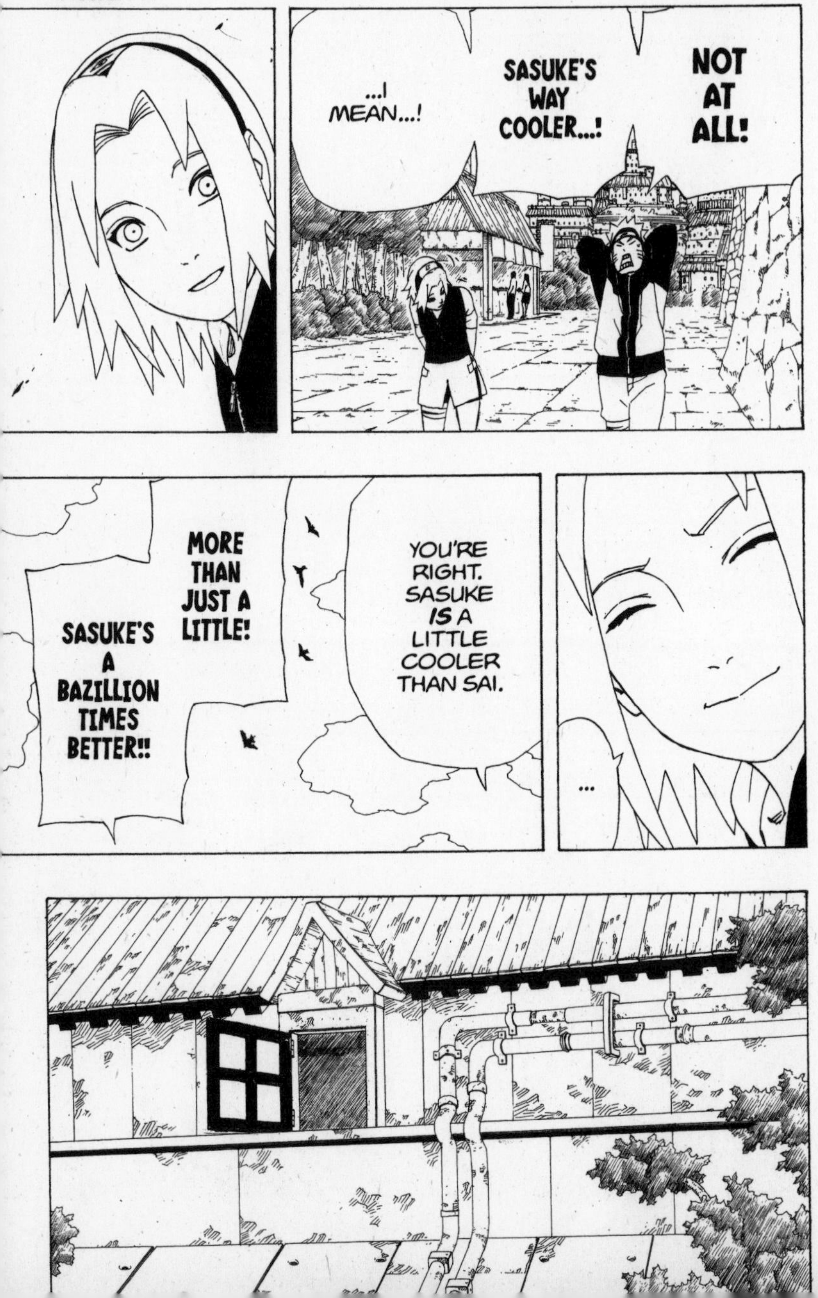
NOT AT ALL!
SASUKE'S WAY COOLER...!
...I MEAN...!
...
YOU'RE RIGHT. SASUKE IS A LITTLE COOLER THAN SAI.
MORE THAN JUST A LITTLE!
SASUKE'S A BAZILLION TIMES BETTER!!

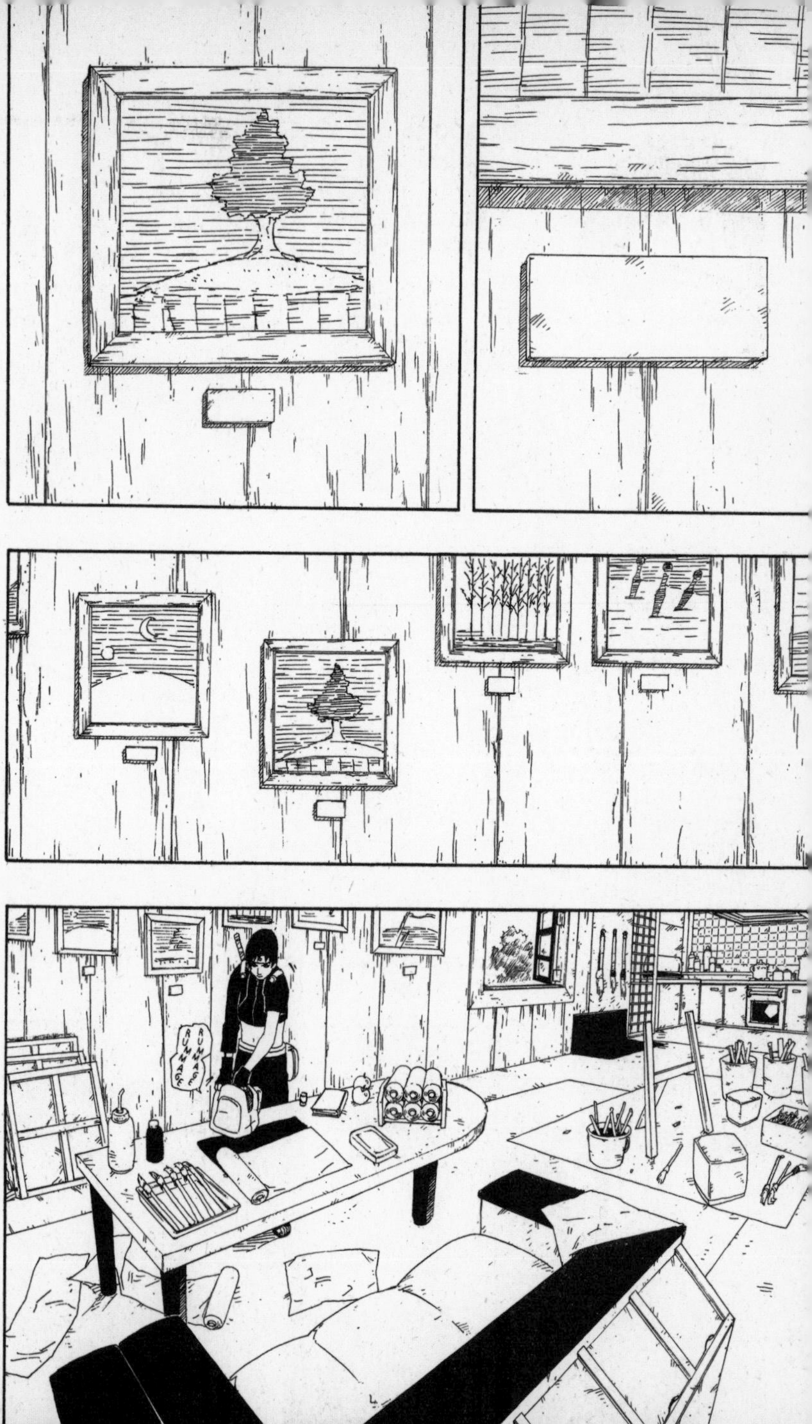
RUMMAGE RUMMAGE

READ THIS WAY

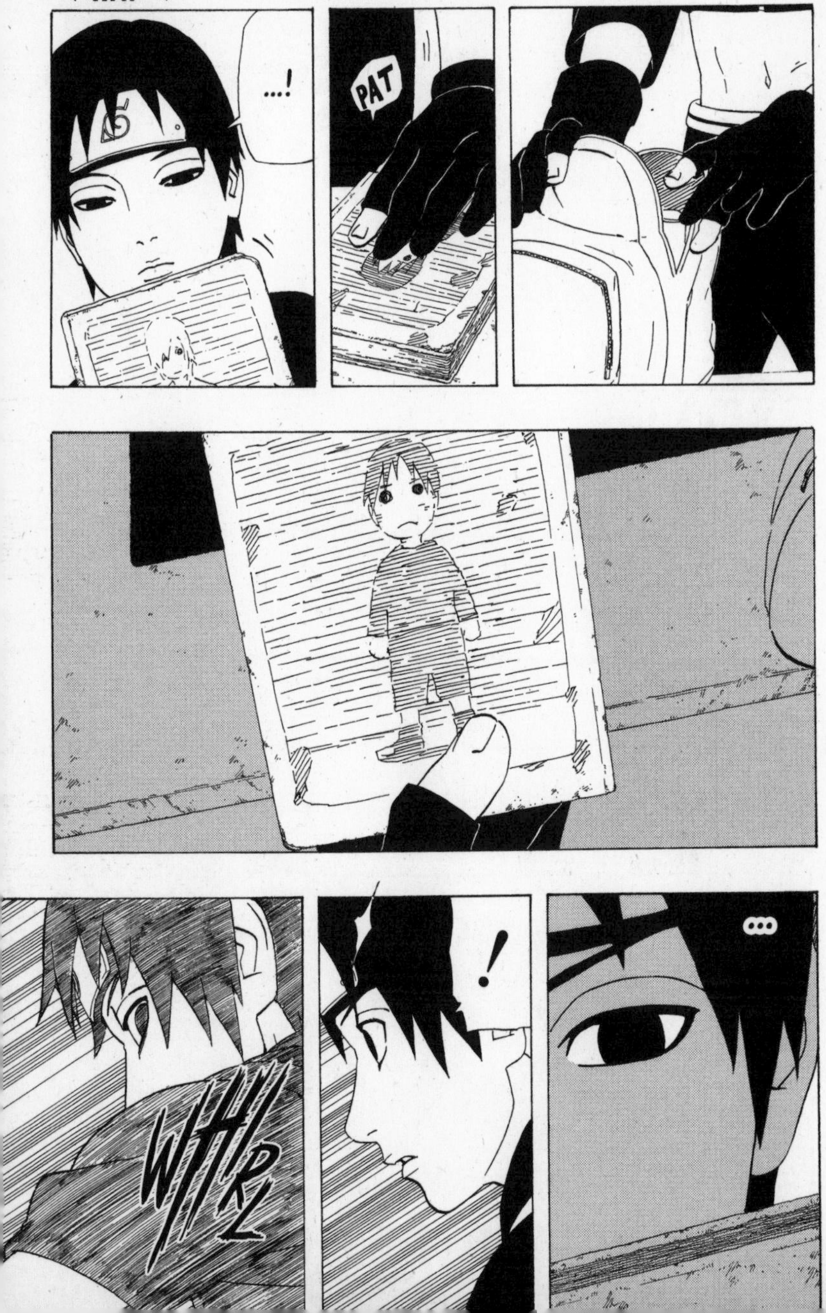
PAT
...!
...
!
WHIRL

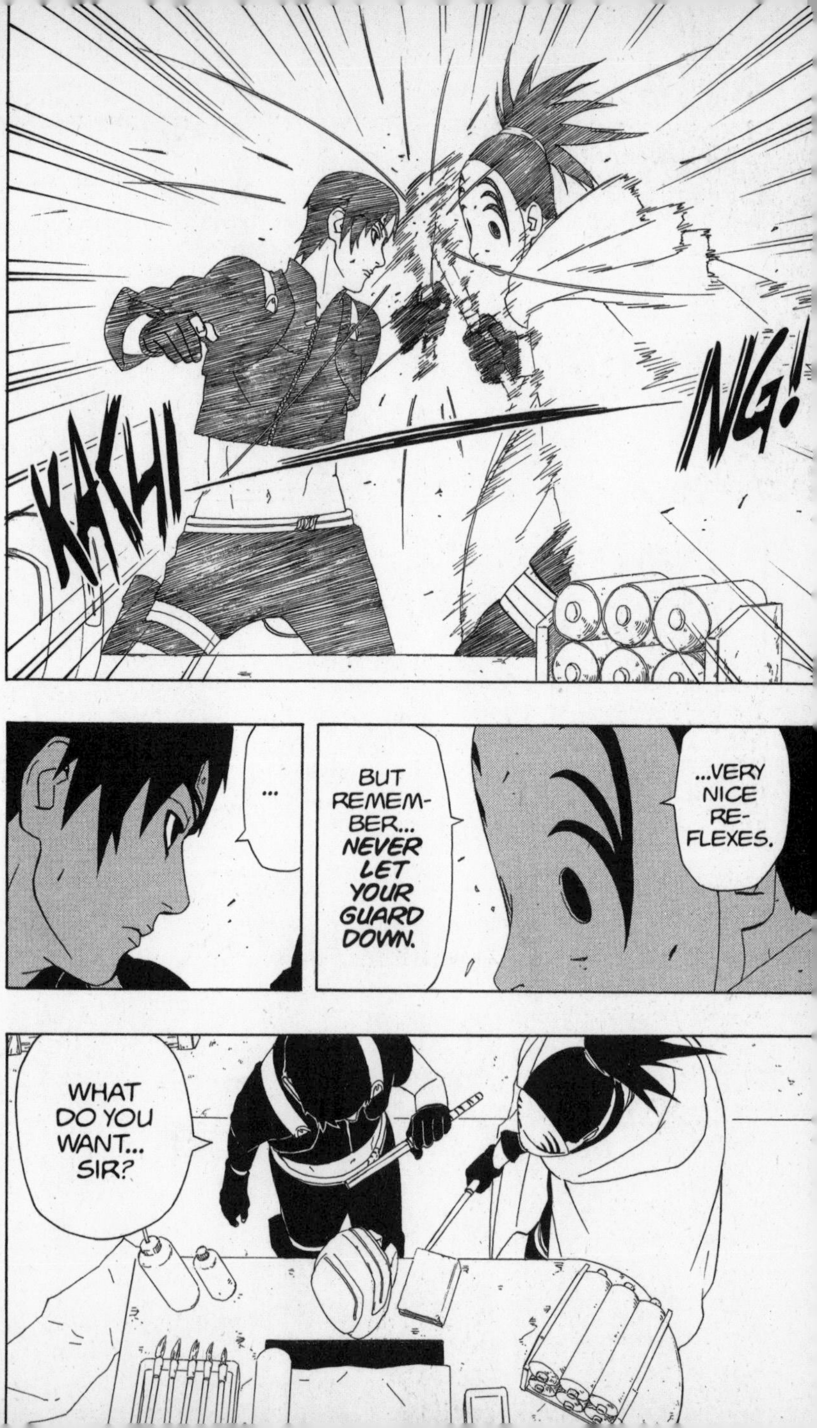
NG!
KACHI
...VERY NICE RE-FLEXES.
BUT REMEM-BER... NEVER LET YOUR GUARD DOWN.
...
WHAT DO YOU WANT... SIR?

READ THIS WAY

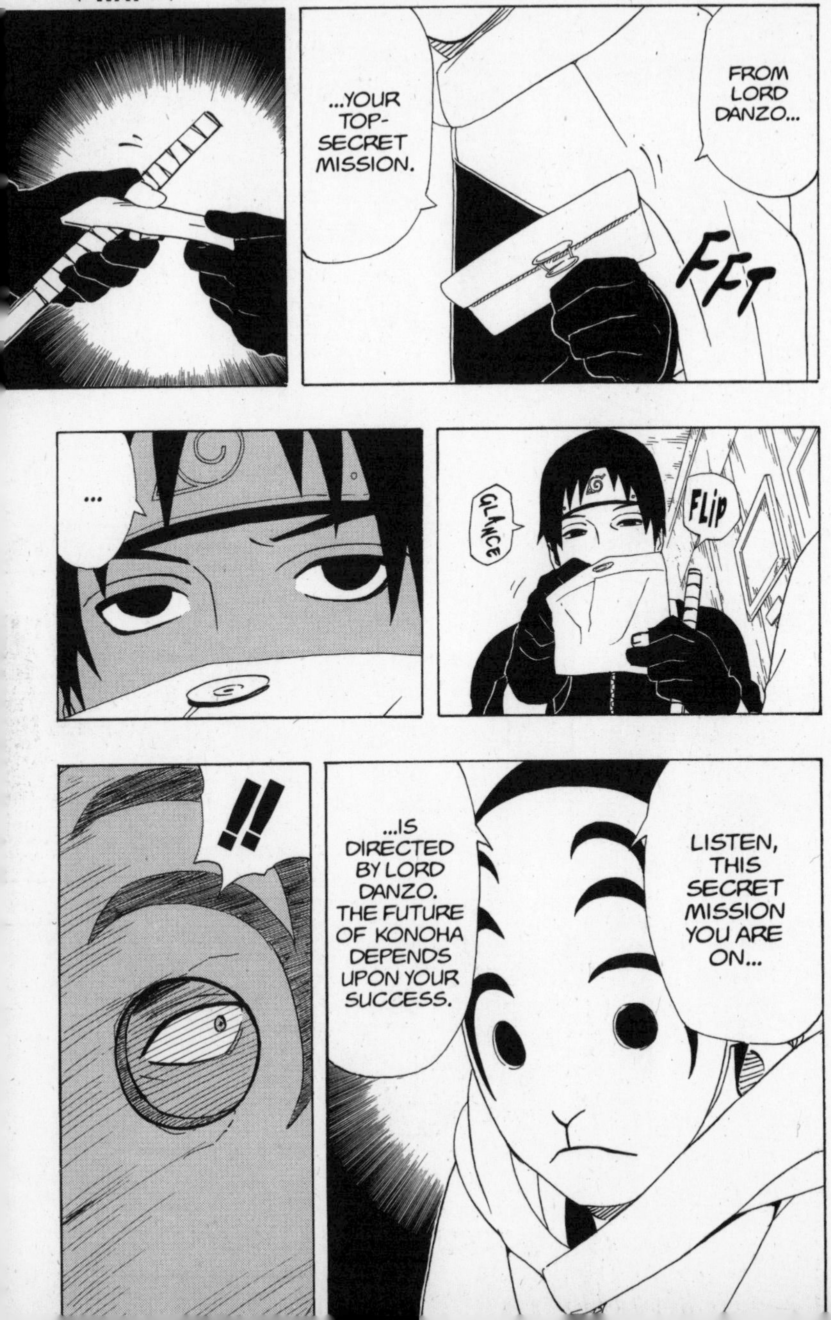
FROM LORD DANZO...
...YOUR TOP-SECRET MISSION.
FFT
FLIP
GLANCE
...
LISTEN, THIS SECRET MISSION YOU ARE ON...
...IS DIRECTED BY LORD DANZO. THE FUTURE OF KONOHA DEPENDS UPON YOUR SUCCESS.
!!

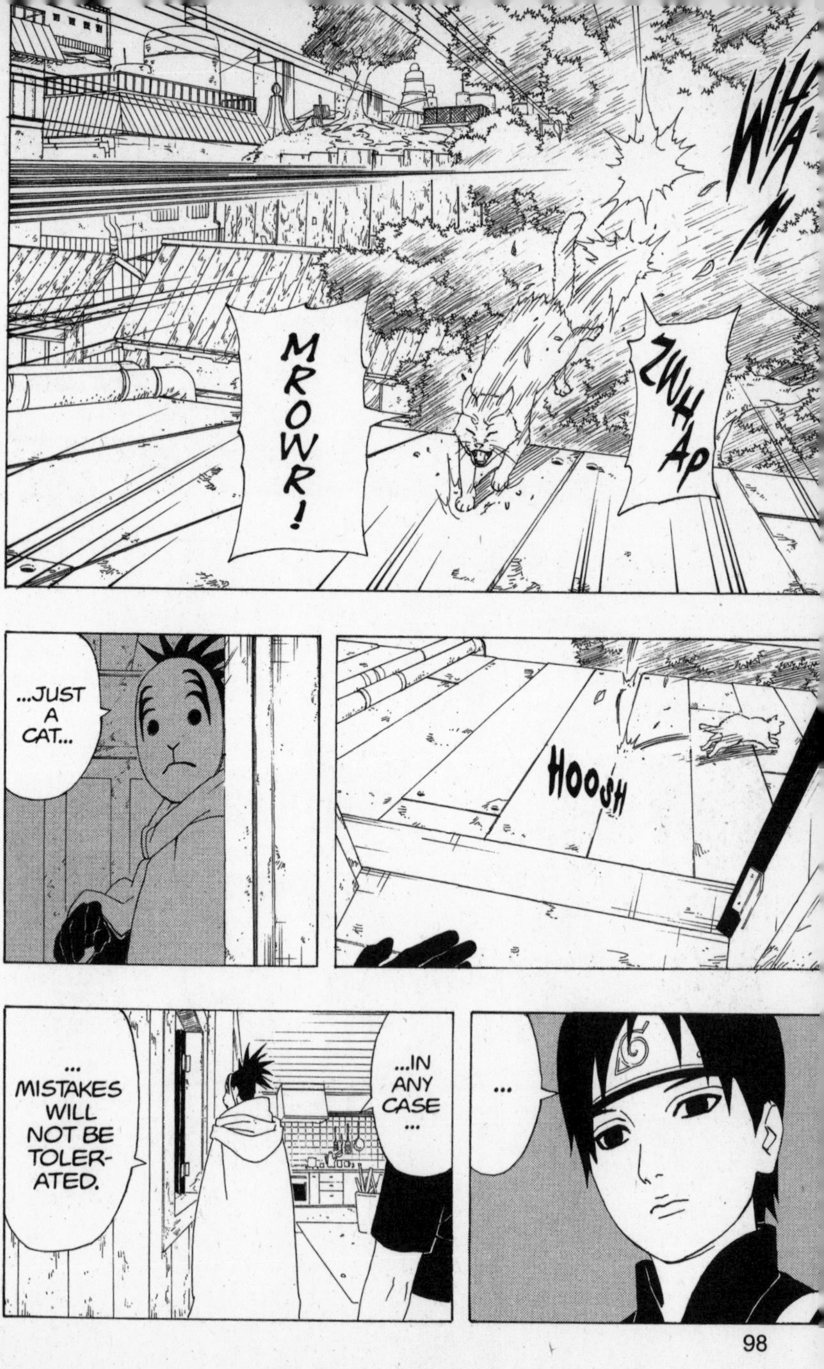
WHAM
ZWHAP
MROWR!
HOOSH
...JUST A CAT...
...
...IN ANY CASE...
...MISTAKES WILL NOT BE TOLERATED.

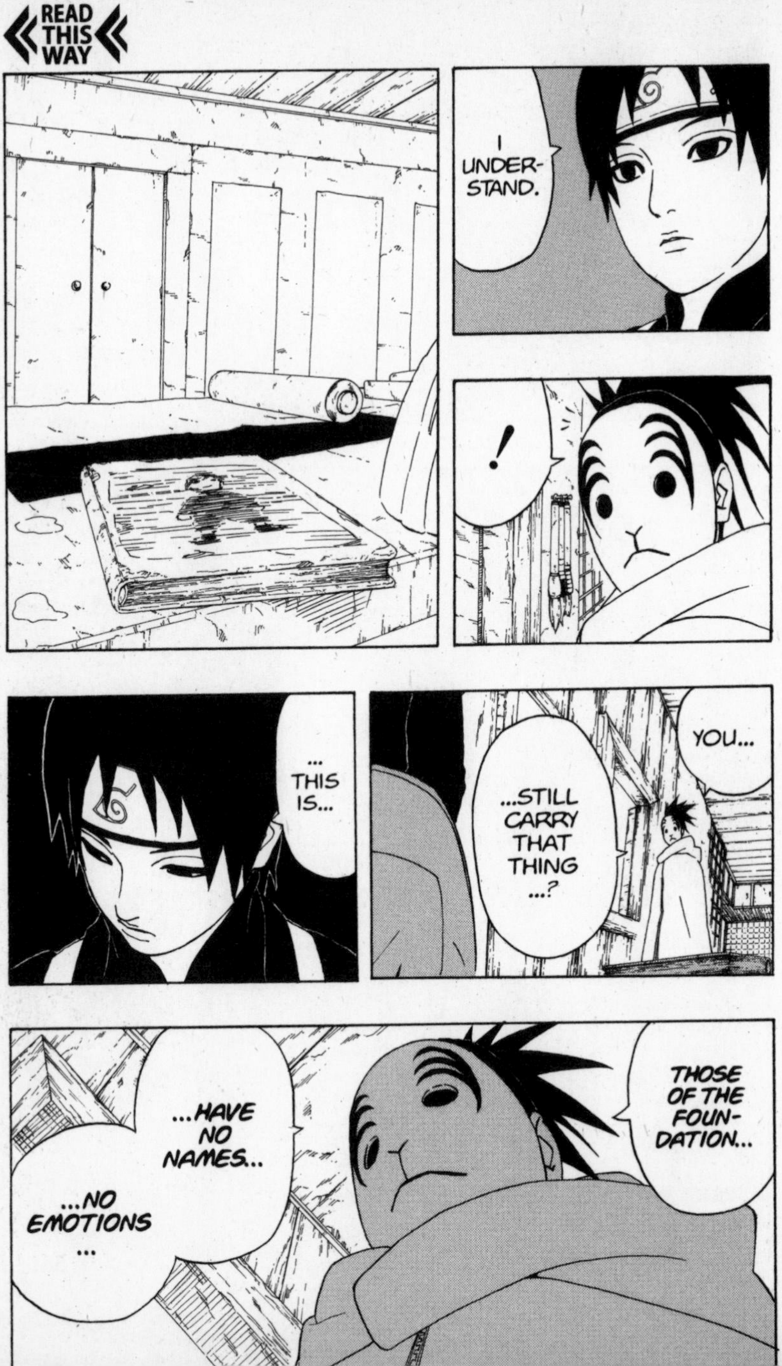
READ THIS WAY
I UNDERSTAND.
!
YOU...
...STILL CARRY THAT THING...?
...THIS IS...
THOSE OF THE FOUNDATION...
...HAVE NO NAMES...
...NO EMOTIONS...

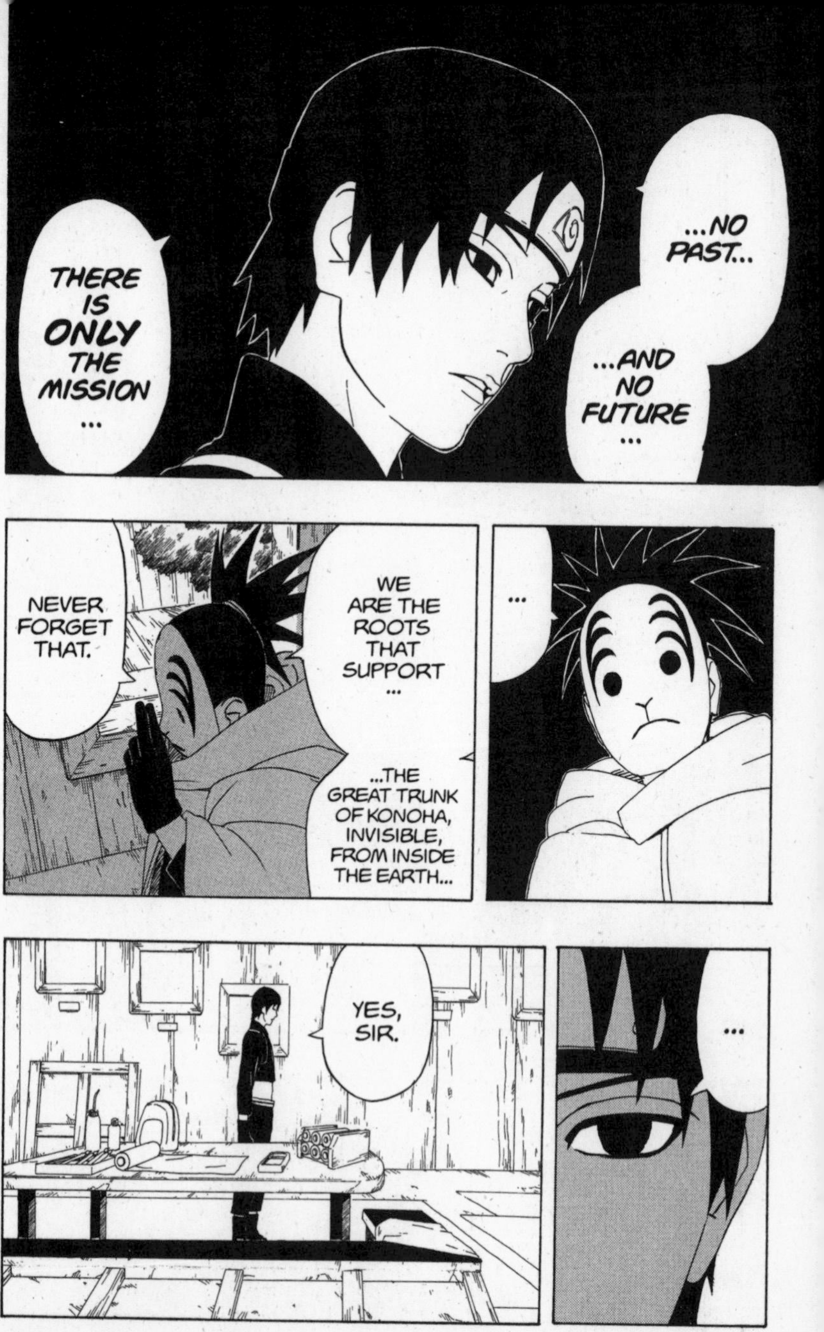
THERE IS ONLY THE MISSION...
...NO PAST...
...AND NO FUTURE...
...
WE ARE THE ROOTS THAT SUPPORT...
...THE GREAT TRUNK OF KONOHA, INVISIBLE, FROM INSIDE THE EARTH...
NEVER FORGET THAT.
...
YES, SIR.

READ THIS WAY

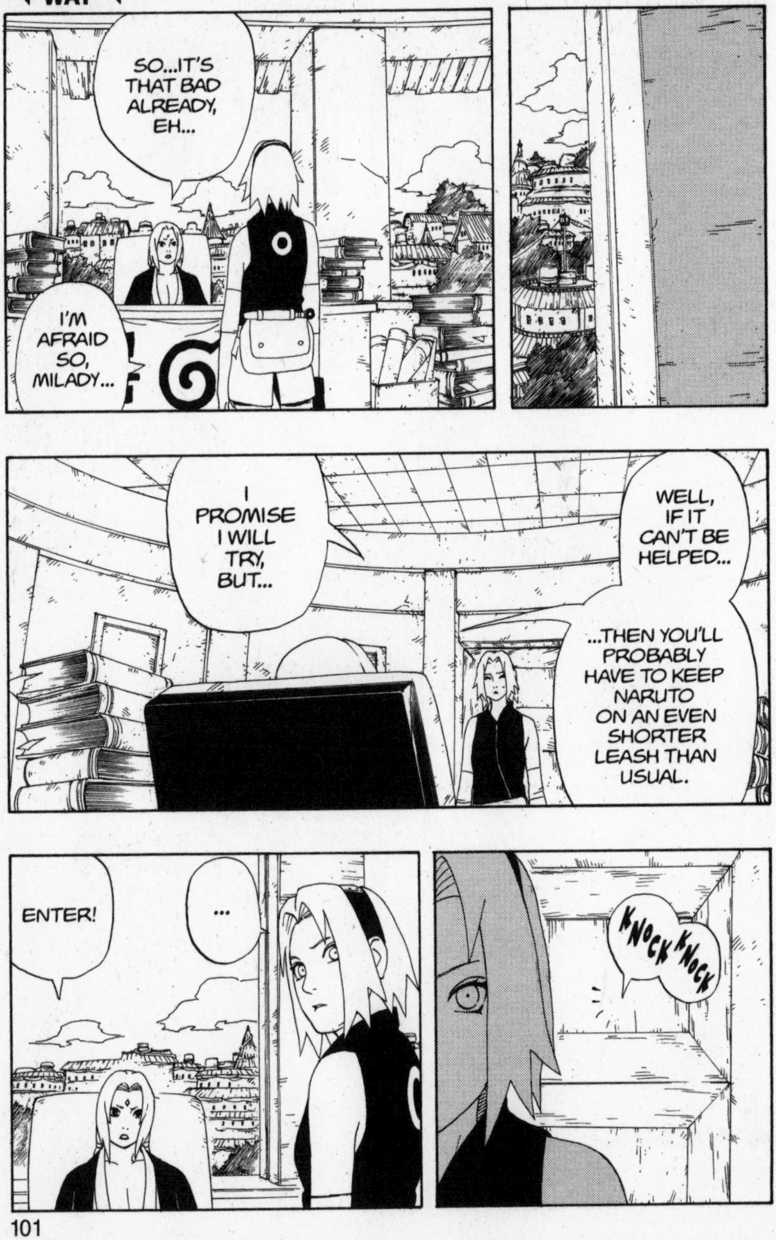
SO...IT'S THAT BAD ALREADY, EH...
I'M AFRAID SO, MILADY...
WELL, IF IT CAN'T BE HELPED...
...THEN YOU'LL PROBABLY HAVE TO KEEP NARUTO ON AN EVEN SHORTER LEASH THAN USUAL.
I PROMISE I WILL TRY, BUT...
KNOCK KNOCK
...
ENTER!

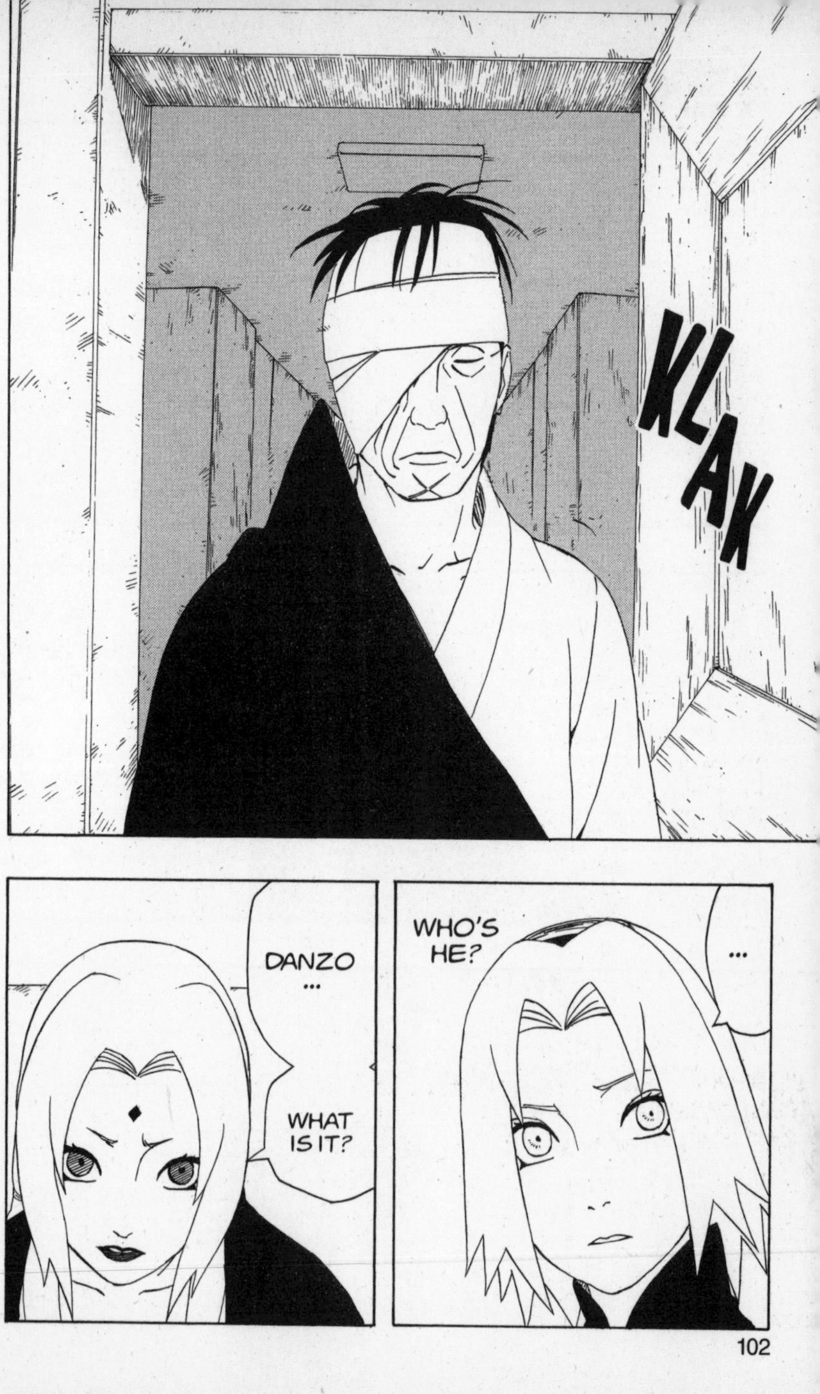
KLAK
...
WHO'S HE?
DANZO ...
WHAT IS IT?

READ THIS WAY

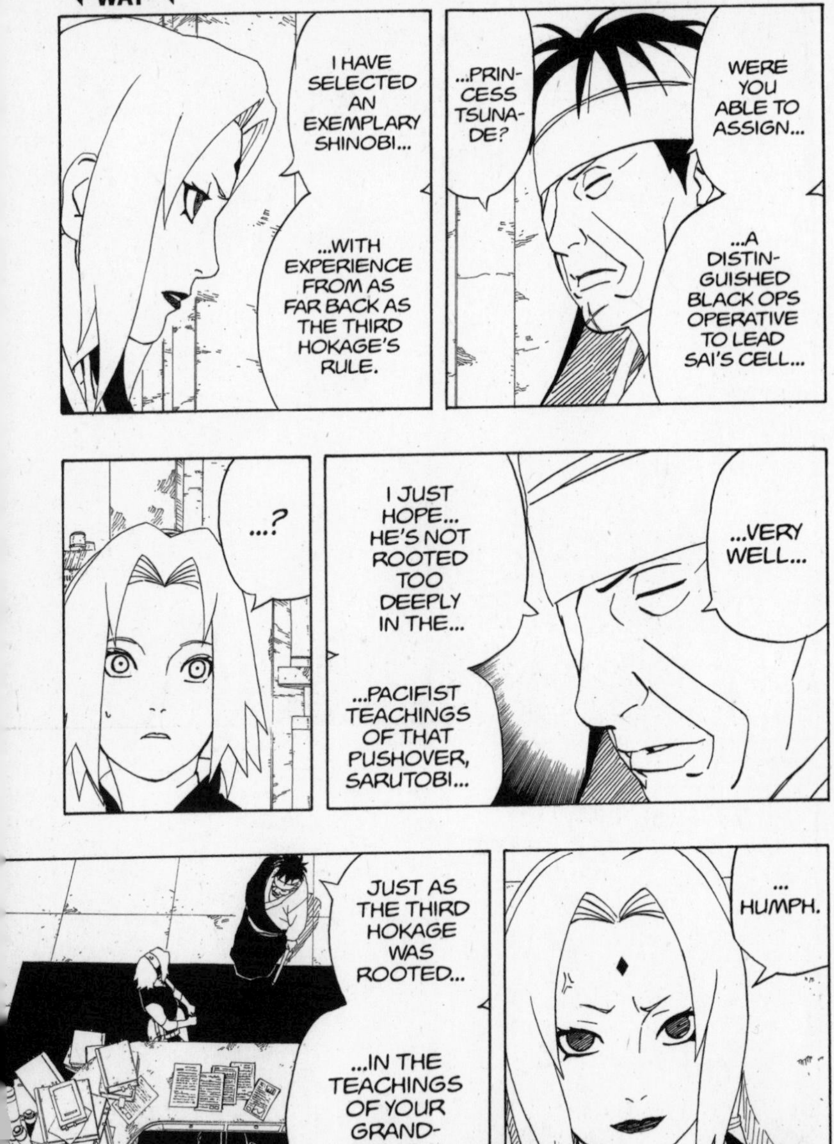
WERE YOU ABLE TO ASSIGN...
...A DISTINGUISHED BLACK OPS OPERATIVE TO LEAD SAI'S CELL...
...PRINCESS TSUNADE?
I HAVE SELECTED AN EXEMPLARY SHINOBI...
...WITH EXPERIENCE FROM AS FAR BACK AS THE THIRD HOKAGE'S RULE.
...VERY WELL...
I JUST HOPE... HE'S NOT ROOTED TOO DEEPLY IN THE...
...PACIFIST TEACHINGS OF THAT PUSHOVER, SARUTOBI...
...?
... HUMPH.
JUST AS THE THIRD HOKAGE WAS ROOTED...
...IN THE TEACHINGS OF YOUR GRANDFATHER.

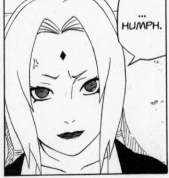

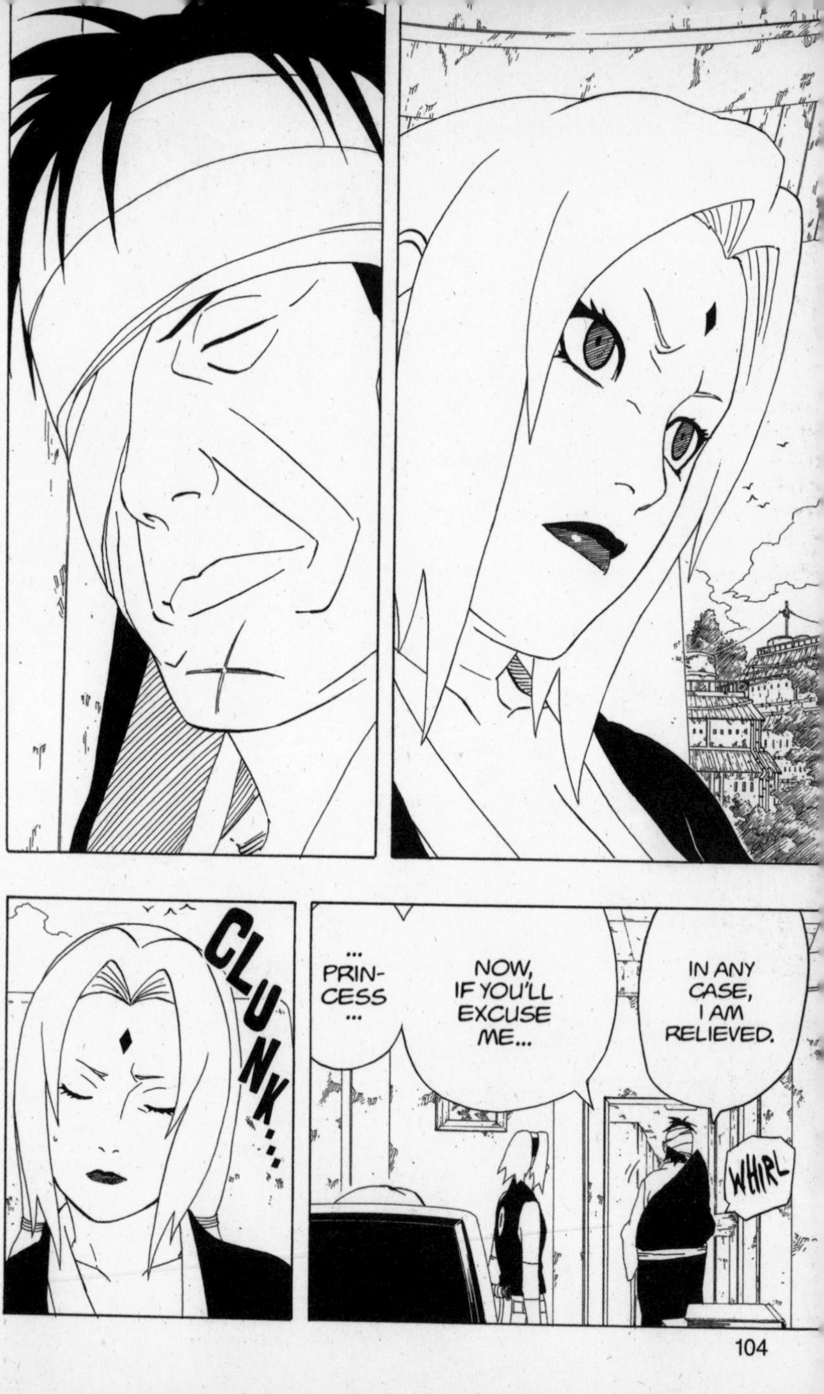
IN ANY CASE, I AM RELIEVED.
WHIRL
NOW, IF YOU'LL EXCUSE ME...
... PRIN-CESS ...
CLUNK...

READ THIS WAY

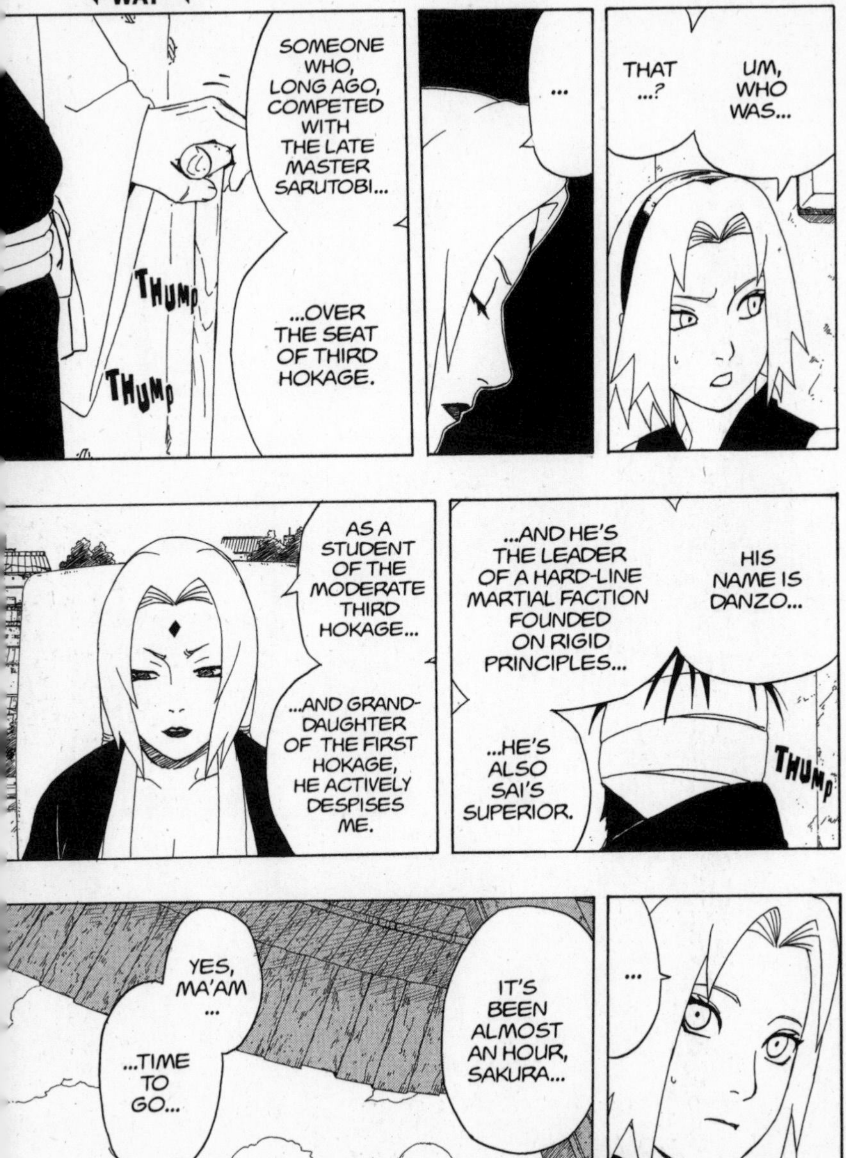
UM, WHO WAS... THAT ...?
...
SOMEONE WHO, LONG AGO, COMPETED WITH THE LATE MASTER SARUTOBI...
...OVER THE SEAT OF THIRD HOKAGE.
THUMP
THUMP
HIS NAME IS DANZO...
...AND HE'S THE LEADER OF A HARD-LINE MARTIAL FACTION FOUNDED ON RIGID PRINCIPLES...
...HE'S ALSO SAI'S SUPERIOR.
THUMP
AS A STUDENT OF THE MODERATE THIRD HOKAGE...
...AND GRAND-DAUGHTER OF THE FIRST HOKAGE, HE ACTIVELY DESPISES ME.
...
IT'S BEEN ALMOST AN HOUR, SAKURA...
YES, MA'AM ...
...TIME TO GO...

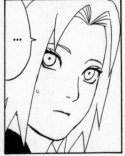

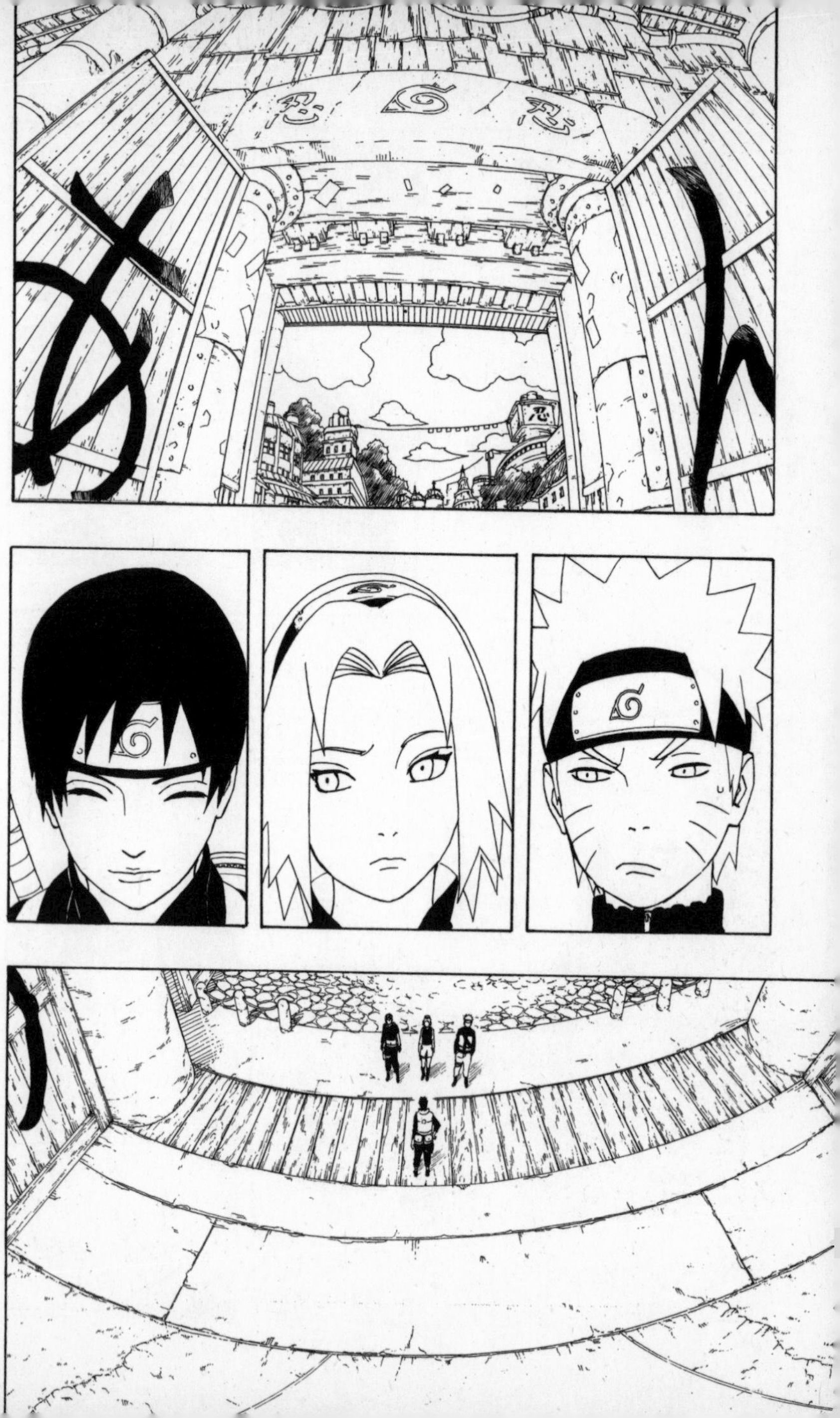
ん
あ

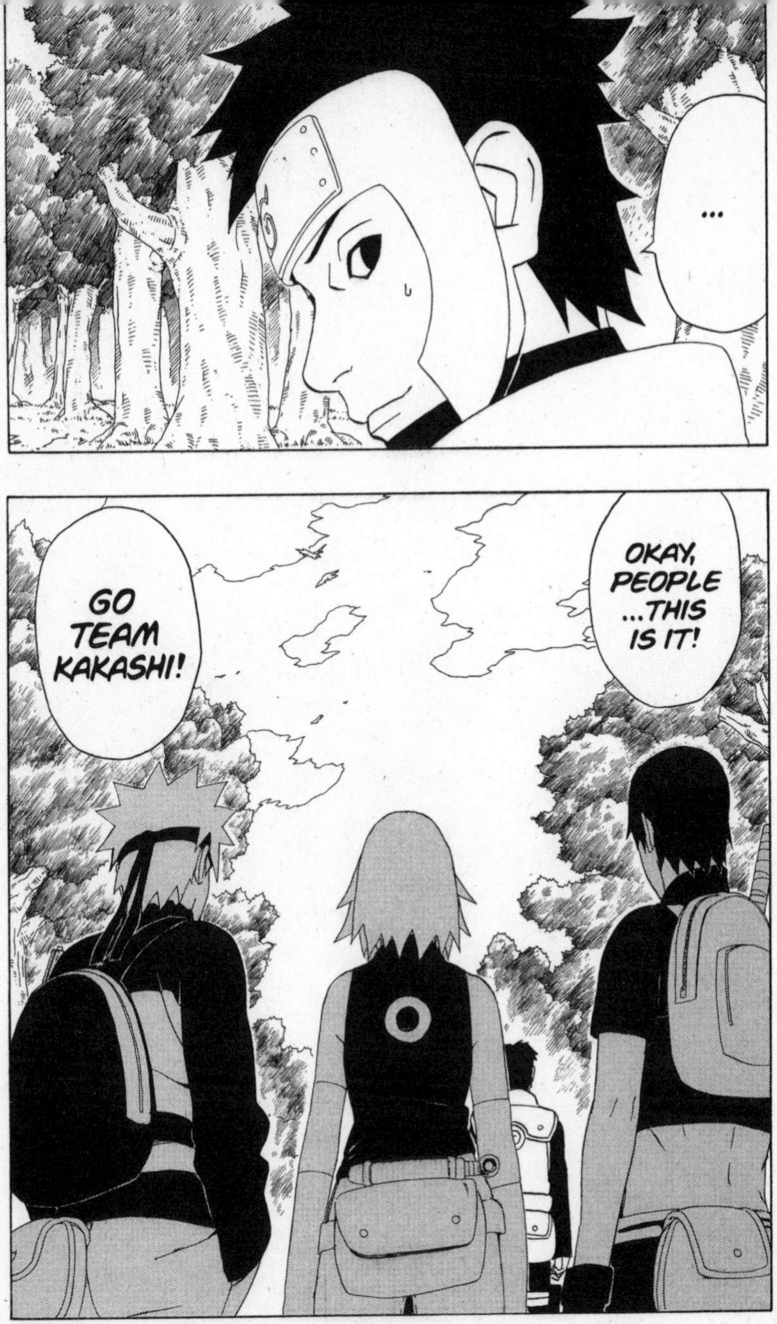
...
OKAY, PEOPLE ...THIS IS IT!
GO TEAM KAKASHI!

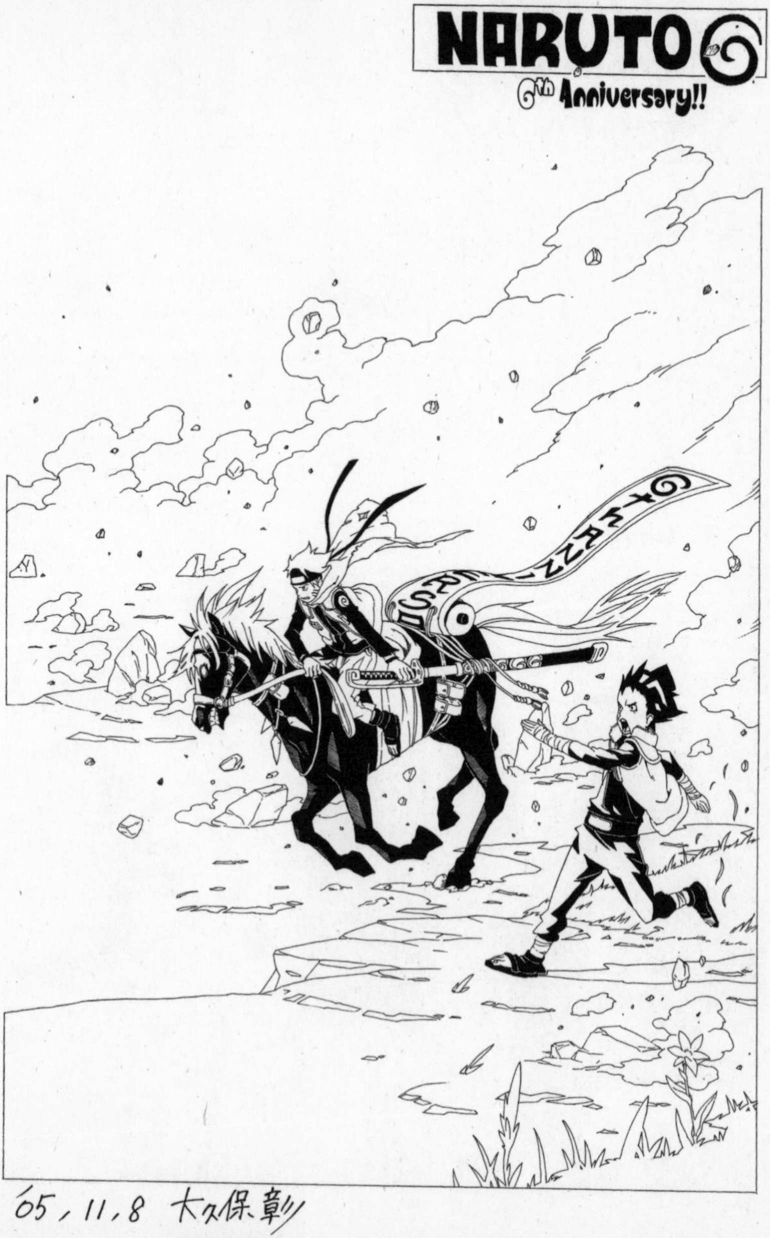
NARUTO
6th Anniversary!!

'05, 11, 8 大久保彰

OHKUBO AKIRA

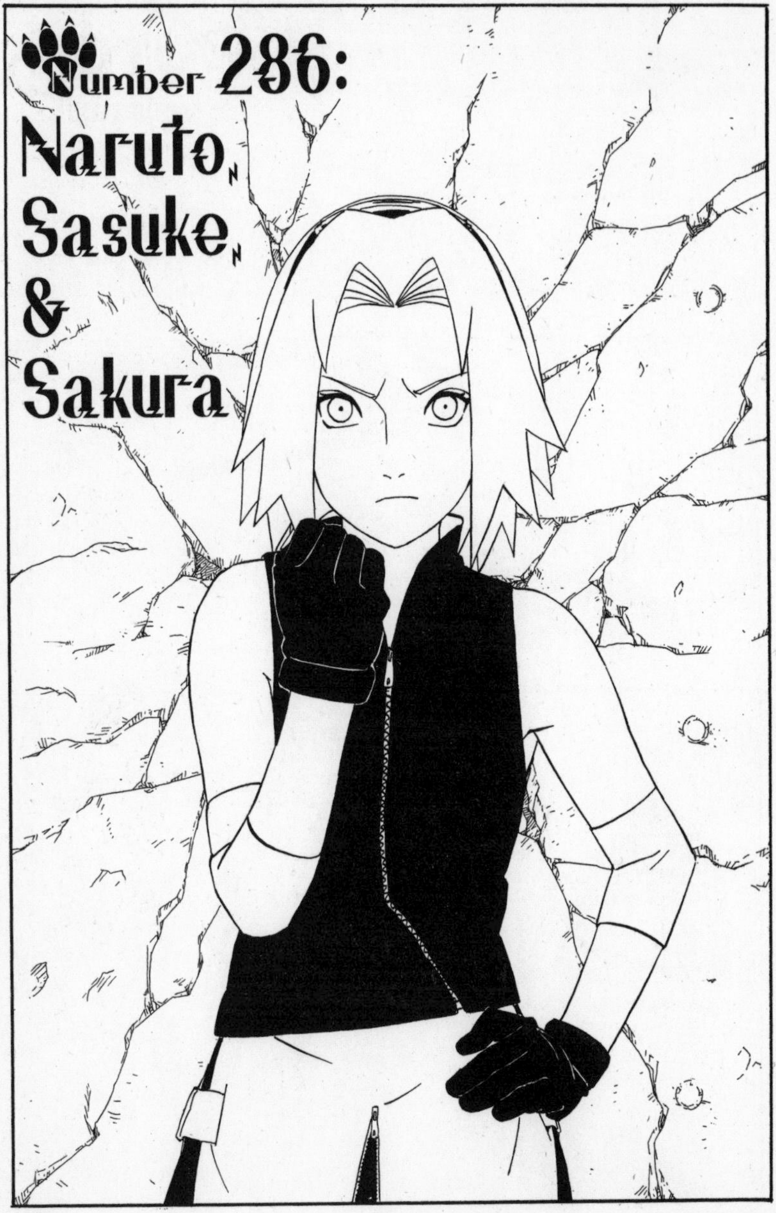
Number 286:
Naruto, Sasuke, & Sakura

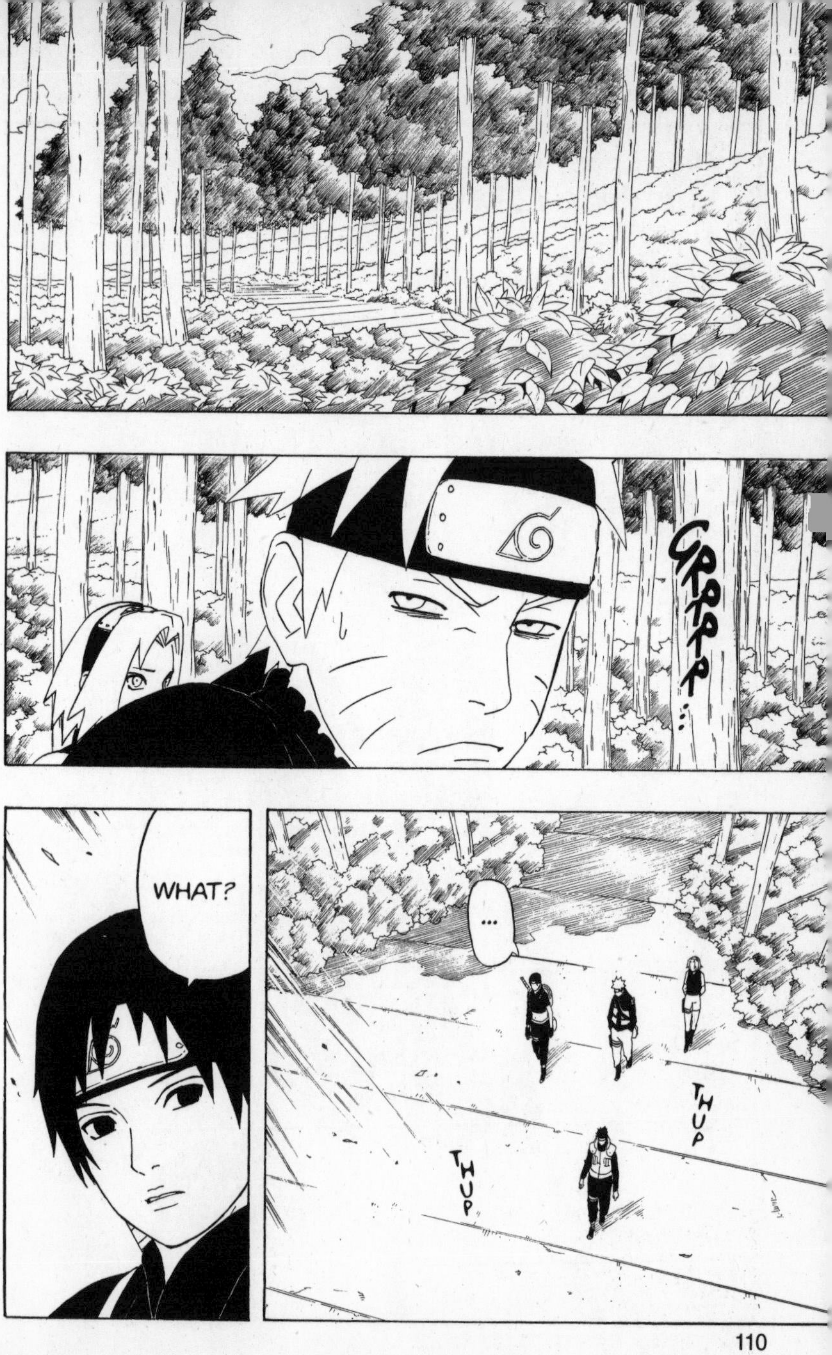
GRRRR...
...
THUP
THUP
WHAT?

READ THIS WAY

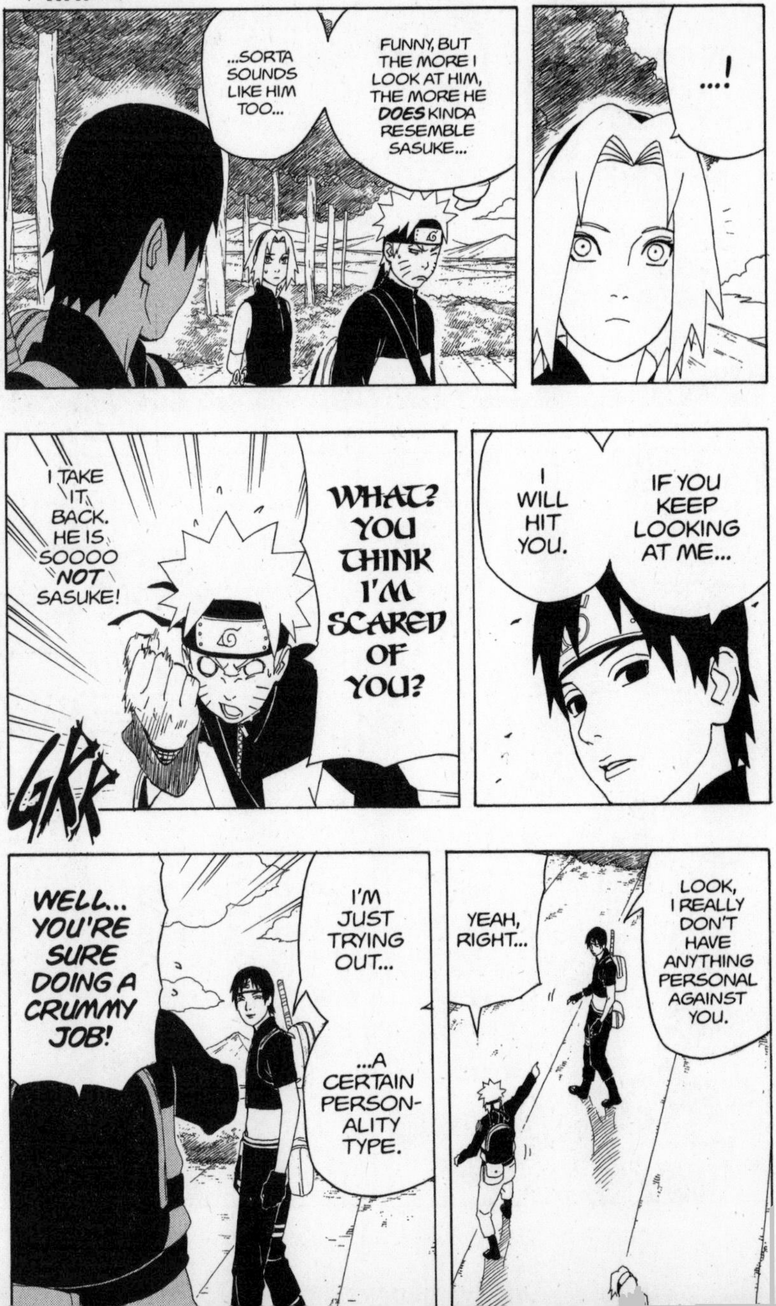
...!
FUNNY, BUT THE MORE I LOOK AT HIM, THE MORE HE DOES KINDA RESEMBLE SASUKE...
...SORTA SOUNDS LIKE HIM TOO...
IF YOU KEEP LOOKING AT ME...
I WILL HIT YOU.
WHAT? YOU THINK I'M SCARED OF YOU?
I TAKE IT BACK. HE IS SOOOO NOT SASUKE!
GRR
LOOK, I REALLY DON'T HAVE ANYTHING PERSONAL AGAINST YOU.
YEAH, RIGHT...
I'M JUST TRYING OUT...
...A CERTAIN PERSONALITY TYPE.
WELL... YOU'RE SURE DOING A CRUMMY JOB!

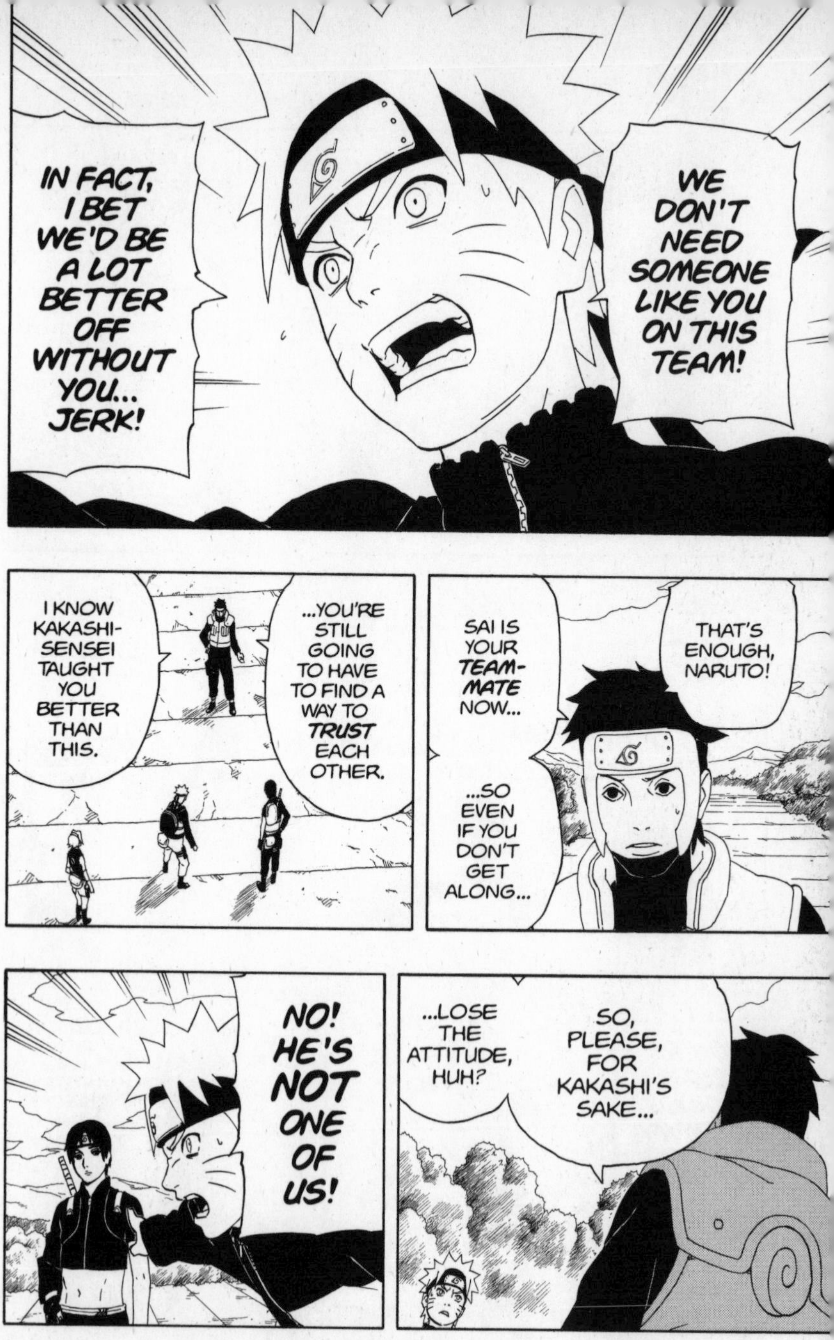
WE DON'T NEED SOMEONE LIKE YOU ON THIS TEAM!
IN FACT, I BET WE'D BE A LOT BETTER OFF WITHOUT YOU... JERK!
THAT'S ENOUGH, NARUTO!
SAI IS YOUR TEAMMATE NOW...
...SO EVEN IF YOU DON'T GET ALONG...
...YOU'RE STILL GOING TO HAVE TO FIND A WAY TO TRUST EACH OTHER.
I KNOW KAKASHI-SENSEI TAUGHT YOU BETTER THAN THIS.
SO, PLEASE, FOR KAKASHI'S SAKE...
...LOSE THE ATTITUDE, HUH?
NO! HE'S NOT ONE OF US!

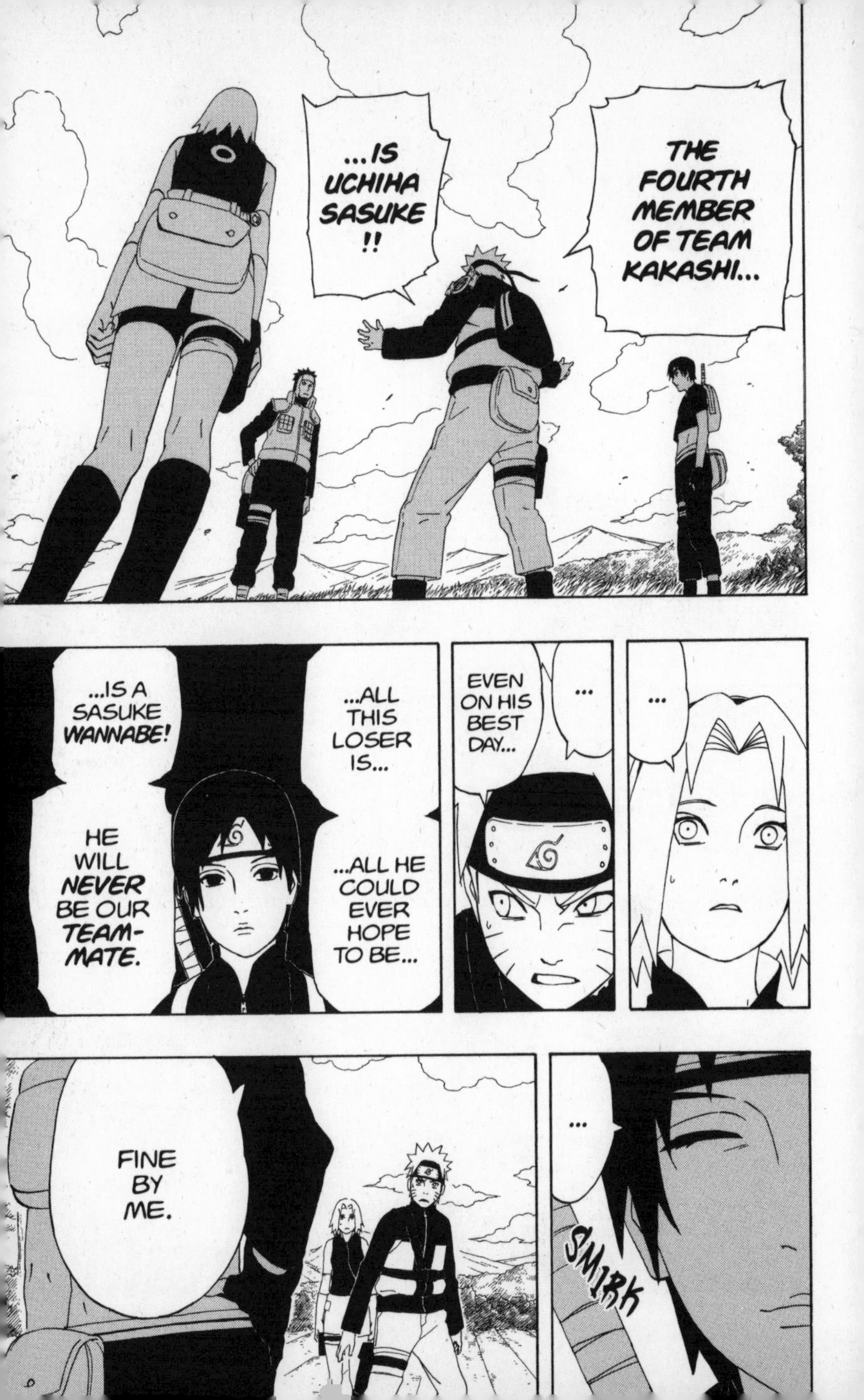
THE FOURTH MEMBER OF TEAM KAKASHI...
...IS UCHIHA SASUKE !!
...
...
EVEN ON HIS BEST DAY...
...ALL THIS LOSER IS...
...ALL HE COULD EVER HOPE TO BE...
...IS A SASUKE WANNABE!
HE WILL NEVER BE OUR TEAM-MATE.
...
SMIRK
FINE BY ME.

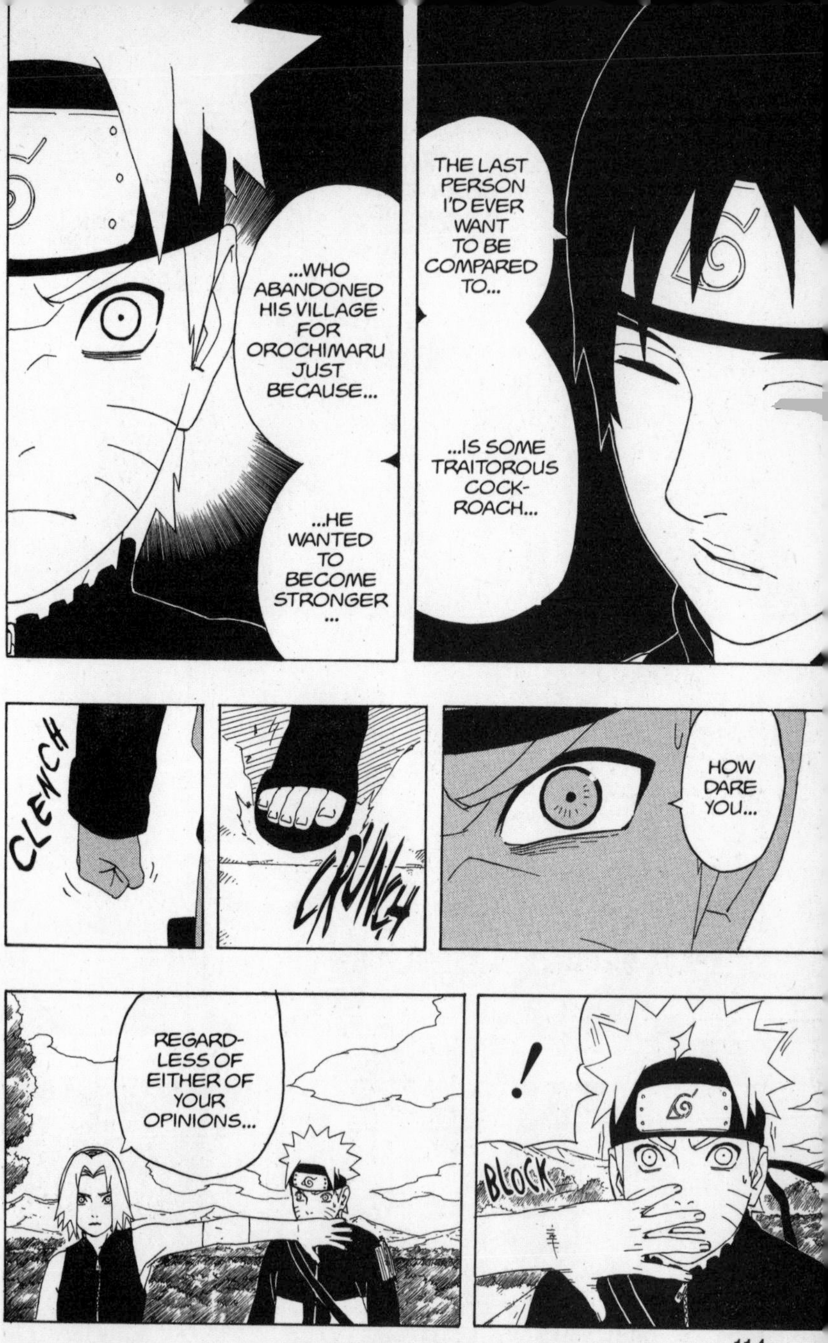
THE LAST PERSON I'D EVER WANT TO BE COMPARED TO...
...IS SOME TRAITOROUS COCK-ROACH...
...WHO ABANDONED HIS VILLAGE FOR OROCHIMARU JUST BECAUSE...
...HE WANTED TO BECOME STRONGER...
HOW DARE YOU...
CRUNCH
CLENCH
!
BLOCK
REGARD-LESS OF EITHER OF YOUR OPINIONS...

READ THIS WAY

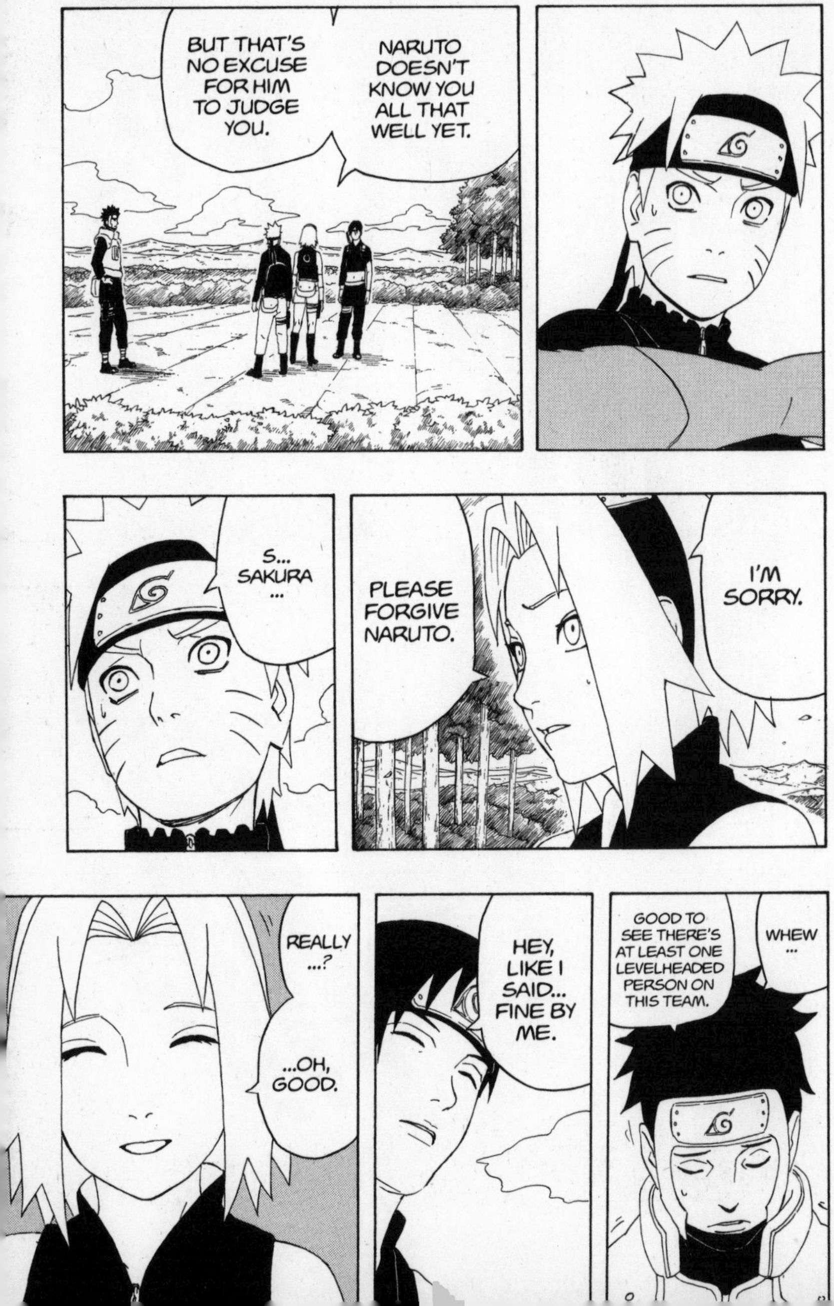
NARUTO DOESN'T KNOW YOU ALL THAT WELL YET.
BUT THAT'S NO EXCUSE FOR HIM TO JUDGE YOU.
I'M SORRY.
PLEASE FORGIVE NARUTO.
S... SAKURA ...
WHEW ...
GOOD TO SEE THERE'S AT LEAST ONE LEVELHEADED PERSON ON THIS TEAM.
HEY, LIKE I SAID... FINE BY ME.
REALLY ...?
...OH, GOOD.

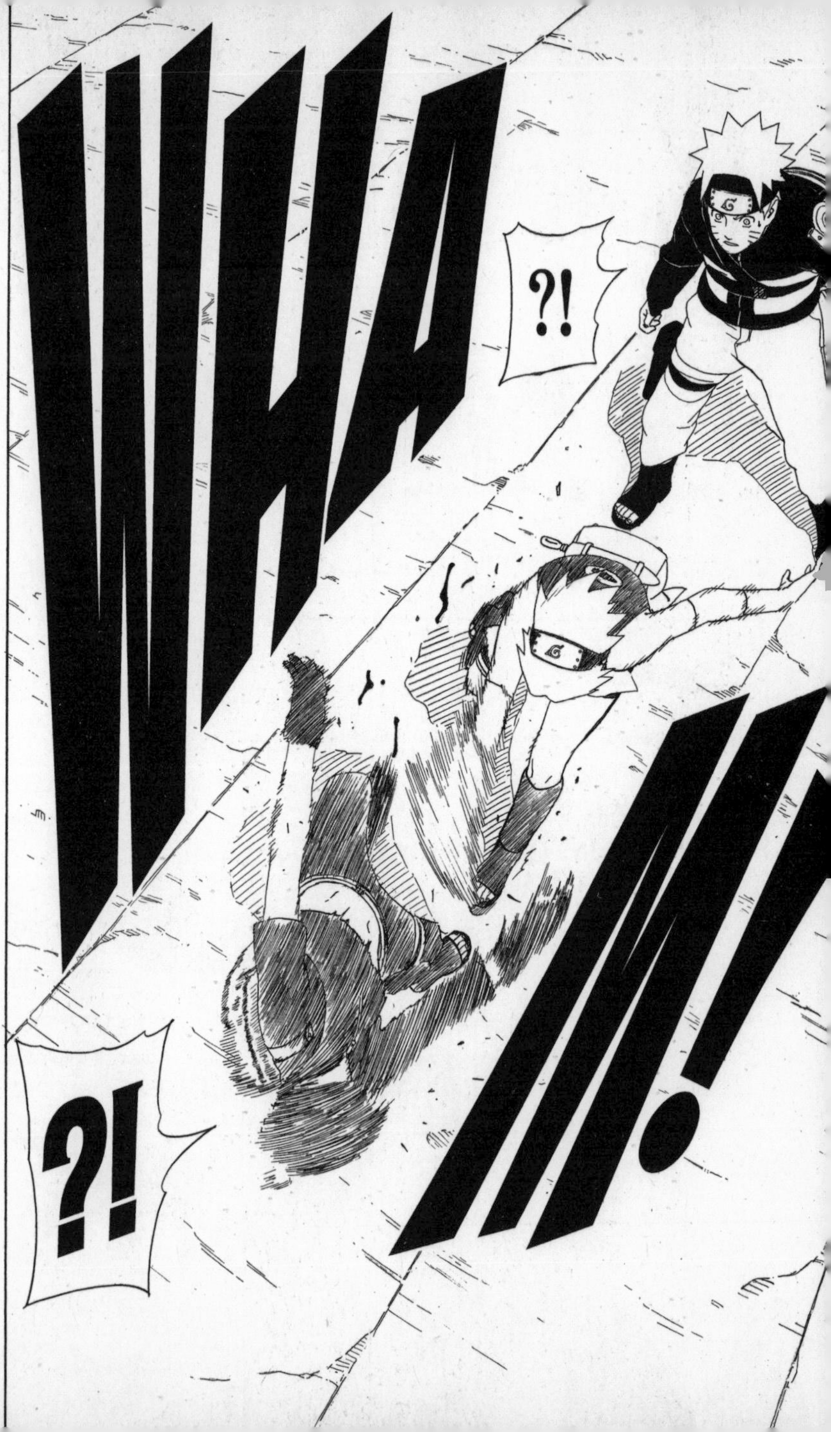
?!
WHHA
AA!
?!

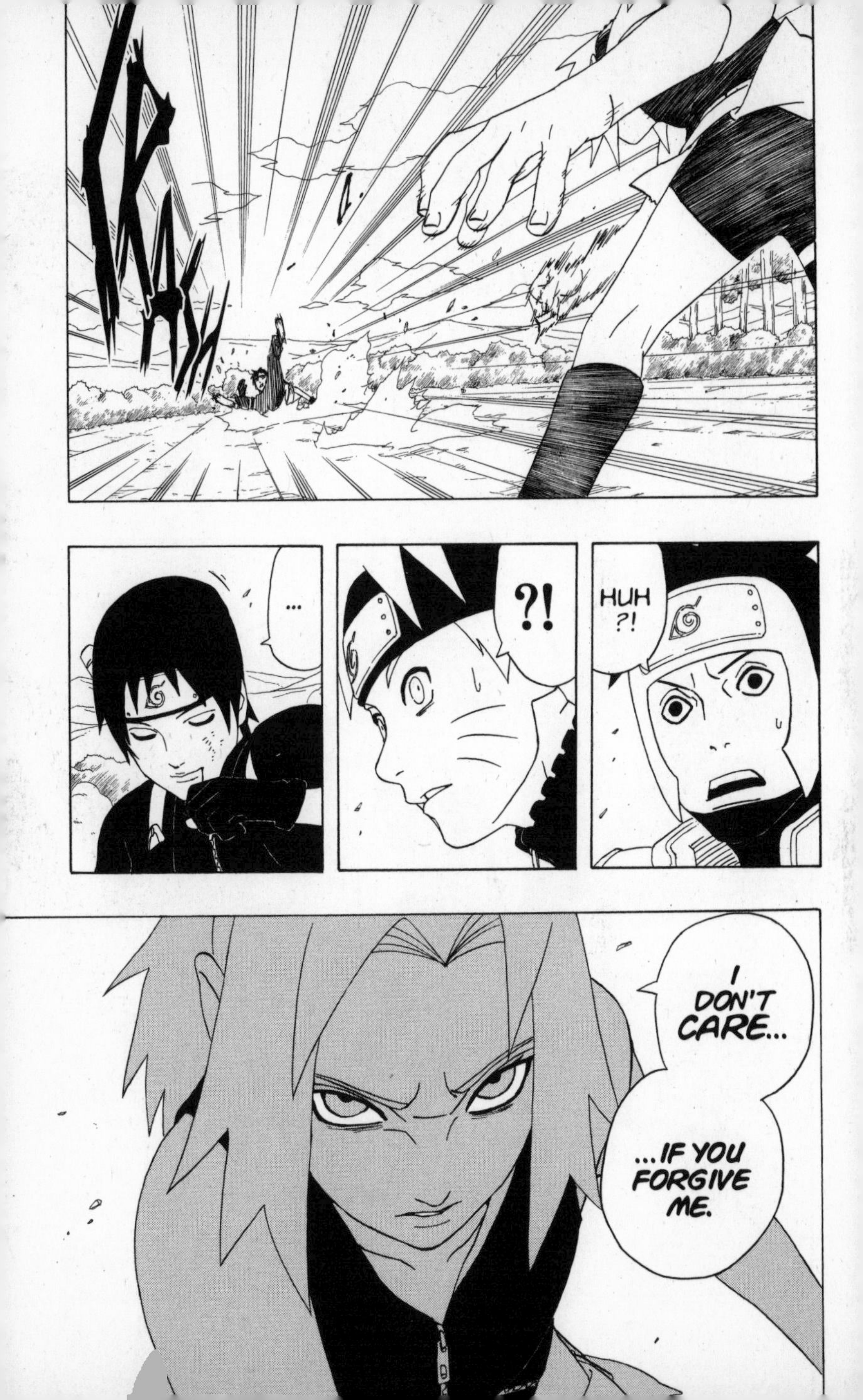
CRASH
HUH ?!
?!
...
I DON'T CARE...
...IF YOU FORGIVE ME.

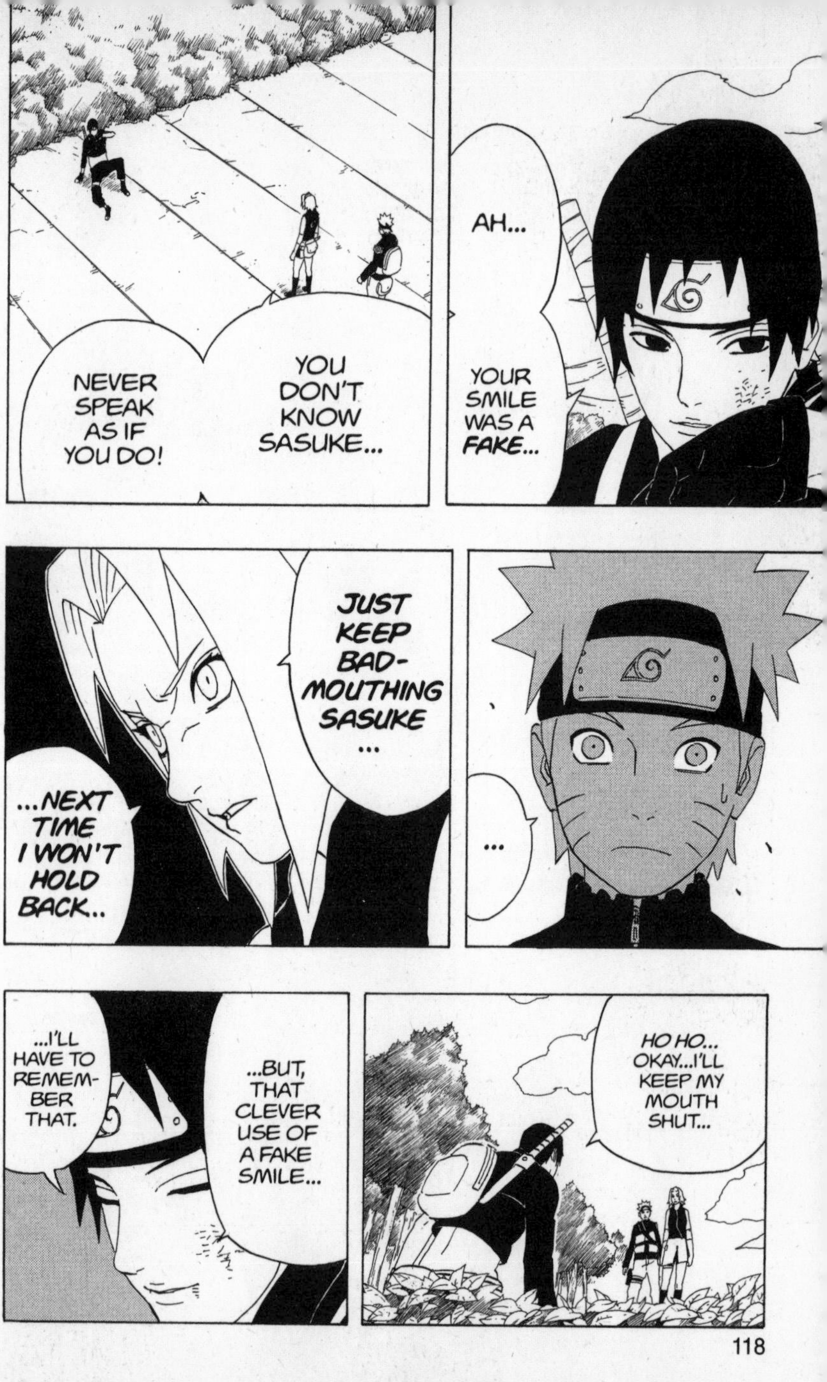
AH...
YOUR SMILE WAS A FAKE...
YOU DON'T KNOW SASUKE...
NEVER SPEAK AS IF YOU DO!
...
JUST KEEP BAD-MOUTHING SASUKE ...
...NEXT TIME I WON'T HOLD BACK..
HO HO... OKAY...I'LL KEEP MY MOUTH SHUT...
...BUT, THAT CLEVER USE OF A FAKE SMILE...
...I'LL HAVE TO REMEMBER THAT.

READ THIS WAY

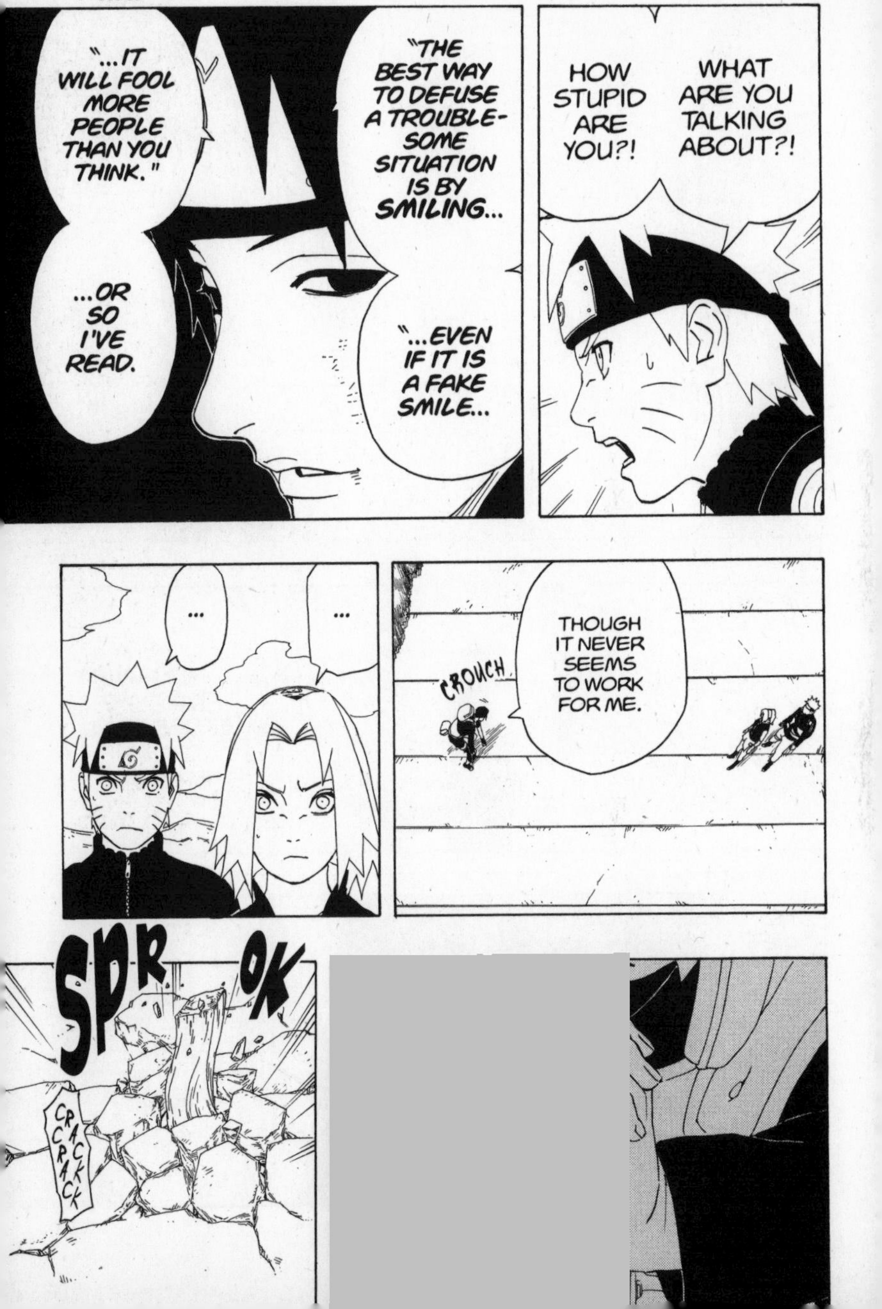
WHAT ARE YOU TALKING ABOUT?!
HOW STUPID ARE YOU?!
"THE BEST WAY TO DEFUSE A TROUBLE-SOME SITUATION IS BY SMILING...
"...EVEN IF IT IS A FAKE SMILE...
"...IT WILL FOOL MORE PEOPLE THAN YOU THINK."
...OR SO I'VE READ.
THOUGH IT NEVER SEEMS TO WORK FOR ME.
CROUCH
...
...
SPROK
CRACK CRACK

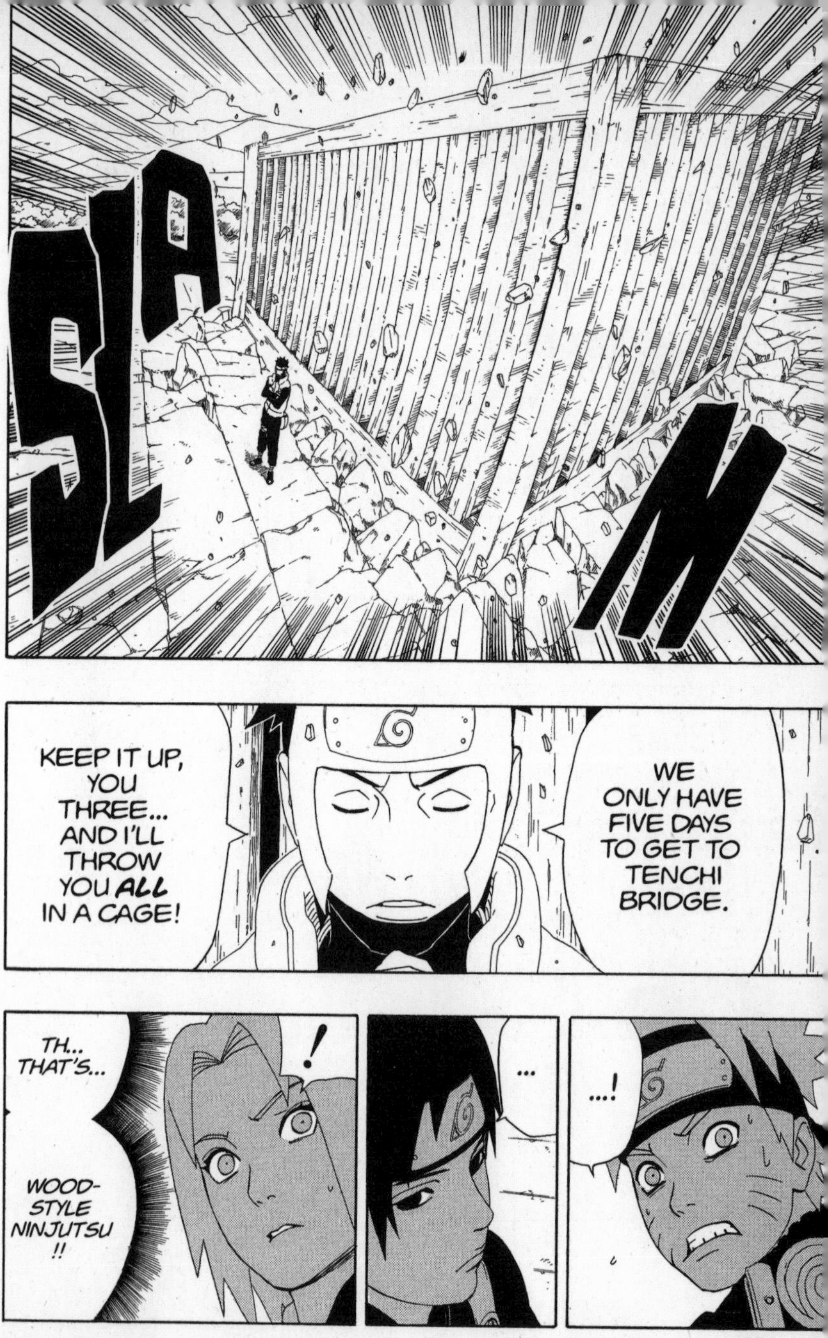
SLAM
WE ONLY HAVE FIVE DAYS TO GET TO TENCHI BRIDGE.
KEEP IT UP, YOU THREE... AND I'LL THROW YOU **ALL** IN A CAGE!
...!
...
!
TH... THAT'S...
WOOD-STYLE NINJUTSU !!

READ THIS WAY

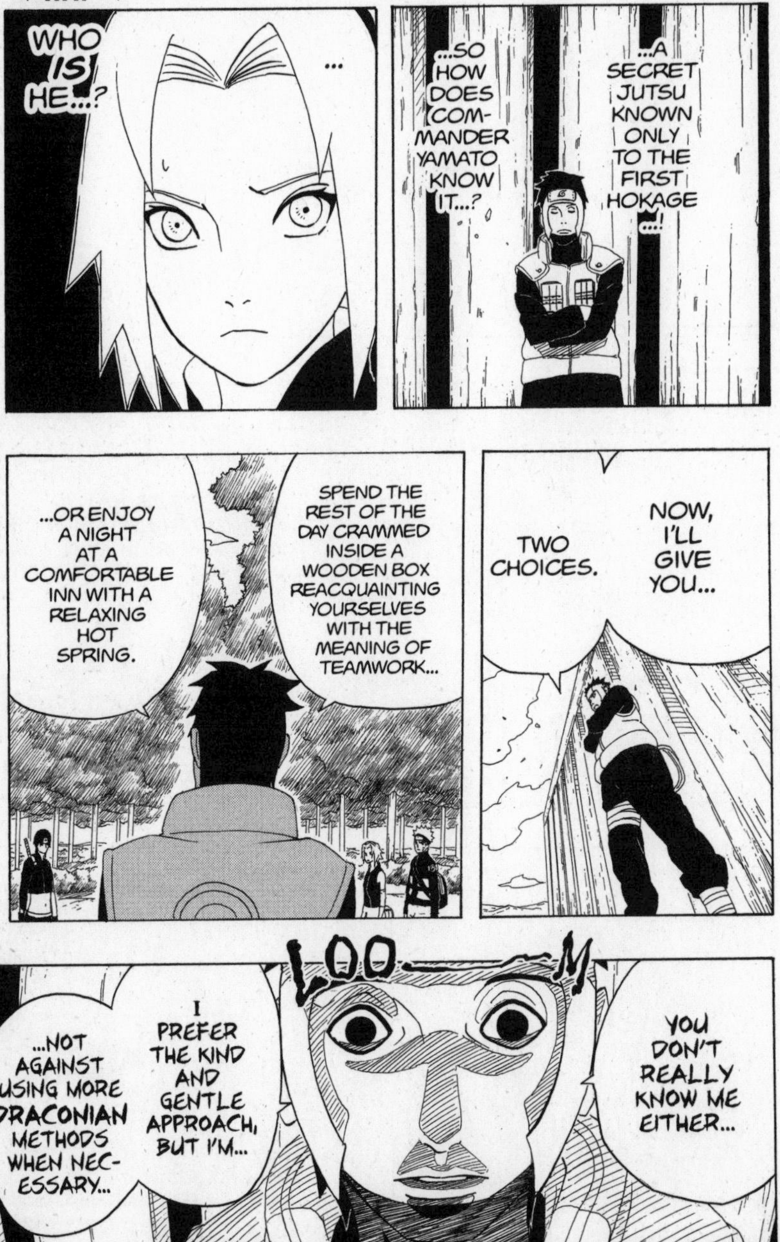

...A SECRET JUTSU KNOWN ONLY TO THE FIRST HOKAGE...!
...SO HOW DOES COMMANDER YAMATO KNOW IT...?
...
WHO IS HE...?
NOW, I'LL GIVE YOU...
TWO CHOICES.
SPEND THE REST OF THE DAY CRAMMED INSIDE A WOODEN BOX REACQUAINTING YOURSELVES WITH THE MEANING OF TEAMWORK...
...OR ENJOY A NIGHT AT A COMFORTABLE INN WITH A RELAXING HOT SPRING.
LOO—M
YOU DON'T REALLY KNOW ME EITHER...
I PREFER THE KIND AND GENTLE APPROACH, BUT I'M...
...NOT AGAINST USING MORE DRACONIAN METHODS WHEN NEC-ESSARY...

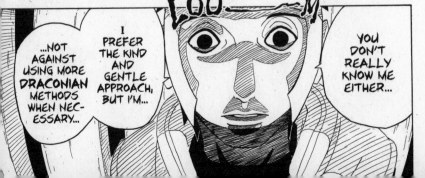

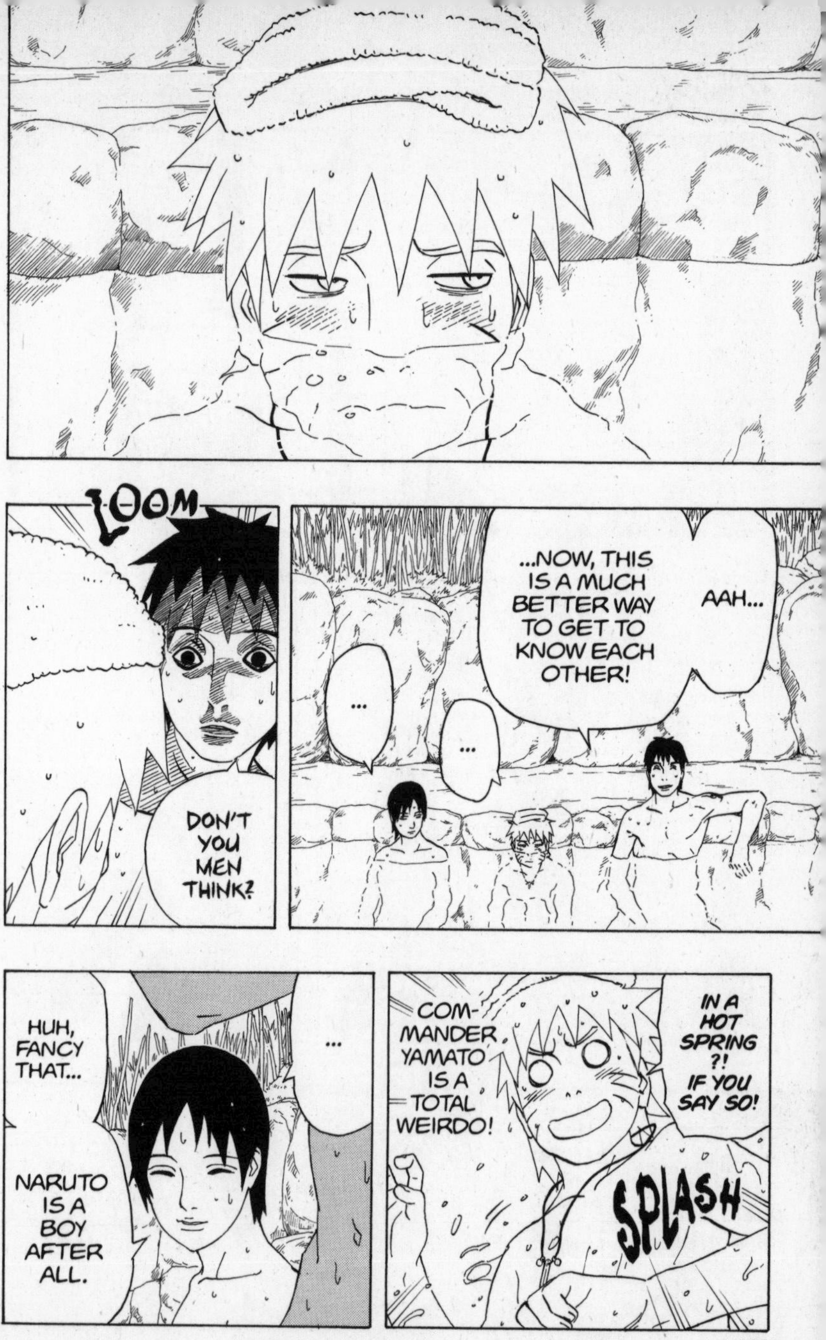
AAH...
...NOW, THIS IS A MUCH BETTER WAY TO GET TO KNOW EACH OTHER!
...
...
LOOM
...
DON'T YOU MEN THINK?
IN A HOT SPRING?! IF YOU SAY SO!
COM-MANDER YAMATO IS A TOTAL WEIRDO!
SPLASH
...
HUH, FANCY THAT...
NARUTO IS A BOY AFTER ALL.

READ THIS WAY

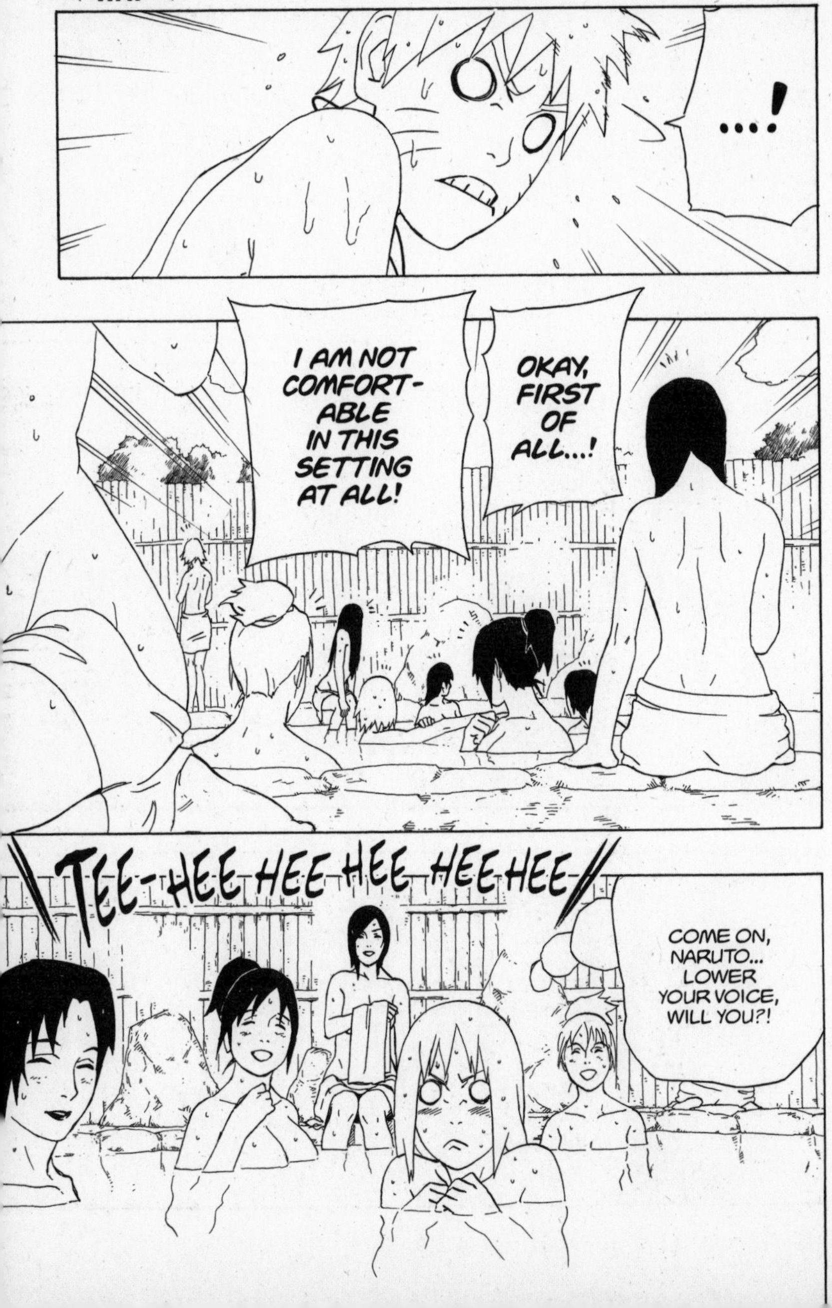
...!
OKAY, FIRST OF ALL...!
I AM NOT COMFORT-ABLE IN THIS SETTING AT ALL!
COME ON, NARUTO... LOWER YOUR VOICE, WILL YOU?!
TEE-HEE HEE HEE HEE HEE

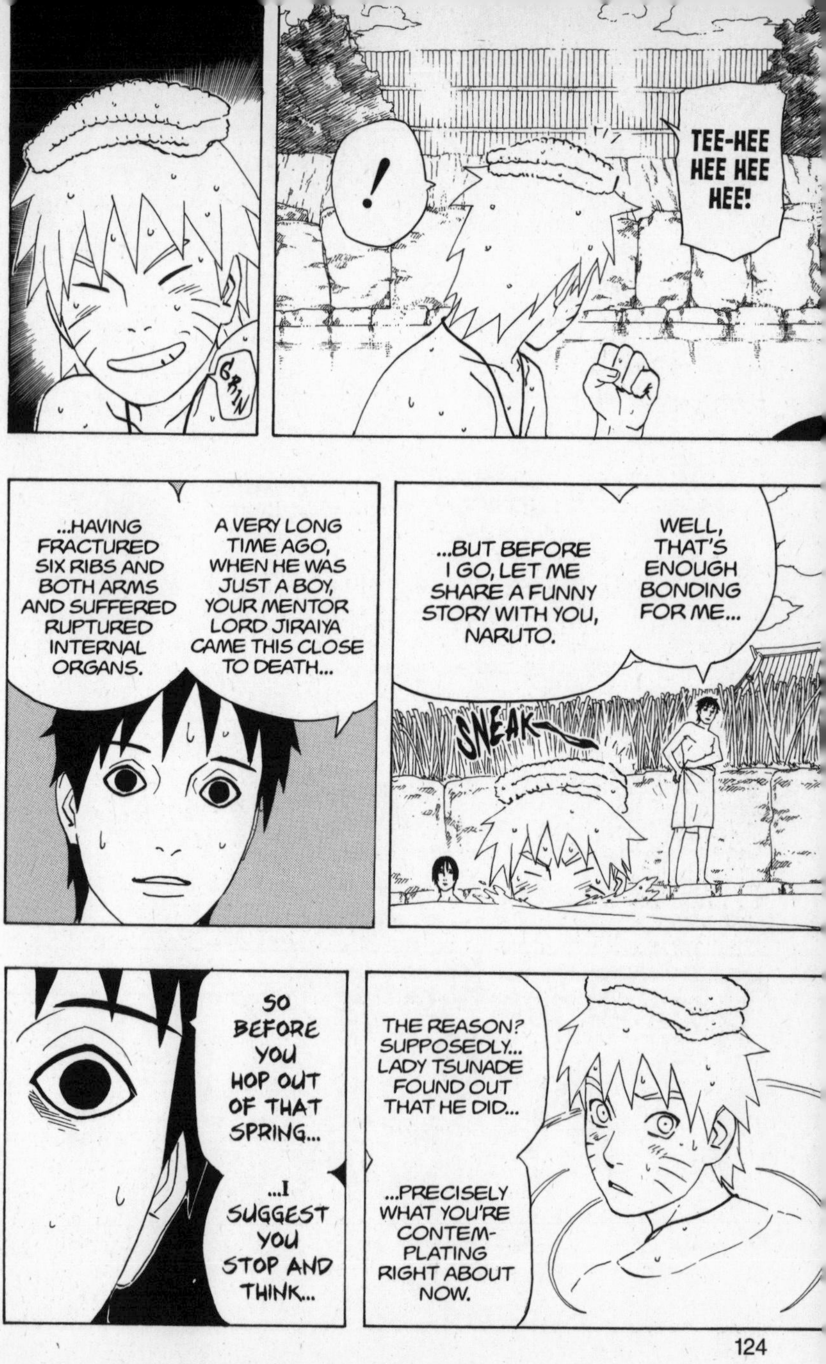
!
TEE-HEE HEE HEE HEE!
GRIN
WELL, THAT'S ENOUGH BONDING FOR ME...
...BUT BEFORE I GO, LET ME SHARE A FUNNY STORY WITH YOU, NARUTO.
SNEAK
A VERY LONG TIME AGO, WHEN HE WAS JUST A BOY, YOUR MENTOR LORD JIRAIYA CAME THIS CLOSE TO DEATH...
...HAVING FRACTURED SIX RIBS AND BOTH ARMS AND SUFFERED RUPTURED INTERNAL ORGANS.
THE REASON? SUPPOSEDLY... LADY TSUNADE FOUND OUT THAT HE DID...
...PRECISELY WHAT YOU'RE CONTEM-PLATING RIGHT ABOUT NOW.
SO BEFORE YOU HOP OUT OF THAT SPRING...
...I SUGGEST YOU STOP AND THINK...

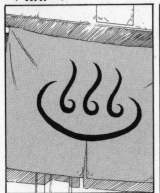

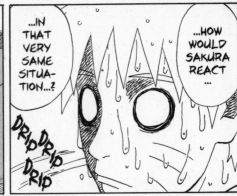

READ THIS WAY

...HOW WOULD SAKURA REACT ...
...IN THAT VERY SAME SITUATION...?
DRIP DRIP DRIP
...A GREAT CHANGE ...
...IS ON THE WIND...

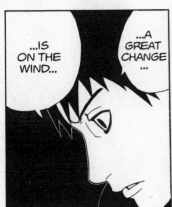

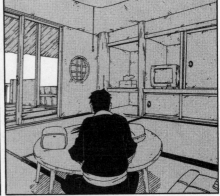

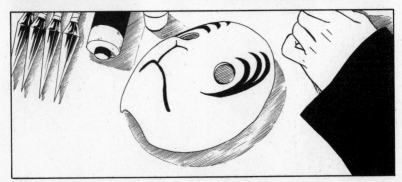

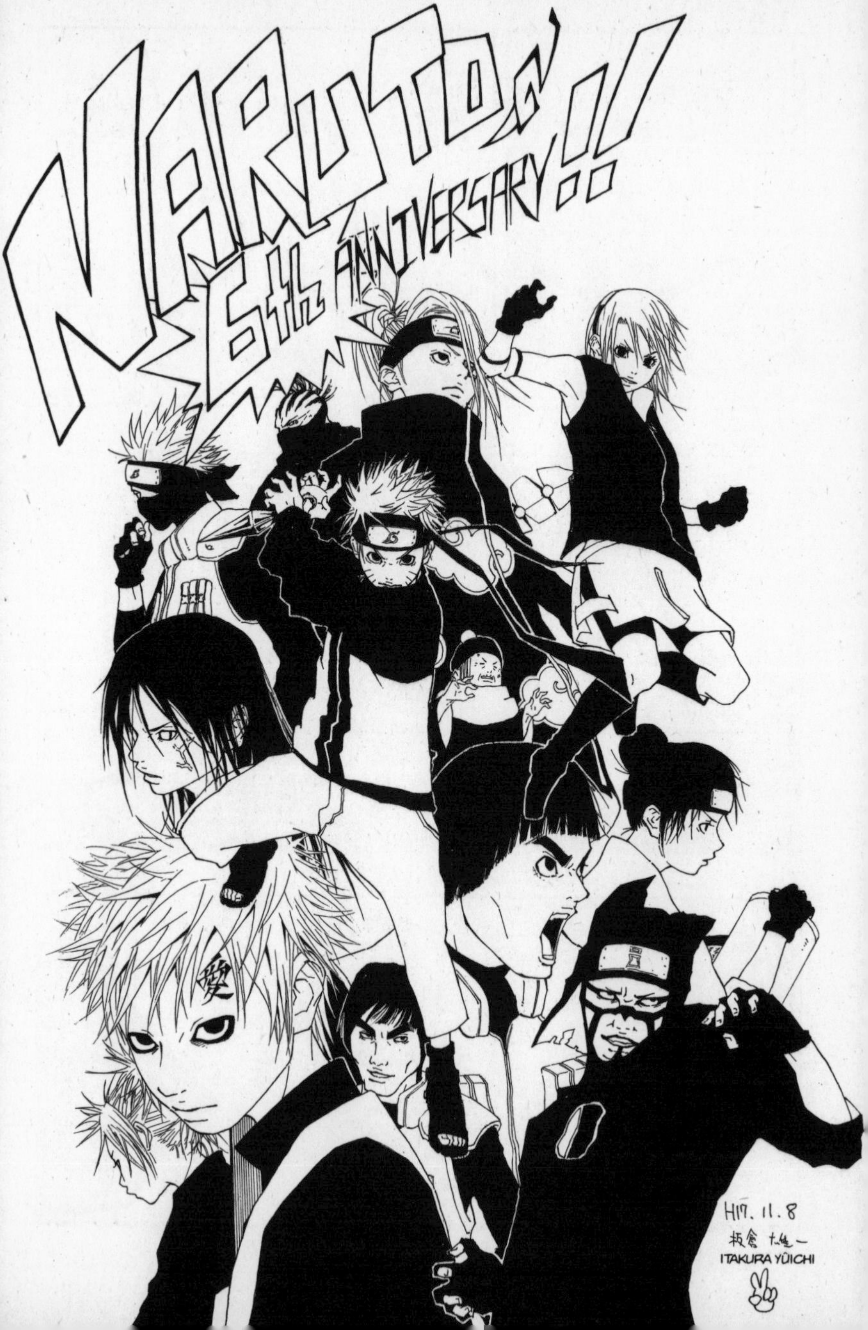
NARUTO
6th ANNIVERSARY!!
H17. 11. 8
板倉 雄一
ITAKURA YÛICHI

Number 287: Untitled

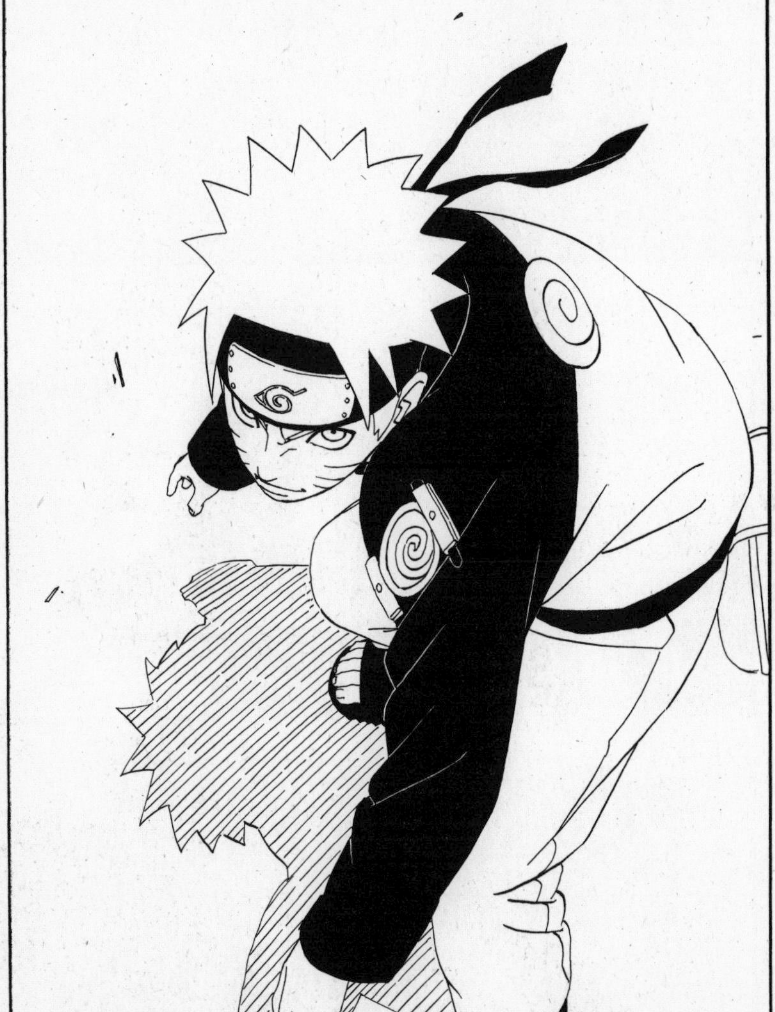

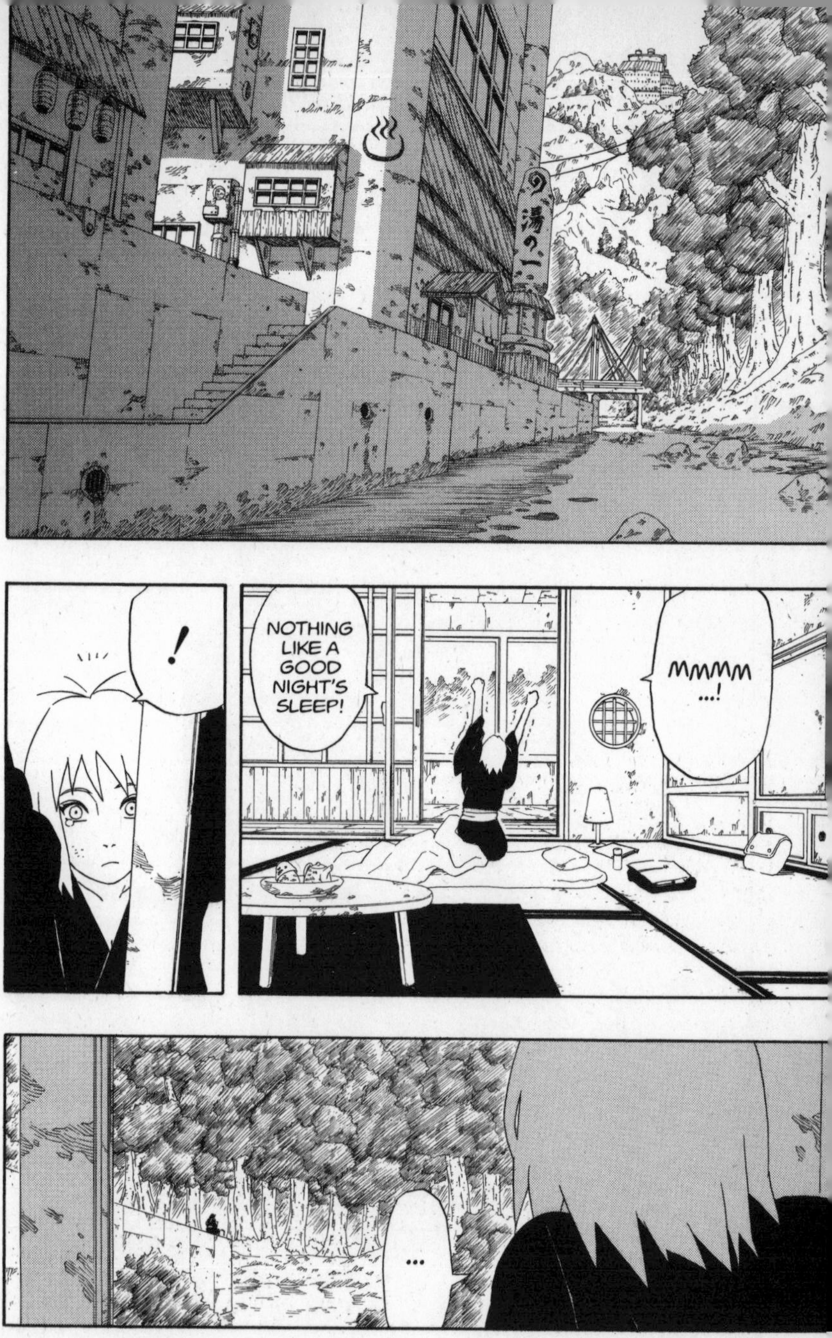
湯の一
MMMM ...!
NOTHING LIKE A GOOD NIGHT'S SLEEP!
!
...

READ THIS WAY

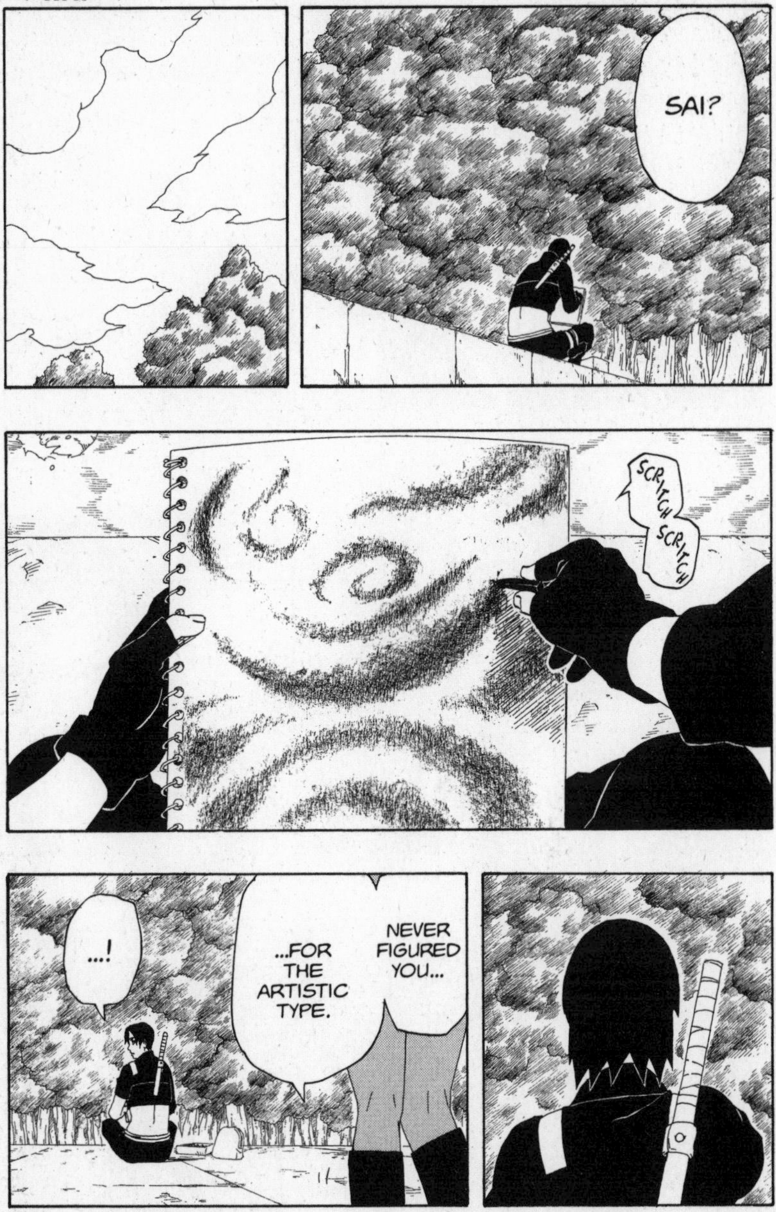
SAI?
SCRITCH SCRITCH
NEVER FIGURED YOU...
...FOR THE ARTISTIC TYPE.
...!

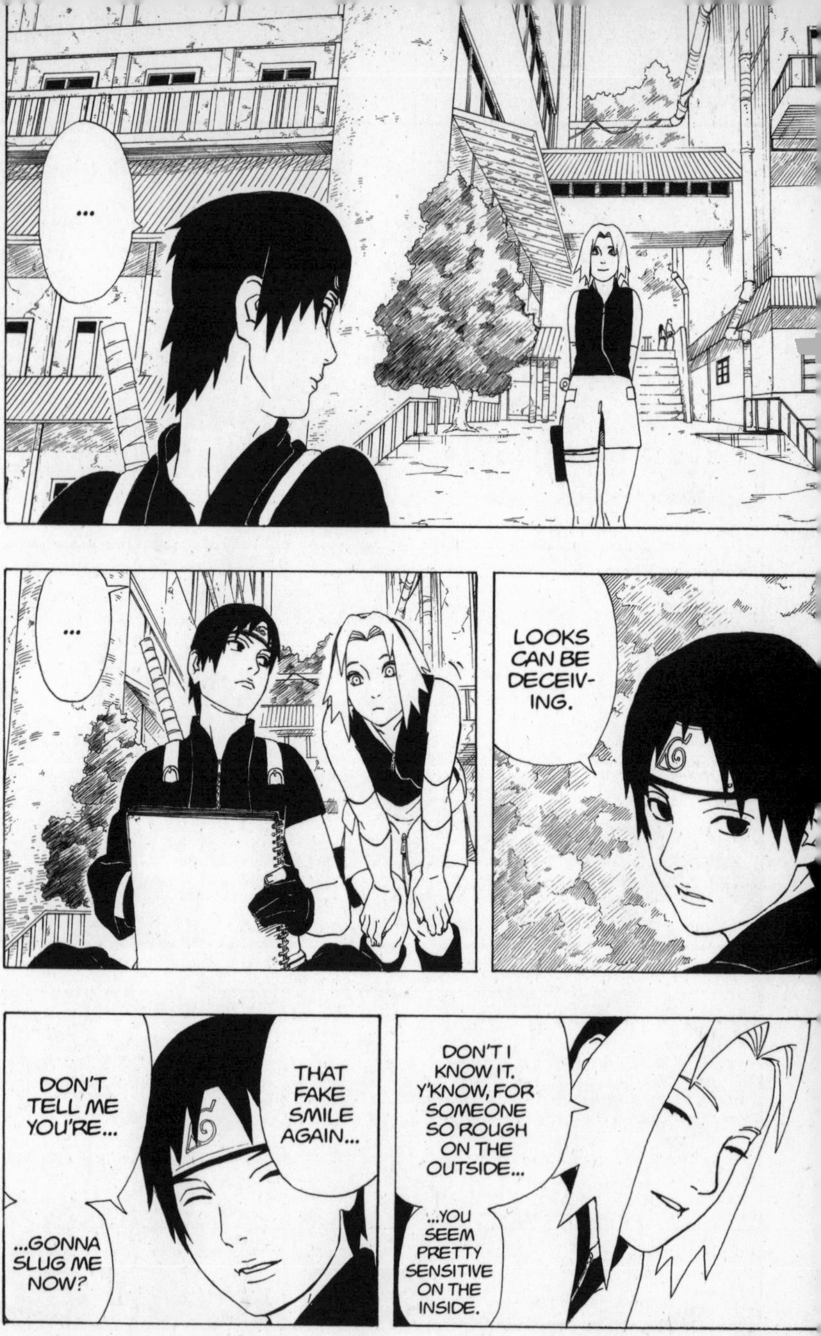
...
LOOKS CAN BE DECEIV-ING.
...
DON'T I KNOW IT. Y'KNOW, FOR SOMEONE SO ROUGH ON THE OUTSIDE...
...YOU SEEM PRETTY SENSITIVE ON THE INSIDE.
THAT FAKE SMILE AGAIN...
DON'T TELL ME YOU'RE...
...GONNA SLUG ME NOW?

READ THIS WAY

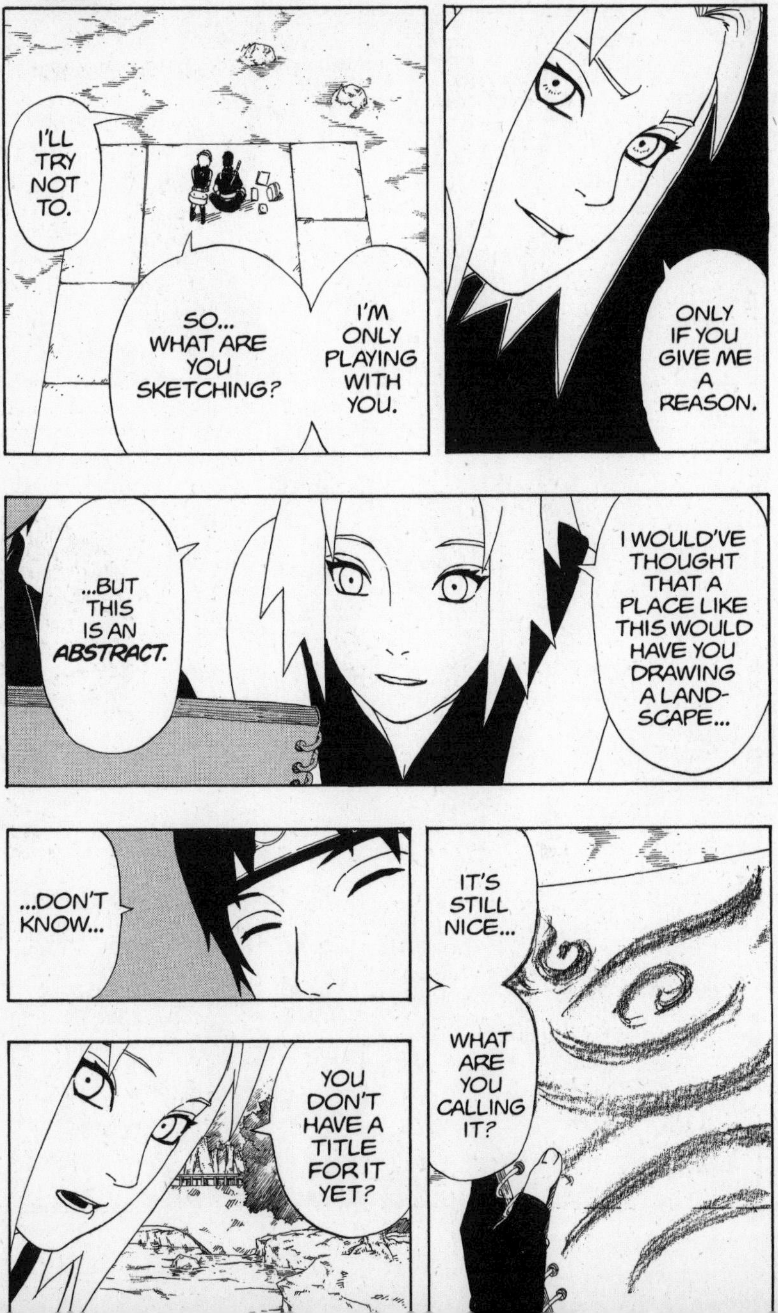
ONLY IF YOU GIVE ME A REASON.
I'LL TRY NOT TO.
I'M ONLY PLAYING WITH YOU.
SO... WHAT ARE YOU SKETCHING?
I WOULD'VE THOUGHT THAT A PLACE LIKE THIS WOULD HAVE YOU DRAWING A LAND-SCAPE...
...BUT THIS IS AN *ABSTRACT.*
IT'S STILL NICE...
WHAT ARE YOU CALLING IT?
...DON'T KNOW...
YOU DON'T HAVE A TITLE FOR IT YET?

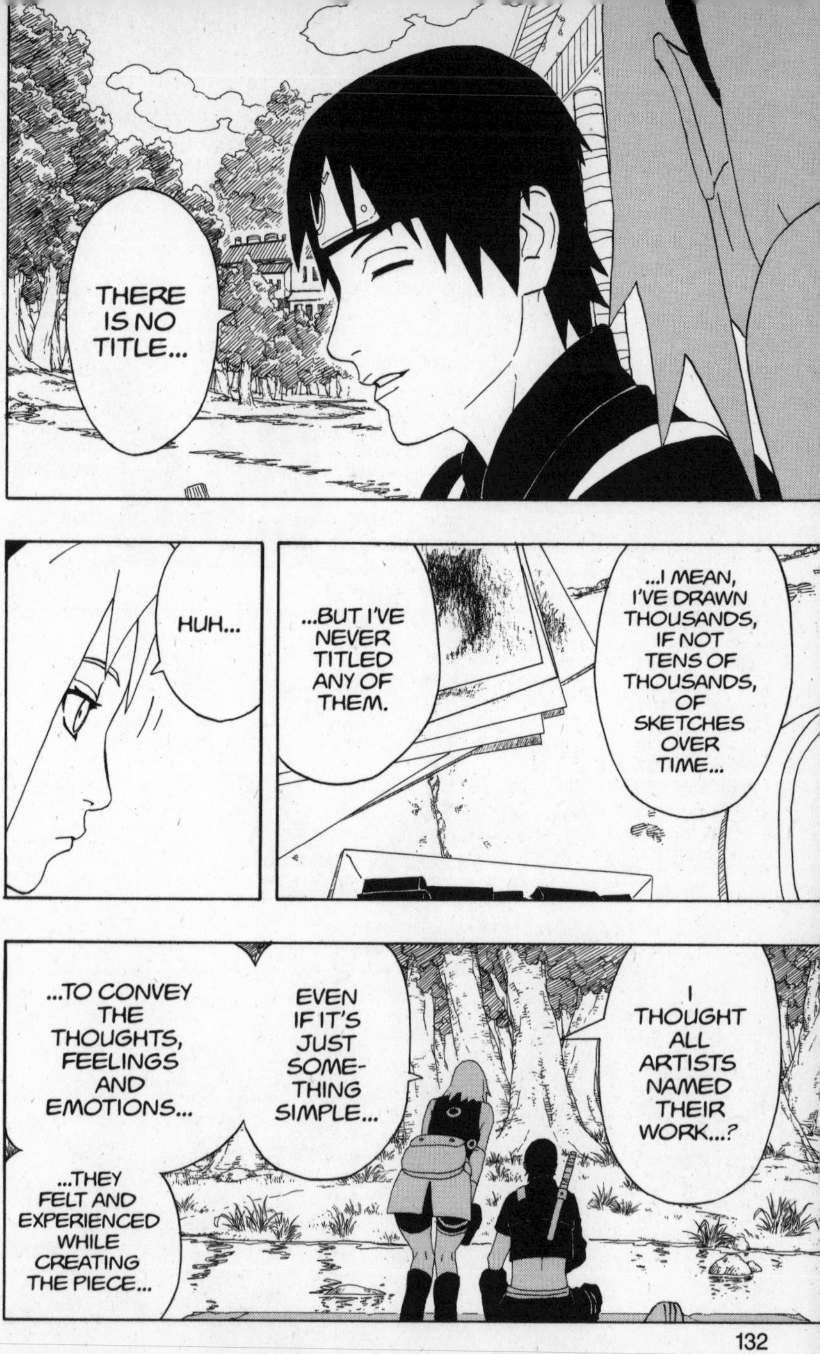
THERE IS NO TITLE...
...I MEAN, I'VE DRAWN THOUSANDS, IF NOT TENS OF THOUSANDS, OF SKETCHES OVER TIME...
...BUT I'VE NEVER TITLED ANY OF THEM.
HUH...
I THOUGHT ALL ARTISTS NAMED THEIR WORK...?
EVEN IF IT'S JUST SOME-THING SIMPLE...
...TO CONVEY THE THOUGHTS, FEELINGS AND EMOTIONS...
...THEY FELT AND EXPERIENCED WHILE CREATING THE PIECE...

READ THIS WAY

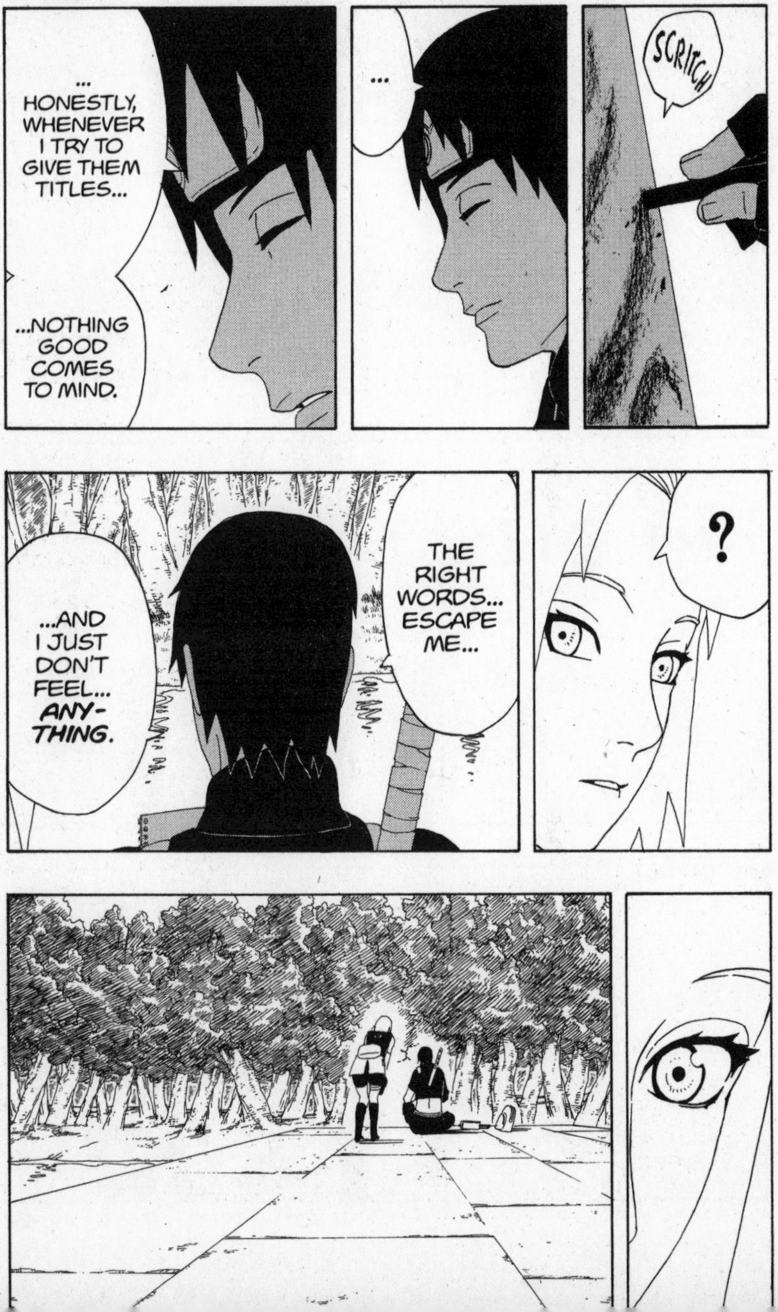

SCRITCH
...
... HONESTLY, WHENEVER I TRY TO GIVE THEM TITLES...
...NOTHING GOOD COMES TO MIND.
?
THE RIGHT WORDS... ESCAPE ME...
...AND I JUST DON'T FEEL... ANYTHING.

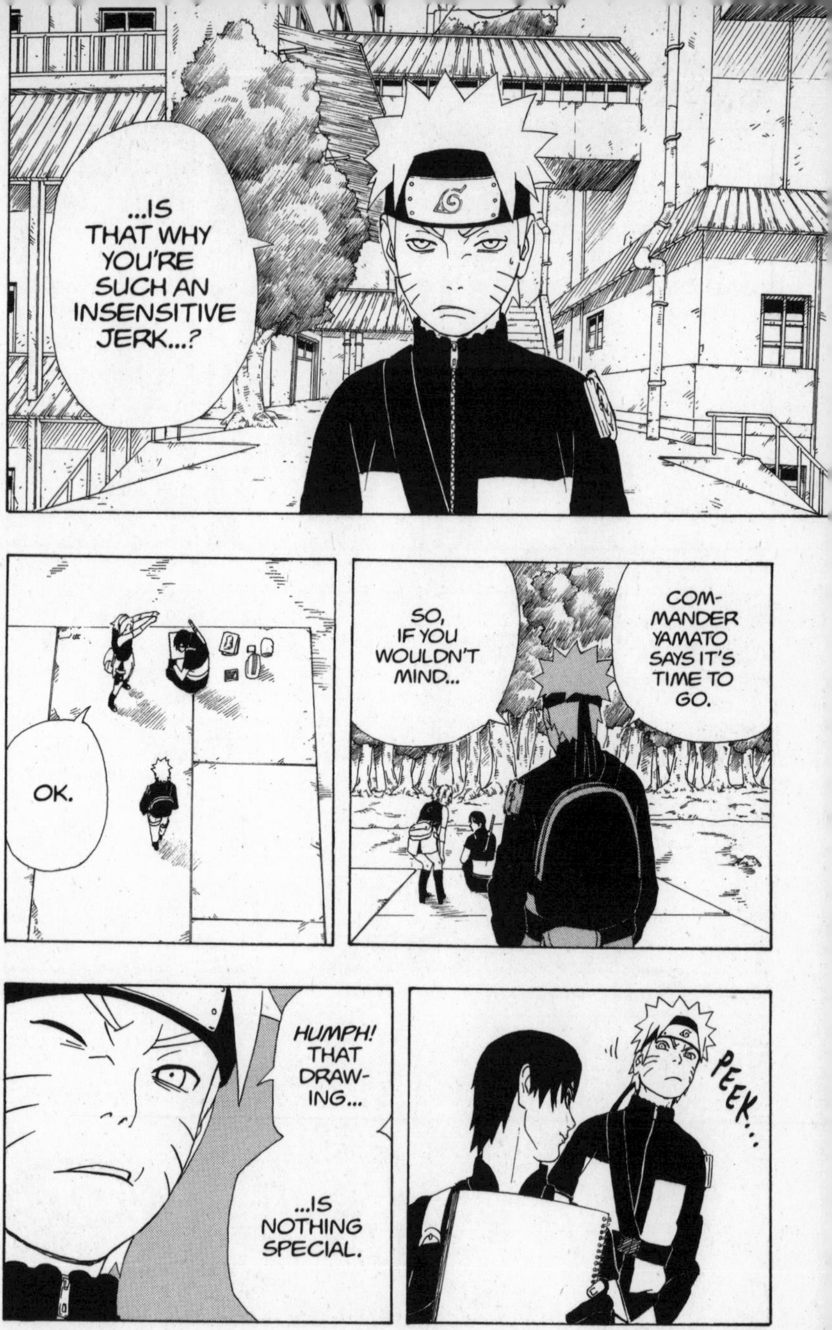
...IS THAT WHY YOU'RE SUCH AN INSENSITIVE JERK...?
COM-MANDER YAMATO SAYS IT'S TIME TO GO.
SO, IF YOU WOULDN'T MIND...
OK.
PEEK...
HUMPH! THAT DRAW-ING...
...IS NOTHING SPECIAL.

READ THIS WAY

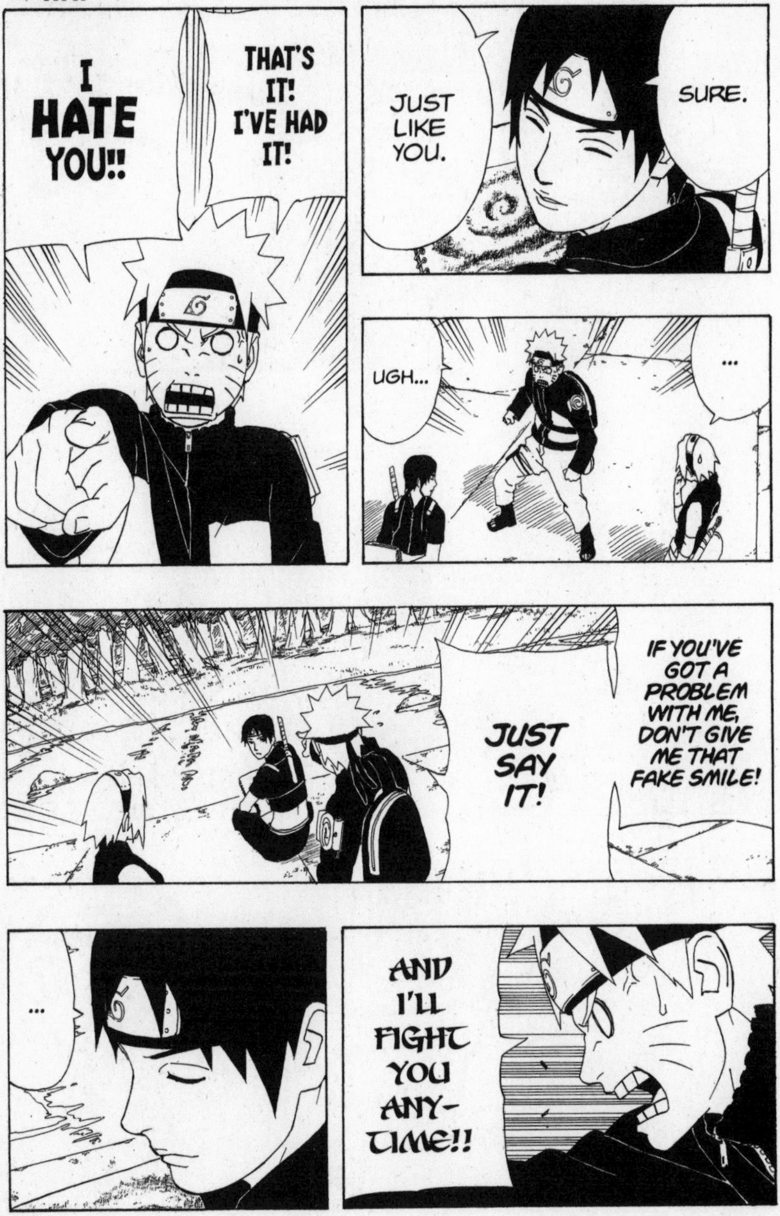

SURE.
JUST LIKE YOU.
...
UGH...
THAT'S IT! I'VE HAD IT!
I HATE YOU!!
IF YOU'VE GOT A PROBLEM WITH ME, DON'T GIVE ME THAT FAKE SMILE!
JUST SAY IT!
AND I'LL FIGHT YOU ANY-TIME!!
...

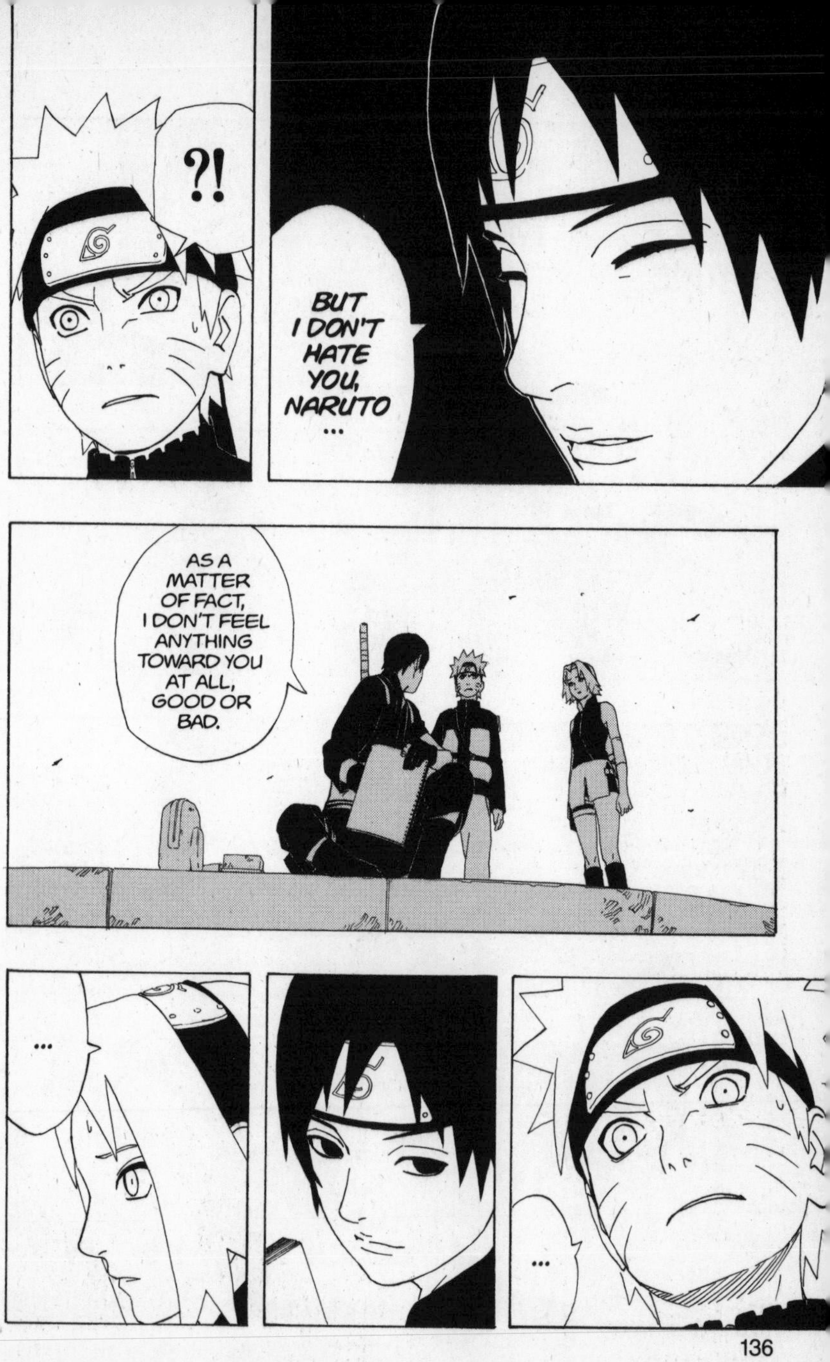
BUT I DON'T HATE YOU, NARUTO ...
?!
AS A MATTER OF FACT, I DON'T FEEL ANYTHING TOWARD YOU AT ALL, GOOD OR BAD.
...
...

READ THIS WAY

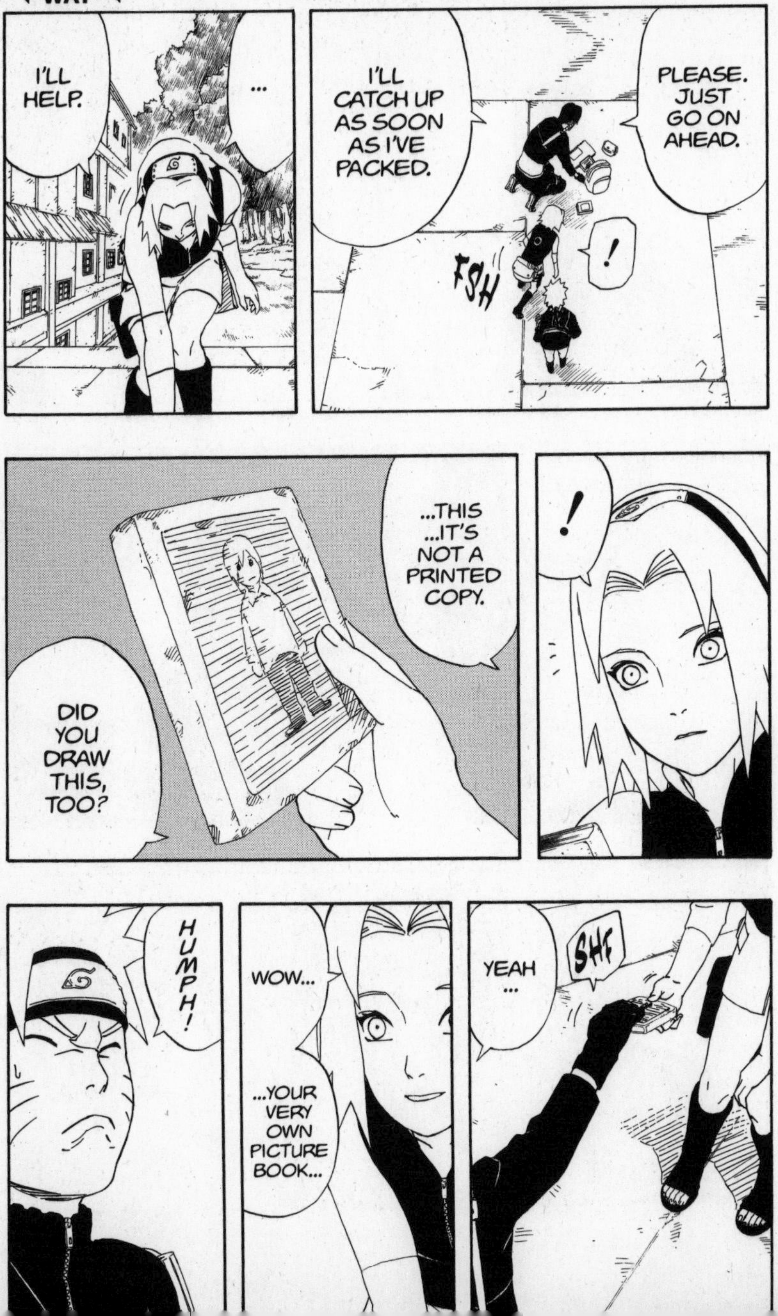
PLEASE. JUST GO ON AHEAD.
I'LL CATCH UP AS SOON AS I'VE PACKED.
!
FSH
...
I'LL HELP.
!
...THIS ...IT'S NOT A PRINTED COPY.
DID YOU DRAW THIS, TOO?
SHF
YEAH ...
WOW...
...YOUR VERY OWN PICTURE BOOK...
HUMPH!

...IT'S NOT FINISHED YET.

SORRY, BUT NO.

HEY...

...WHILE WE'RE ON THE ROAD, IS IT OKAY IF I FLIP THROUGH THIS?

?

PLUS, I DON'T REALLY SHOW IT TO OTHERS...

...BECAUSE IT BELONGS TO MY OLDER BROTHER.

READ THIS WAY

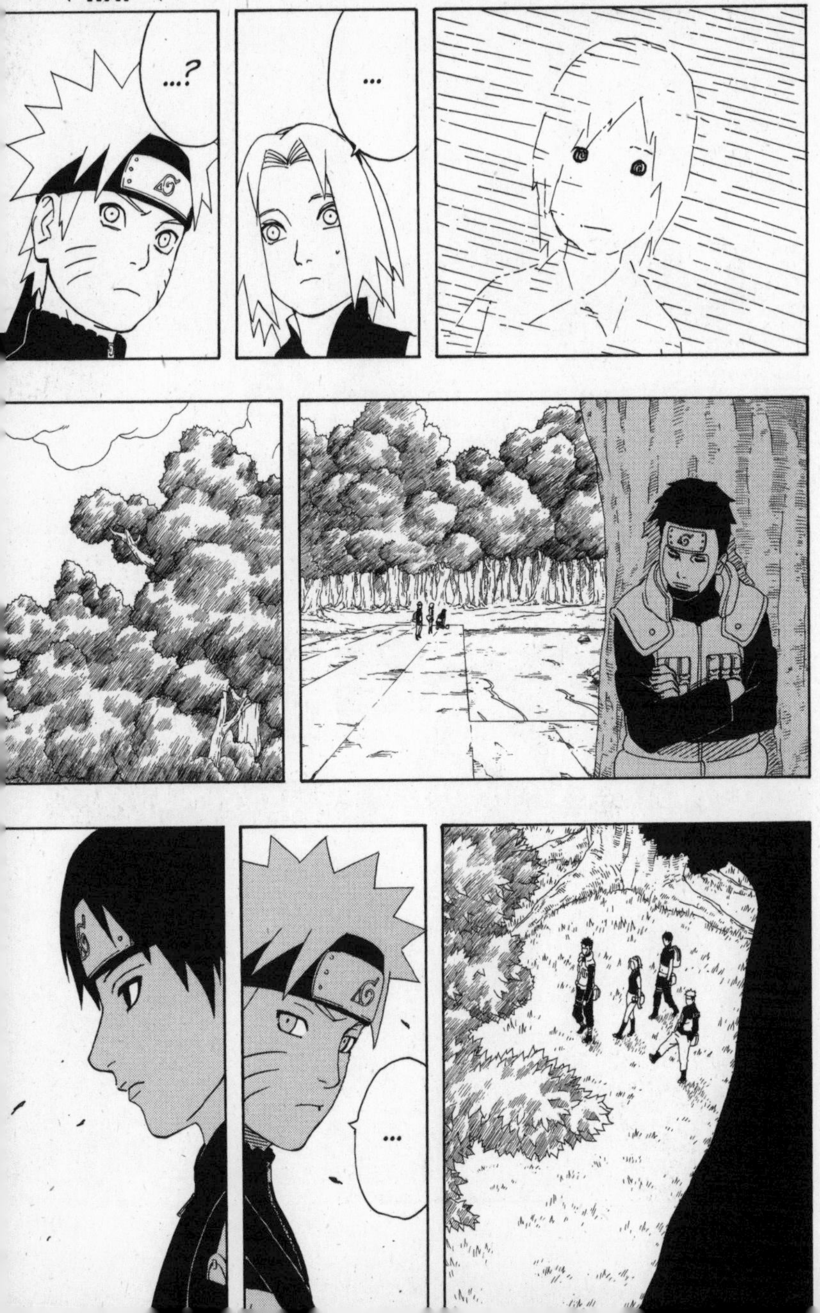
...
...?
...

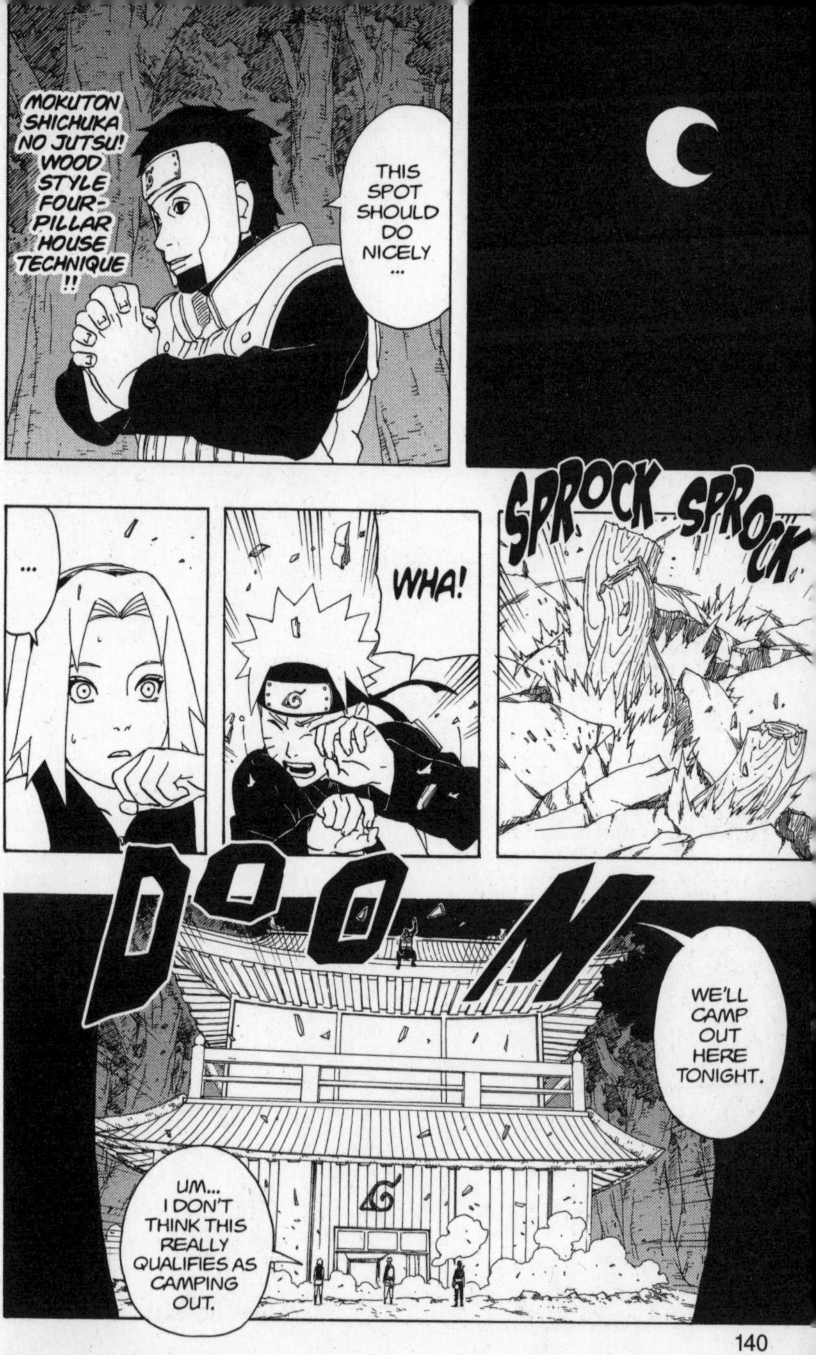
THIS SPOT SHOULD DO NICELY...
MOKUTON SHICHUKA NO JUTSU! WOOD STYLE FOUR-PILLAR HOUSE TECHNIQUE!!
SPROCK SPROCK
WHA!
...
DOOM
WE'LL CAMP OUT HERE TONIGHT.
UM... I DON'T THINK THIS REALLY QUALIFIES AS CAMPING OUT.

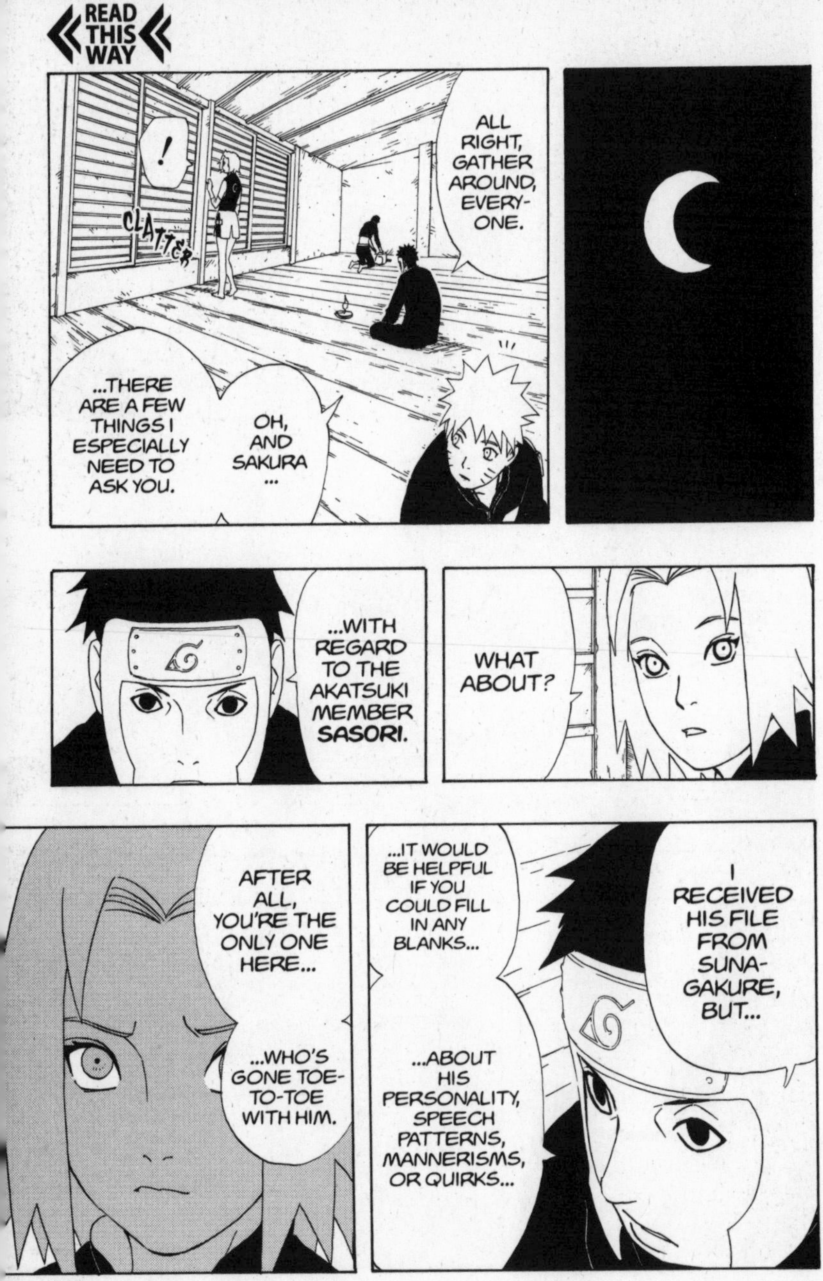
READ THIS WAY
ALL RIGHT, GATHER AROUND, EVERY-ONE.
!
CLATTER
OH, AND SAKURA ...
...THERE ARE A FEW THINGS I ESPECIALLY NEED TO ASK YOU.
WHAT ABOUT?
...WITH REGARD TO THE AKATSUKI MEMBER **SASORI**.
I RECEIVED HIS FILE FROM SUNA-GAKURE, BUT...
...IT WOULD BE HELPFUL IF YOU COULD FILL IN ANY BLANKS...
...ABOUT HIS PERSONALITY, SPEECH PATTERNS, MANNERISMS, OR QUIRKS...
AFTER ALL, YOU'RE THE ONLY ONE HERE...
...WHO'S GONE TOE-TO-TOE WITH HIM.

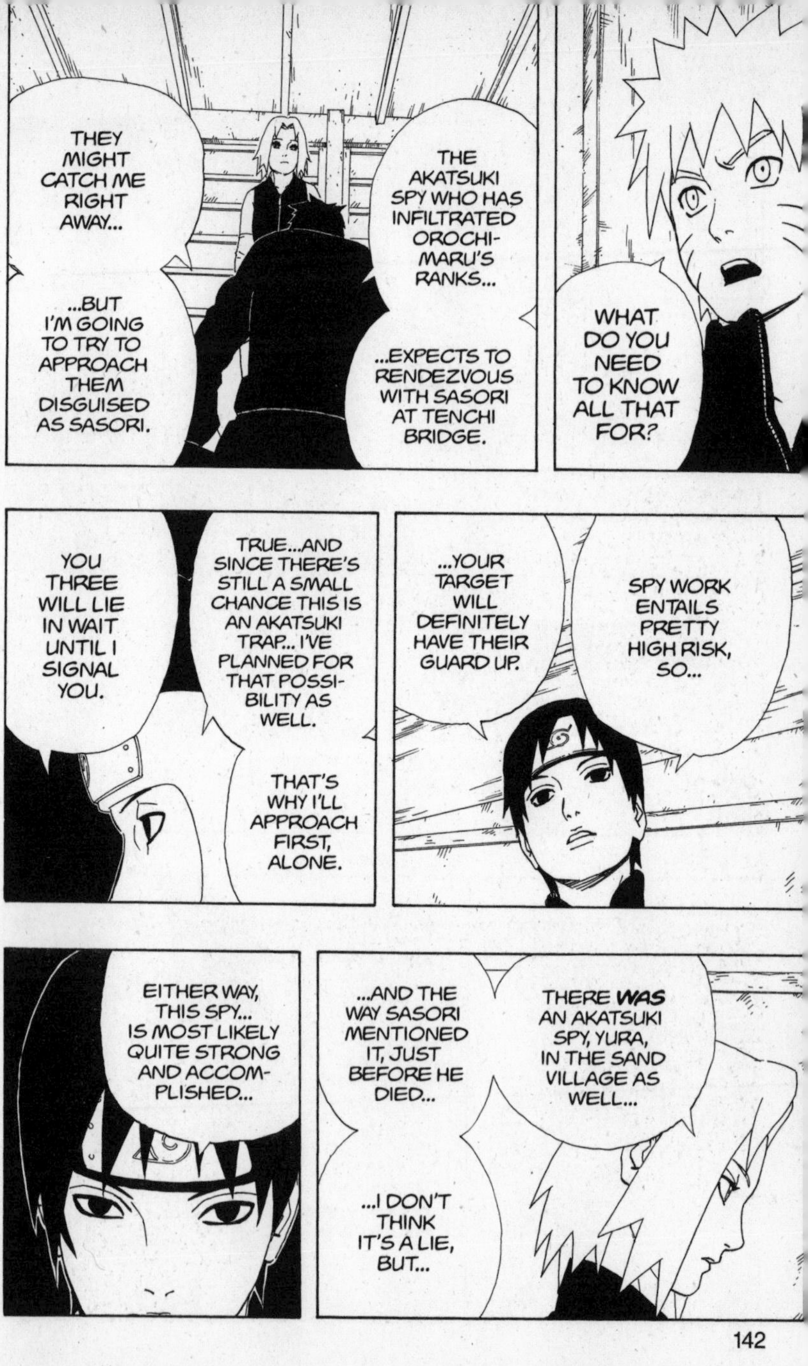
WHAT DO YOU NEED TO KNOW ALL THAT FOR?
THE AKATSUKI SPY WHO HAS INFILTRATED OROCHI-MARU'S RANKS...
...EXPECTS TO RENDEZVOUS WITH SASORI AT TENCHI BRIDGE.
THEY MIGHT CATCH ME RIGHT AWAY...
...BUT I'M GOING TO TRY TO APPROACH THEM DISGUISED AS SASORI.
SPY WORK ENTAILS PRETTY HIGH RISK, SO...
...YOUR TARGET WILL DEFINITELY HAVE THEIR GUARD UP.
TRUE...AND SINCE THERE'S STILL A SMALL CHANCE THIS IS AN AKATSUKI TRAP... I'VE PLANNED FOR THAT POSSI-BILITY AS WELL.
THAT'S WHY I'LL APPROACH FIRST, ALONE.
YOU THREE WILL LIE IN WAIT UNTIL I SIGNAL YOU.
THERE ***WAS*** AN AKATSUKI SPY, YURA, IN THE SAND VILLAGE AS WELL...
...AND THE WAY SASORI MENTIONED IT, JUST BEFORE HE DIED...
...I DON'T THINK IT'S A LIE, BUT...
EITHER WAY, THIS SPY... IS MOST LIKELY QUITE STRONG AND ACCOM-PLISHED...

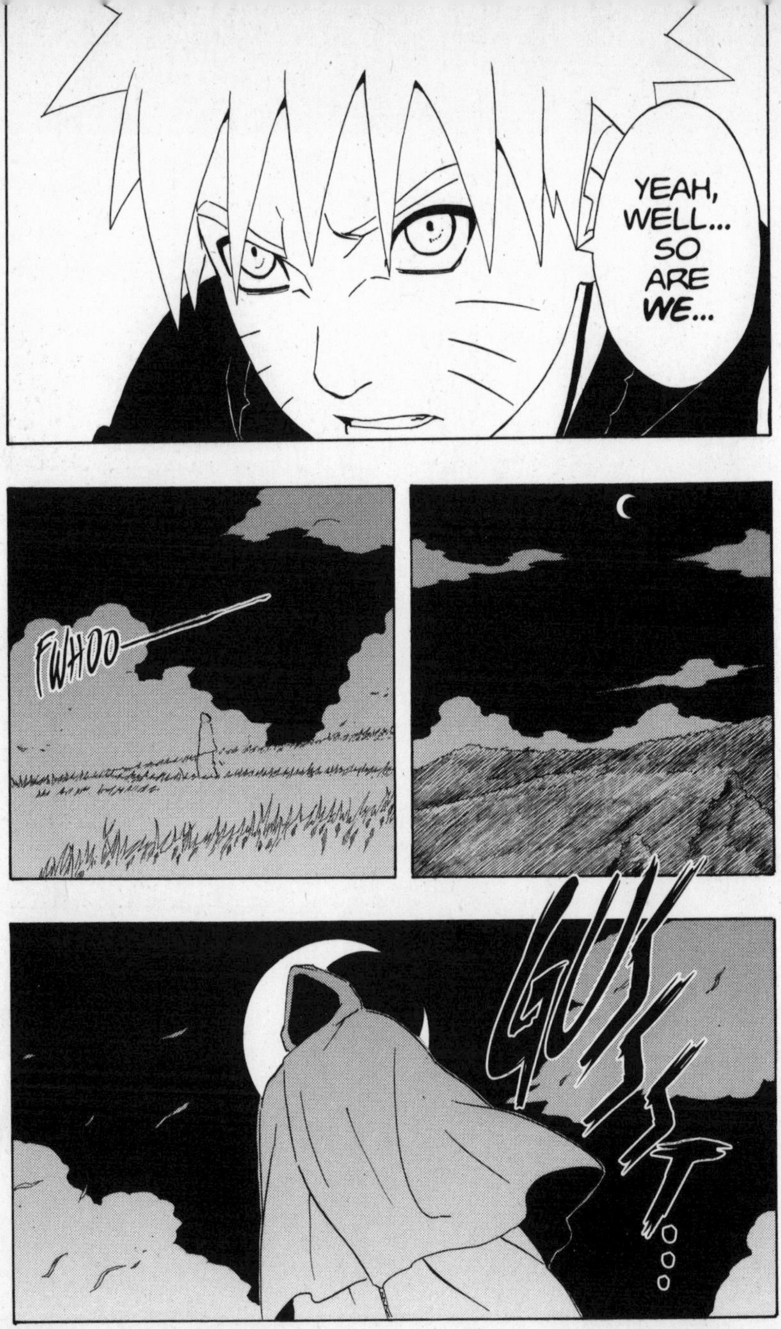
YEAH, WELL... SO ARE WE...
FWHOO
GUSST...

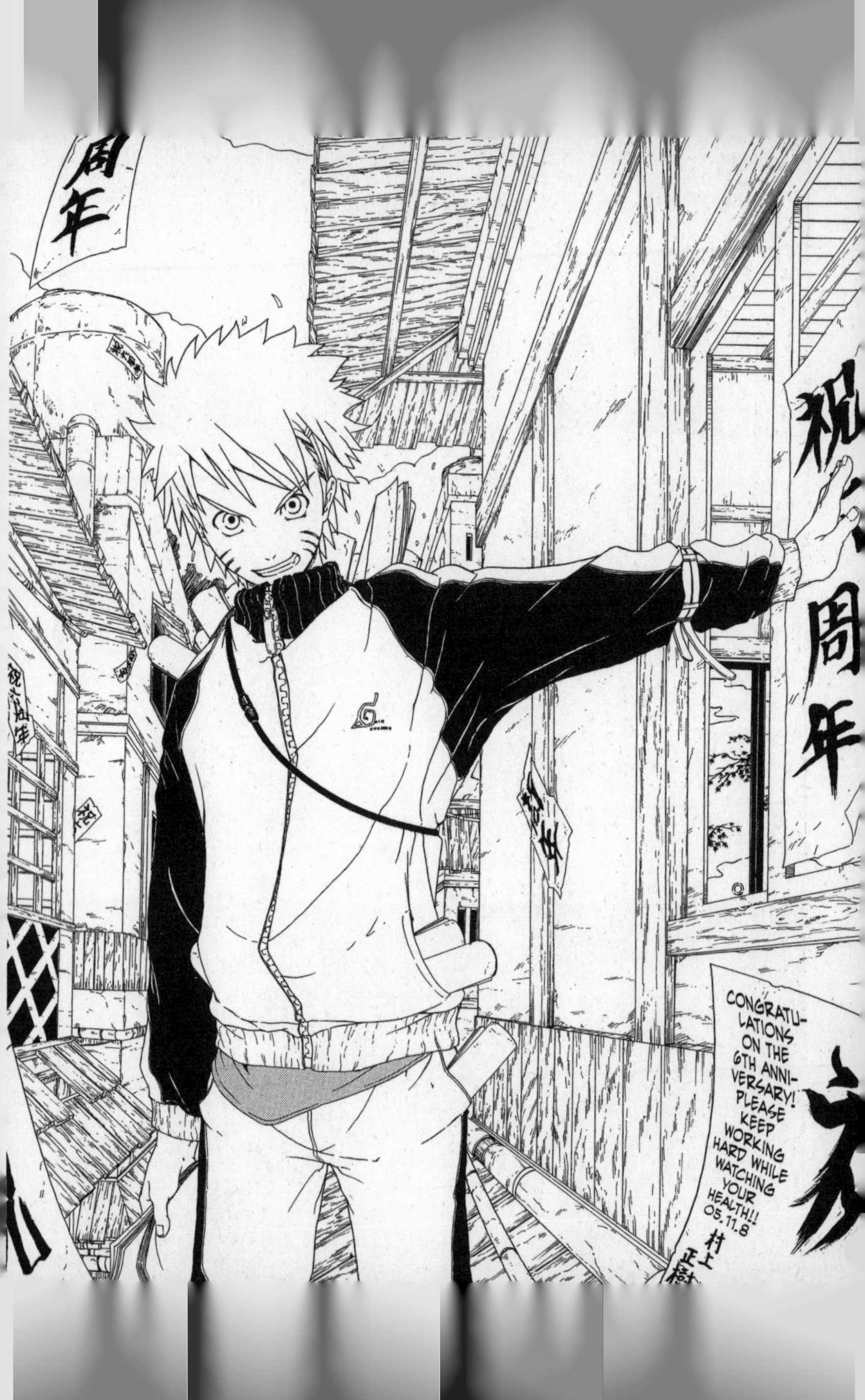
周年
CONGRATULATIONS ON THE 6TH ANNIVERSARY! PLEASE KEEP WORKING HARD WHILE WATCHING YOUR HEALTH!! 05.11.8
村上正樹

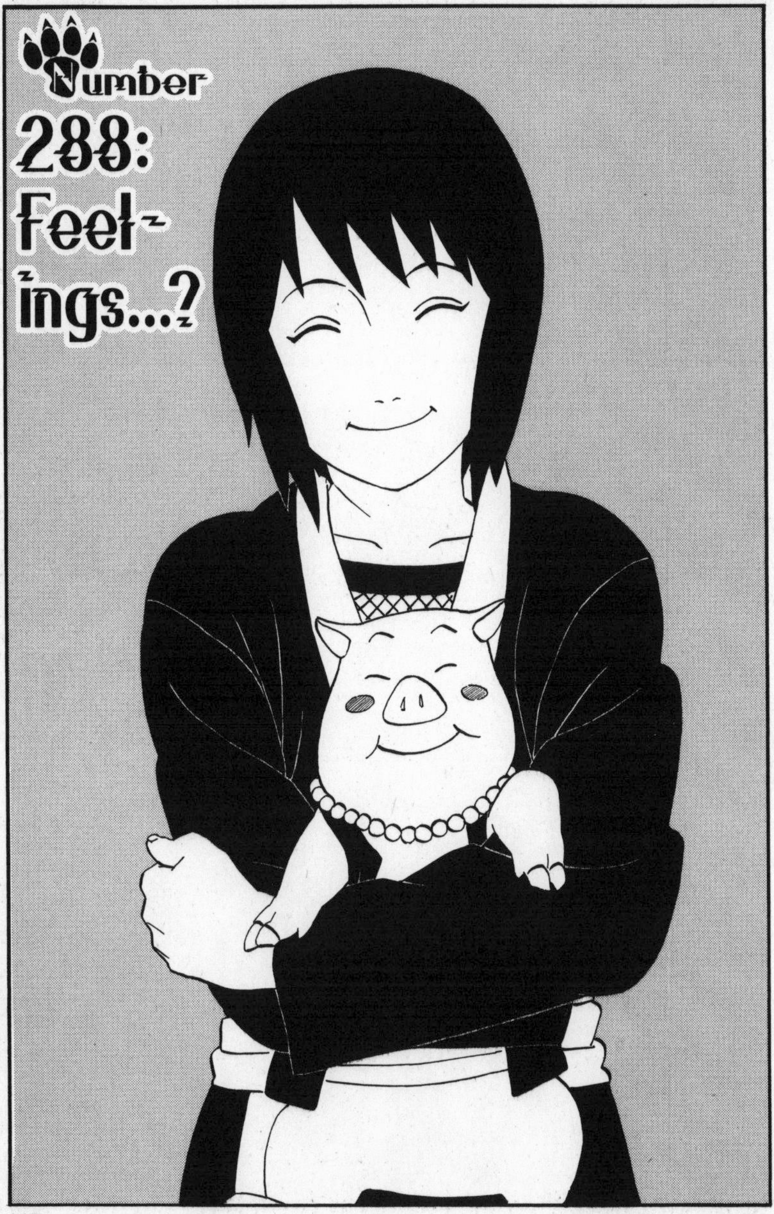
Number 288: Feel-ings...?

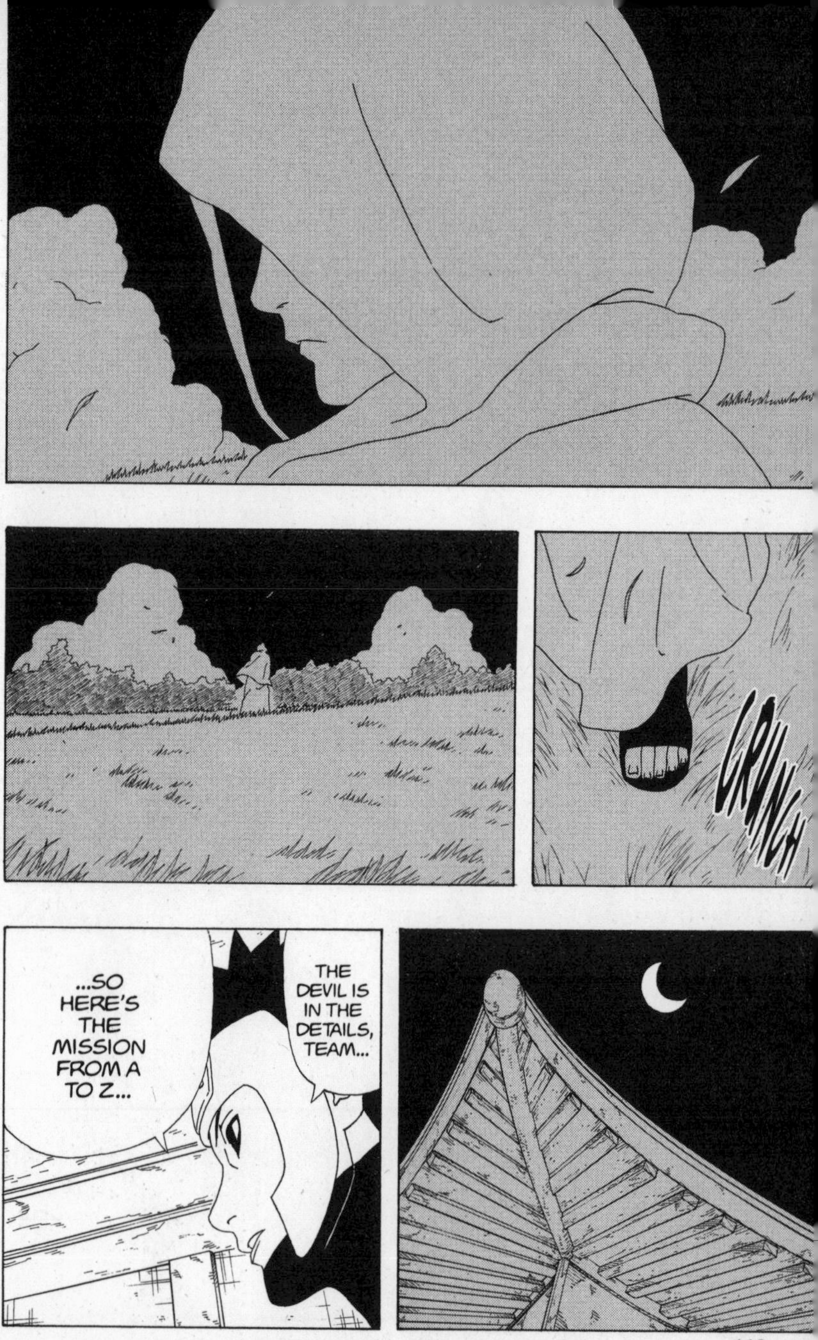
CRUNCH
THE DEVIL IS IN THE DETAILS, TEAM...
...SO HERE'S THE MISSION FROM A TO Z...

READ THIS WAY

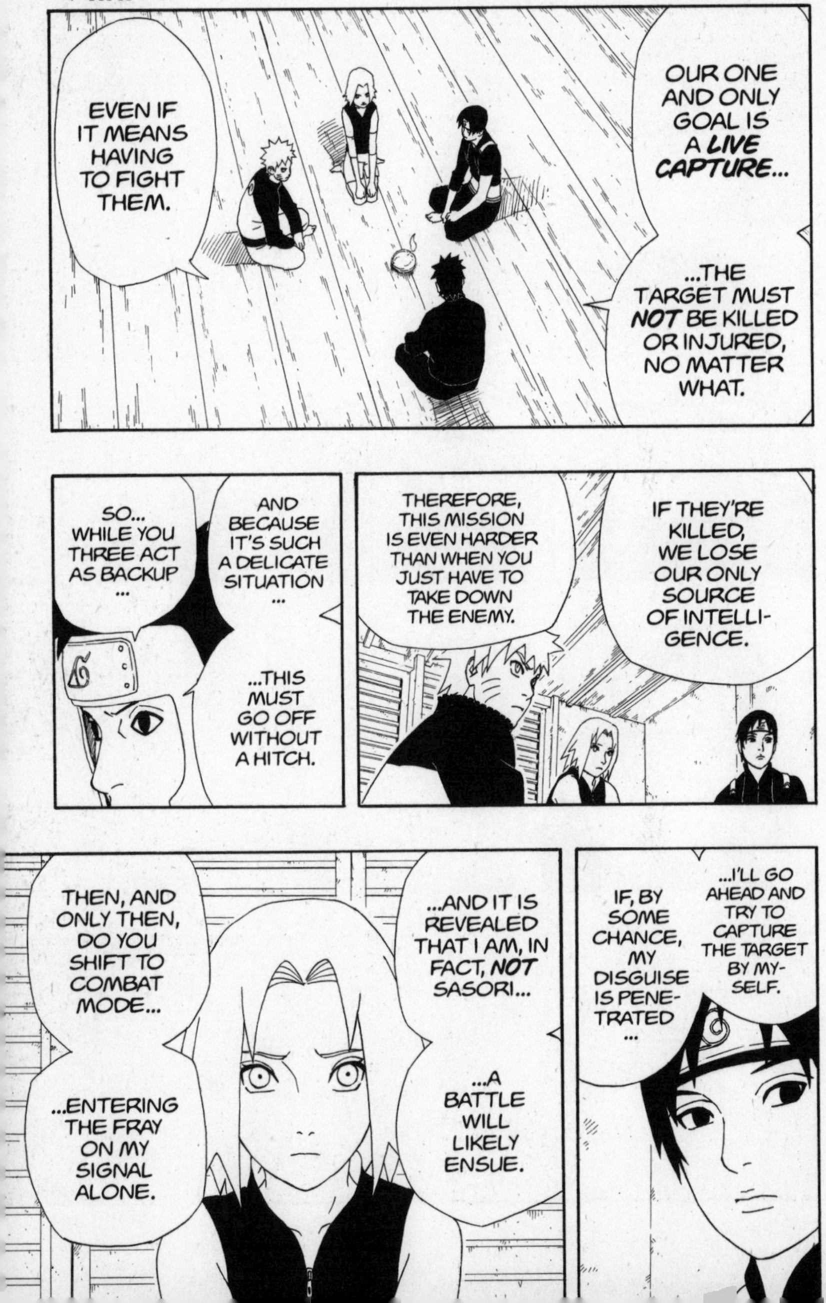
OUR ONE AND ONLY GOAL IS A *LIVE CAPTURE*...
...THE TARGET MUST *NOT* BE KILLED OR INJURED, NO MATTER WHAT.
EVEN IF IT MEANS HAVING TO FIGHT THEM.
IF THEY'RE KILLED, WE LOSE OUR ONLY SOURCE OF INTELLI-GENCE.
THEREFORE, THIS MISSION IS EVEN HARDER THAN WHEN YOU JUST HAVE TO TAKE DOWN THE ENEMY.
AND BECAUSE IT'S SUCH A DELICATE SITUATION ...
...THIS MUST GO OFF WITHOUT A HITCH.
SO... WHILE YOU THREE ACT AS BACKUP ...
IF, BY SOME CHANCE, MY DISGUISE IS PENE-TRATED ...
...I'LL GO AHEAD AND TRY TO CAPTURE THE TARGET BY MY-SELF.
...AND IT IS REVEALED THAT I AM, IN FACT, *NOT* SASORI...
...A BATTLE WILL LIKELY ENSUE.
THEN, AND ONLY THEN, DO YOU SHIFT TO COMBAT MODE...
...ENTERING THE FRAY ON MY SIGNAL ALONE.

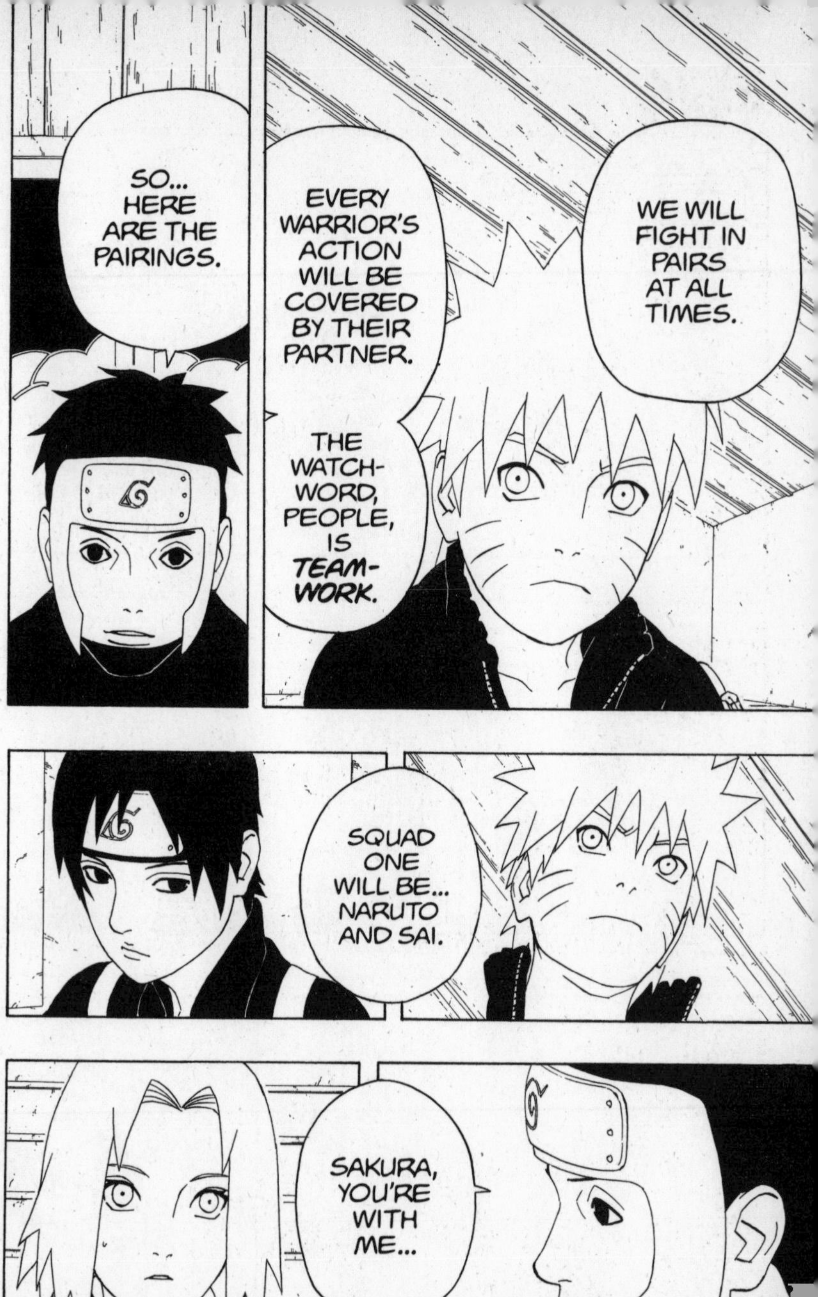
WE WILL FIGHT IN PAIRS AT ALL TIMES.
EVERY WARRIOR'S ACTION WILL BE COVERED BY THEIR PARTNER.
THE WATCH-WORD, PEOPLE, IS *TEAM-WORK*.
SO... HERE ARE THE PAIRINGS.
SQUAD ONE WILL BE... NARUTO AND SAI.
SAKURA, YOU'RE WITH ME...

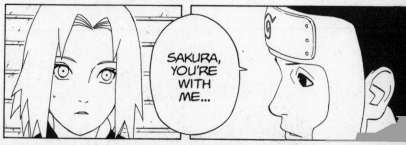

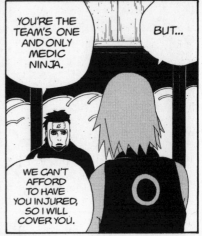

YOU'RE THE TEAM'S ONE AND ONLY MEDIC NINJA.

BUT...

WE CAN'T AFFORD TO HAVE YOU INJURED, SO I WILL COVER YOU.

PART-NER.

!

...

OH, C'MON, COM-MANDER!

TEAM ME UP WITH ANYONE... JUST NOT HIM!

...

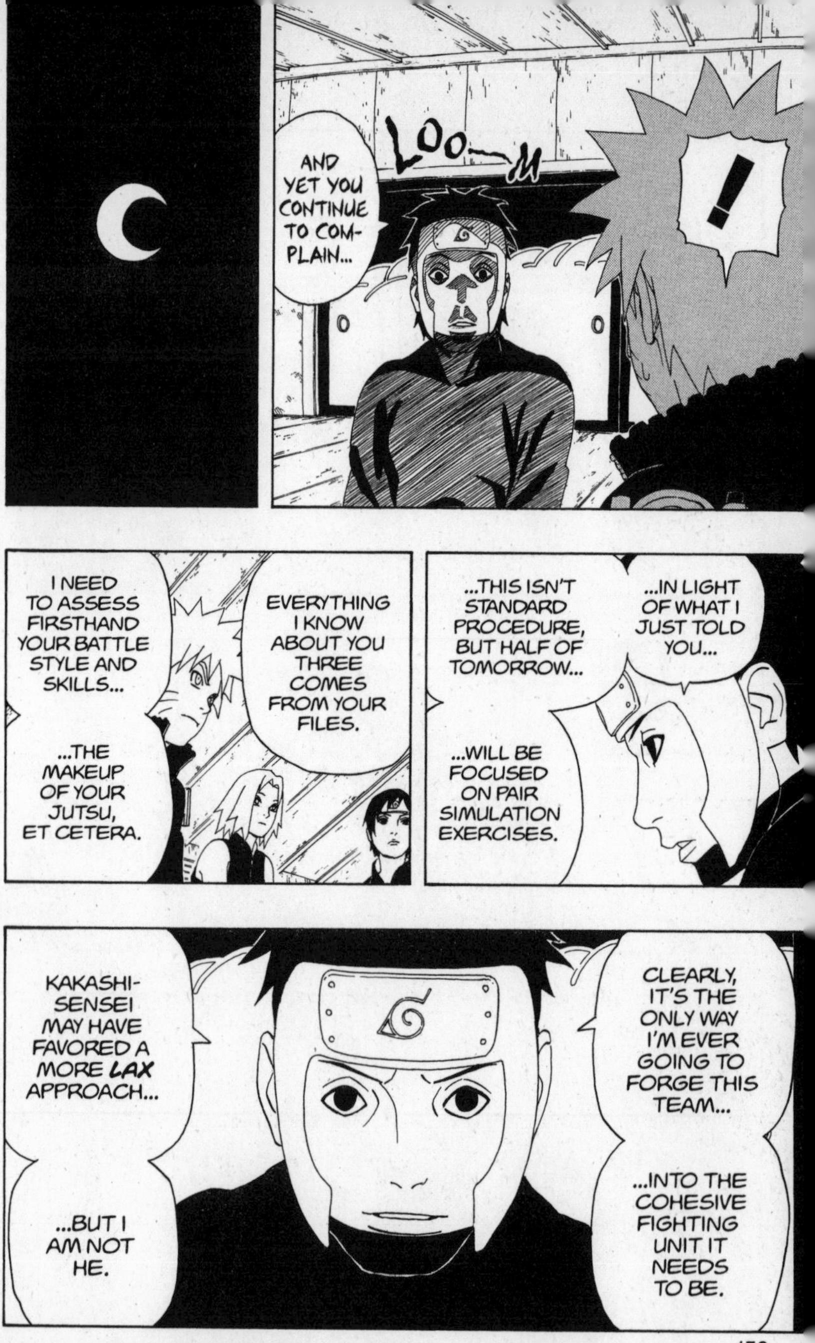
!
LOO—M
AND YET YOU CONTINUE TO COMPLAIN...
...IN LIGHT OF WHAT I JUST TOLD YOU...
...THIS ISN'T STANDARD PROCEDURE, BUT HALF OF TOMORROW...
...WILL BE FOCUSED ON PAIR SIMULATION EXERCISES.
EVERYTHING I KNOW ABOUT YOU THREE COMES FROM YOUR FILES.
I NEED TO ASSESS FIRSTHAND YOUR BATTLE STYLE AND SKILLS...
...THE MAKEUP OF YOUR JUTSU, ET CETERA.
CLEARLY, IT'S THE ONLY WAY I'M EVER GOING TO FORGE THIS TEAM...
...INTO THE COHESIVE FIGHTING UNIT IT NEEDS TO BE.
KAKASHI-SENSEI MAY HAVE FAVORED A MORE *LAX* APPROACH...
...BUT I AM NOT HE.

READ THIS WAY

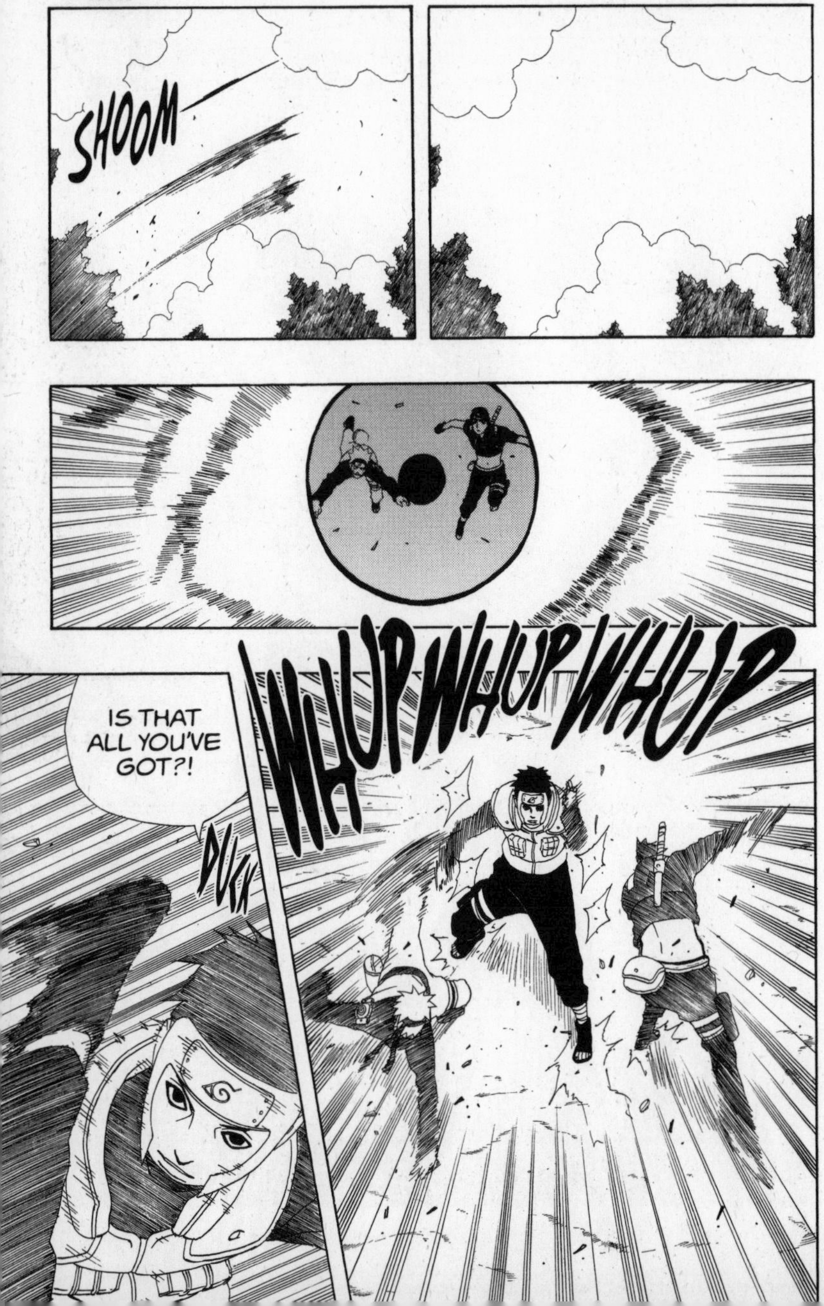
SHOOM
WHUP WHUP WHUP
IS THAT ALL YOU'VE GOT?!
DUCK

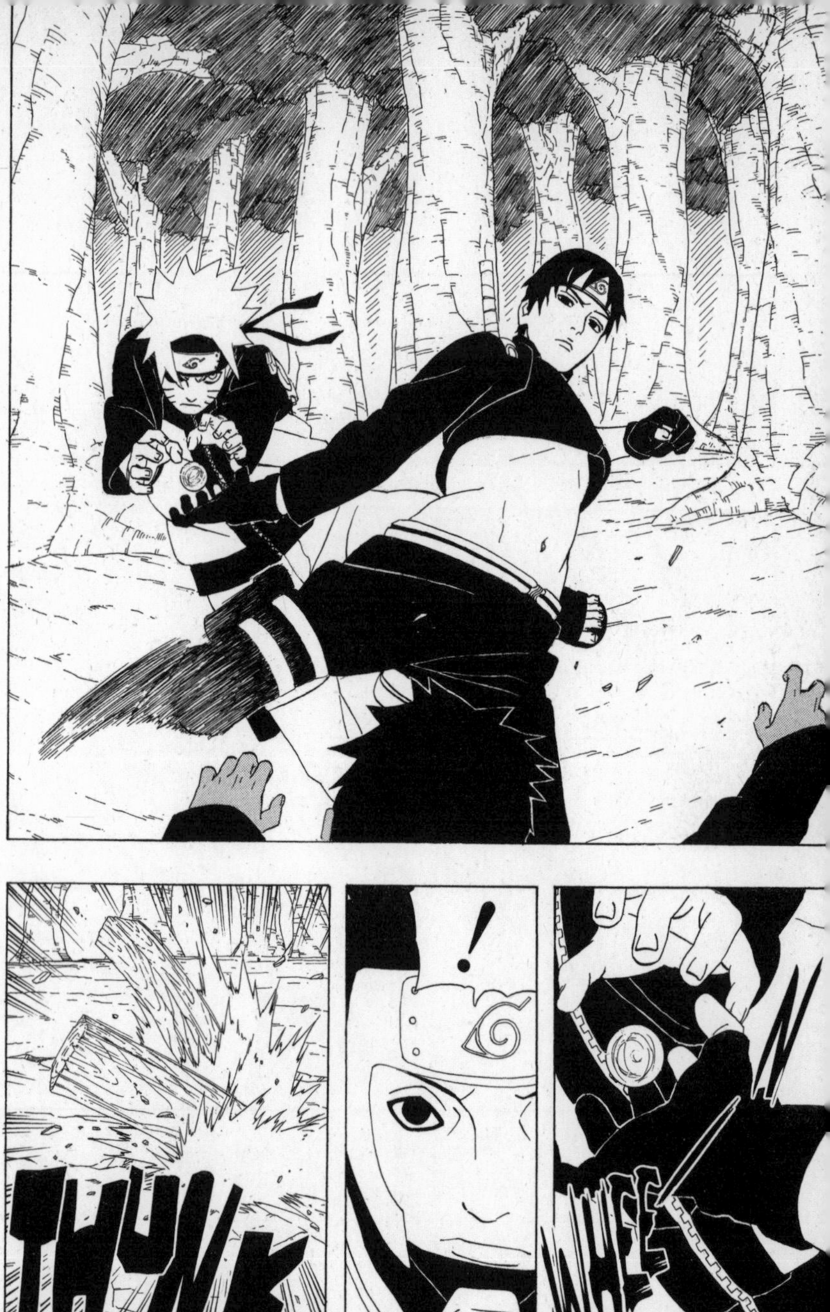
WHEEN
!
THUNK

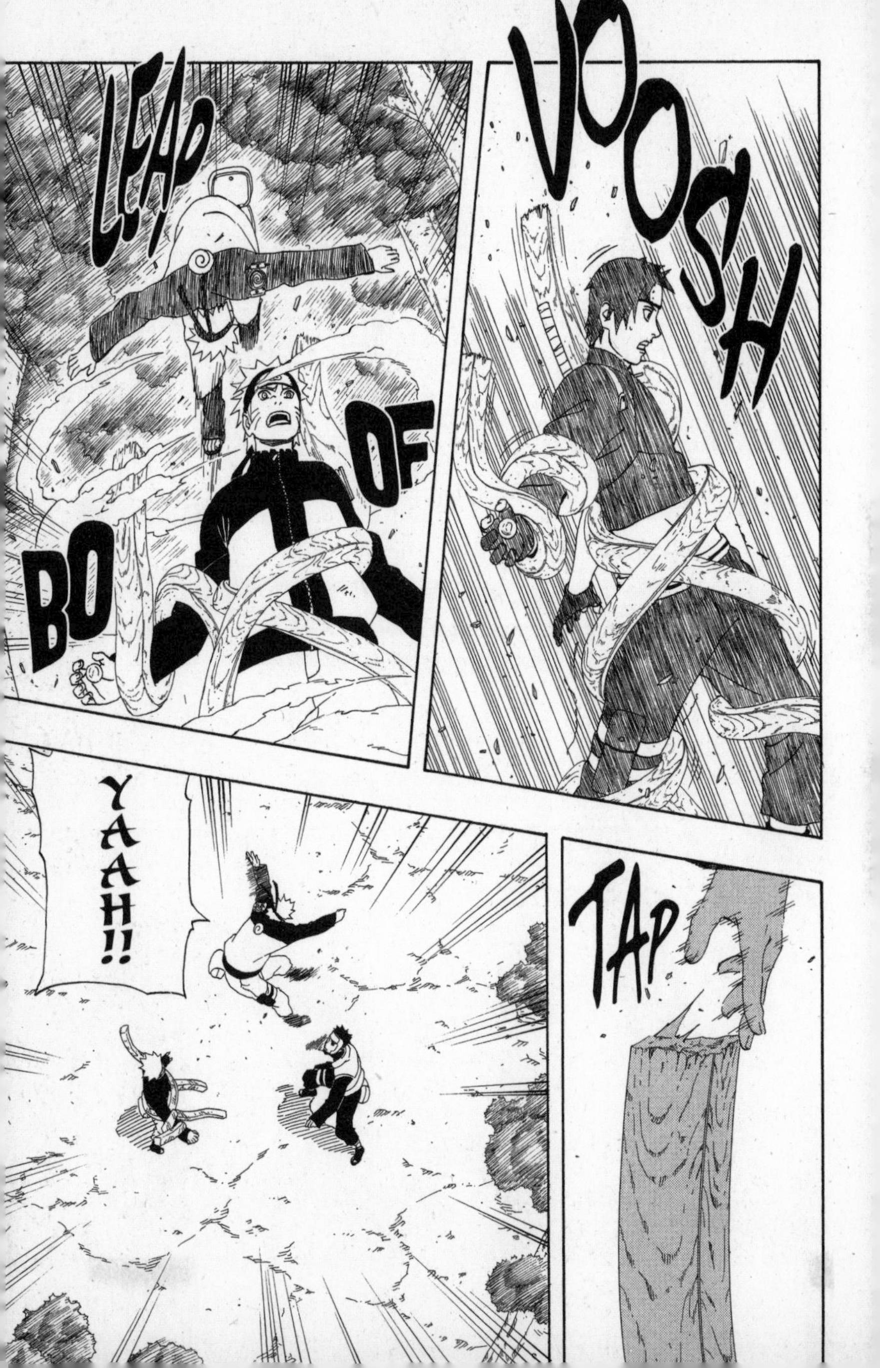
VOOSH
LEAP
BOOF
TAP
YAAAH!!

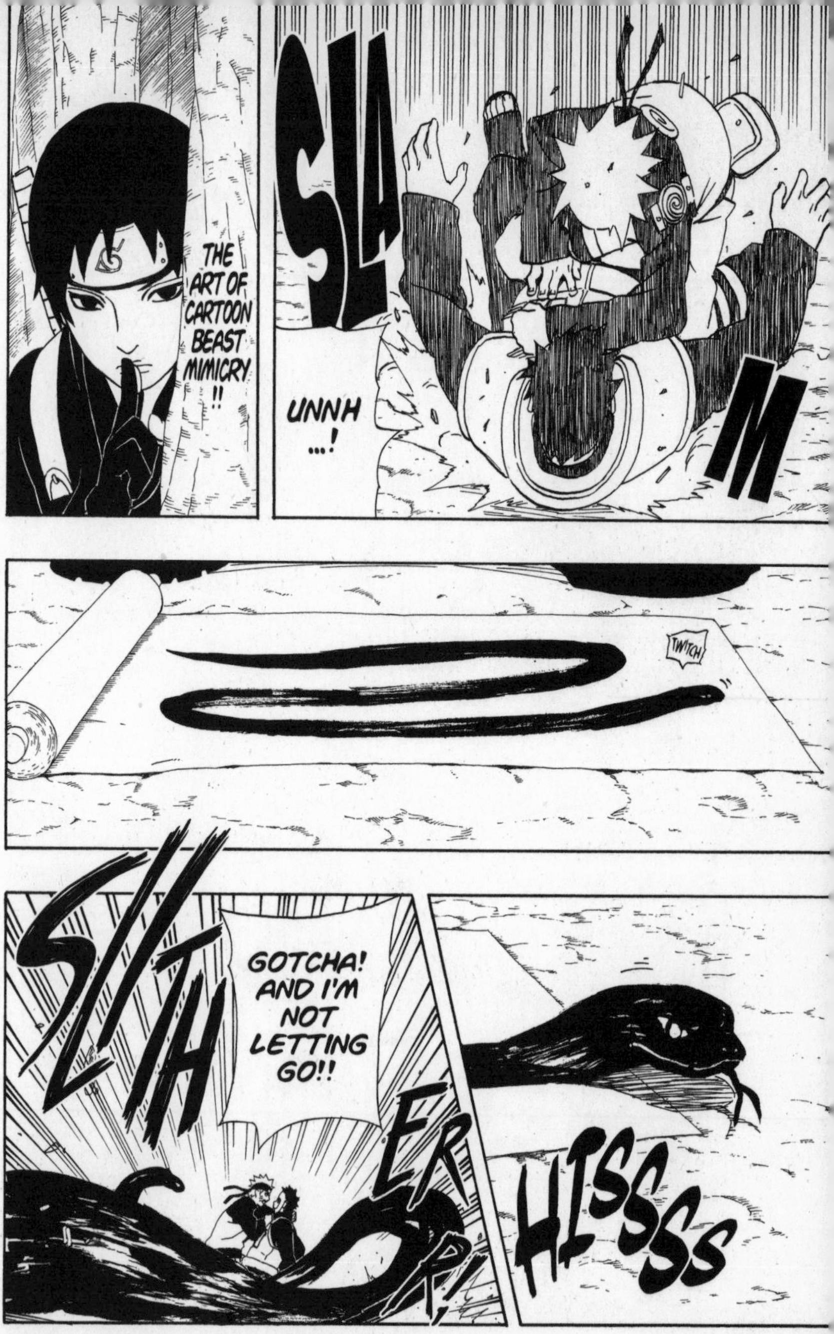
SLAM
UNNH ...!
THE ART OF CARTOON BEAST MIMICRY!!
TWITCH
HISSSSS
SLITHERR!
GOTCHA! AND I'M NOT LETTING GO!!

READ THIS WAY

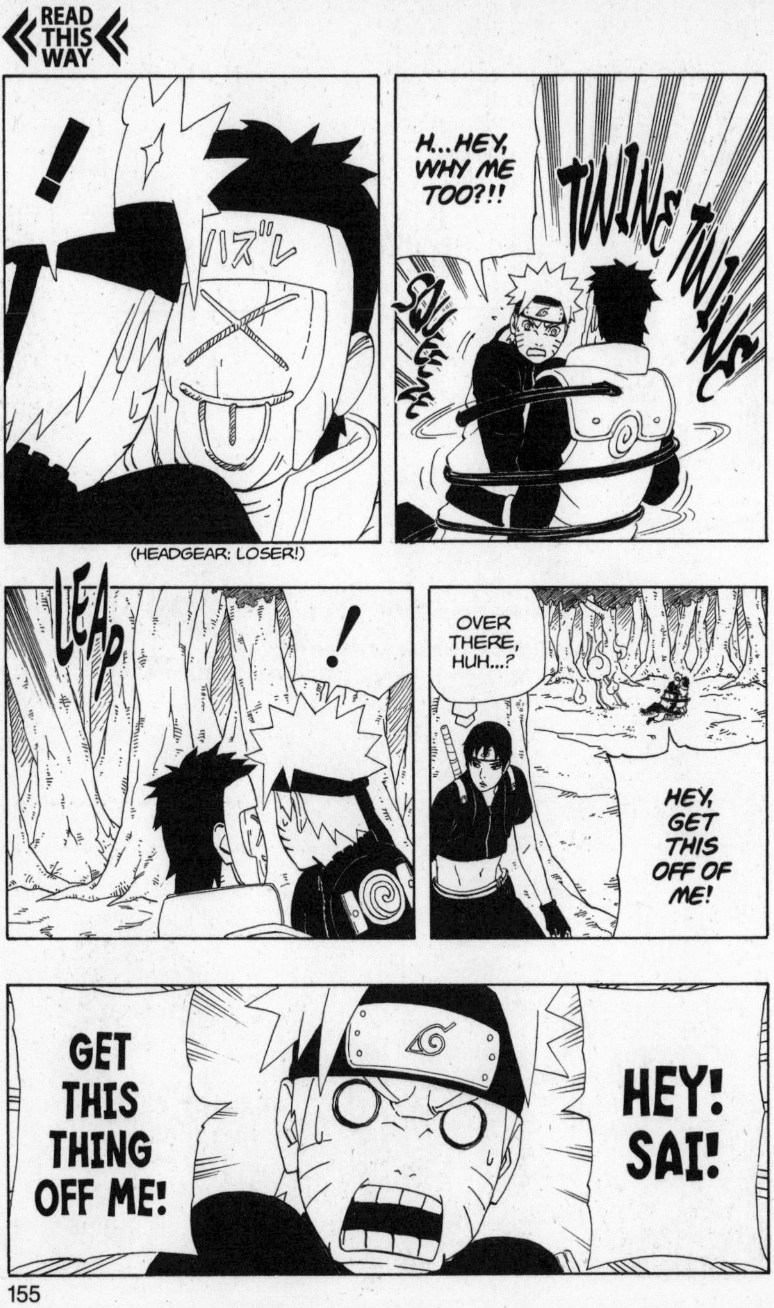

H...HEY, WHY ME TOO?!!
TWINE TWINE
!
ハズレ
(HEADGEAR: LOSER!)
OVER THERE, HUH...?
HEY, GET THIS OFF OF ME!
LEAP
!
HEY! SAI!
GET THIS THING OFF ME!

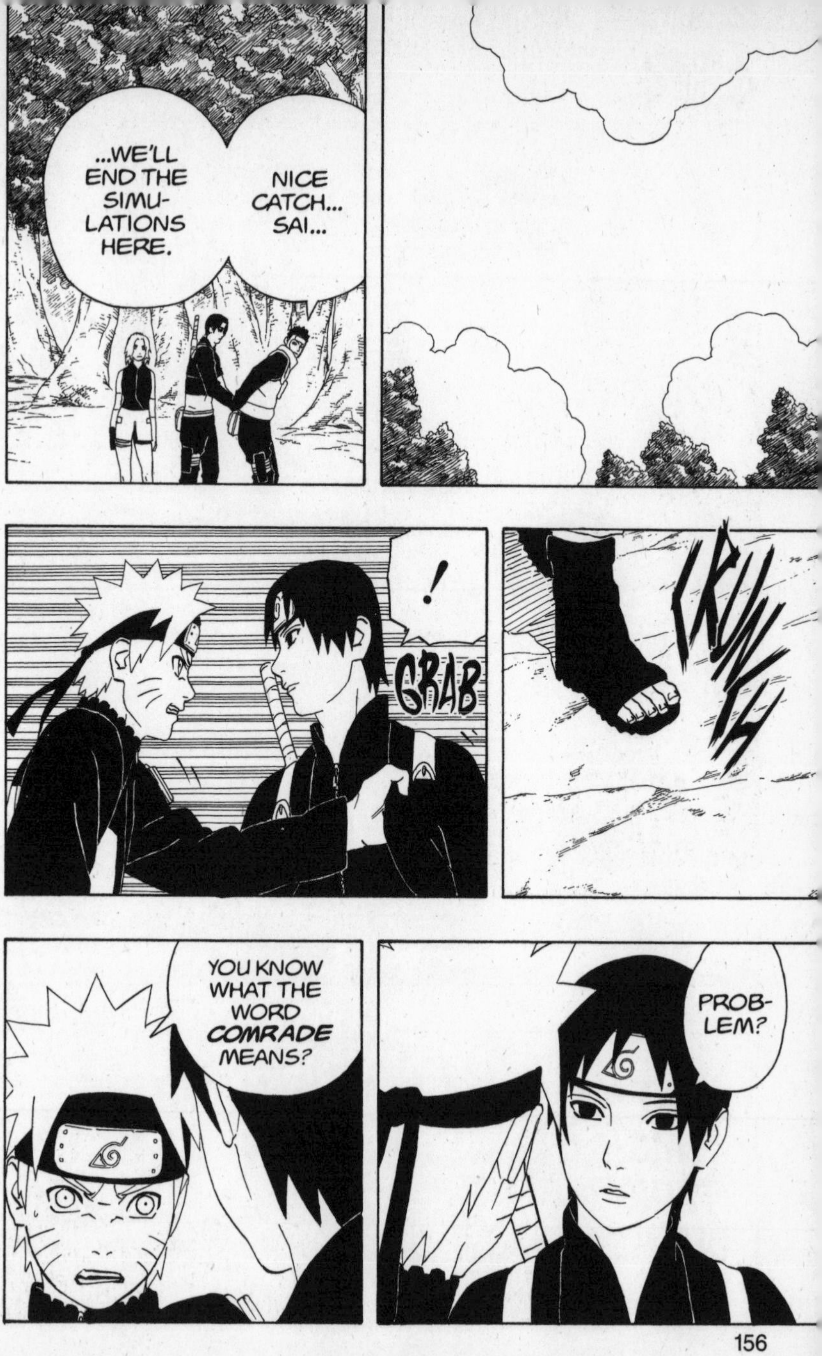
NICE CATCH... SAI...
...WE'LL END THE SIMU-LATIONS HERE.
CRUNCH
!
GRAB
PROB-LEM?
YOU KNOW WHAT THE WORD **COMRADE** MEANS?

READ THIS WAY

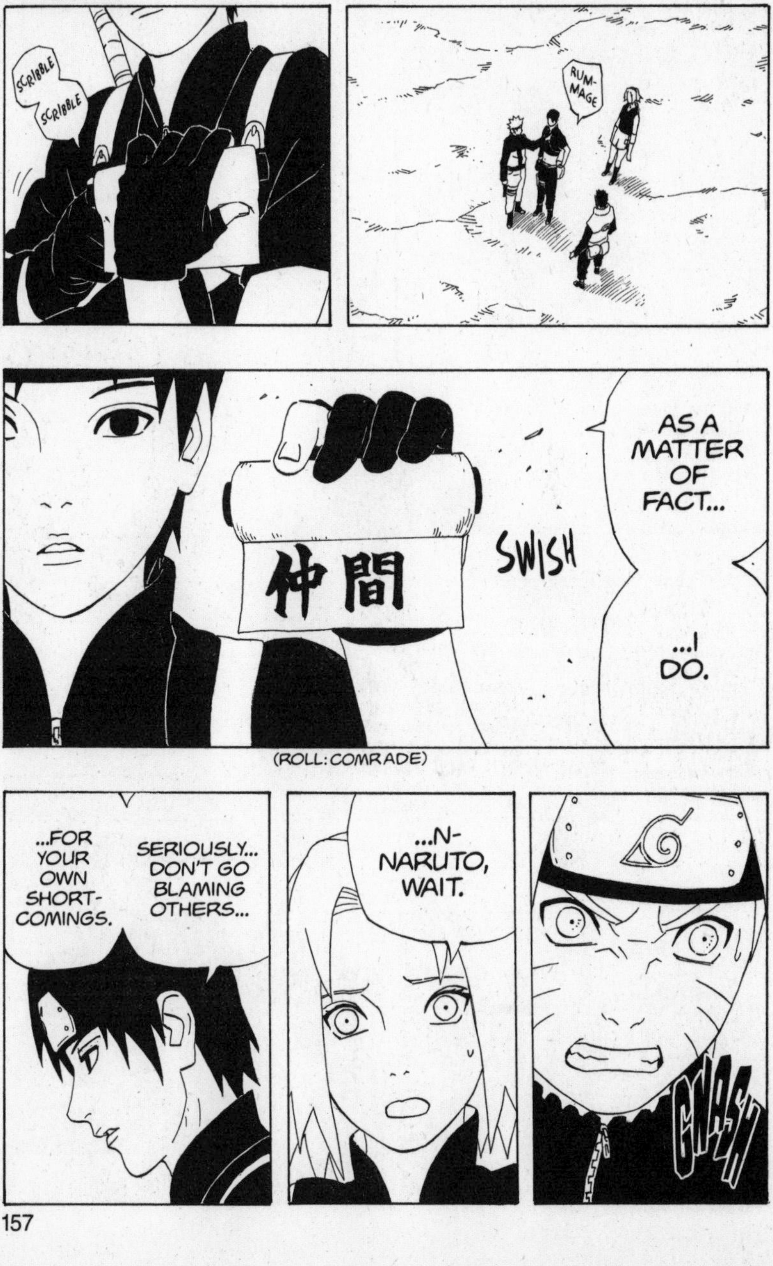
RUM-MAGE
SCRIBBLE SCRIBBLE
AS A MATTER OF FACT...
...I DO.
SWISH
仲間
(ROLL: COMRADE)
GNASH
...N-NARUTO, WAIT.
SERIOUSLY... DON'T GO BLAMING OTHERS...
...FOR YOUR OWN SHORT-COMINGS.

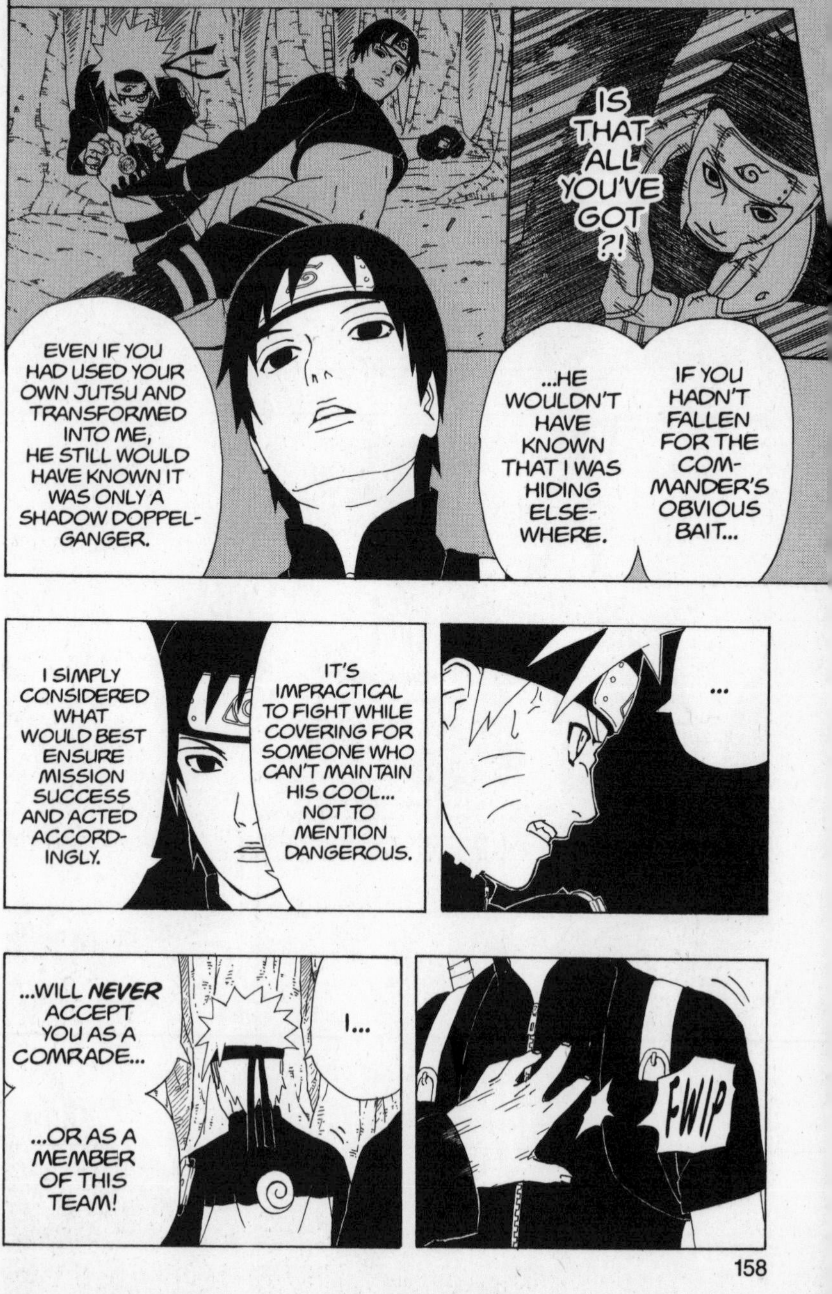

IS THAT ALL YOU'VE GOT ?!
IF YOU HADN'T FALLEN FOR THE COM-MANDER'S OBVIOUS BAIT...
...HE WOULDN'T HAVE KNOWN THAT I WAS HIDING ELSE-WHERE.
EVEN IF YOU HAD USED YOUR OWN JUTSU AND TRANSFORMED INTO ME, HE STILL WOULD HAVE KNOWN IT WAS ONLY A SHADOW DOPPEL-GANGER.
...
IT'S IMPRACTICAL TO FIGHT WHILE COVERING FOR SOMEONE WHO CAN'T MAINTAIN HIS COOL... NOT TO MENTION DANGEROUS.
I SIMPLY CONSIDERED WHAT WOULD BEST ENSURE MISSION SUCCESS AND ACTED ACCORD-INGLY.
FWIP
I...
...WILL ***NEVER*** ACCEPT YOU AS A COMRADE...
...OR AS A MEMBER OF THIS TEAM!

READ THIS WAY

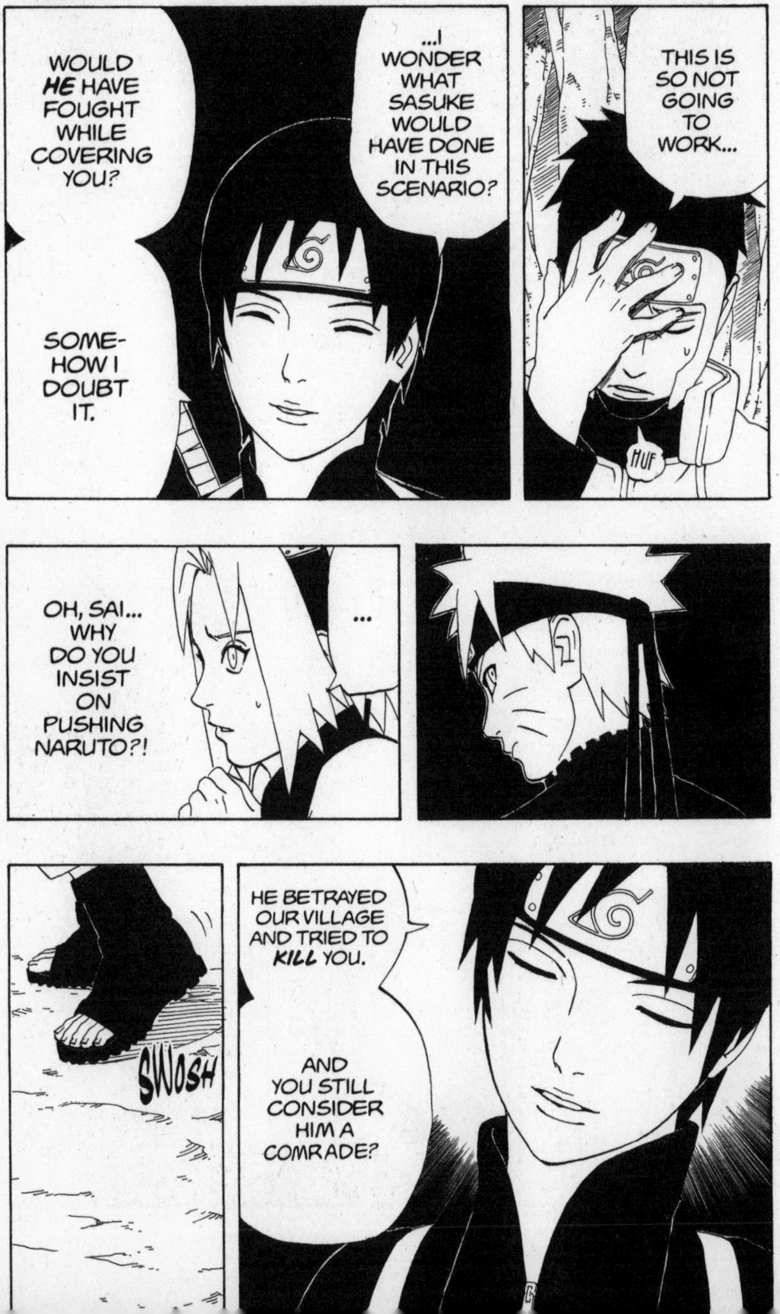
THIS IS SO NOT GOING TO WORK...
HUF
...I WONDER WHAT SASUKE WOULD HAVE DONE IN THIS SCENARIO?
WOULD *HE* HAVE FOUGHT WHILE COVERING YOU?
SOME-HOW I DOUBT IT.
...
OH, SAI... WHY DO YOU INSIST ON PUSHING NARUTO?!
HE BETRAYED OUR VILLAGE AND TRIED TO *KILL* YOU.
AND YOU STILL CONSIDER HIM A COMRADE?
SWOSH

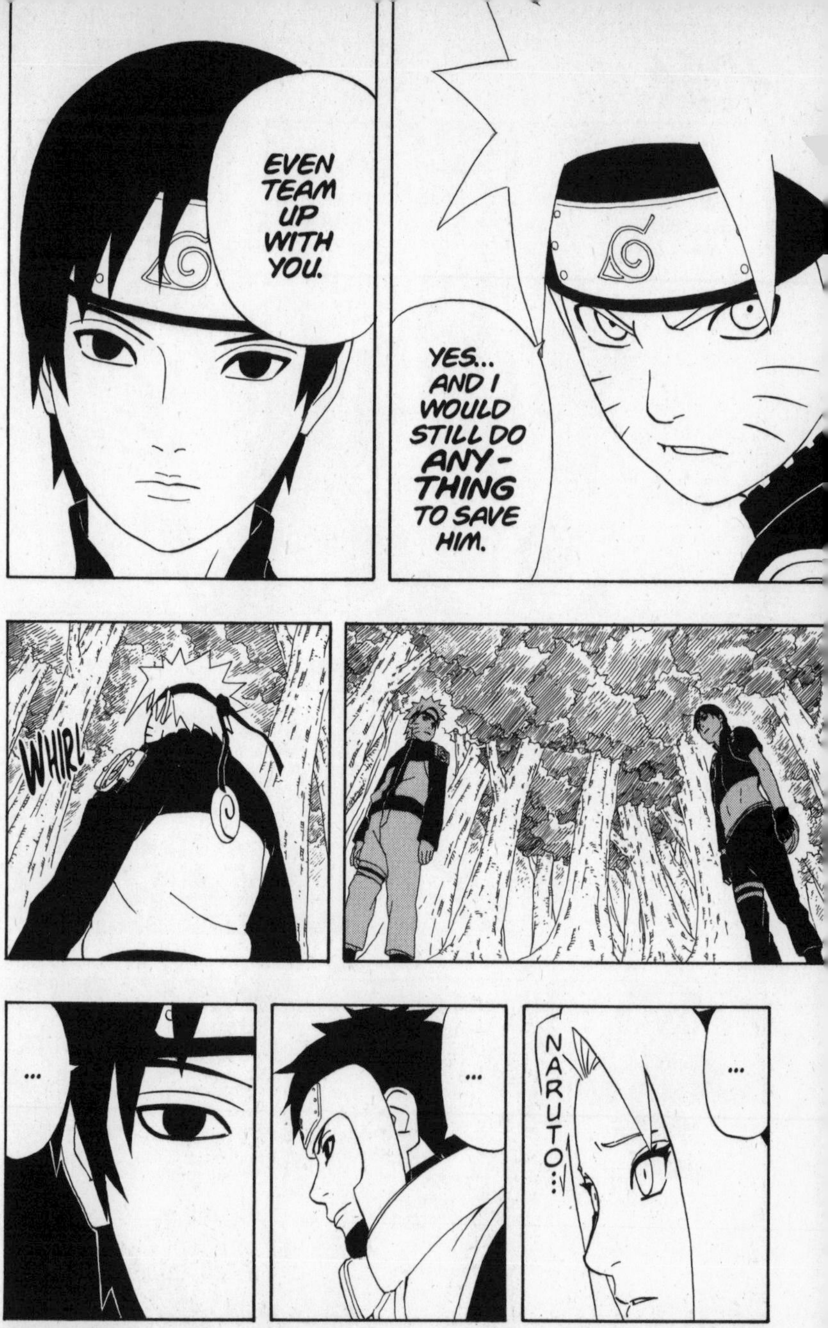

YES... AND I WOULD STILL DO ANYTHING TO SAVE HIM.
EVEN TEAM UP WITH YOU.
WHIRL
...
NARUTO...
...
...

READ THIS WAY

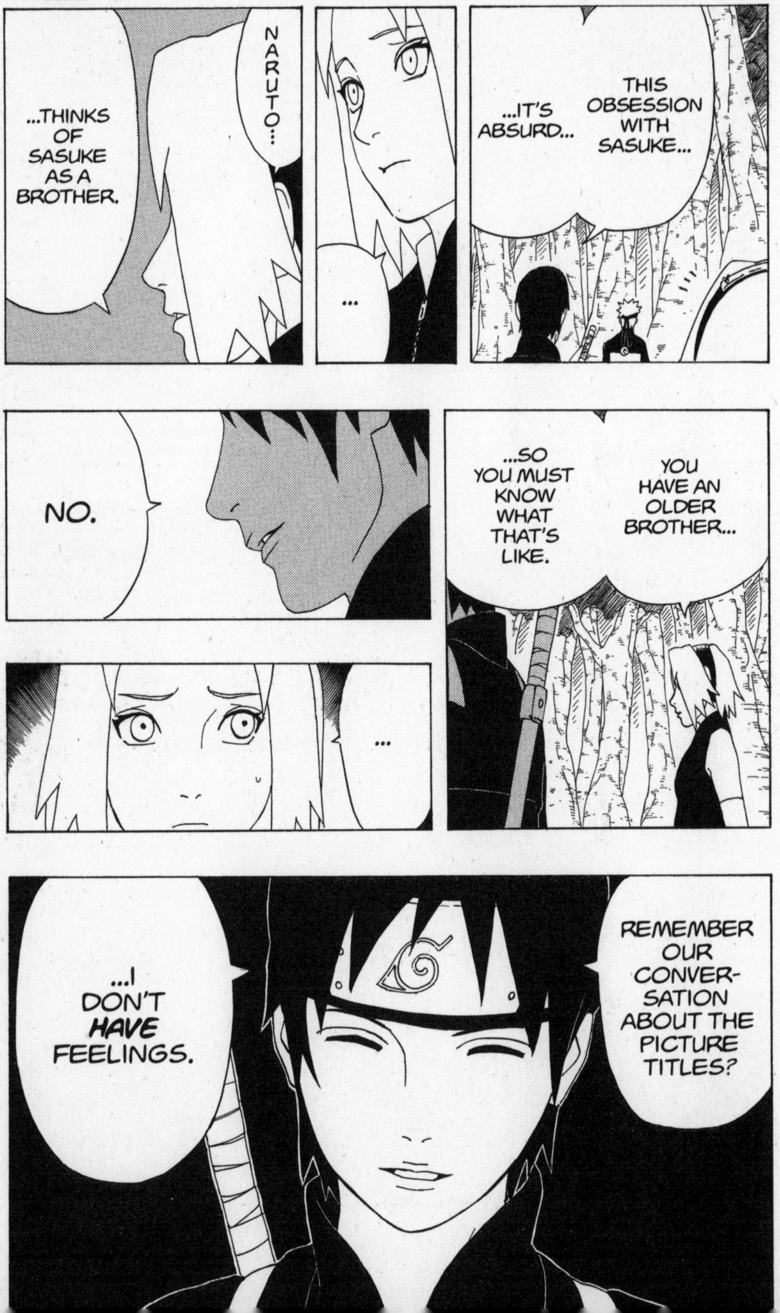
THIS OBSESSION WITH SASUKE...
...IT'S ABSURD...
NARUTO...
...
...THINKS OF SASUKE AS A BROTHER.
YOU HAVE AN OLDER BROTHER...
...SO YOU MUST KNOW WHAT THAT'S LIKE.
NO.
...
REMEMBER OUR CONVER-SATION ABOUT THE PICTURE TITLES?
...I DON'T *HAVE* FEELINGS.

NARUTO

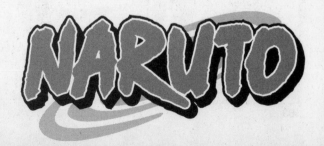

Number 289: The Akatsuki Spy!!

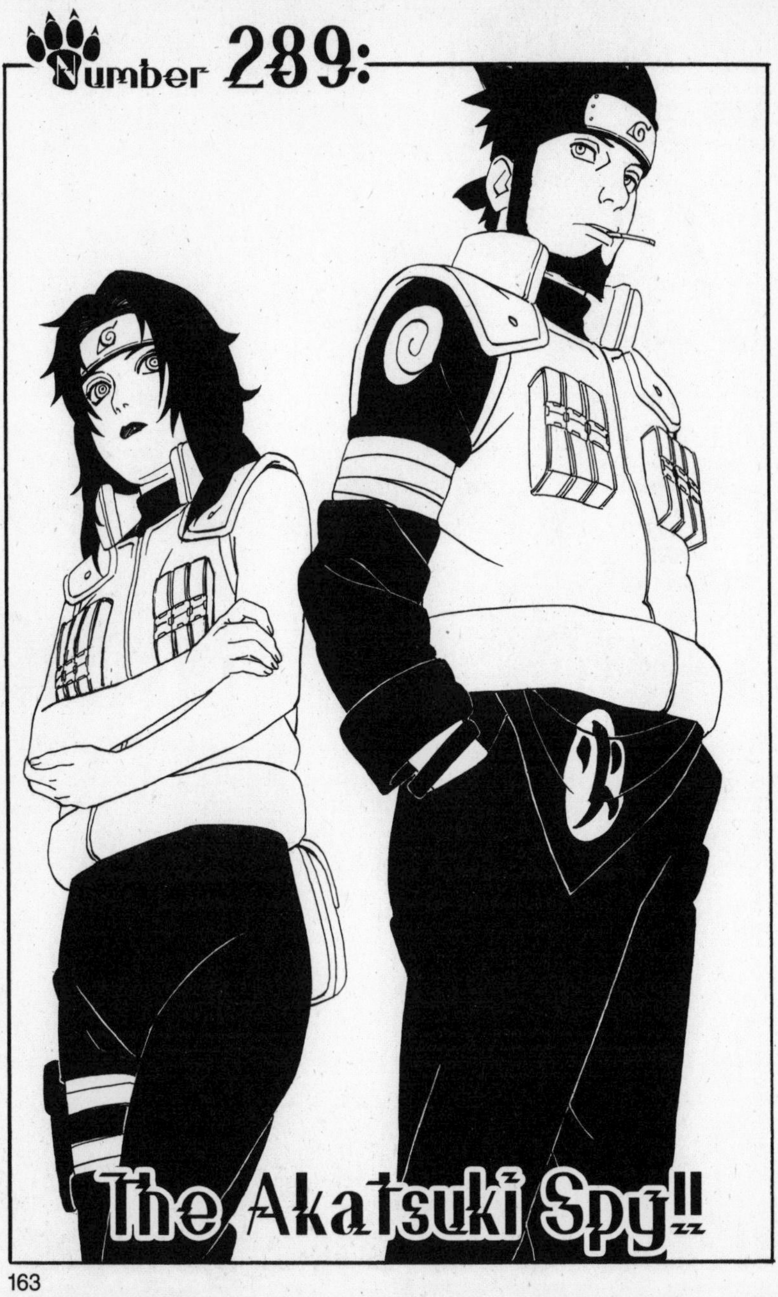

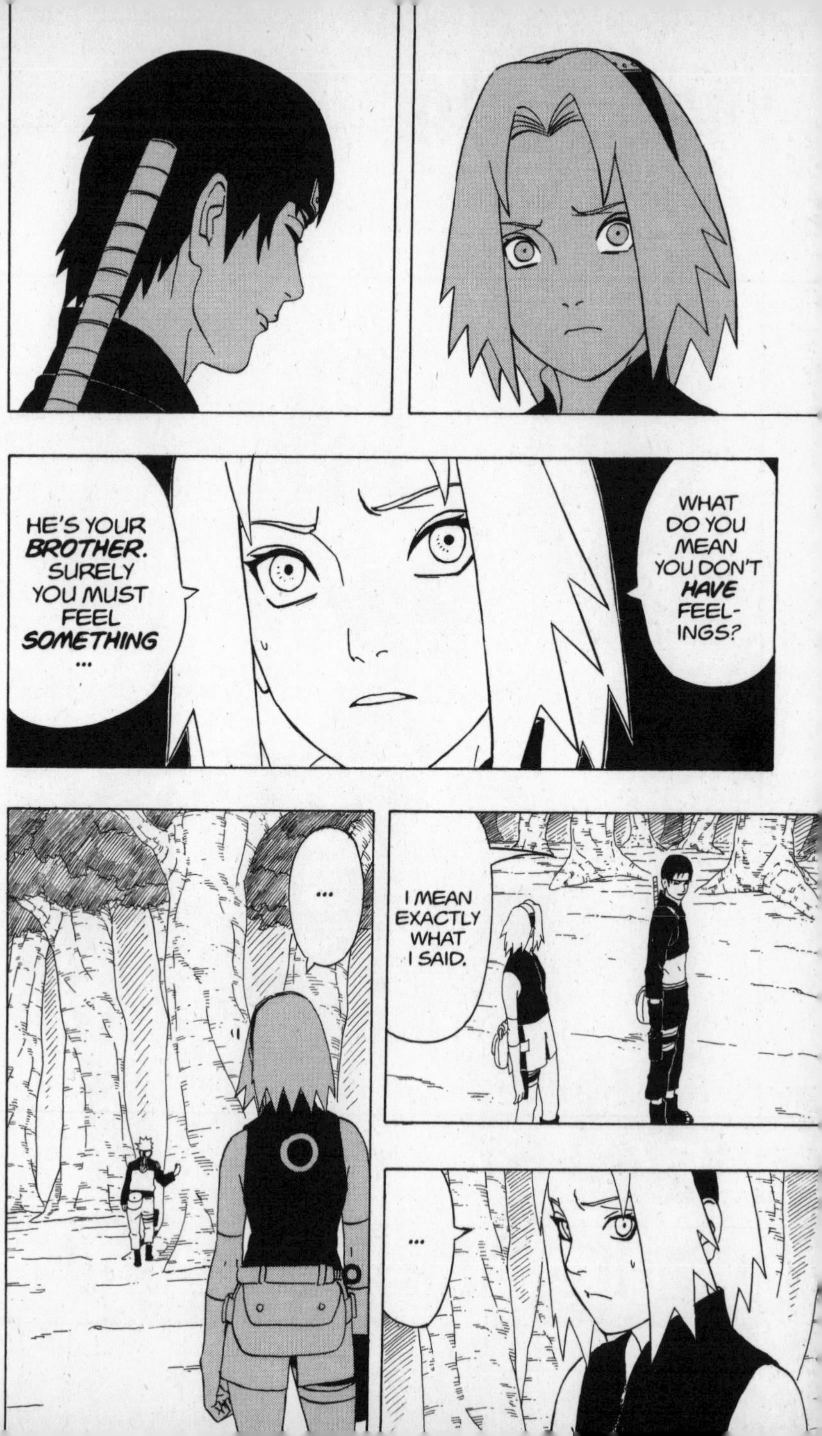
WHAT DO YOU MEAN YOU DON'T **HAVE** FEELINGS?
HE'S YOUR **BROTHER.** SURELY YOU MUST FEEL **SOMETHING**...
I MEAN EXACTLY WHAT I SAID.
...
...

READ THIS WAY

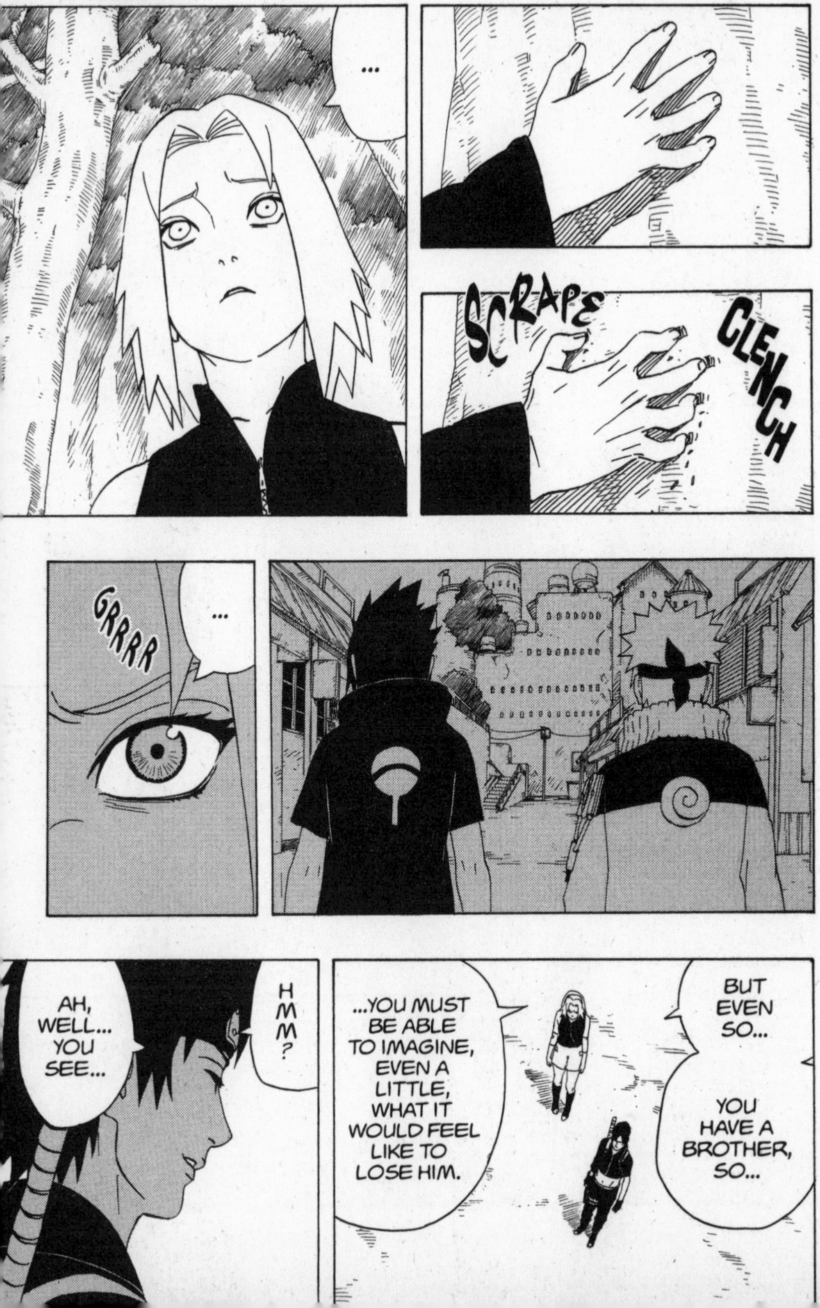
CLENCH
SCRAPE
...
...
GRRRR
BUT EVEN SO...
YOU HAVE A BROTHER, SO...
...YOU MUST BE ABLE TO IMAGINE, EVEN A LITTLE, WHAT IT WOULD FEEL LIKE TO LOSE HIM.
HMM?
AH, WELL... YOU SEE...

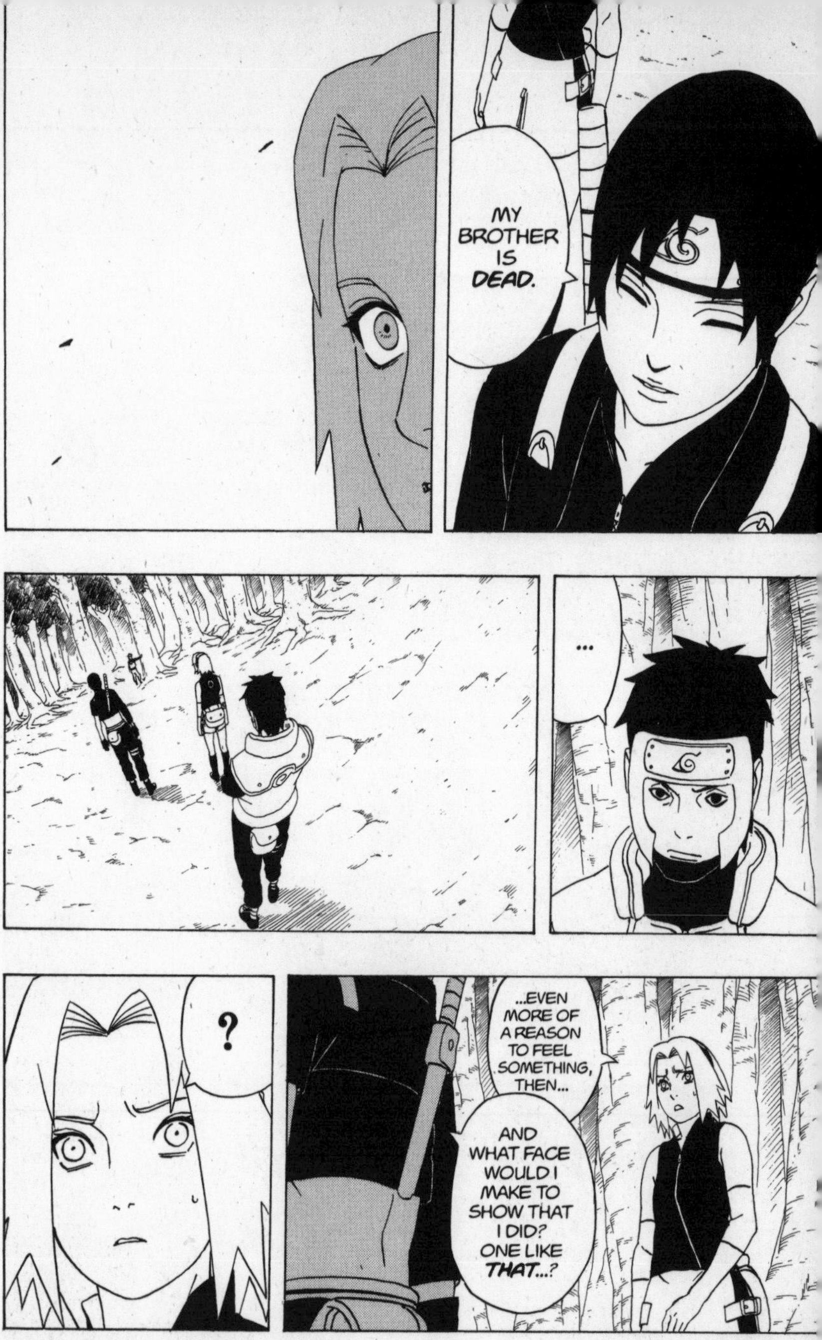
MY BROTHER IS DEAD.
...
...EVEN MORE OF A REASON TO FEEL SOMETHING, THEN...
AND WHAT FACE WOULD I MAKE TO SHOW THAT I DID? ONE LIKE THAT...?
?

READ THIS WAY

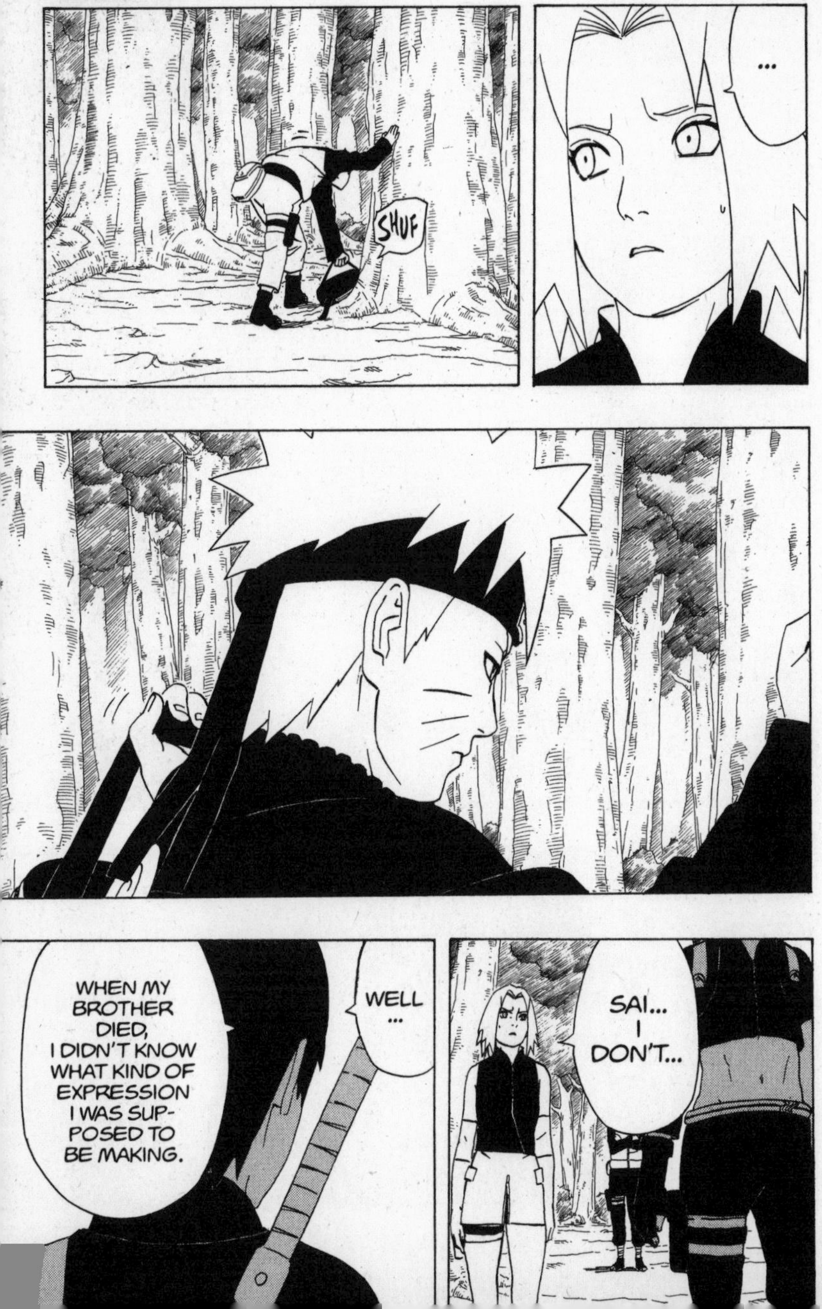
...
SHUF
SAI... I DON'T...
WELL ...
WHEN MY BROTHER DIED, I DIDN'T KNOW WHAT KIND OF EXPRESSION I WAS SUP-POSED TO BE MAKING.

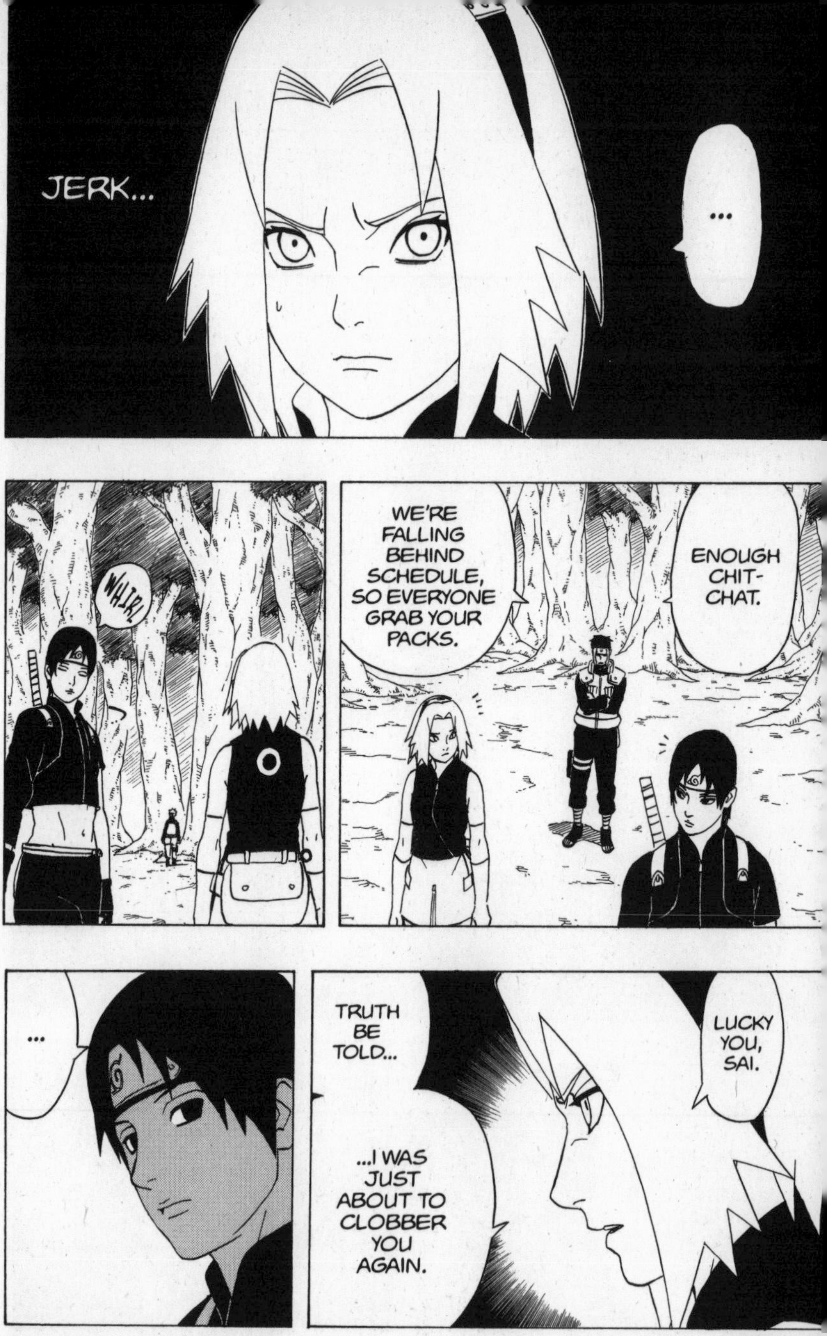
...
JERK...
ENOUGH CHIT-CHAT.
WE'RE FALLING BEHIND SCHEDULE, SO EVERYONE GRAB YOUR PACKS.
WHIRL
LUCKY YOU, SAI.
TRUTH BE TOLD...
...I WAS JUST ABOUT TO CLOBBER YOU AGAIN.
...

READ THIS WAY

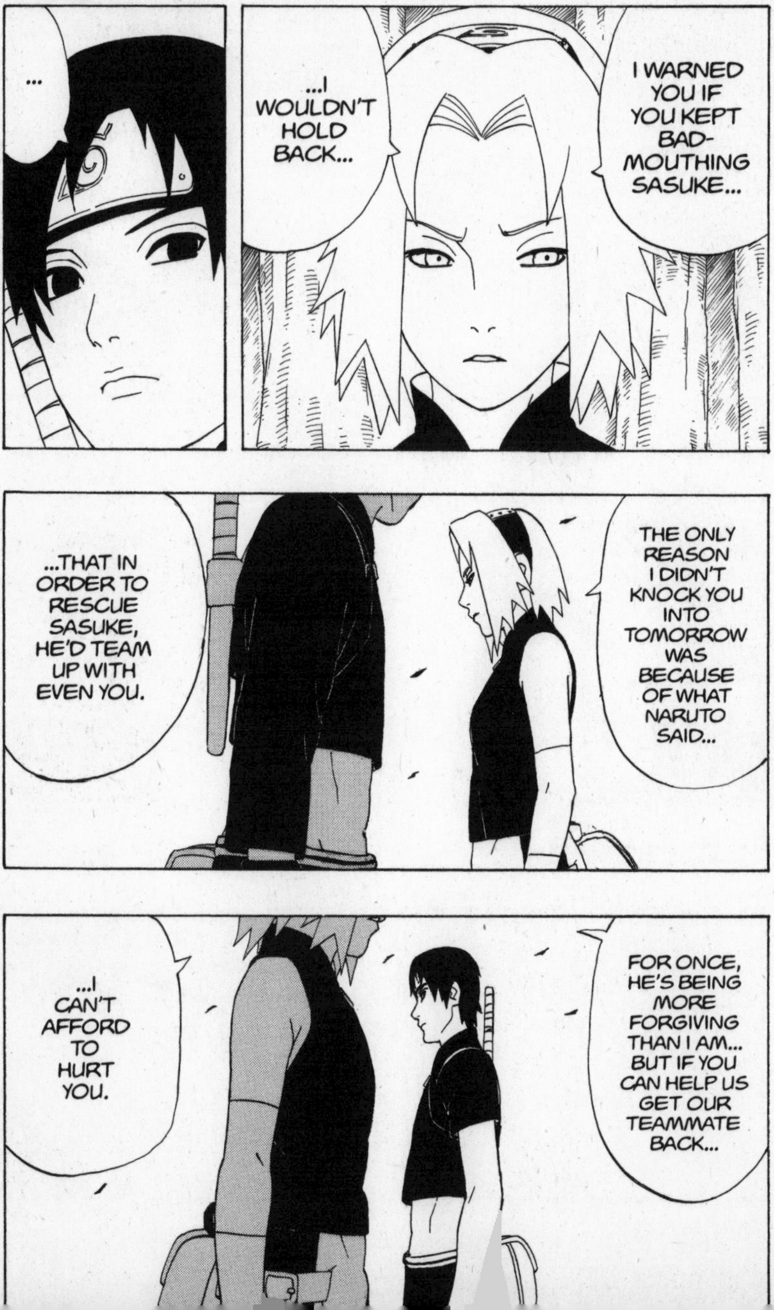
I WARNED YOU IF YOU KEPT BAD-MOUTHING SASUKE...
...I WOULDN'T HOLD BACK...
...
THE ONLY REASON I DIDN'T KNOCK YOU INTO TOMORROW WAS BECAUSE OF WHAT NARUTO SAID...
...THAT IN ORDER TO RESCUE SASUKE, HE'D TEAM UP WITH EVEN YOU.
FOR ONCE, HE'S BEING MORE FORGIVING THAN I AM... BUT IF YOU CAN HELP US GET OUR TEAMMATE BACK...
...I CAN'T AFFORD TO HURT YOU.

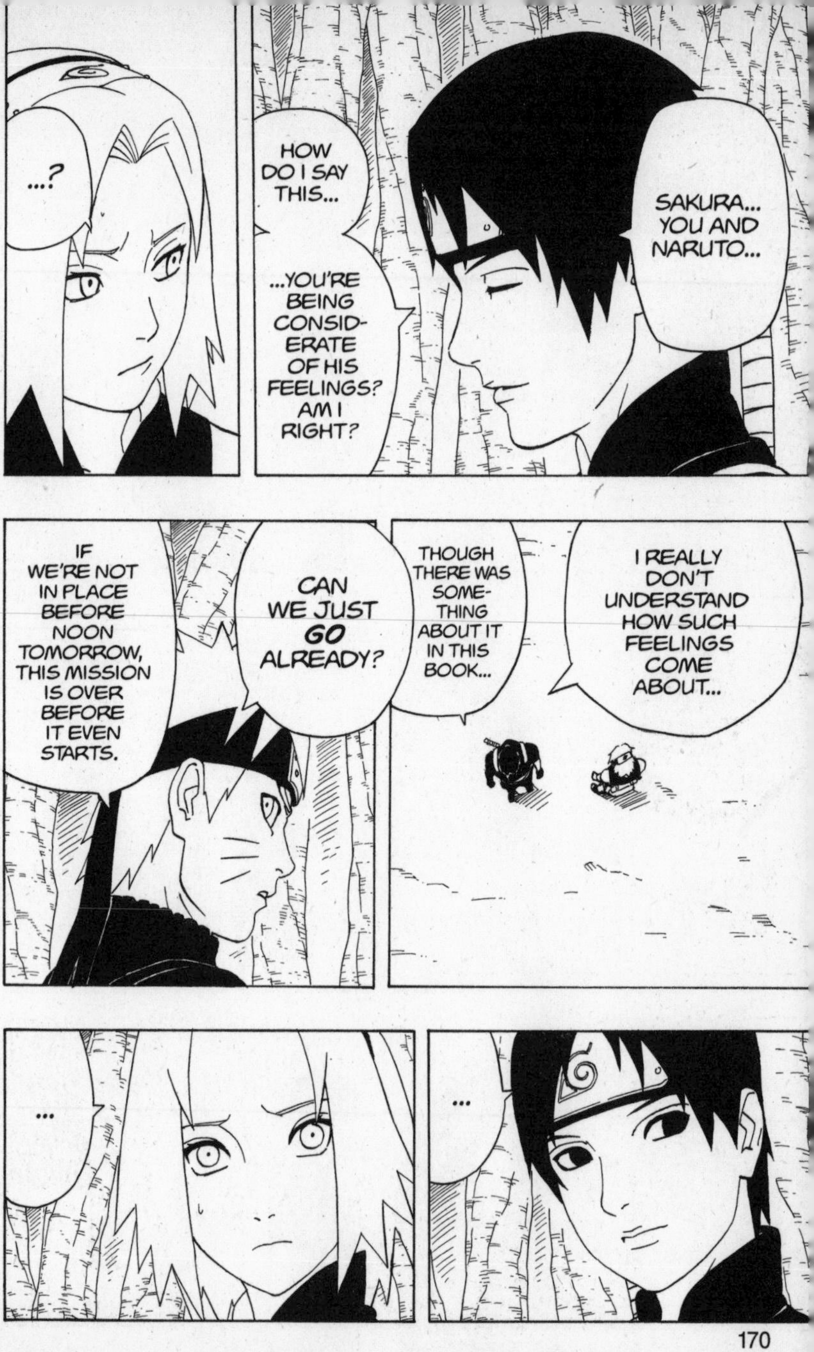
SAKURA... YOU AND NARUTO...
HOW DO I SAY THIS...
...YOU'RE BEING CONSIDERATE OF HIS FEELINGS? AM I RIGHT?
...?
I REALLY DON'T UNDERSTAND HOW SUCH FEELINGS COME ABOUT...
THOUGH THERE WAS SOMETHING ABOUT IT IN THIS BOOK...
CAN WE JUST GO ALREADY?
IF WE'RE NOT IN PLACE BEFORE NOON TOMORROW, THIS MISSION IS OVER BEFORE IT EVEN STARTS.
...
...

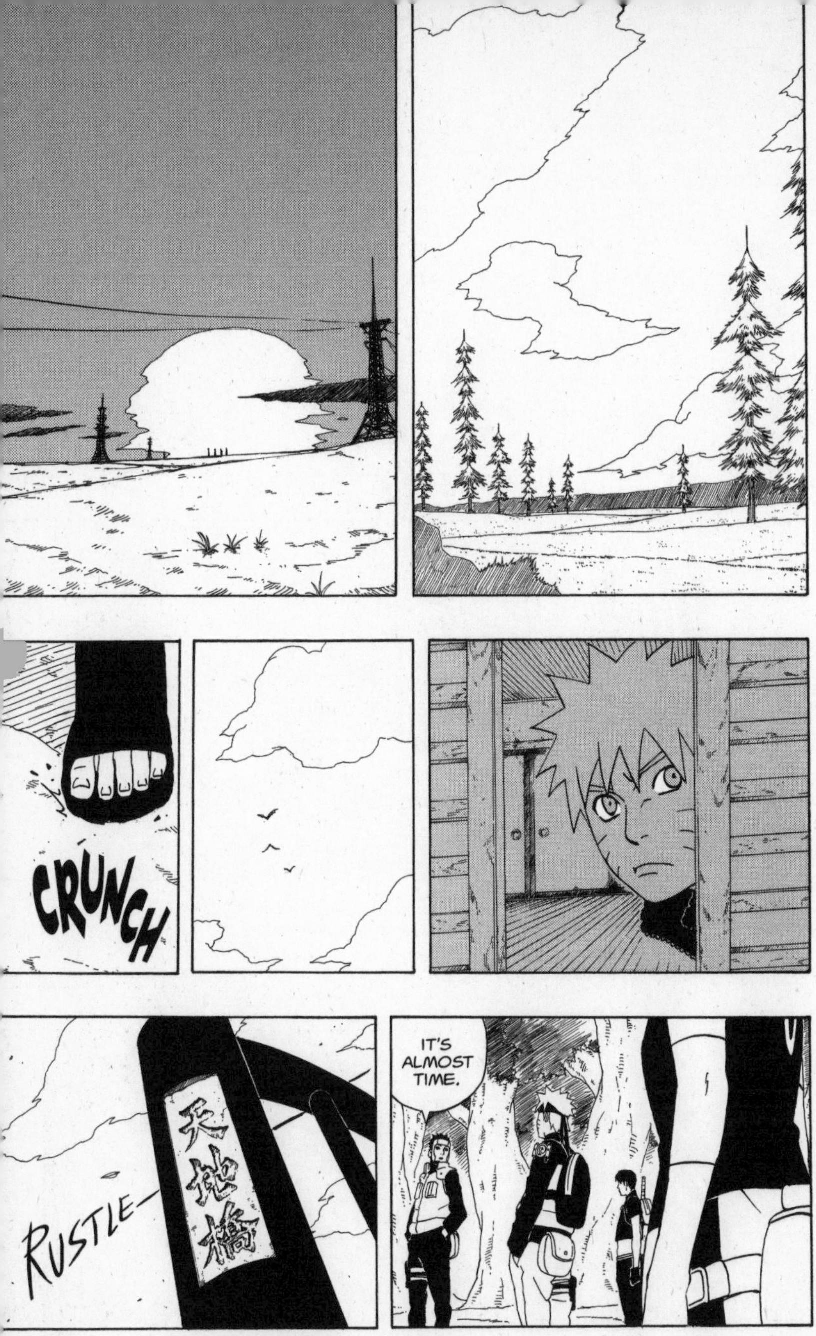
CRUNCH
IT'S ALMOST TIME.
RUSTLE
天地橋

(POST: TENCHI BRIDGE)

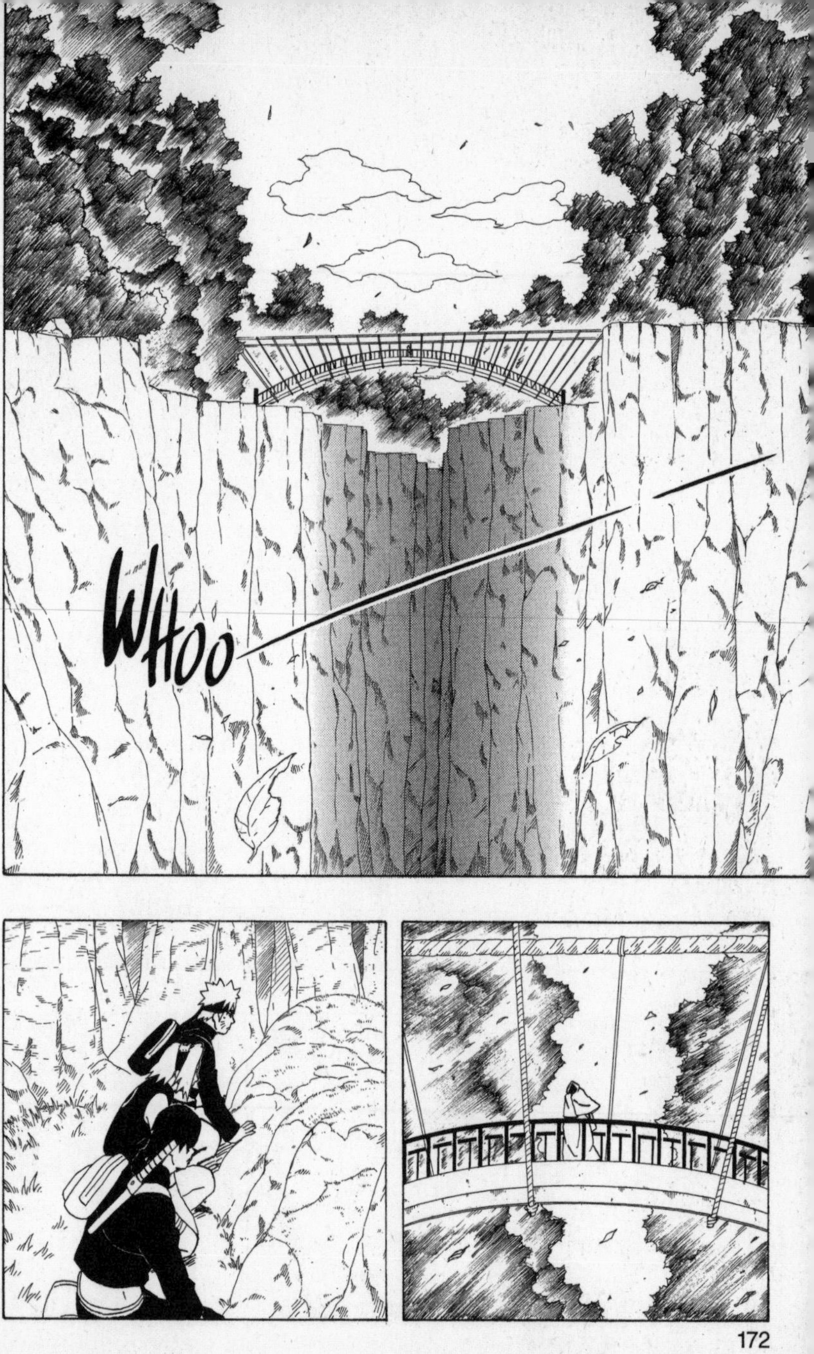
WHOO

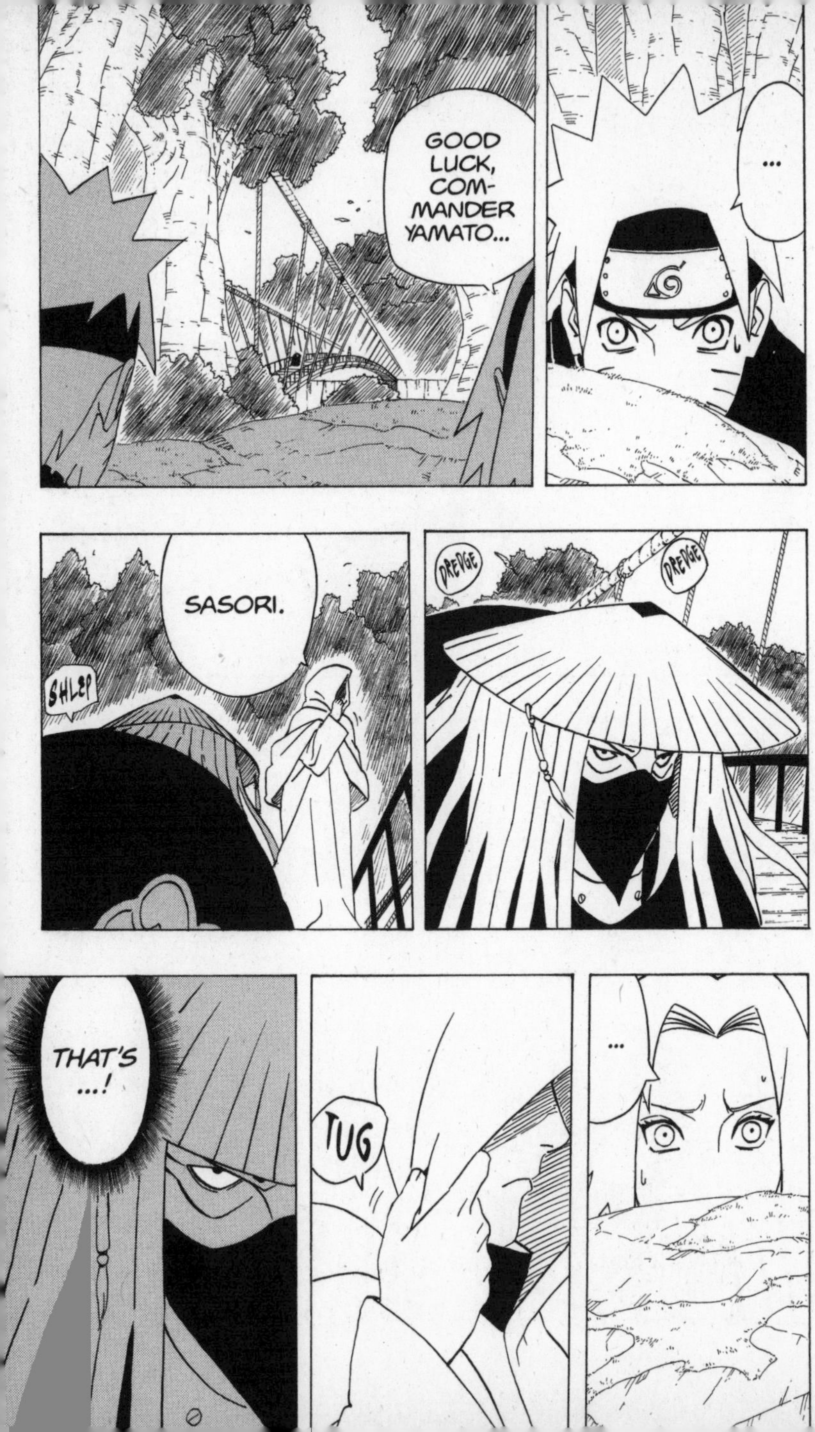
...
GOOD LUCK, COM-MANDER YAMATO...
DREDGE
DREDGE
SASORI.
SHLEP
...
TUG
THAT'S ...!

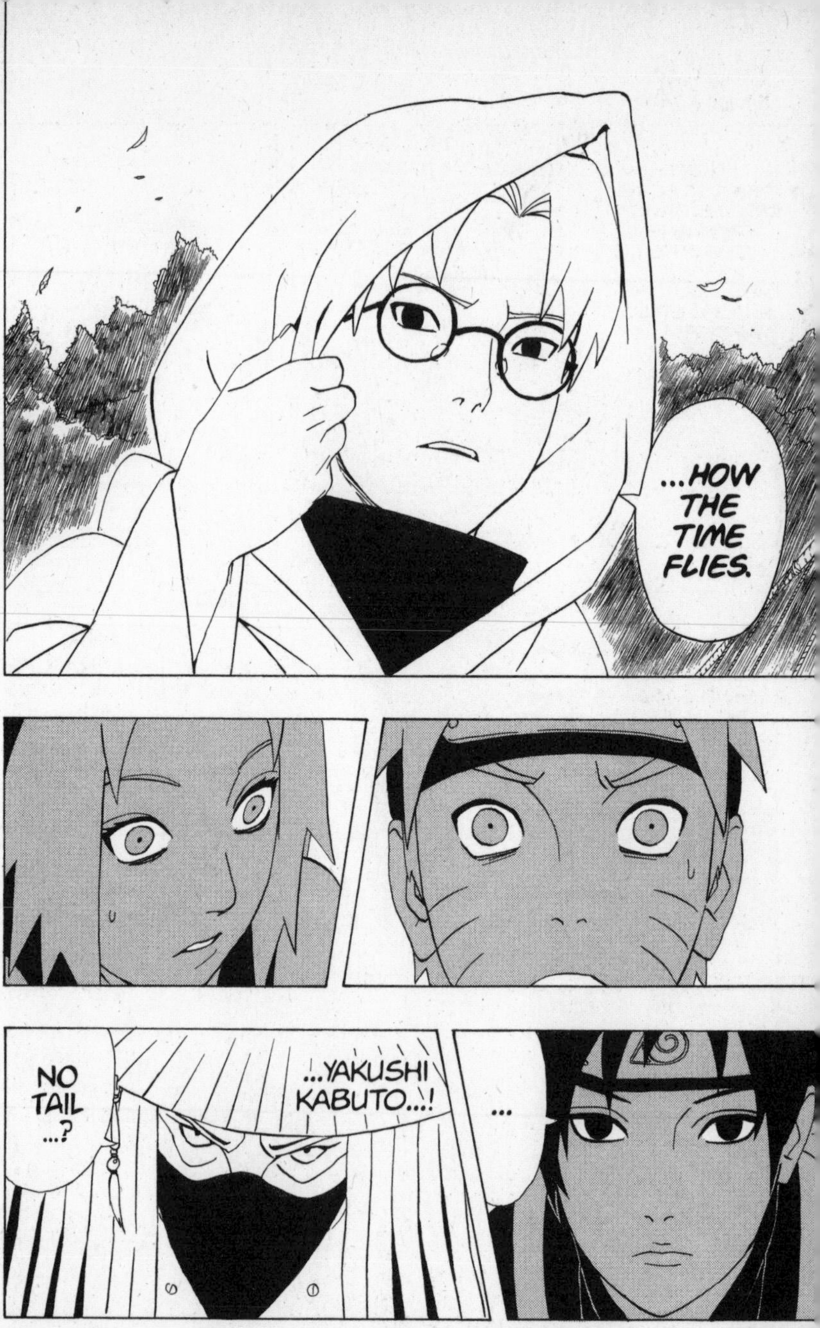
...HOW THE TIME FLIES.
...
...YAKUSHI KABUTO...!
NO TAIL ...?

READ THIS WAY

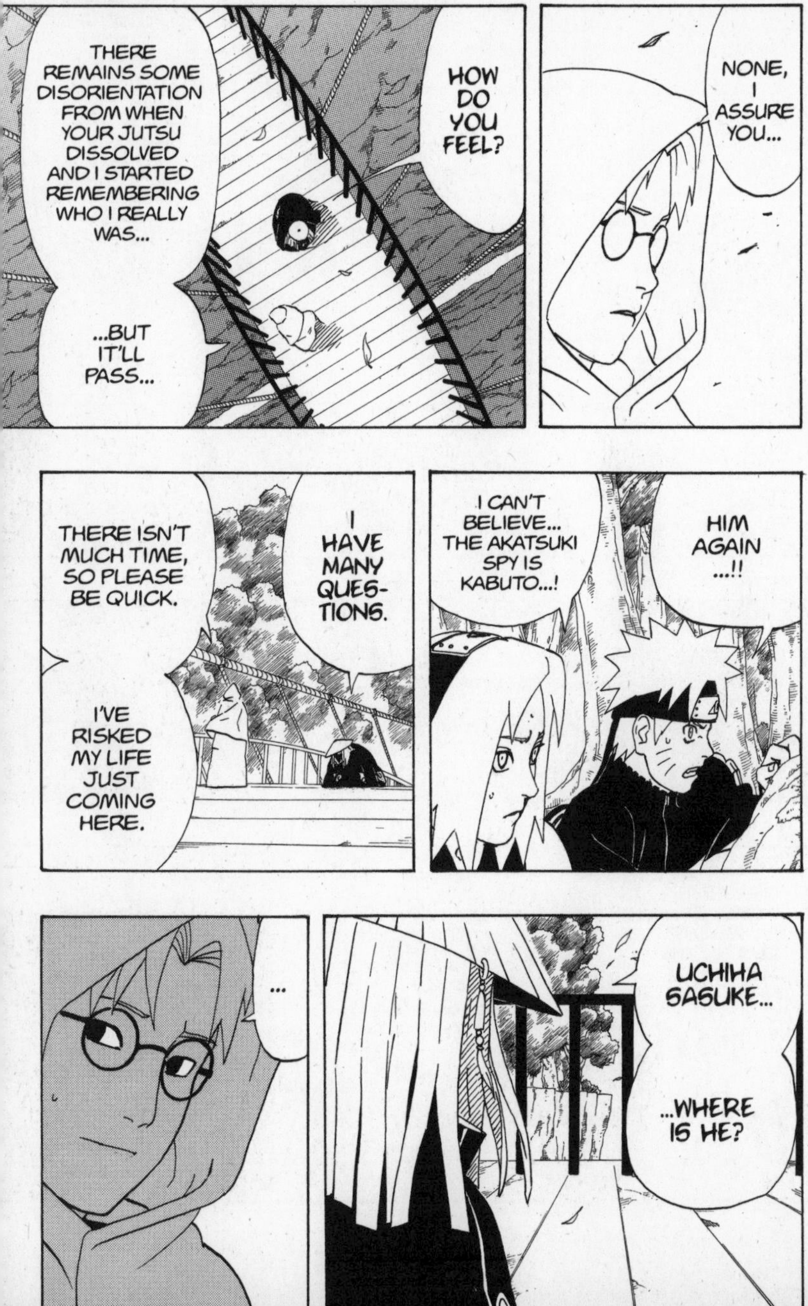

NONE, I ASSURE YOU...
HOW DO YOU FEEL?
THERE REMAINS SOME DISORIENTATION FROM WHEN YOUR JUTSU DISSOLVED AND I STARTED REMEMBERING WHO I REALLY WAS...
...BUT IT'LL PASS...
HIM AGAIN ...!!
I CAN'T BELIEVE... THE AKATSUKI SPY IS KABUTO...!
I HAVE MANY QUES-TIONS.
THERE ISN'T MUCH TIME, SO PLEASE BE QUICK.
I'VE RISKED MY LIFE JUST COMING HERE.
UCHIHA SASUKE...
...WHERE IS HE?
...

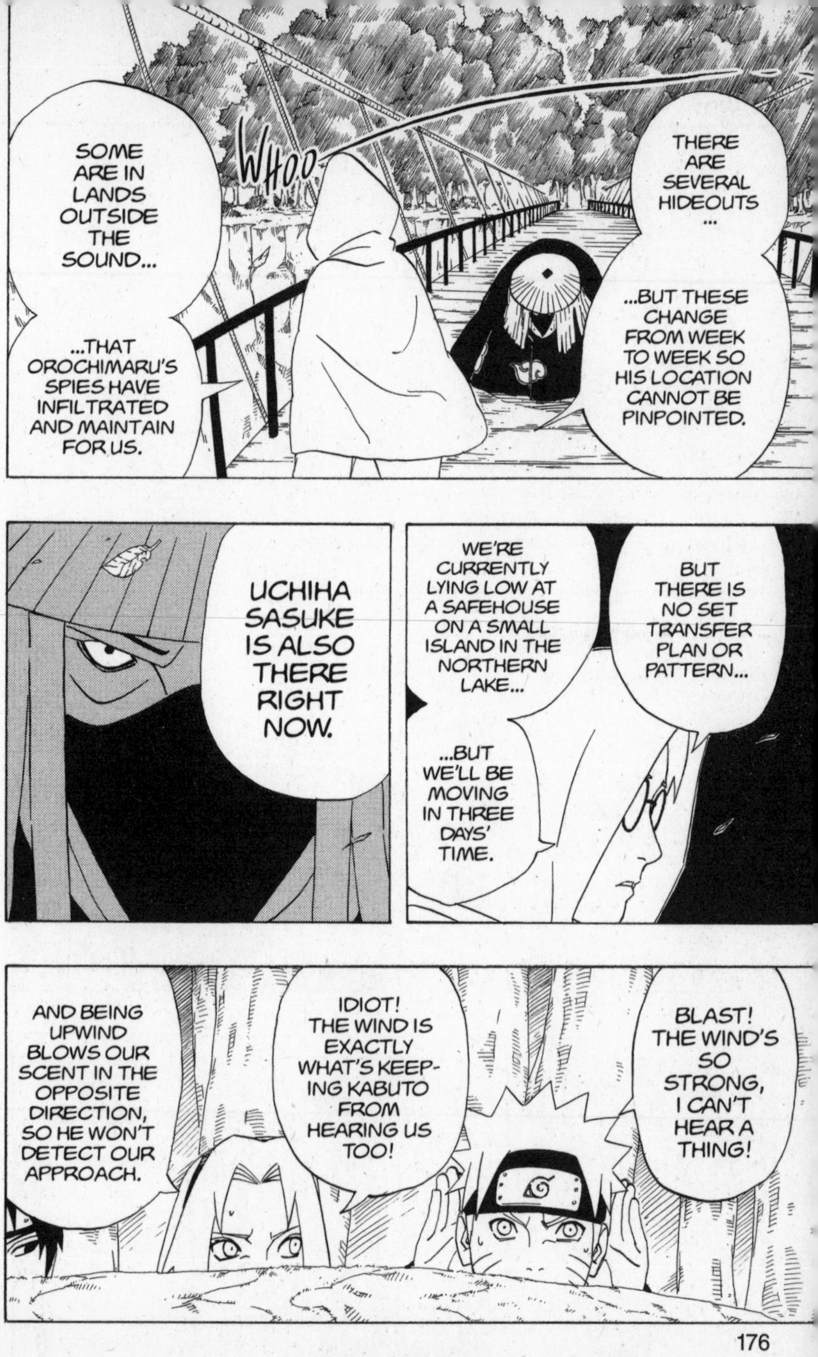
THERE ARE SEVERAL HIDEOUTS ...
...BUT THESE CHANGE FROM WEEK TO WEEK SO HIS LOCATION CANNOT BE PINPOINTED.
WHOO
SOME ARE IN LANDS OUTSIDE THE SOUND...
...THAT OROCHIMARU'S SPIES HAVE INFILTRATED AND MAINTAIN FOR US.
BUT THERE IS NO SET TRANSFER PLAN OR PATTERN...
WE'RE CURRENTLY LYING LOW AT A SAFEHOUSE ON A SMALL ISLAND IN THE NORTHERN LAKE...
...BUT WE'LL BE MOVING IN THREE DAYS' TIME.
UCHIHA SASUKE IS ALSO THERE RIGHT NOW.
BLAST! THE WIND'S SO STRONG, I CAN'T HEAR A THING!
IDIOT! THE WIND IS EXACTLY WHAT'S KEEP-ING KABUTO FROM HEARING US TOO!
AND BEING UPWIND BLOWS OUR SCENT IN THE OPPOSITE DIRECTION, SO HE WON'T DETECT OUR APPROACH.

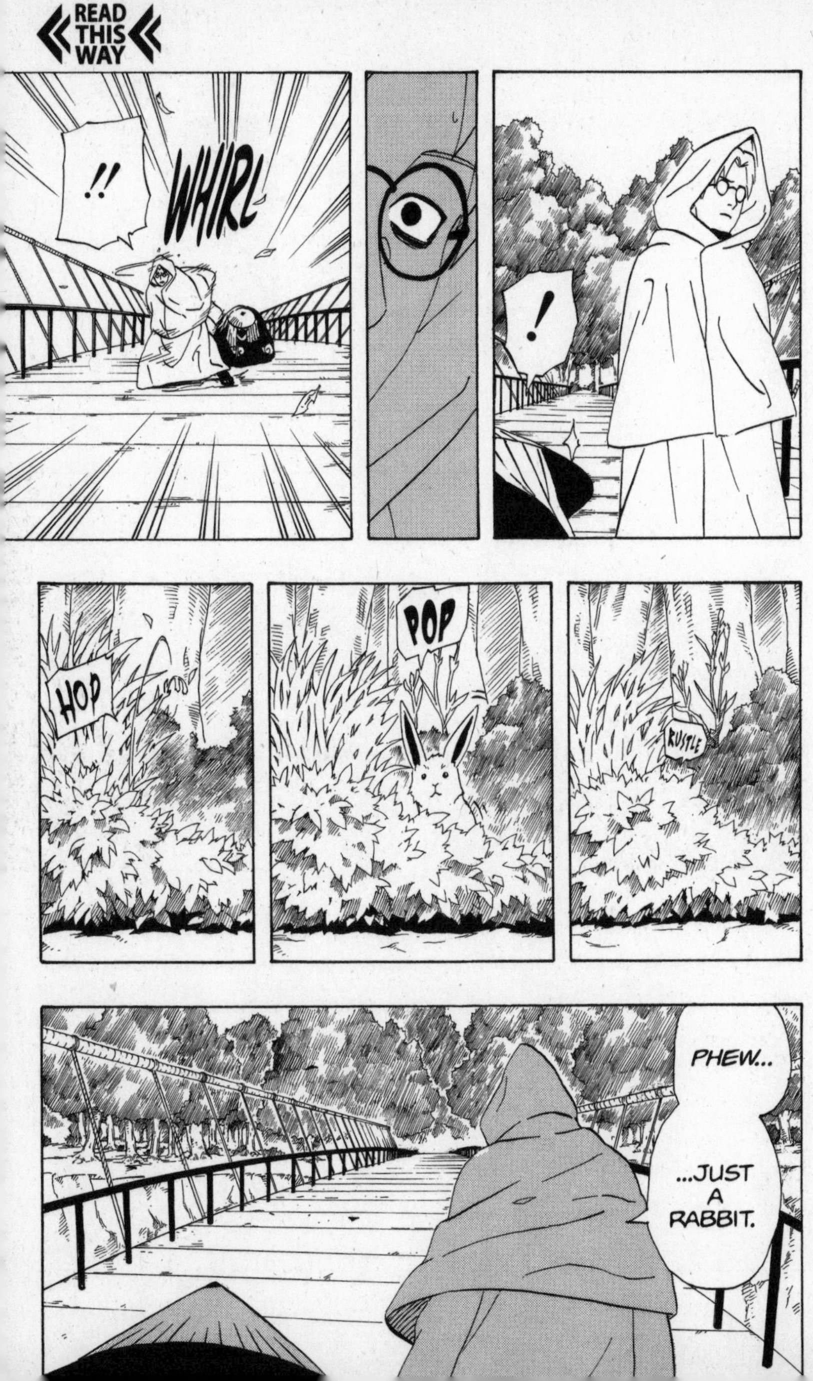
READ THIS WAY
!
!!
WHIRL
RUSTLE
POP
HOP
PHEW...
...JUST A RABBIT.

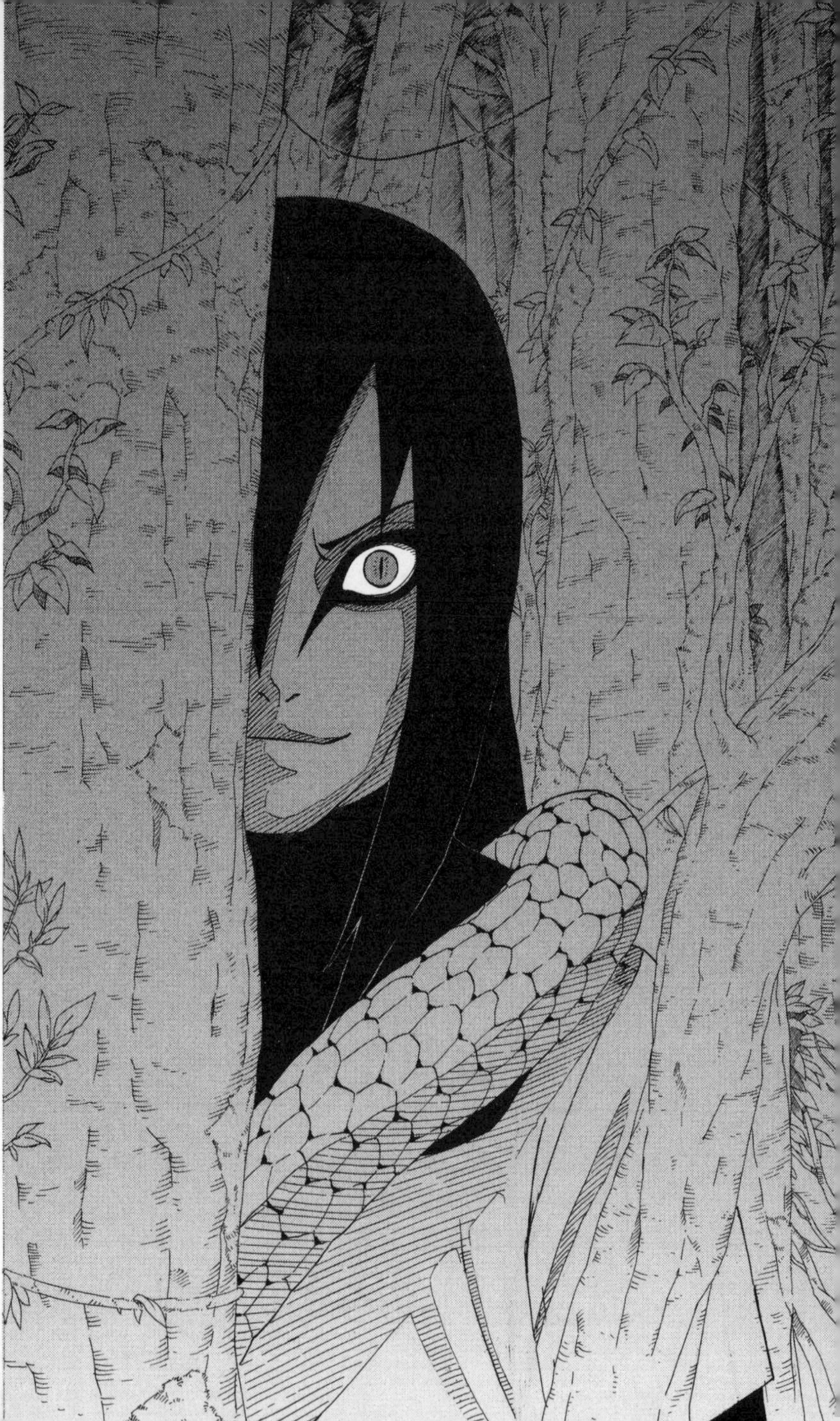

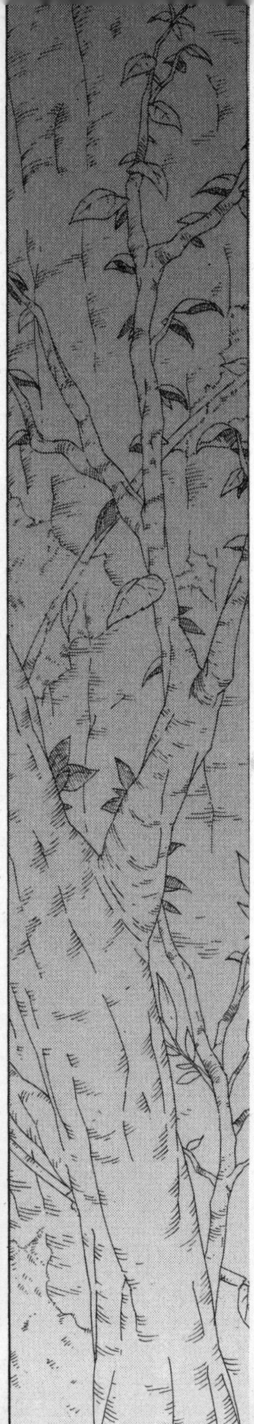

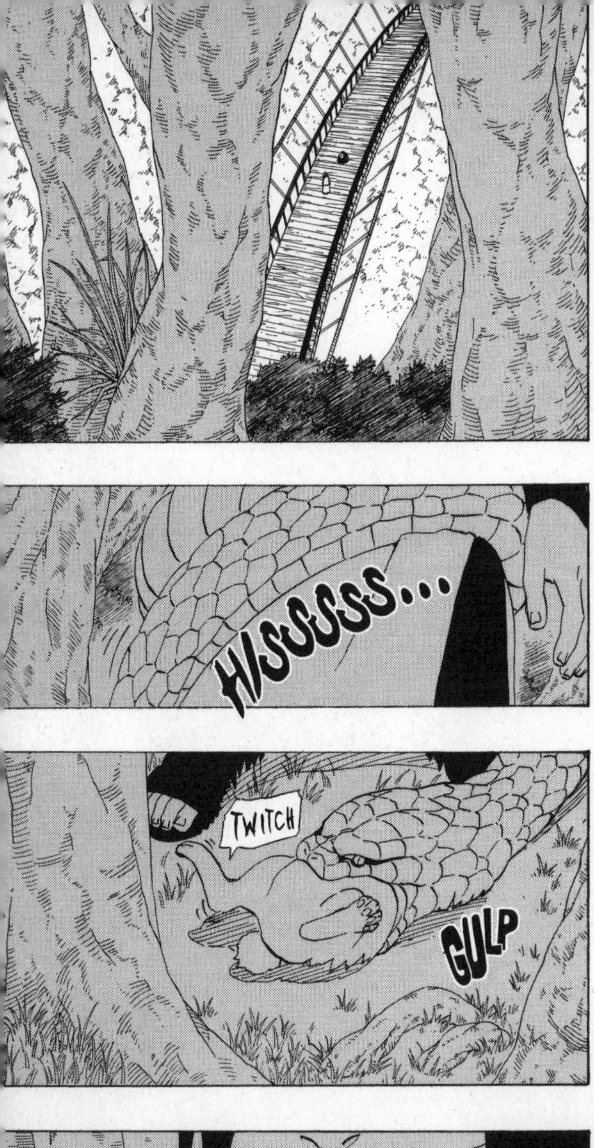
HISSSSS...
TWITCH
GULP

TO BE CONTINUED IN *NARUTO* VOLUME 33!

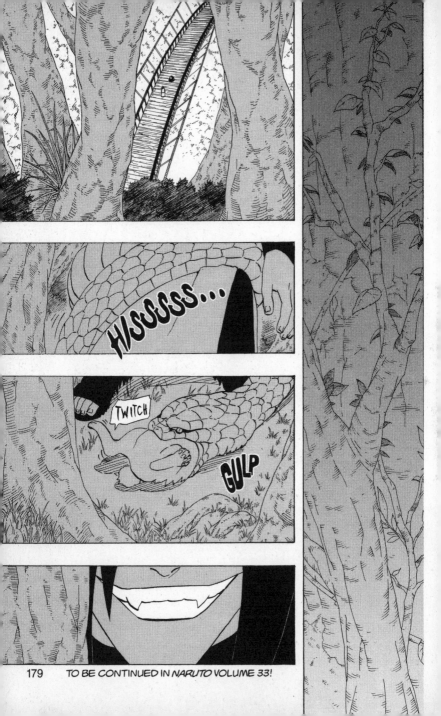

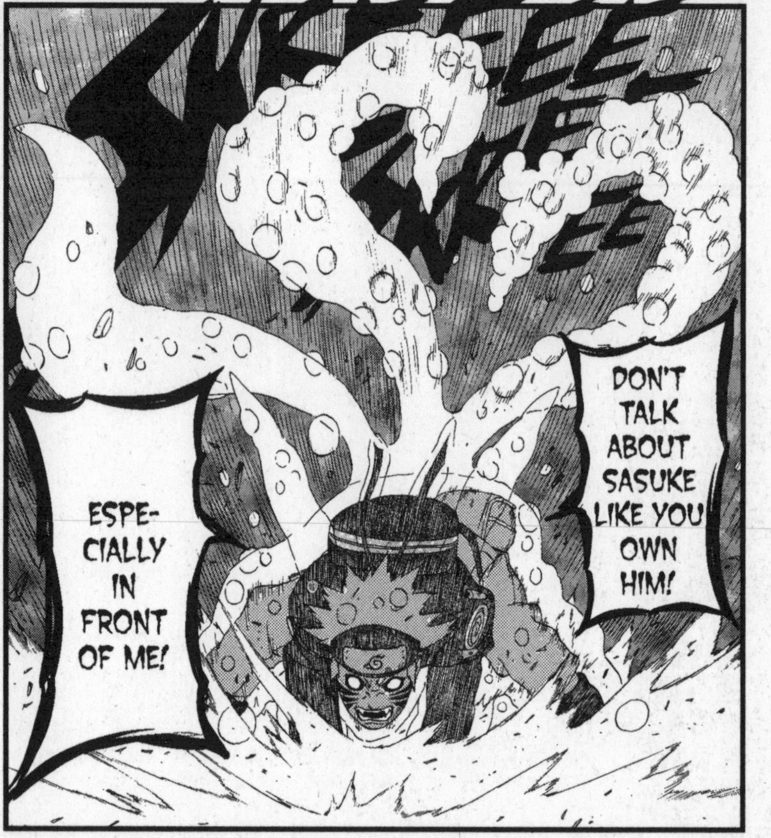
DON'T TALK ABOUT SASUKE LIKE YOU OWN HIM!
ESPE-CIALLY IN FRONT OF ME!

IN THE NEXT VOLUME...

THE SECRET MISSION

Morphing out of control, a stronger-than-ever Naruto turns on his own teammates! Orochimaru triggers a frightening change in Naruto as he reveals a sinister plot that's been the death of far more people than anyone knew.

AVAILABLE DECEMBER 2008!

Read it first in SHONEN JUMP magazine!

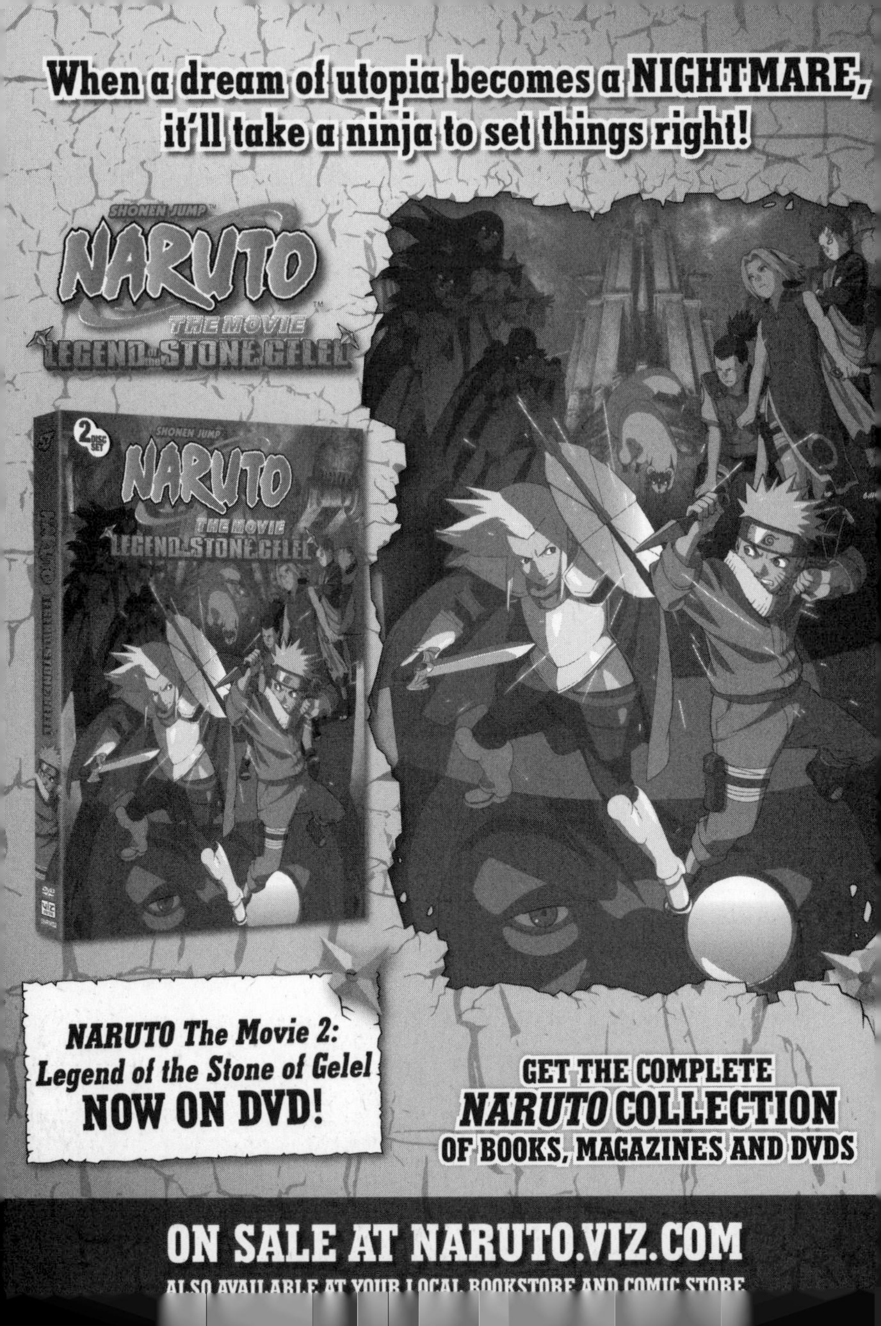
When a dream of utopia becomes a NIGHTMARE,
it'll take a ninja to set things right!
SHONEN JUMP
NARUTO
THE MOVIE
LEGEND OF THE STONE GELEL
2 DISC SET
NARUTO The Movie 2:
Legend of the Stone of Gelel
NOW ON DVD!
GET THE COMPLETE
NARUTO COLLECTION
OF BOOKS, MAGAZINES AND DVDS
ON SALE AT NARUTO.VIZ.COM
ALSO AVAILABLE AT YOUR LOCAL BOOKSTORE AND COMIC STORE